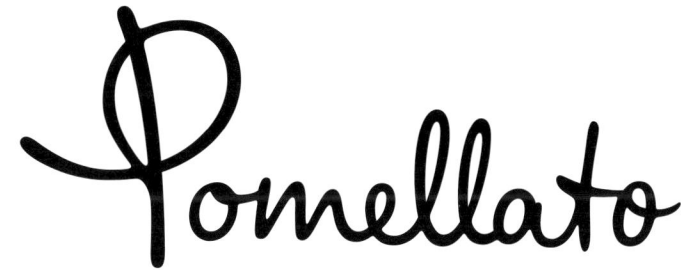

MILANO JEWELRY SINCE 1967

Pomellato: Since 1967

First published in the United States of America in 2018
by Rizzoli International Publications Inc.
300 Park Avenue South, New York, NY 10010
www.rizzoliusa.com

© 2018 Pomellato

Introduction © 2018 Pino Rabolini with Giusi Ferré
"The Gentle Revolution of 1967" © 2018 Sheila Weller
"The Year When Everything Changed in Milan" © 2018 Giusi Ferré

Publisher: Charles Miers
Editorial Direction: Catherine Bonifassi
Production Director: Maria Pia Gramaglia
Design: Campbell-Rey
Picture Editors: Ruby Cohen Cirici & Kate McCusker
Editor: Victorine Lamothe
Editorial Coordination: CASSI EDITION, Vanessa Blondel

ISBN: 978-0-8478-6263-4
Library of Congress Control Number: 2017950145
2018 2019 2020 2021 / 10 9 8 7 6 5 4 3 2 1
Printed in Italy

Pomellato

SINCE

1967

WITH TEXTS BY SHEILA WELLER AND GIUSI FERRÉ

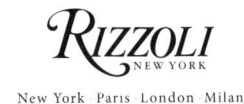

RIZZOLI
NEW YORK

New York · Paris · London · Milan

Happy Anniversary Pomellato!

Fifty years of inspired jewelry for the independent, audacious, and fashionably chic woman who believes that beauty and craftsmanship prevail over trends and status.

Fifty years of unique creativity shaped into sensual mountings, opulent yet minimal aesthetics, and infinitely colorful precious gemstones facetted for a kaleidoscopic and playful effect or carved into the purest essence of a cabochon.

Fifty years of complicity and friendly dialogue with women eager to mark their major life milestones with a ring, a necklace, or a bracelet carefully chosen to reward themselves and to be kept as a symbol, a talisman, or a partner of their personal path.

Fifty years of expansion and international success ignited by Pino Rabolini's unique creative idea in 1967, and pursued by a dedicated team of passionate master goldsmiths in the everlasting tradition of the Italian school of jewelry.

Fifty years of excellence and flawless reputation as a company and as a brand.

Happy anniversary Pomellato, with immense pride and honor for having been part of a moment of your never-ending, unconventional story.

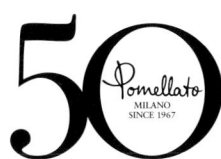

—Sabina Belli
Pomellato's CEO since 2015

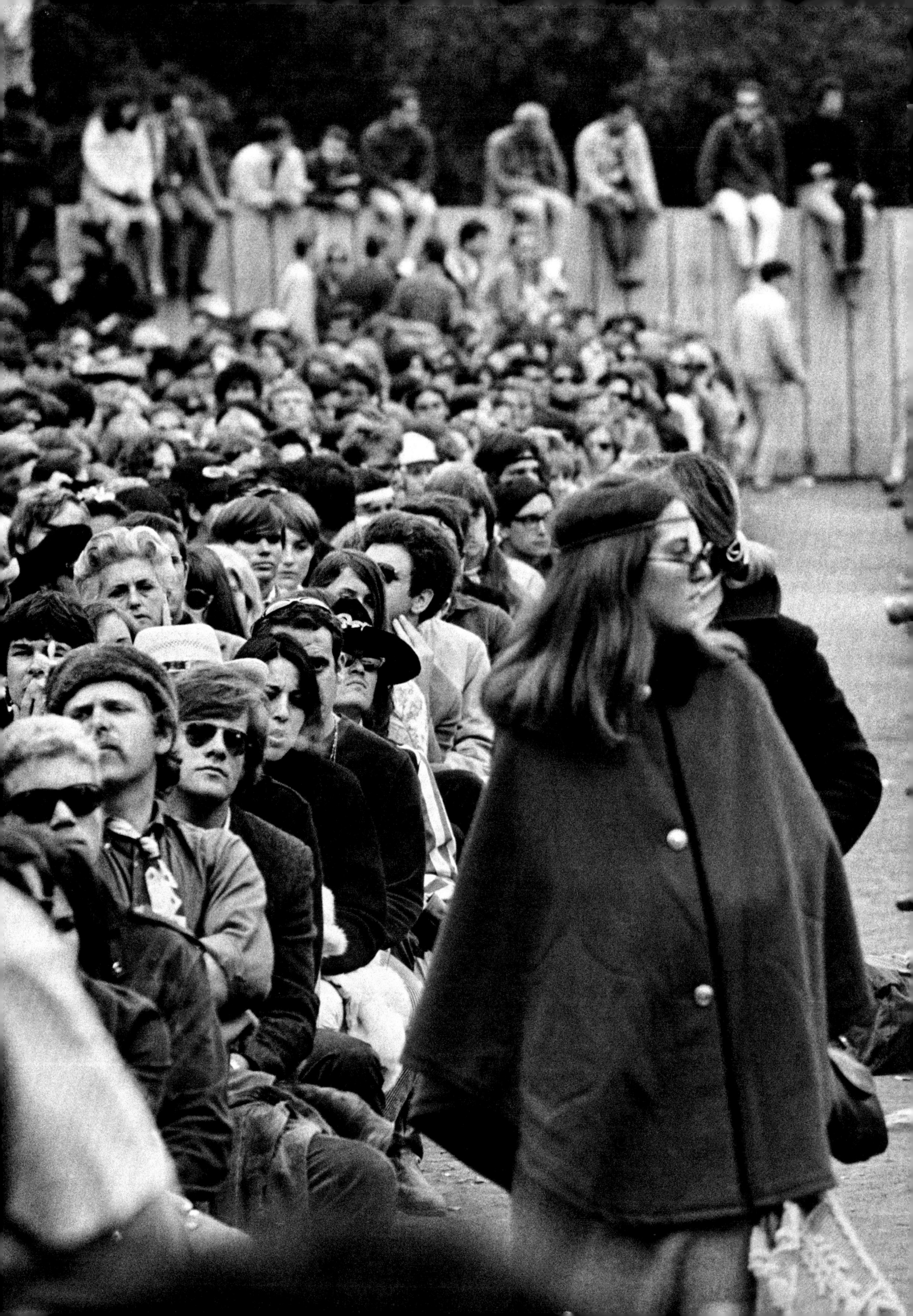

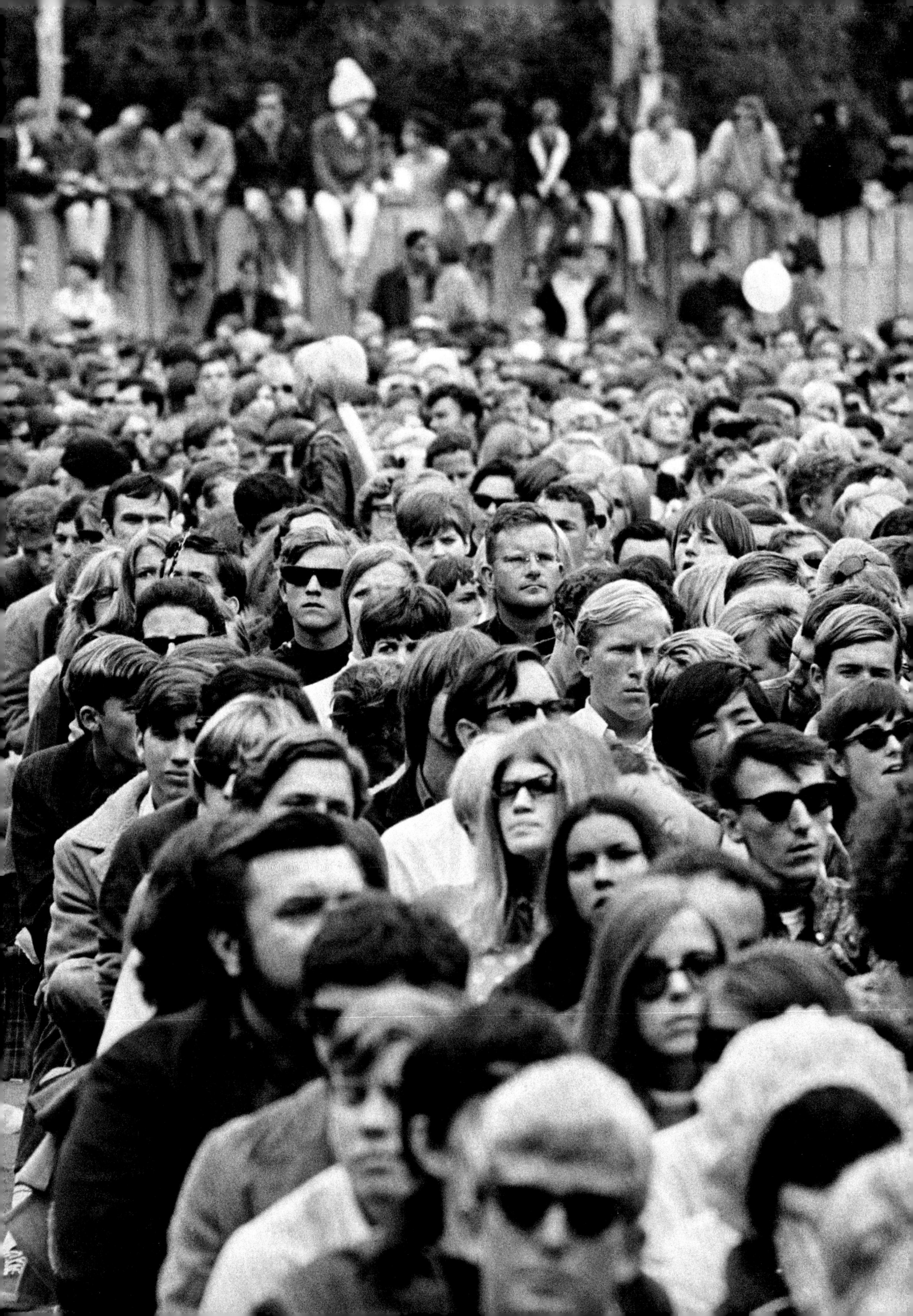

INTRODUCTION

BY PINO RABOLINI, AS TOLD TO GIUSI FERRÉ

There are words that open your mind and inspire you to cross every possible boundary. For me, it was the discovery of prêt-à-porter. I grew up in an era when the terms of fashion were haute couture—garments for divas and princesses—and the Italian word *confezione*, clothing for everyone else. Then the term prêt-à-porter, or "ready-to-wear," started to circulate and it intrigued me, because it offered insight into a surprising focus on style, quality, and elegance. Pierre Cardin talked about it in a long interview published in *Vogue Paris* in 1963; I still have that clipping. Because it is the answer to intuitions and observations, gestures and behaviors, that I could see around me and that I wanted to understand and interpret.

After the tough years of poverty and rebirth, of the reconstruction that wasn't only about houses and industries, but was also on an ethical and cultural level, society was opening up to innovation and to a strong female presence, composed of capable and intelligent women. These were generations that were put to the test and had a growing sense of freedom. They were the women I ran into at the Bar Jamaica, near the Brera Academy, which the papers nicknamed the "Montmartre of Milan." The café attracted the likes of Gigina Baj and Antonia Mulas, the singer and actress Maria Monti, the ceramicist Giorgina Lattes, and the then-debuting actress Mariangela Melato, who enjoyed the encounters and evenings there that helped turn this eccentric young woman into the extraordinary figure she was.

I admired them all, even though, given my character, I never needed a muse to inspire me. I always devoted my Pomellato creations to women in general, and not to one woman in particular, starting with the first collection launched in 1967: thirty pieces in which I concentrated the rebellions of that crucial decade and the experience of tradition. Mine was a family of goldsmiths. My maternal grandfather, who cast gold—necessitating a melting temperature reaching 1,050° Celsius (1,922° Fahrenheit)—between the two world wars, had perfected a more advanced system for the industrial production of wedding rings, which also had softer and more beautiful forms. In fact, depending on how rounded the edges were, they were called *tonda, tondella,* and *tondellissima*: rounded, rounder, and roundest.

This delicate workmanship became one of our distinctive features.

In 1946, the first year to commence without the horror of war, my father opened a wholesale company, where I worked and learned so much. But I would think about my legendary grandfather and I wanted to follow in his footsteps. I wanted to create something unexpected. And to do it, in 1965 I set up my own company and prepared my first collection. The first problem I had to immediately address was what to name it. My brother, with the distance of anyone who is not involved firsthand, grabbed a dictionary and, since I wanted to include a horse's head in my logo, he started reading out definitions: sorrel, bay, black horse, roan, dapple—*pomellato* in Italian. In essence, it reminded me of that smooth, satin expression, and I decided it might be the perfect name.

At this point, it was the eve of 1968 and women were changing before my very eyes: they were dynamic, they traveled, they drove cars. I sensed that dynamic jewelry was ideal for them, things like chains, charms, and *gourmette* chains. But

I also understood that design, high-quality execution, and accessibility were fundamental. I told myself that this was the prêt-à-porter of jewelry, which transforms gold into pure modernity. I could have opted for silver, as several friends later suggested, and as we have done for certain special collections. Yet in order to fully express itself, silver needs large surfaces, while gold demands sophisticated hand craftsmanship, a subtle sense of proportion, and great creativity.

During my time at the Bar Jamaica in the company of its habitués—painters like Lucio Fontana, Gianni Dova, Roberto Crippa, and Cesare Peverelli, as well as photographers like Mario Dondero, Alfa Castaldi, Ugo Mulas, and Jacqueline Vodoz—I had seen the power that can be unleashed by the imagination. However, the entrepreneur is a person who reasons based on intuition, on what can be glimpsed in everyday reality, and is able to do the math. I have never considered this to be a drawback, but the real tool to allow the imagination to work. Fifty years later, now that it has changed hands, yet is always the same, Pomellato has never been so young.

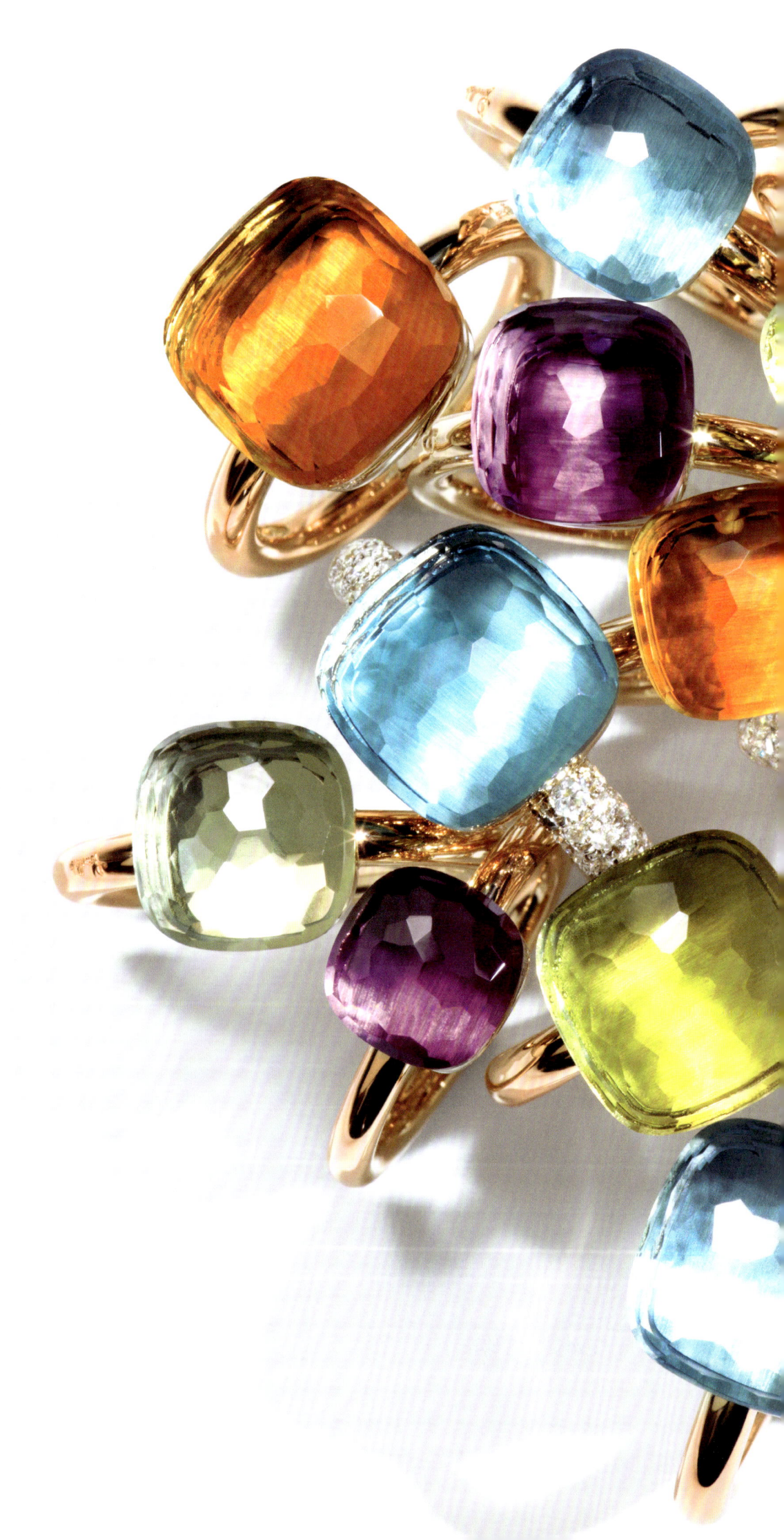

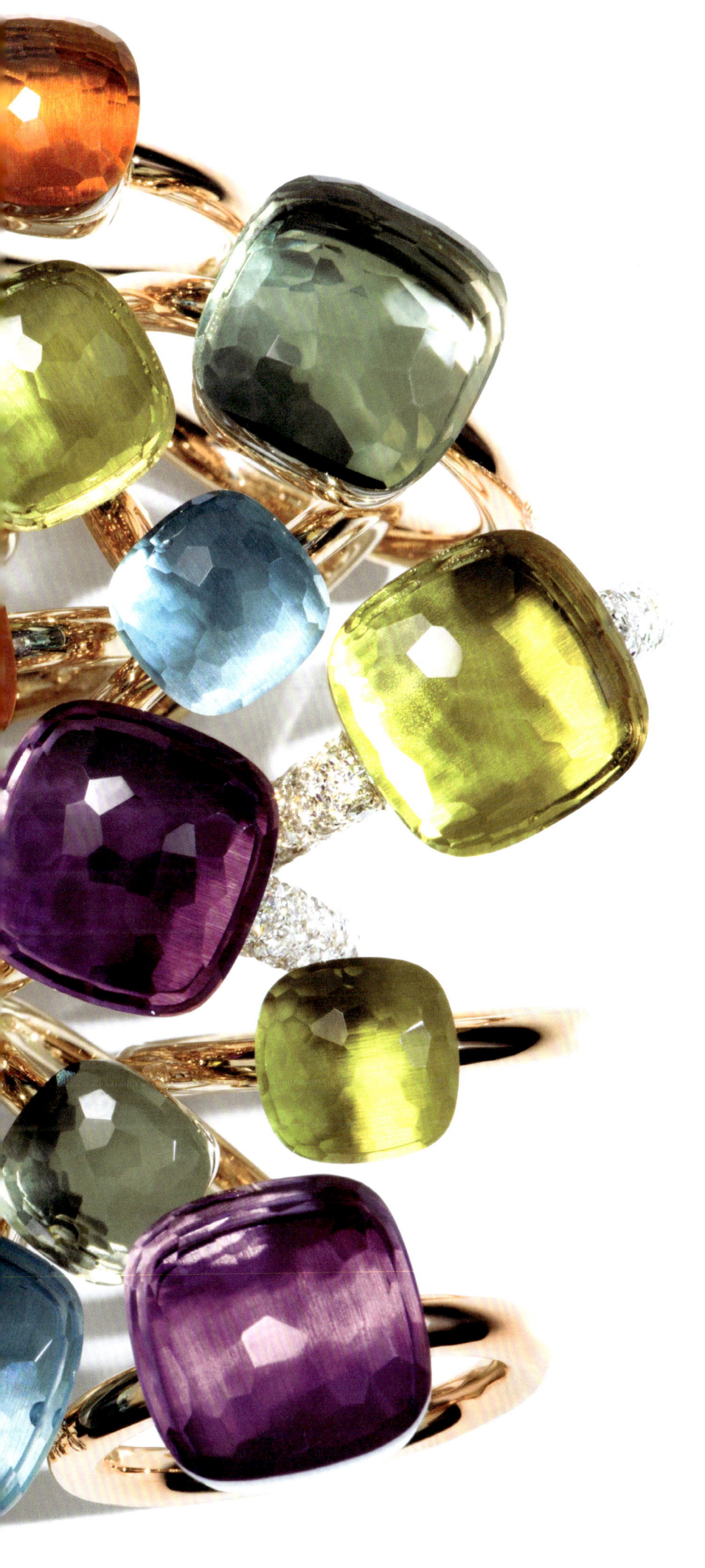

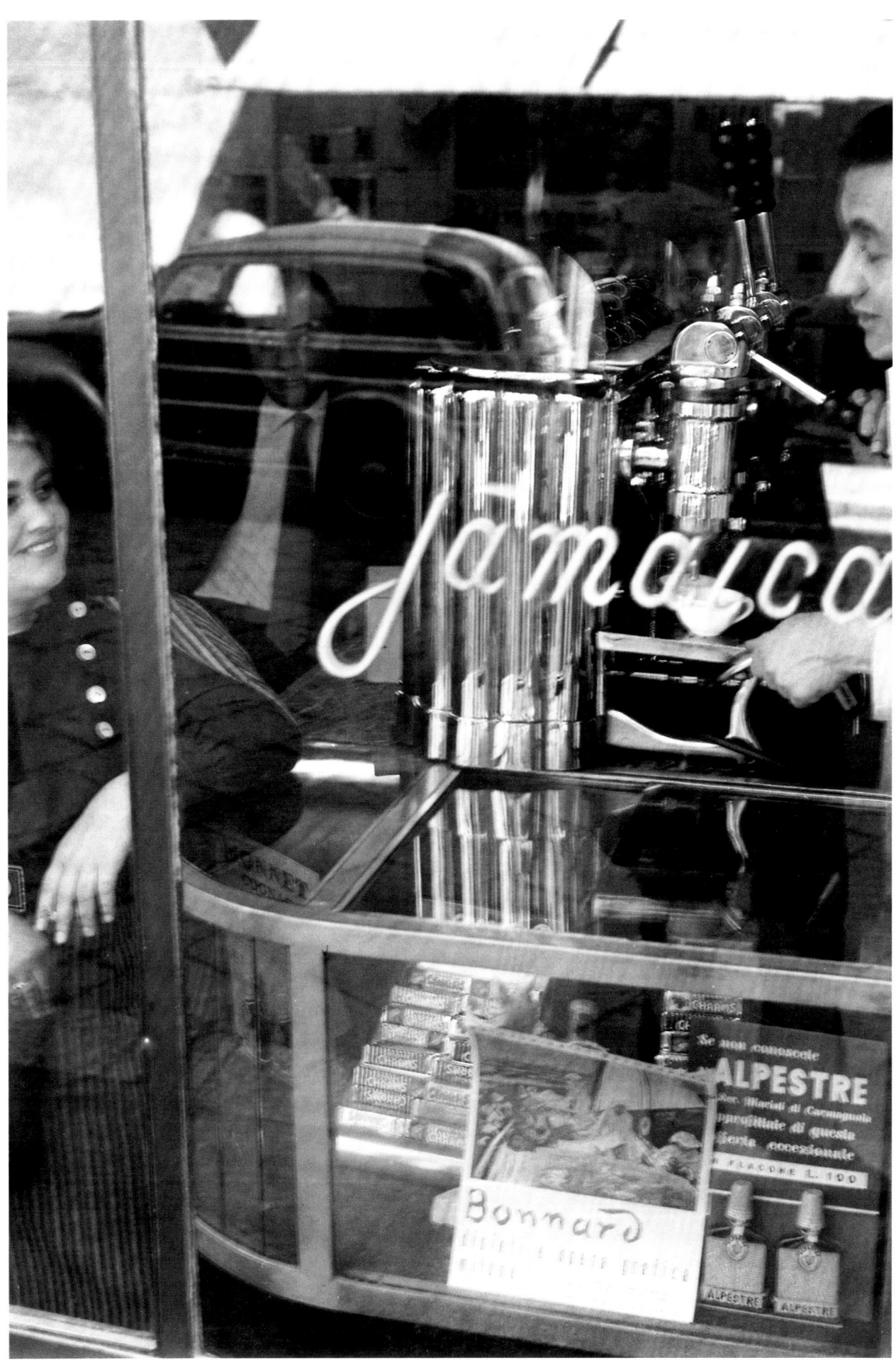

THE GENTLE REVOLUTION OF 1967

BY SHEILA WELLER

PAGES 6–7: Where everything started: the Summer of Love, Monterey Pop Festival crowd, 1967

PREVIOUS SPREAD: Pomellato's signature icon, *Nudo*

OPPOSITE: The seat of the mid-twentieth-century Italian intelligentsia: Bar Jamaica, Milan

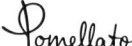

One day in 1967, a young man named Pino Rabolini was sitting as usual with a group of friends at the Bar Jamaica in Milan. Rabolini was the grandson of a goldsmith. He had an aesthete's soul, an idealist's, and was part of an elite group of artists and intellectuals who almost daily patronized the iconic café. Many were students at the nearby Milan Art Academy. Boundary-pushing photographers, painters, sculptors, writers, and designers, they clutched demitasses of espresso or glasses of Spritz or Negroni as they vigorously debated the political and cultural events of the moment. They felt a bit arrogantly on top of the world—the *changing* world.

The Bar Jamaica was at the center of Milan's creative ferment. It achieved that prominence in the late 1940s when its owner organized an exhibition called *Post-Award Guernica*, which became a cause célèbre in a city already renowned for its confident cultivation of the avant-garde.

Inspired by this environment, Pino Rabolini decided to create a jewelry company named Pomellato to cater to the new kind of young woman he was beginning to see all around him: free spirits who existed not just in Milan, but also in London, Paris, San Francisco, New York, and Los Angeles. He chose the name because of his deep appreciation of horses (the word "*pomellato*" refers to a dappled horse). Rabolini's passion for horses was equal to his passion for an attitude and a lifestyle in which elegance, allure, and personality are key components of distinction. The witty, chic women who embodied that elegance were suddenly rebellious, revolting against the old order—but in an elegantly sensual and, it would soon turn out, spiritually and politically principled way.

This new style of a modern, idealistic woman was running from the entrenched culture of her parents and grandparents, with its strict status hierarchy, its propriety, and its insistence that women must marry (and early!) to have respectable—even legitimate—lives. She didn't want to inherit her mother's dowager diamonds and gold, the totems of a class system she now eschewed, or to have a wealthy fiancé patronizingly grace her fingers, wrists, ears, and neck with ostentatious baubles, as if he could own and control her with his largesse. No. This new woman wanted to buy *her own* jewelry—colorful jewelry that matched her beatific sense of adventure. This new young woman believed that *she* owned and controlled *herself*. That sentiment would flourish in this momentous year. It would be tested, and it would morph into a liberation movement—feminism—that would bring about profound changes, which still affect us today.

The 1967 revolution was played out most "mediagenically" in America, but it had European influences. It was a two-way cultural dance. Europe looked to the headline-making Be-Ins and rock festivals in the U.S. while American women were fueled by their infatuation with the soigné life in continental cafés. Here is the story of that year and how it led to a generation of women reveling in their freedom—women for whom Pomellato jewelry expressed their new independence.

The Long "Before"

Any female who felt liberated in 1967 knew there *was* a Before: a *long* Before. It started when they were little girls, wearing saddle shoes, being spoon-fed an image of female life that was more oppressed and desperate than had existed in decades.

In 1956, when the American versions of young women Pino Rabolini sat gazing at in Milan were ten years old, dissemination of information about birth control, even to married women, was a crime in some states. Women in shirtwaist dresses and high heels kissed their brand-new refrigerators in television commercials.

Contained in the kitchen, but not for long: portrait of a housewife, 1957

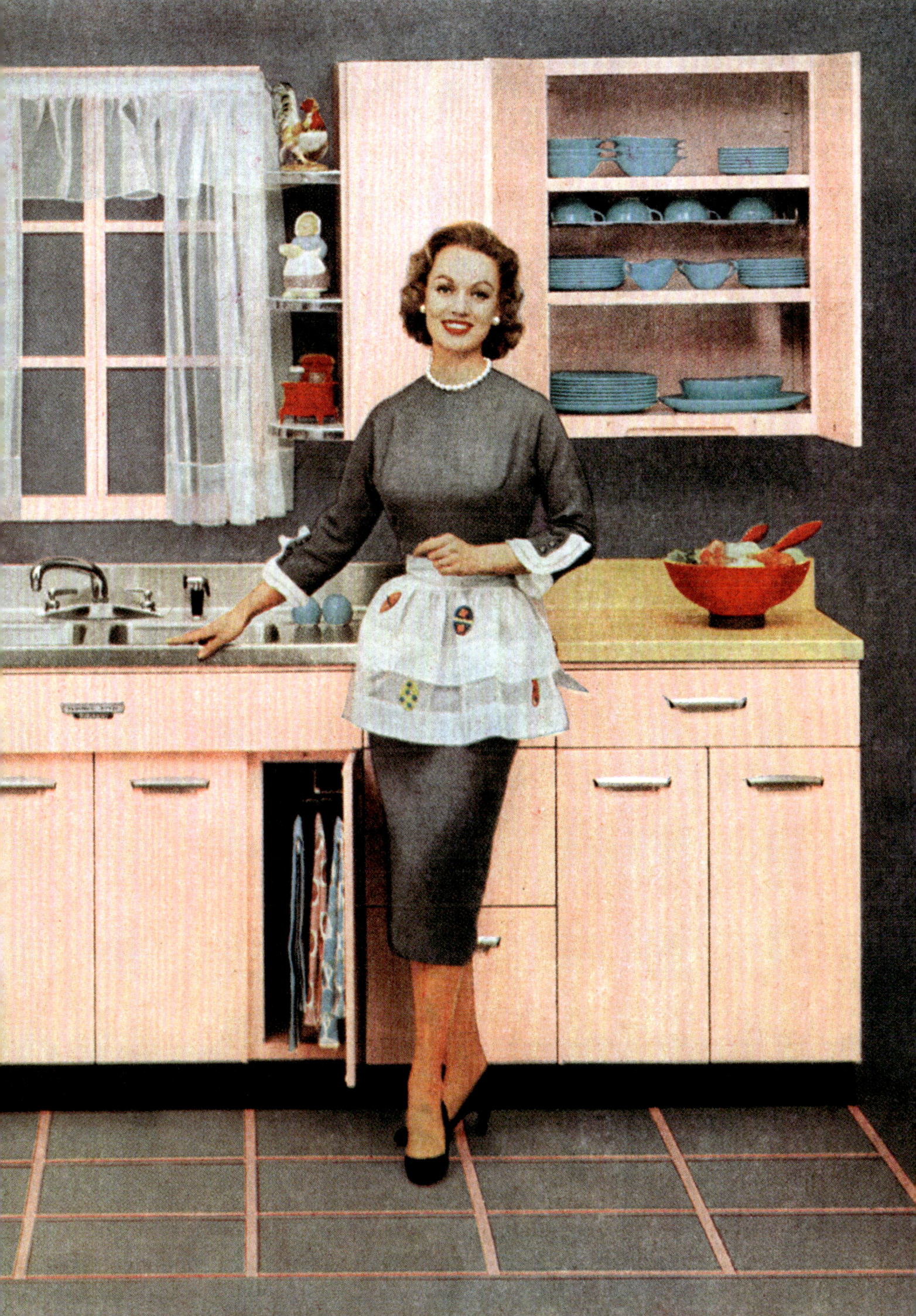

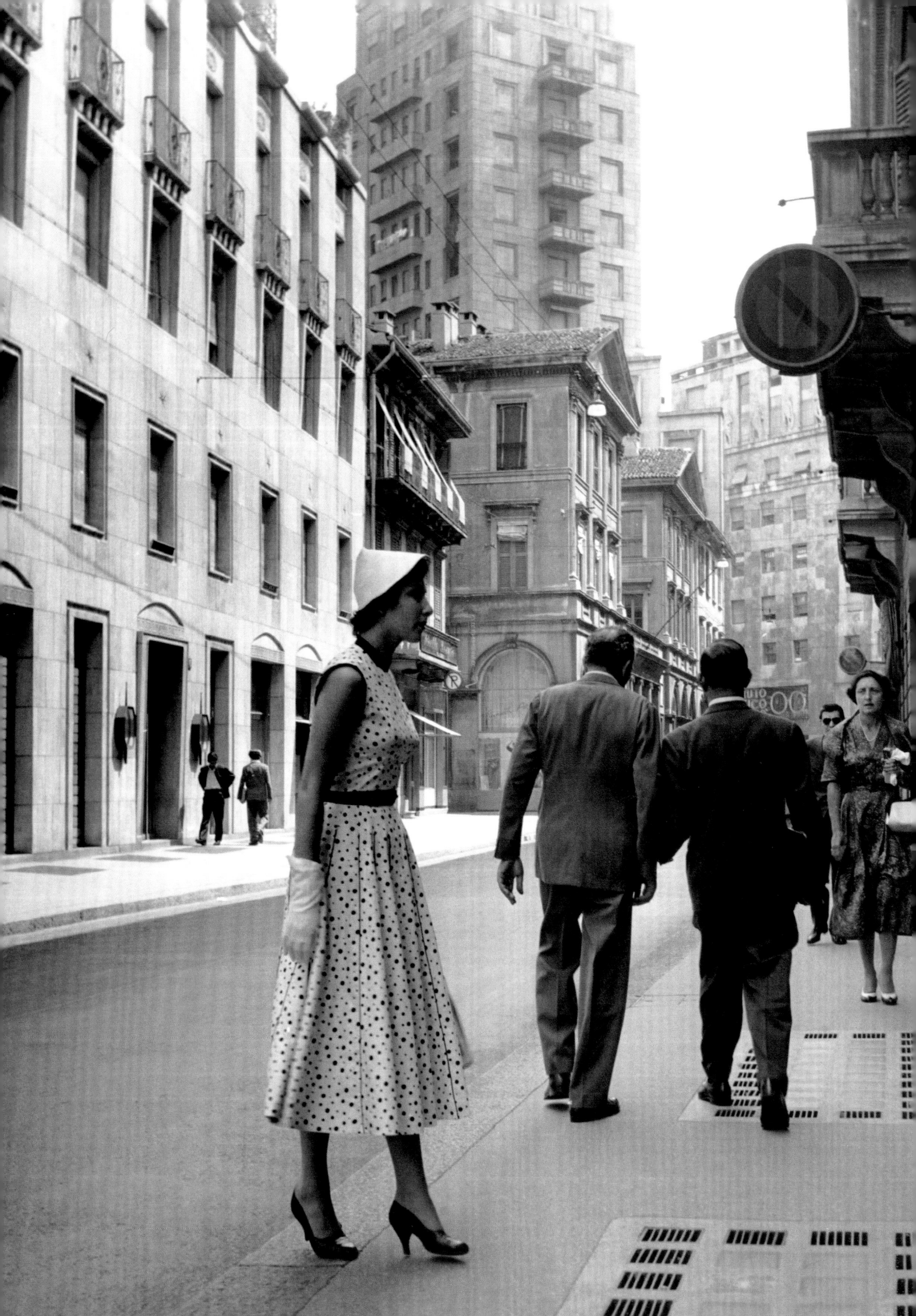

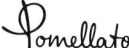

That's how much the culture of the 1950s revered domesticity. Every word of *Seventeen* magazine was vetted by a pastor. In garment factories, union inspectors checked skirt lengths before job lots were shipped to department stores.

Elvis may have been singing and swinging his hips, Jack Kerouac writing about drugs and sex, and James Dean's rebel movies still being shown—even after his fatal car crash—but there were no female analogues. Virginal Doris Day pluckily kept wolves at bay; The Chordettes crooned like a quartet of Perry Comos on estrogen. There was no comparison.

The 1920s had their fabulous flappers, the 1930s their fox-stole-draped society aviatrixes cheerfully trundling off to Reno for divorces. The 1940s, on one hand, had Rosie the Riveter soldering aircraft parts together in a defense plant, and on the other swing-dancing girls who waxed near-orgasmic for a young Frank Sinatra. All of those decades had *some* symbols of female adventure, tough-mindedness, and sexuality. But the middle of the 1950s—a convention-venerating time in America when Senator Joseph McCarthy was carrying out paranoid Communist witch hunts—produced the most moribund images of women of all the previous four decades. Only from this distance does it seem, perhaps poetically, that those little girls might eventually view this low point as a springboard: there was nowhere to go but up—*way* up. Thinking to themselves, "I don't want this for *my* life," they were brewing a majestic rebellion.

These young American girls sensed that Europe was different. Italy was a source of awe. The 1953 movie *Roman Holiday* starred the wonderfully, imperfectly beautiful Belgian-Dutch-English actress Audrey Hepburn, someone so distinctive she seemed to invent a new ideal form of femininity. Hepburn, the genteel cosmopolite in toreador pants, takes a ride on a Vespa and a vacation from her princess status to become a (decorous) rebel. A year later, another movie set in Rome, *Three Coins in the*

Fountain, depicted a trio of American women who came to the Eternal City to seek adventure and love. Europe—and especially with its romantic superstitions, like that about the Trevi Fountain—promised a thrilling break from an American church wedding and a set of casserole dishes. American women of the previous generation would have died to have that continental experience, figuratively speaking. (In *Revolutionary Road*, Richard Yates's era-limning novel of the Silent Generation, the tragic heroine *literally* dies trying to attain it.) The average ten-year-old American in 1956, wearing her poodle skirt and Peter Pan–collar blouse, grew up with a mother who made meatloaf with Campbell's soup. Coq au vin, paella, or veal Milanese in a "café" was a beckoning to a world beyond suburban hula hoop America.

In 1960, an invention arrived that would power 1967 like almost no other: the Enovid birth control pill. Taking "the Pill" meant that lovemaking needn't have *anything* to do with making babies; erotic pleasure was a respectable, physician-approved female goal. At almost precisely that same time, a Brooklyn girl named Carole King cowrote the wistfully melodious song "Will You Love Me Tomorrow," which became a number-one hit. It was the first popular song to say a girl could proudly risk going to bed with a boy even if he didn't ultra-convincingly pledge his love to her.

The other biggest fashion-changing event of the new decade was the inauguration of President John F. Kennedy. Never had such a glamorous, iconic, youthful man ascended to that office. Twice as important to the girls who would be twenty-one in 1967 was his wife, Jacqueline. She was uniquely beautiful with her wide-set eyes, off-the-charts chic, and serene, almost-naughty half-smile—the opposite of her dowdy predecessors Mamie Eisenhower, Bess Truman, and Eleanor Roosevelt. Jackie was almost as European as American: Pablo Casals performed at her parties; Christian Dior and Oleg Cassini dressed her; and her French was flawless (not a

Via Montenapoleone, Milan, 1950s

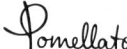

complete surprise considering her maiden name was Bouvier).

There was, however, a catch: with her whispery, almost juvenile voice and kittenish ways, her awed deference to her husband, and her opinion that women should devote themselves to culture, child-rearing, and entertaining (nothing approaching power—she disparaged women she thought acted too "masculine"), she advanced a sensibility that doubled-down on the attitudes of the 1950s while *seeming* to lift American women above it. Then, too, there was JFK's constant infidelity, which Jackie, we now know, endured with pain and stoicism.

This would be the pattern for the next seven years, a time that is now known as the *Mad Men* era, named for the historically astute TV series of that name: make things playful and sexy and modern but keep the male–female rules intact. Women must "snag" men but then work hard to please them. You can have fun, and even have a career that might rise a notch above secretary or (this breezy term said it all) "Gal Friday," but you are a version of a moll. Thus came the glut of surfer movies with names like *How to Stuff a Wild Bikini*, in which beauties in bathing suits (many aspiring fruitlessly to be serious actresses) jumped up and down in thrall to conceited surfboard-carrying hunks. Helen Gurley Brown's wildly popular *Sex and the Single Girl* (book, 1962; movie, 1964) encouraged women to be financially and sexually independent, yes, but to cajole and manipulate men in the process. Brown's hugely successful takeover of *Cosmopolitan* magazine in 1965 brought that kittenish, manipulative form of getting ahead to millions of American women. Socialites—*and* teenage girls—wore short chemise dresses and high-teased flip coiffures and danced the Twist at parties, but you had to get married right after college or you were thought desperate. Upon becoming brides, girls who'd earned top marks at top universities often took jobs as teachers, secretaries, or social workers to put husbands who were often less sharp than they through law or med school. Teased-haired, Pucci-

clad Jacqueline Susann promoted her soon-to-be-a-movie book *Valley of the Dolls* to multi-million-dollar bestseller status. Its three female protagonists uttered lines like, "A man must feel he runs things, but as long as you control yourself, you control him," and nobody complained.

Then there were the entertainment world's coolest guys, the Rat Pack: Frank Sinatra, Dean Martin, Peter Lawford, and Sammy Davis, Jr. They called women "broads," and those desperately game "broads" who were invited to their Vegas tables were gruffly deemed dispensable. (Sinatra's very young wife, Mia Farrow—who, in one year's time, would become a meditating flower child—was very uncomfortable with the image of worthlessness that came with that nickname, and sensed the women's vulnerability.)

There was so much jaunty sexism that a female book publicist who would later become a major early feminist and abidingly close friend of Gloria Steinem's, Letty Cottin Pogrebin, promoted a novel by hiring a model who was willing to stand topless in New York's Times Square and let men come up and paint her flesh. ("I can't believe I did that—I'm ashamed of it now," says Pogrebin, who has been active in feminist reform for over forty solid years, her chagrin at herself underscoring the sharp attitude change.)

In swinging London, enjoying its full bloom for several years by now, Mary Quant's miniskirts were lofted onto the pages of every fashion magazine. Infatuated American eyes turned to The Beatles and The Stones—and their girlfriends. In the same half-liberated way the pre-1967 culture existed in America, Carnaby Street teemed with feisty young working-class girls from northern England who were discarding their prim parents' postwar drear. They were proud to be called "birds" by blokes who could break their hearts like the snap of a guitar string. The 1966 movie *Blow Up*, directed by Michelangelo Antonioni, glamorized the London

"I Was Lord Kitchener's Valet" boutique on London's swinging Portobello Road, 1967

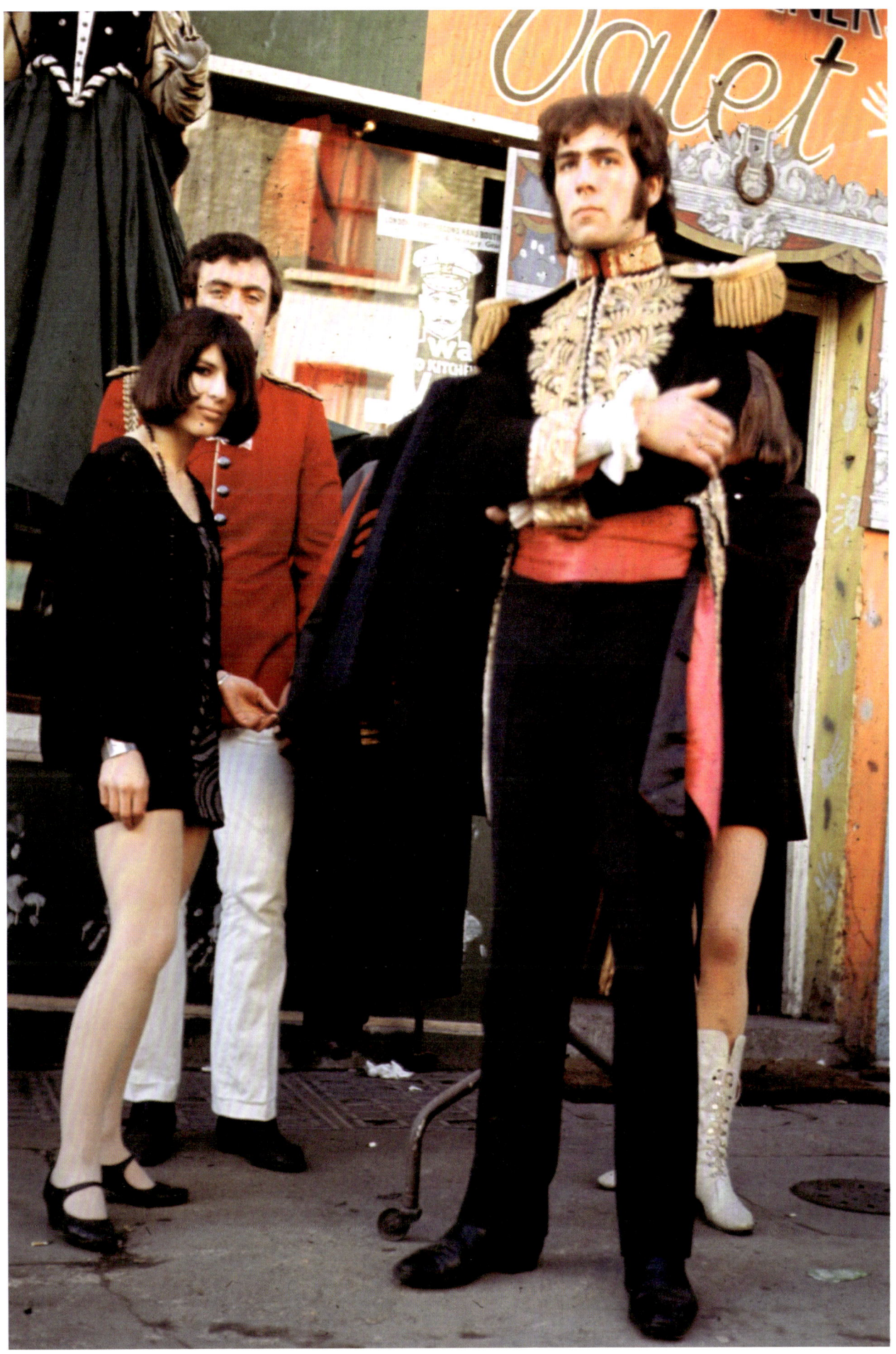

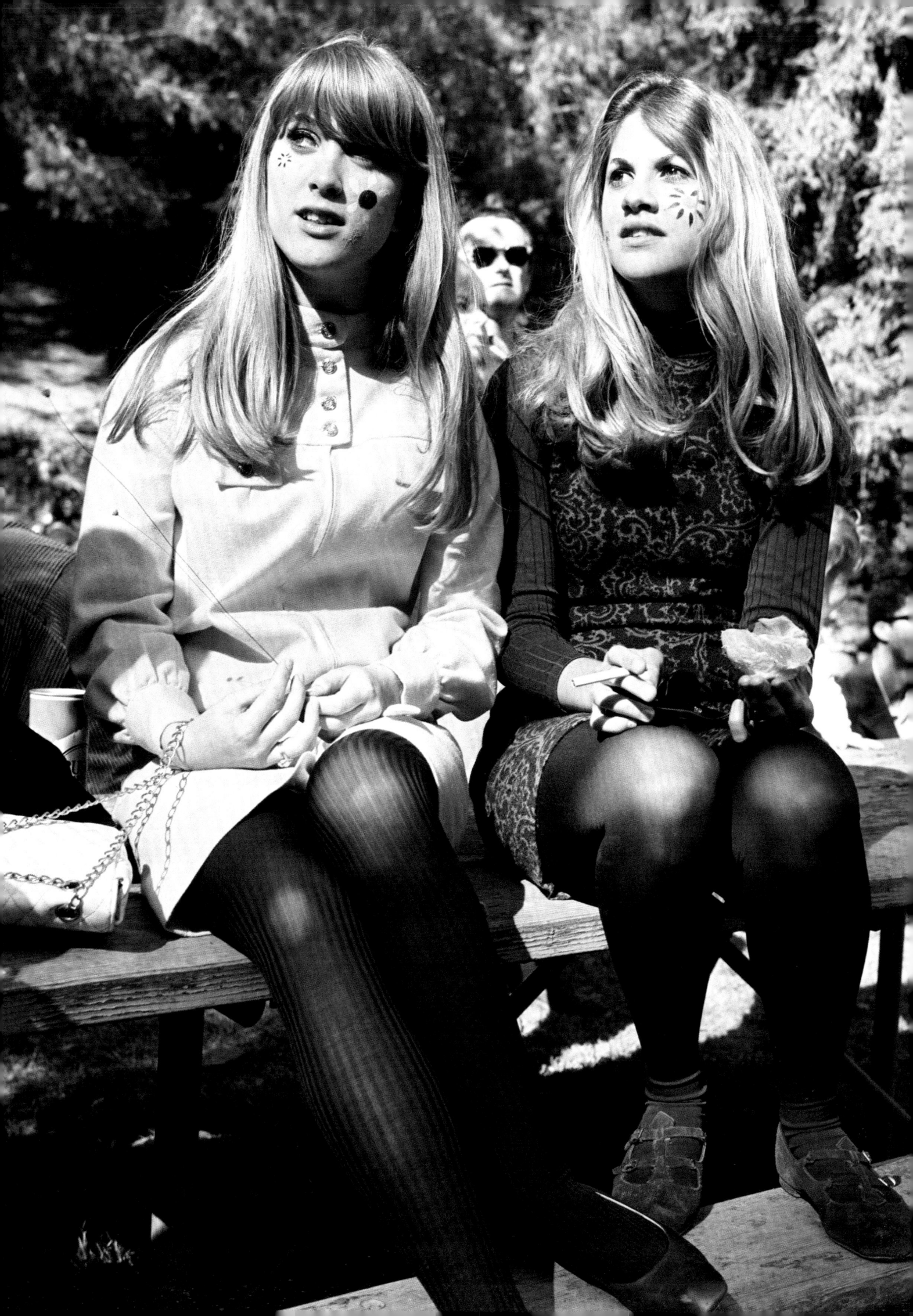

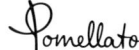

fashion world, which had given America its most mold-breaking models, Jean Shrimpton and Twiggy. Here, too, were clues to a change. Shrimpton had a soft seriousness. Twiggy and her American look-alikes, Penelope Tree and Andy Warhol's muse Edie Sedgwick (both aristocratic girls), were waifs with huge, wonder-filled, Keene-painting eyes. They looked innocent, the opposite of Vegas broads and *Cosmo* girls. The coupling of guilelessness with sexuality meant being a female adventurer needn't be "cheap," but Sweet Sixteen party winsome.

The girl that everyone wanted to be was Julie Christie. So stunning, so classy in the contemporary film *Darling* and romantic period piece *Dr. Zhivago*. Her self-possession beamed like radar to female viewers who might have correctly predicted that she was the only female so elusive and unownable that even one of the era's most notable lotharios, Warren Beatty, was dumped by her. Christie previewed what was about to bloom, the idea that a woman could have as many lovers as a man yet retain her dignity, mystique, and one more advantage—her heart.

The Magical Year

The values of "responsible adulthood" gave way to ecstatic youthfulness in 1967. Style-wise, and in terms of the new liberation for women, things happened the opposite way. In London, The Beatles' *Sergeant Pepper's Lonely Hearts Club Band*, the album of the year, featured John, Paul, George, and Ringo in nineteenth-century military uniforms. Young women in London were following suit. The miniskirt was being replaced by romantic period gowns, many by Barbara Hulanicki of Biba, the boutique so popular with rock stars' girlfriends that Betsey Johnson, one of the hippest designers in New York, stood in line for over an hour to get in. *Elvira Madigan* and *Far from the Madding Crowd* (the latter starring Julie Christie)—these

movies influenced Hulanicki and the girls in London, who wore street-sweeping gowns as if out of *Wuthering Heights*. "My romantic clothes were historical: Victorian, mid-late nineteenth century," Hulanicki says. "Art Nouveau was terribly important. Alfonse Mucha, who is Czech like I am: that's who my influence was."

The Haight-Ashbury district of San Francisco was a thrilling center of action for the dawning West Coast culture. For several years before they burst out in public, esoteric young art students, poets, and hipsters (some in a commune nicknamed "The Family Dog") took to dressing in their city's analogue to London's historicism. They wore the thrift-store-rescued clothes of the 1849 Gold Rush prospectors, with the period-accurate, long-haired men in high hats, vests, and watch fobs and the girls in wagon-train-worthy gowns, Victorian bonnets, velvet capes, and lace-up boots. Folk-singing women like Judy Collins and Joan Baez had always worn what Collins calls "Maid Marian" dresses; now other girls did too.

Joni Mitchell, the Canadian singer-songwriter who was thriving under the public radar—and who, as a friend from those years put it, "had a propriety that was so natural, you didn't notice it"—charmed audiences at the Second Fret coffeehouse in Philadelphia with her long, straight blonde hair, her gosh-golly patter, and her delicate vintage clothes. Yet, at the same time, she was ditching a marriage to an older man and taking lovers. Like Joni, more and more young women were strolling around the Haight-Ashbury and New York's East Village as if attired from Brontë-era trunks.

For many young people in 1967, the first day you saw your peers dressed in clothes from other centuries was surreal. This was especially true for women, whose personal behavior was as new as their clothes were old. These women were seekers and nonconformists, girls who chose the life that writer Sara Davidson described in her 1967-set memoir *Loose Change:*

Peace and love, Elysian Park, Los Angeles, 1967

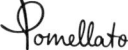

"We would not marry for security or be hampered by convention. It's almost as if we took vows: we were going to make life as interesting a journey as possible and were willing to suffer pain if necessary." Armed with the Pill (which had been made safer seven years after its original manufacture), these girls were taking boyfriend after boyfriend. That they dressed with the quaint decorum of maidens who used smelling salts was in deliciously obfuscating contradiction to the social and erotic barriers they were breaking. "Free love"—and that was the new clarion call (along with "free" *everything*)—was now dignified; a packaging that cleansed premarital recreational sex of shame and guilt and reframed it as classically romantic and heartfully questing.

Although it had been brewing underground in the Bay Area for several years, the buoyant, psychedelic counterculture seemed to have popped out of the oven fully baked one magical day in early 1967, with the same suddenness as the Beatles-borne stealth British Invasion to the States in early 1964. The idealism was astonishing. At the first Human Be-In that January in San Francisco, ten thousand costumed, om-chanting, cavorting, marijuana- and LSD-imbibing young people convened, and free food, drugs, bells, and (sometimes loin-locking) embraces were distributed. "No drunks!" the influential and skeptical eminent local jazz reporter Ralph Gleason marveled, anointing the scene with his surprised approval. Timothy Leary intoned his famous motto— "Turn on, tune in, drop out"—to the crowd, and the call to action, from the beautifully art-directed alternative newspaper *The San Francisco Oracle* was so earnest, it sounds shockingly quaint to today's snark-weathered ears: "When in the course of human events it becomes necessary for people to cease [obeying] obsolete social patterns which have isolated man from his consciousness . . . we the citizens of the Earth declare our *love and compassion for all hate-carrying men and women*." Love and compassion. Love, love, love. Free, free, free.

The euphoric elevation of a word that stood for kindness, adoration, and mother–child bonding, along with the elevation of a word that stood for selfless refusal to profit and an act that had been thought of as funky and raw—sex was turned almost religious. Sex became a rite of generosity, vulnerability, and precious human connection. To give yourself away carnally was *good* and "hip" and self-confident and pure. There was no such thing as promiscuity anymore—what a fusty word that was. The last thing a 1967 girl wanted to be was "uptight."

It wasn't just the change in the perception of sex from raunchy to generosity. There was a subtle feminine coloration of the 1967 counterculture from the start, beginning with the graphic designs of the posters for the Fillmore and Avalon Ballroom rock concerts—for Jefferson Airplane, The Grateful Dead, Big Brother and the Holding Company, and other bands. Although the graphic artists were all male (Wes Wilson, Rick Griffin, Stanley Mouse, Alton Kelley, Victor Moscoso), their style was feminine; everything swirled or was sinewy in homage to the Art Nouveau movement. (Alfonse Mucha, Barbara Hulanicki's clothing inspiration, also inspired these poster artists.) The new dancing style, too, was so different from the angular, thumping Twist. It was sensual and languorous, and so feminine that when The Byrds toured the Midwest, some of the long-haired, undulating male backup dancers were pounced on by macho locals. Girls appreciated boys who took the risk (even if those boys used their long hair and groovy vibes as a pretext to get in the girls' pants).

The culture was feminine in other ways: LSD and marijuana prompted rumination and thoughtfulness, the opposite of the macho surliness that liquor often brings out. The new images—flowers in hair, rainbows on cheeks, bells tied to fingertips—were traditionally feminine. So were the accessories and pastimes: tarot and astrology, Tiffany lamps, Beardsley prints. With these subtle cues, the new culture

OPPOSITE: **Model Samantha Jones in Udaipur, India, wearing Emilio Pucci, 1967**

PAGES 26–27: **Shoppers on Carnaby Street in London's Soho, 1967**

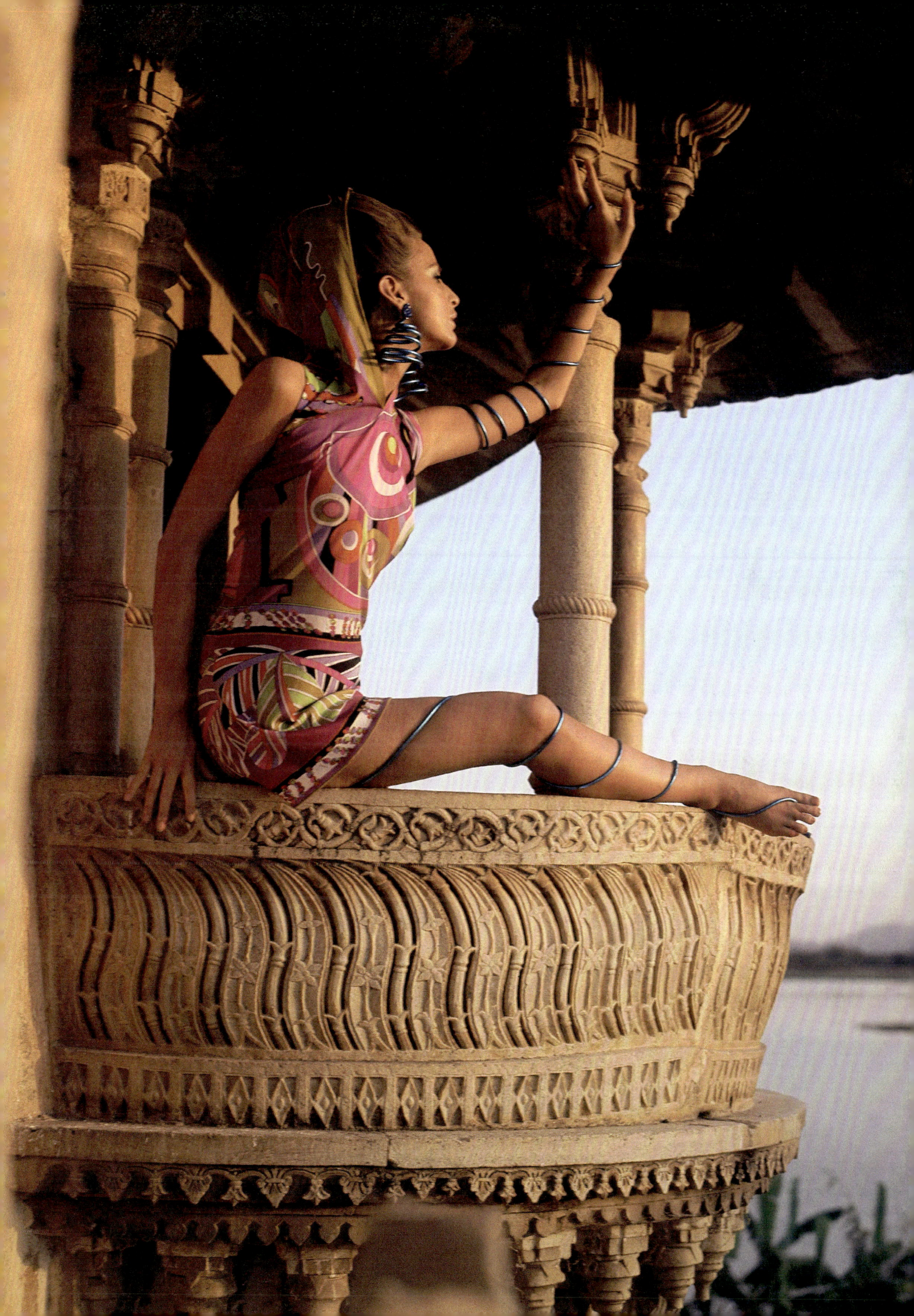

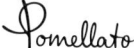

entranced girls who'd spent their previous years as insecure, dutifully beer-sipping, madras-clad sorority pledges. They wafted, dreamlike, through a door that had suddenly sprung open at the exact moment they were ready for it to do so. The highpoint of this Summer of Love was the Monterey Pop Festival in late June. It was the first-ever of its kind; there had been jazz and folk festivals but never pop or rock. It was the brainchild of John Phillips, leader of The Mamas and Papas—the hit-making quartet famous for "California Dreaming" and for pioneering the shift from folk rock to a '50s-style, close-harmonized, psychedelic hybrid—and the group's producer, Lou Adler. John Phillips's wife and singing partner, Michelle Phillips, also had a big hand in organizing the festival. The lineup was chock-full of now-legendary rock groups—The Jimi Hendrix Experience, The Who, The Grateful Dead, Eric Burdon and the Animals, Jefferson Airplane—many of whom had never met the wide U.S. public, or even one another.

The Monterey Pop Festival made an overnight star of Janis Joplin, who was a wild, lovable, middle-class white girl from Texas who sang like a black blues veteran. Though she wore a pantsuit to perform (that's how innocent of her own nascent charisma she was), she would soon be known for her fabulous bell bottoms, big floppy hats, and flamboyant tops. The other queen of the summer, Joplin's opposite in so many ways, was Jefferson Airplane's lead singer, Grace Slick. A former finishing school graduate, socialite, and couture model, she was as icy as Janis was warm and vulnerable, as chic as Janis was shabby, as arrogant about her looks as Janis was almost tragically insecure about her own. Both sent messages to their non-celebrity female peers. Janis's message was that an unbeautiful girl with heart and soul can be a superstar. Grace's message was to fellow debutantes: stop that corny crap and join the hip rebellion.

The festival's biggest message may have come from filmmaker D. A. Pennebaker's documentary *Monterey Pop*. Virtually every face—whether performer or audience member—looked beautiful, cultivated, and serene. From the orchids laid out on each seat to the lobster in the green room, this was an elite event. The festival marked the new counterculture not as an assemblage of, as some people scorned, dirty hippies, but as a highly aspirational new movement for the young people who had been the "popular kids" in top American high schools. The long gowns, the straight hair, the calm entitlement, and élan behind the grooving to the music—this was a bit of *Vogue* magazine in the Monterey, California, campgrounds.

Actress Peggy Lipton noticed something else: it was a bonding of look-alike soulmates. "My God!" she says, recalling it euphorically. "You saw people just like yourself for the *first* time. And it was *glam*! All these gorgeous long, straight-haired girls—I looked just like them and they looked just like me! All these gorgeous guys in bandanas and no shirts." Peggy's friend, the actress Salli Sachse, had appeared in seven surfer movies, but her sensibility had hairpin-turned along with the changes in the year. Hearing Peggy rave about the concert, Salli moved to Laurel Canyon, joined a commune, and eventually left an on-brink-of-stardom Jackson Browne crestfallen when she insisted on going to Morocco alone. A Twist-dancing, hunk-fawning extra in *Beach Blanket Bingo* morphing into a solo globetrotter? In one year? Yes! 1967 did that!

These girls plunged into traveling, as Salli would do, journeying to Morocco, Afghanistan, Ibiza, or, like Joni Mitchell did at the height of her fame several years later, to Crete. While there she lived in a cave with a churlish, mischievous boyfriend who mocked her fame. Joni wrote two songs—"Carey" and "California"—about this man. Her wanderlust, her folding in with a community of hip expatriates from every country in Europe, on bucolic islands and other off-the-grid meccas was part of the new internationalism that sprang from that year. The folks at the Bar Jamaica understood it. The impulse was

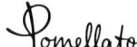

shared. What was different is that before 1967 women were the minority of travelers and solo café-sitters; after 1967 many were female. Djellabas, jewel-dotted sheepskin vests, ethnic scarfs wrapped around the head, boutique finds picked up in Milan, Paris, and Barcelona . . . these modern women dressed as if out of the dreamy Crosby, Stills & Nash songs "Marrakesh Express" and "Wooden Ships." Jewelry to match this spirit was required.

After

With travel came the desire to stay free, and for longer than previous generations of women ever had. Marriage rates dropped. Women proudly stayed single through their twenties. As the spirit of 1967 edged into the compatible new political movement, Second Wave Feminism started to take off. *Ms.* magazine was on the drawing board; Gloria Steinem gained prominence as a woman whose beauty and enjoyment of the most coveted men in New York proved to a prejudiced American public that serious feminists weren't ugly man haters. Betty Friedan's National Organization for Women (NOW) began to rectify legal and judicial sexism hiding in plain sight.

Several years after the barrier-breaking of 1967, a young singer named Carly Simon wrote a conventionally elegant, deceptively Sondheim-like, song, "That's the Way I've Always Heard It Should Be." The song had a 1967-capping theme: a young upscale woman was rejecting marriage because such a bond would keep her on a shelf, would deny her freedom. After decades of men getting marital cold feet while women cajoled them to go through with their weddings, here was a woman poignantly expressing doubts about the institution. And she was doing so at the very moment that many of her friends were dissolving their marriages because sexism was finally being recognized like a thorn in the shoe—and no one could turn back the clock and forget that their husbands expressed it.

Carly Simon was the perfect person to represent this position. She was the daughter of the cofounder of the publishing house Simon & Schuster and a Civil Rights activist, a sophisticated, witty young Sarah Lawrence-college-educated woman raised amid such convention-breaking. Beautiful, sexy as hell (her legs went on for miles), and stylish, she represented the top-drawer New York intellectual. Before, during, and just after 1967, Carly traveled to Europe with lovers, lost lovers, dumped lovers, and felt alternatively elegiacally affirmed and heartbreakingly rejected. She remained single. Freedom was worth the bumpy ride to her. Like the male Beats, like the nineteenth-century Transcendentalists, life lessons burnished wisdom and character.

"That's the Way I've Always Heard It Should Be" seemed such a clarion call to women that Elektra Records executive Jac Holzman sent it to radio stations' secretaries (in the 1970s most females in offices were secretaries). The secretaries badgered their bosses to get the record played on their stations. The song became a hit because women identified with it. Carly Simon became the 1971 Girl of the Hour just as *Ms.* magazine's first issue was being printed, becoming feminism's media outreach to Middle America. She had many lovers—Cat Stevens, Warren Beatty, Jack Nicholson, Kris Kristofferson—before marrying her counterpart man of the hour, the American Heathcliffe, James Taylor. The promise of 1967—independent women relinquishing none of their classiness while becoming as free, experimental, and sexual as men—was fulfilled in her and in her peers.

Pomellato's delicate, jubilant, witty jewelry was made, and continues to be made, for all the women who grabbed that emotional, experimental brass ring fifty years ago and never let it go, and for their daughters who have inherited the lessons and the lifestyle.

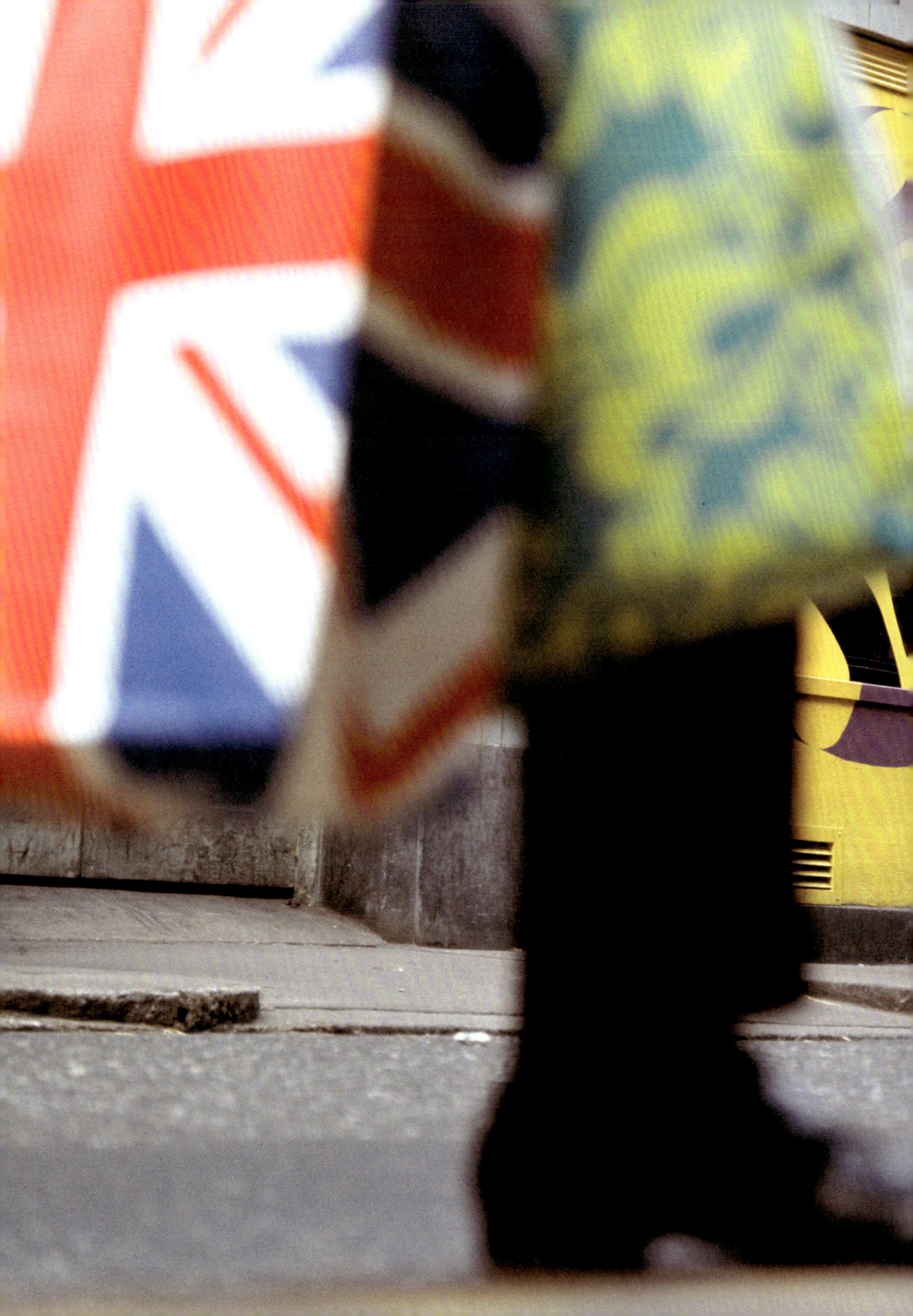

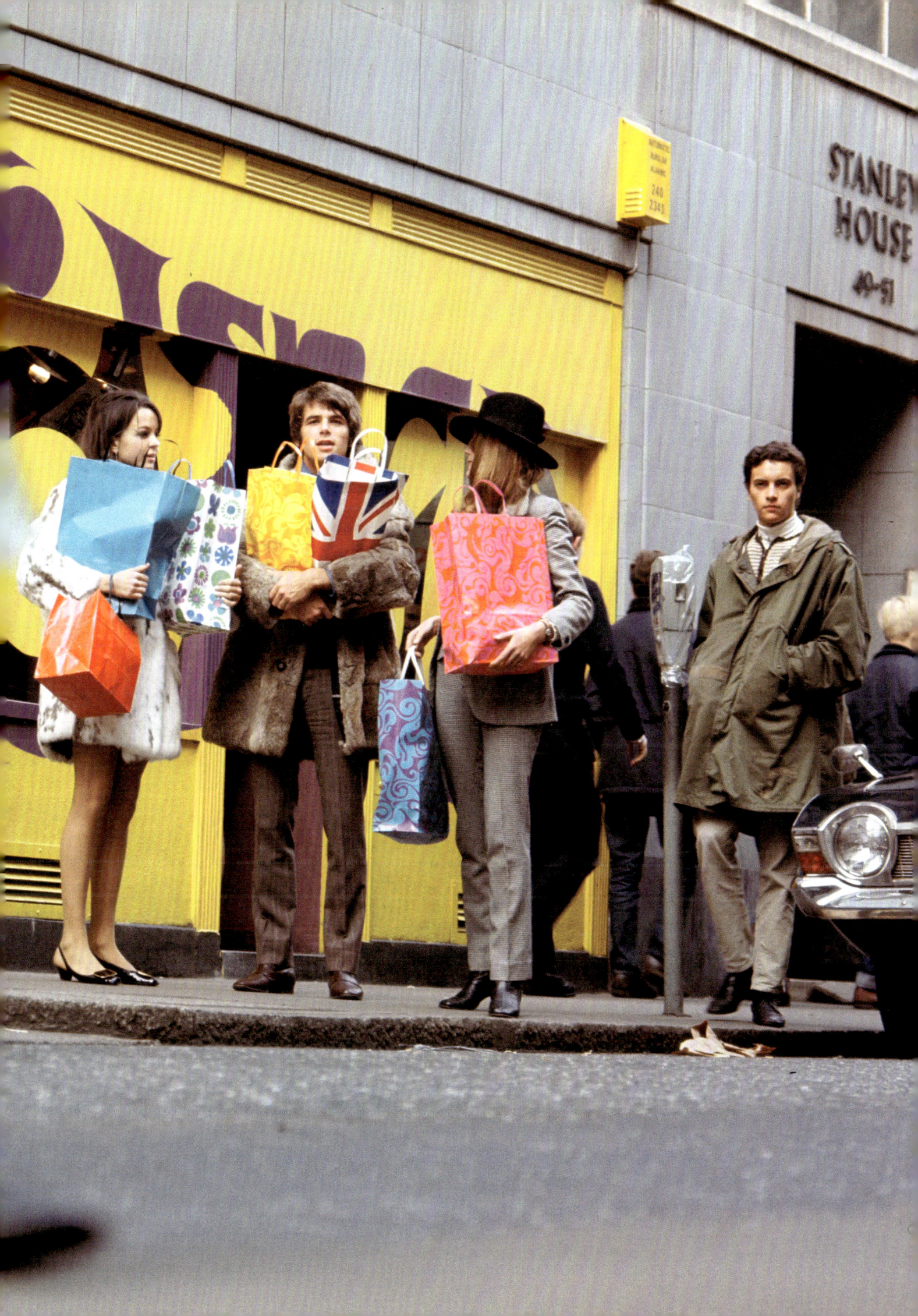

THE YEAR *W*HEN EVERYTHING CHANGED IN *M*ILAN

BY GIUSI FERRÉ

Calendars are sentimental yet rational. They force us to deal with time, changing moods, and memories that stay with us, because there is a lot of the past in these lists that have been created to keep us imprisoned in the present. In 1967, Milan was prepared for the powerful changes that would sweep through politics and the economy, which would become a system of production activities established around creativity, ranging from design to fashion. The media projected these developments into a troubled reality in which many snapshots— different and not harmonious—overlap: the important presence of workers and the first protests, the advent of alternative experiences, and the forms of socially diverse fashion. This phenomenon no longer trickled down from the top, but rose from below, driven by a stormy evolution of customs that deserve to be investigated with curiosity and freedom of thought.

Back then, Milan was a city of factories, veritable cathedrals of labor: Carlo Erba, Magneti Marelli, Caproni, Breda, Enel, Innocenti. Now these work yards are being completely restored or are awaiting transformation or repurposing. One example is the glorious Caproni, which built planes and now holds the magical universe of Gucci's creativity.

It is important to remember this, because it defines the city's character. The quintessentially Milanese virtue that the nineteenth-century philosopher Carlo Cattaneo grasped is the relationship between mind and hand. At 5 a.m. garbage collectors and workers would make their way through the foggy city streets on their bicycles. The factory whistles blew. There were discussions about the center-left party at the Palazzo Marino, now the City Hall and mentioned in Alessandro Manzoni's *The Betrothed* as the seventeenth-century family

Present throughout the history of Pomellato, the sensual *Iconica* gold collection is relaunched in 2017 to celebrate the jeweler's fiftieth anniversary

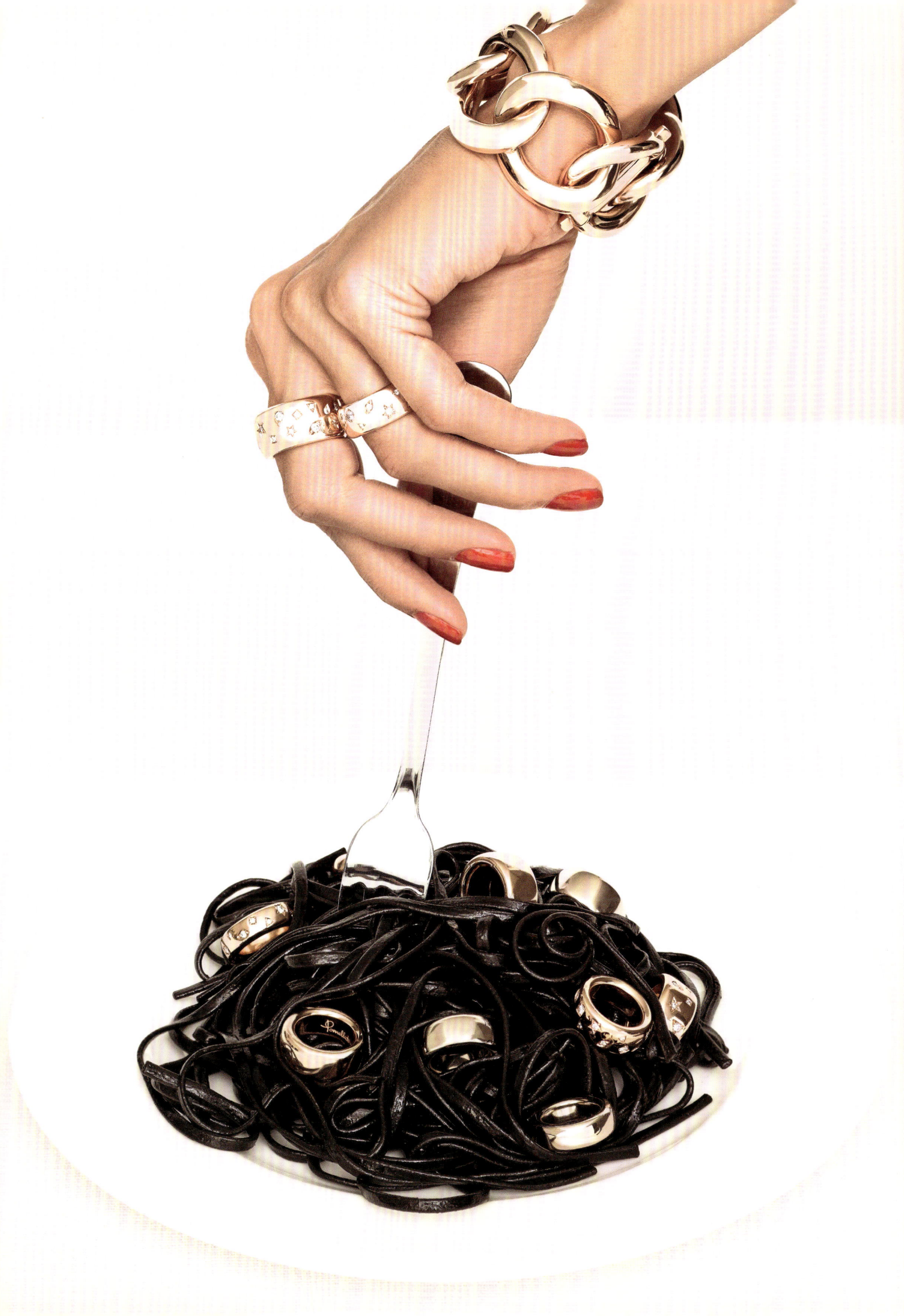

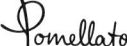

home of the Nun of Monza. There was a long debate that commenced during Mayor Ferrari's tenure and culminated with the appointment of Aldo Aniasi.

The year 1967 was a "young" year: Italian schools had the highest number of enrollments ever recorded. Nearly six million children had been born between 1947 and 1952 and, at this point, those aged fifteen to twenty were entering high school and college. In February, the sweeping occupations of the universities began while awaiting the reforms promised by Minister Luigi Gui. The movement started in Pisa, home to the "Normale," one of Italy's most prestigious universities. In February hundreds of students stopped all activities at the Palazzo Campana, the venue of the Humanities Departments at the University of Turin, for twenty days. The rector asked the police to step in to clear them out, but the students held a massive sit-in, showing passive resistance. Two hundred students were carried out bodily and charged. In Viareggio, the protests were taken up by high school students, who sided with the university students. On November 1, the University of Sociology in Trento—the only one in Italy offering studies in this new field—was occupied. On November 17, it was the Catholic University of Milan's turn, when its students discovered their tuition fees had been doubled.

A wave seemed to run through the entire city, touching key points like Brera and the Academy. This place is the heart of our history, as it was rife with surprising intellectual activity that managed to transform a geography of little streets into a space of the imagination, where the aspiration of living within art could perhaps come true. The sort of Latin Quarter between the Bar Jamaica and the little restaurant run by the Pirovini sisters, who generously jotted down people's bills in a notebook, knowing full well they would never be paid, between the Brera Art Gallery and the Botanical Garden, attracted painters who had been habitués there before or immediately after World War II. There was

Roberto Crippa, Ennio Morlotti, Alik Cavaliere, Andrea Cascella, Guido and Sandro Somaré, and Bruno Cassinari. It was the generation that represented modernization as far back as the 1930s, when, thanks to professors such as Achille Funi, Carlo Carrà, Aldo Carpi, and Marino Marini, the Academy opened its doors to students with a cultural education and a very different social background with respect to the past.

It was in this thriving environment, this crossroads of hopes and dreams, this joyful and feverish atmosphere, that Pino Rabolini immersed himself: this was the man who came up with the idea of bringing jewelry into the up-and-coming world of prêt-à-porter. Like all revolutionaries, he knew the rules, in this case of the goldsmith's art, and mastered them so he could move beyond them. This was an idea that flashed through his mind a number of times, after evenings spent talking—and listening—at the Jamaica. He was a child of the hardworking upper middle class that led Milan from postwar reconstruction to the consumer society, but that also wanted information and entertainment to satisfy the thirst for modernity. At the age of eighteen, Rabolini went off to live on his own.

Yet he had been brought up in a progressive and inquisitive family that loved to examine the paths of art and international thought. His father was a friend of Antonio Ghiringhelli, superintendent at the opera house La Scala, as well as Paolo Grassi and Giorgio Strehler, the geniuses behind the Piccolo Teatro that, through a close network of relations, linked the world of Milanese theater and art with that of other European cities and the United States. In 1956, he had given his son season tickets for two in the fourth row at the Piccolo. One evening a man with round spectacles sat down behind Rabolini: it was Bertold Brecht, who had come to check the staging of his *Threepenny Opera*.

It was natural that this young man in search of beauty would gravitate to Brera and the Jamaica, to the narrow streets where cheap boarding houses offered rooms to aspiring artists, and working-class taverns also welcomed professors, intellectuals, and art lovers. Those seeking modernity would gather in this district, in the middle-class neighborhood between Via Borgonuovo and Via dell'Orso, Via Pontaccio and the church of San Marco. One of them was Pino Rabolini, who pictured a new life and new passions for jewelry—authentic jewelry in the quintessential noble metal: gold. In the meantime, the fantasy bijou straddled the line between spatial and yé-yé. On May 13, 1967, during the Beat Fashion Parade at the Piper Club in Turin, the artist Piero Gilardi presented clothes and earrings made of foam rubber, which artificially reproduced the forms of nature. In a cross between irony and provocation, he called them *Vestiti Natura:* Nature Dresses. He sent out a dress made of foam-rubber tree trunks covering the body from the shoulders to the knees, and cinched at the waist by a chain, which probably symbolized the harshness and pressure of human intervention. For the earrings, he invented two enormous phytomorphic protuberances, two bright green cabbages that tripled the size of the model's head. These outfits had been preceded in 1964 by *Vestiti Stati d'Animo*—Mood Dresses—that reproduced the characteristics of figures ranging from the Explorer to the Woman in a Spiritual Crisis.

These were operations at the very edge, but they showed that clothing and decorations were becoming more and more closely linked. "Pomellato's approach is different," says Vincenzo Castaldo, currently creative director and responsible for the brand's entire aesthetic approach. "We're close to fashion because we stem from a similar idea, from an unconventional vision that blends artistic ability and innovative boldness, dedication, and craftsmanship. We are proud to play according to our own rules. But we are always well aware that jewelry will have a long life and will endure, unlike clothes, which are outdated in a season." This is the challenge Castaldo faces every day, just as the great creative director Sergio Silvestris

did for many years before him, all thanks in no small part to the skill of expert hands that converge to create exceptional teamwork, where constant updating must go hand in hand with tradition. It is no longer a question of ego, and the inspiration responds to the identity and method of Pomellato. "They are so precise that, thanks to them, you never get lost. In this task, the contribution of over one hundred master craftspeople working in-house is fundamental. This allows us to test innovative solutions, giving each piece an organic, slightly irregular, and human look. Most of our craftspeople have been with us for decades and, in some cases, sons have taken over from their fathers. I think that this continuity is part of what I'm proud to define as *irresistible charm.*"

It is the concept of emotion on which Rabolini founded his Pomellato, convinced that softness had to be the distinctive feature of everything that touches a woman, even when metal is involved. There is a perfect understanding—that is always renewed—between a woman and Pomellato. Because, while the idea is what promotes the design, what is so appealing is not status, but a free and playful sense of taste. "Overturning standards has always been a method and objective for us," the creative director comments. "Wearing jewelry every day, transforming it into a lifestyle element, means juxtaposing creativity with the quotidian, without any fear of being overwhelmed or of confusing art for an excess of design. Pomellato is not a cold exercise in design, but the chain you can fiddle with, the sautoir you can wrap around your neck twice, the clasps that become a decoration. It's what makes a woman beautiful and strong."

The balance between these two extremes is one of the key elements of the brand and its Milanese essence on the one hand, almost Calvinist and sober-minded, but on the other Mediterranean and Catholic. The basic rule here is not to show off the wealth and beauty that is nevertheless there. Milan is not a source of inspiration, but something more: a state of mind."

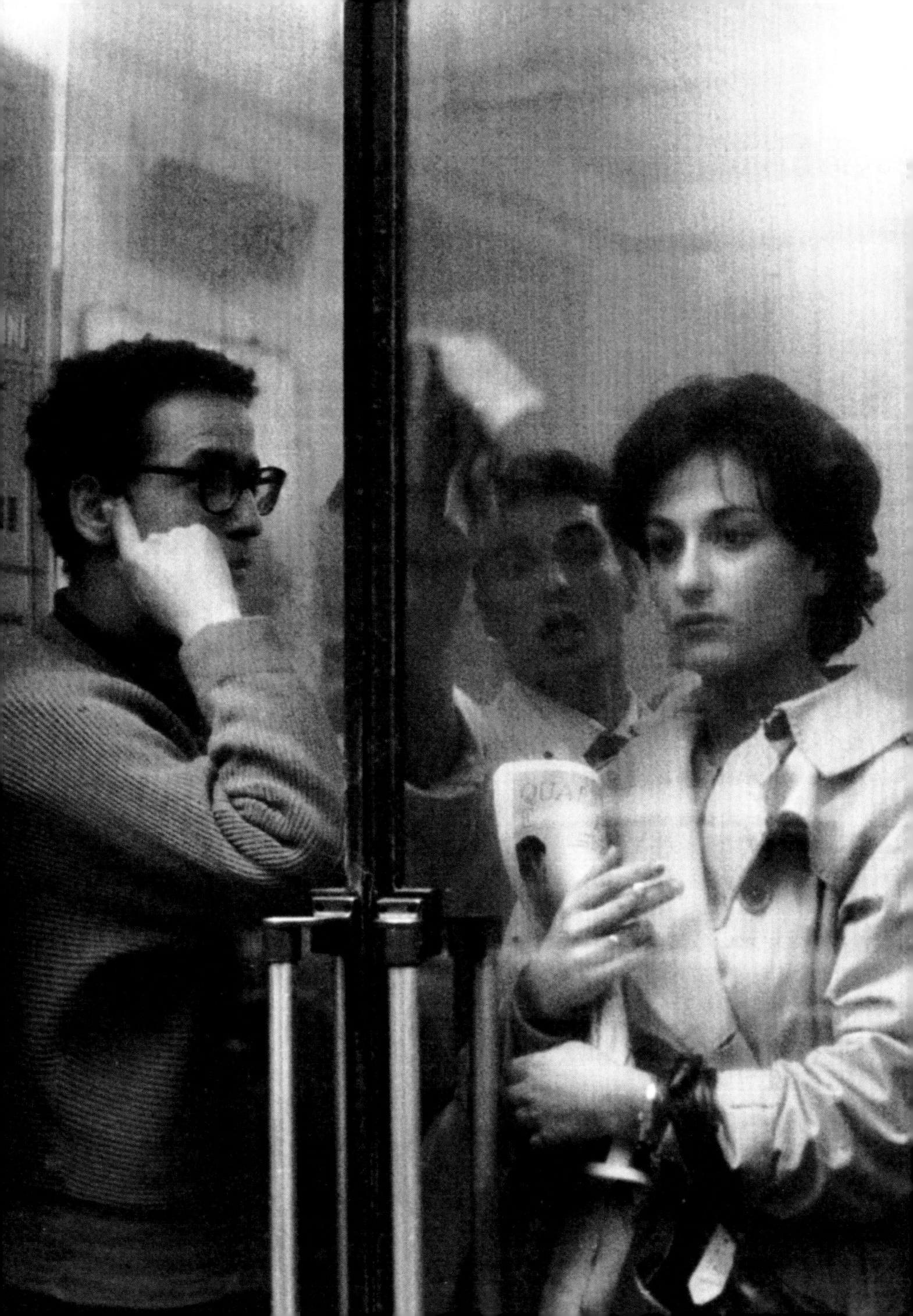

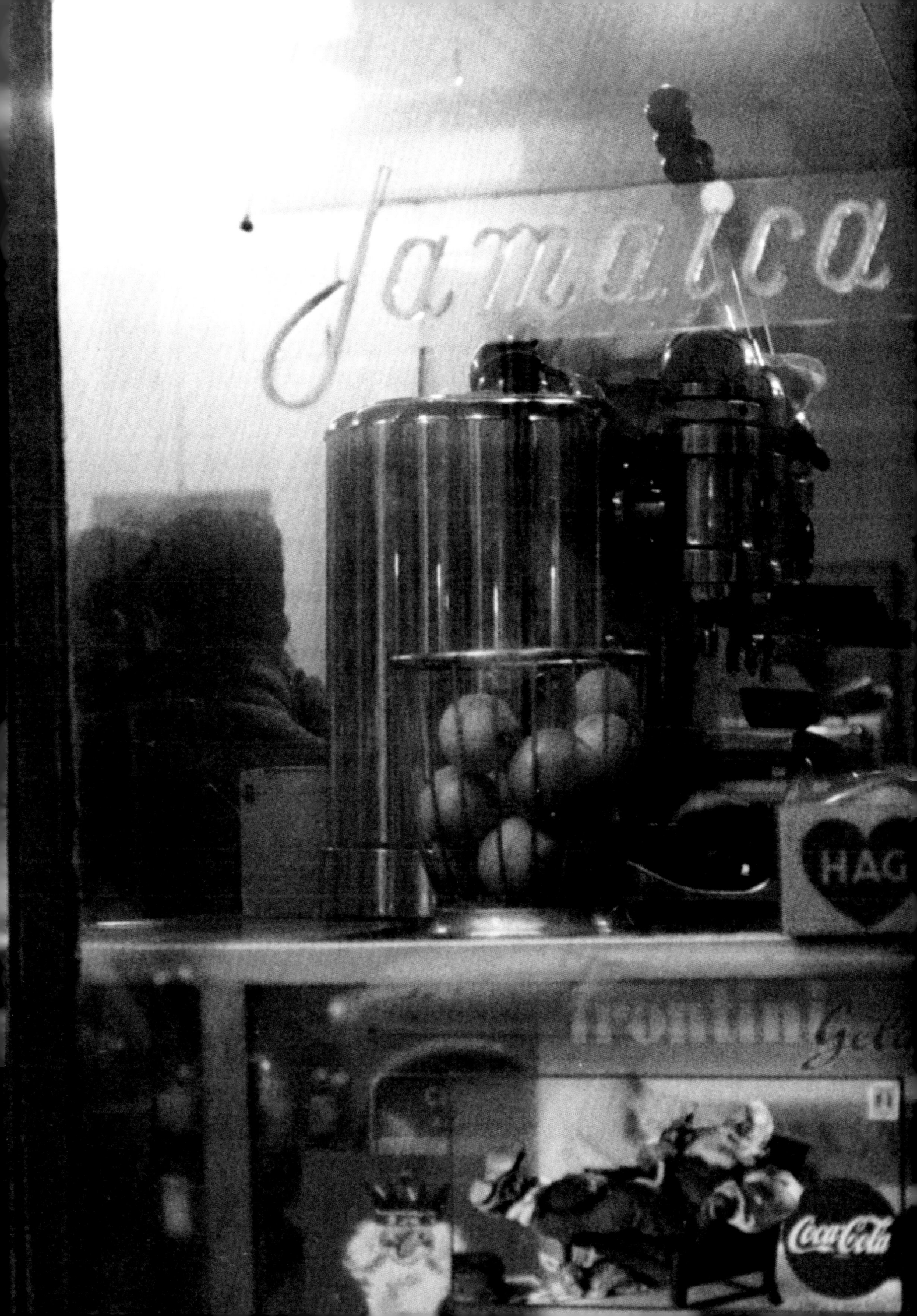

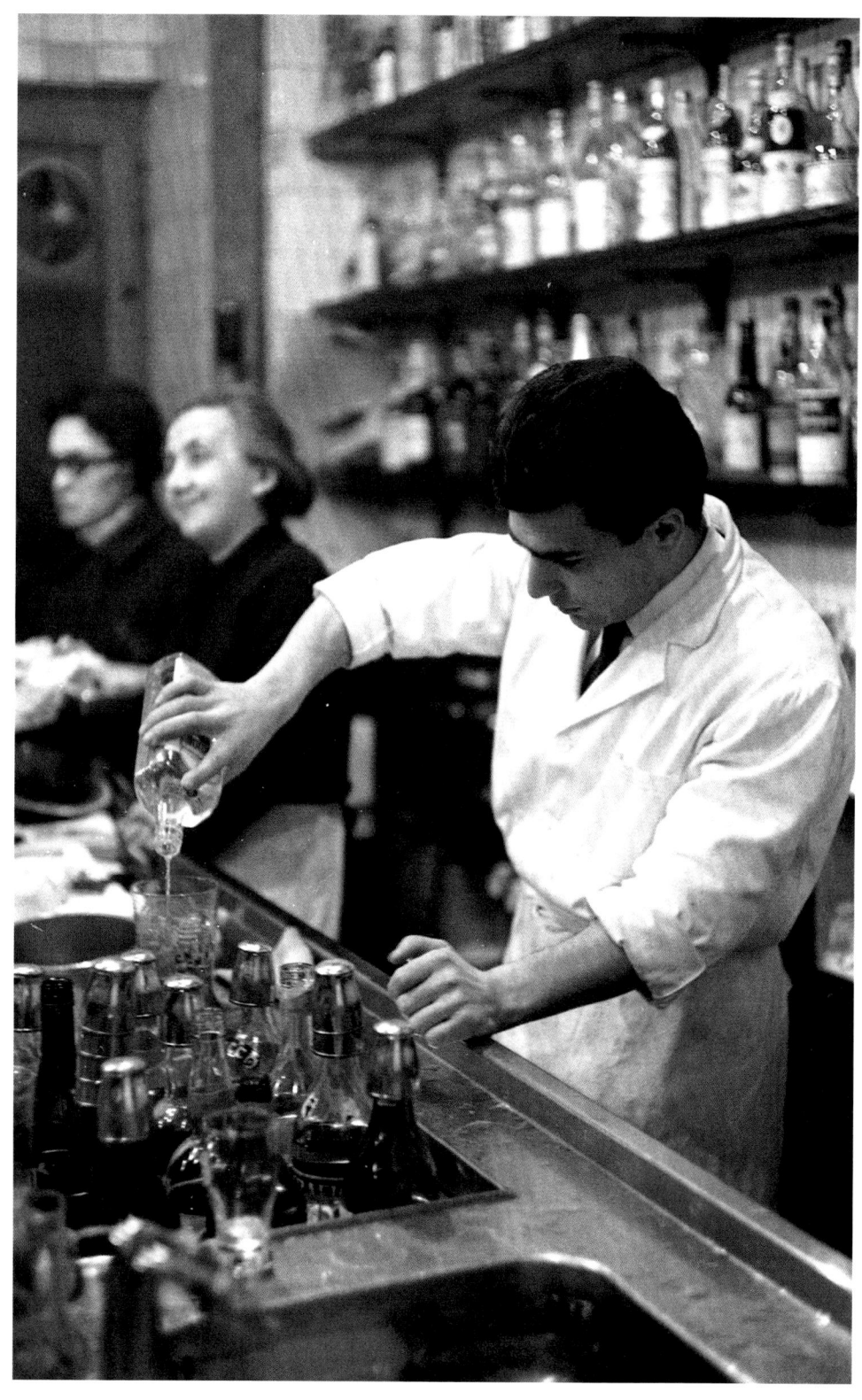

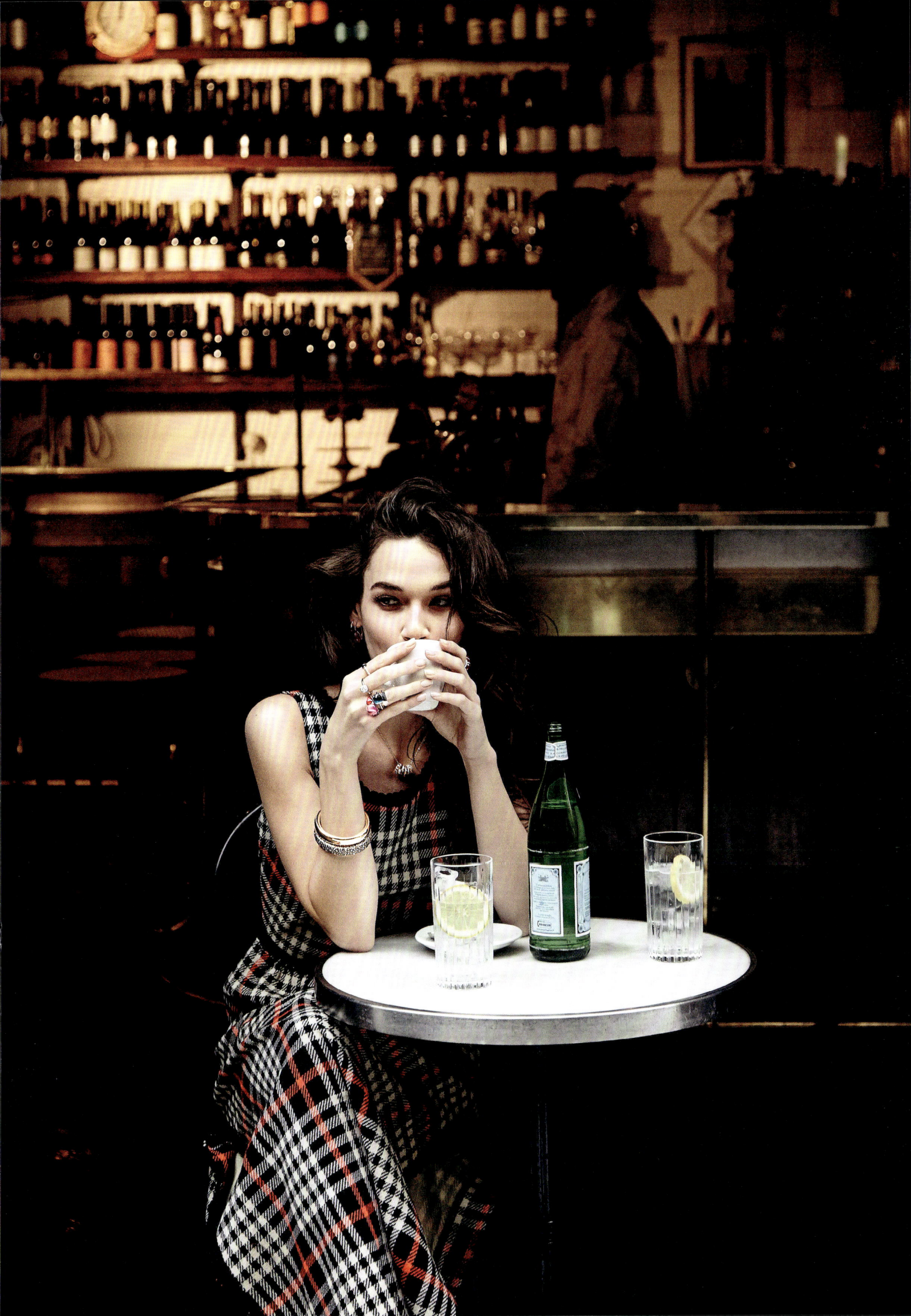

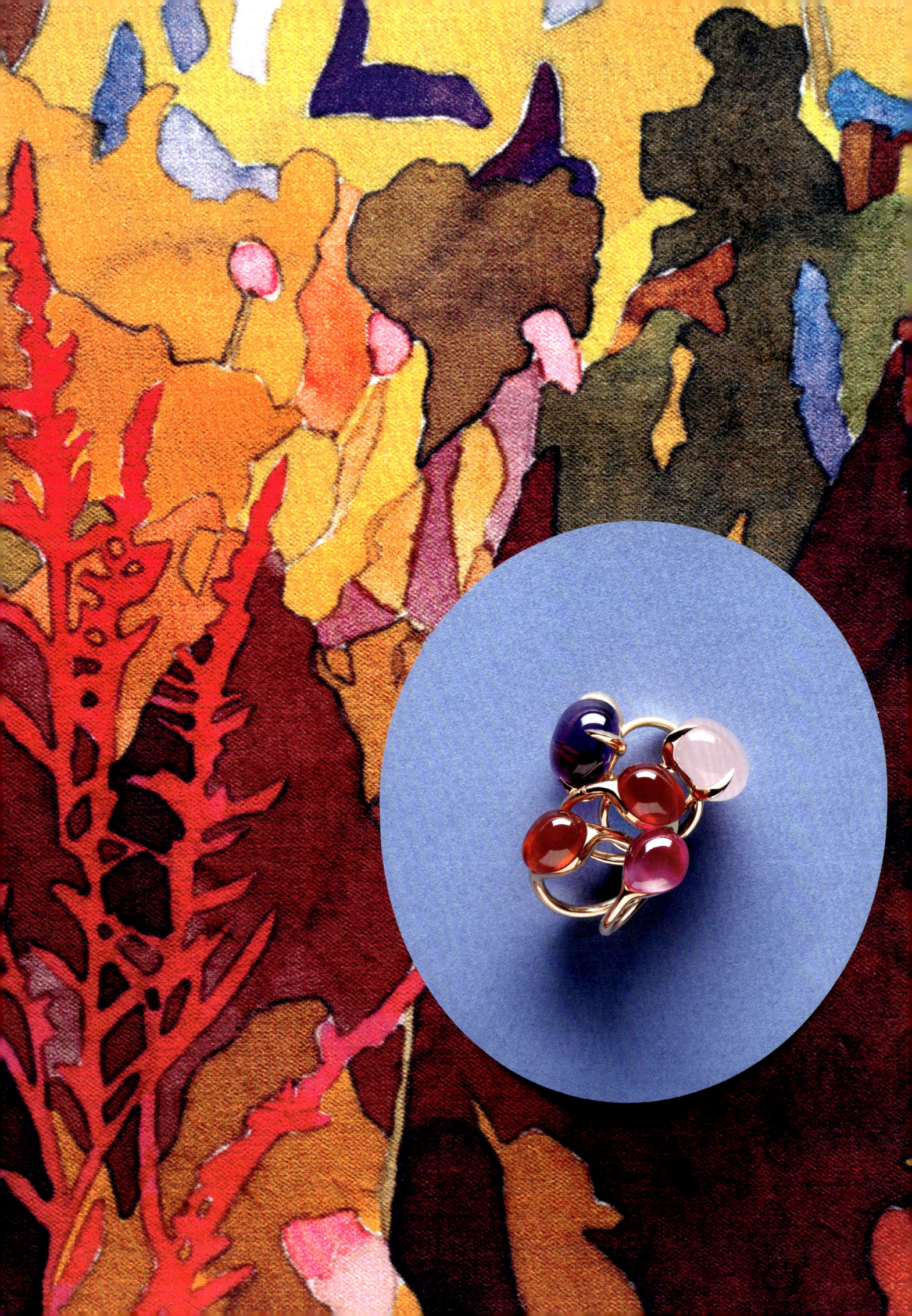

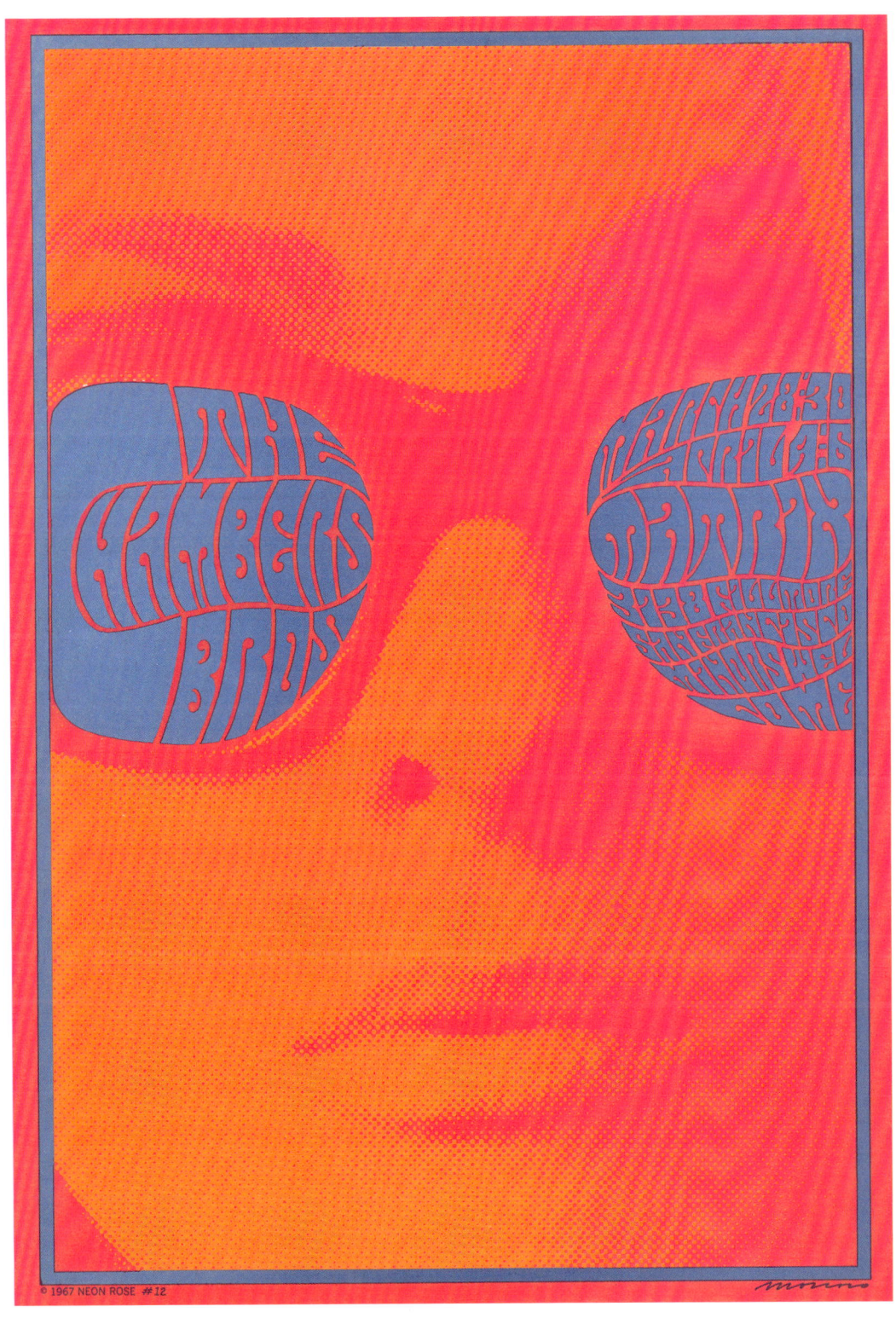

© 1967 NEON ROSE #12

OPPOSITE: Pomellato *Rouge Passion* and *Veleno* collections

ABOVE: Looking toward a bright future: *Neon Rose #12* by Victor Moscoso, 1967

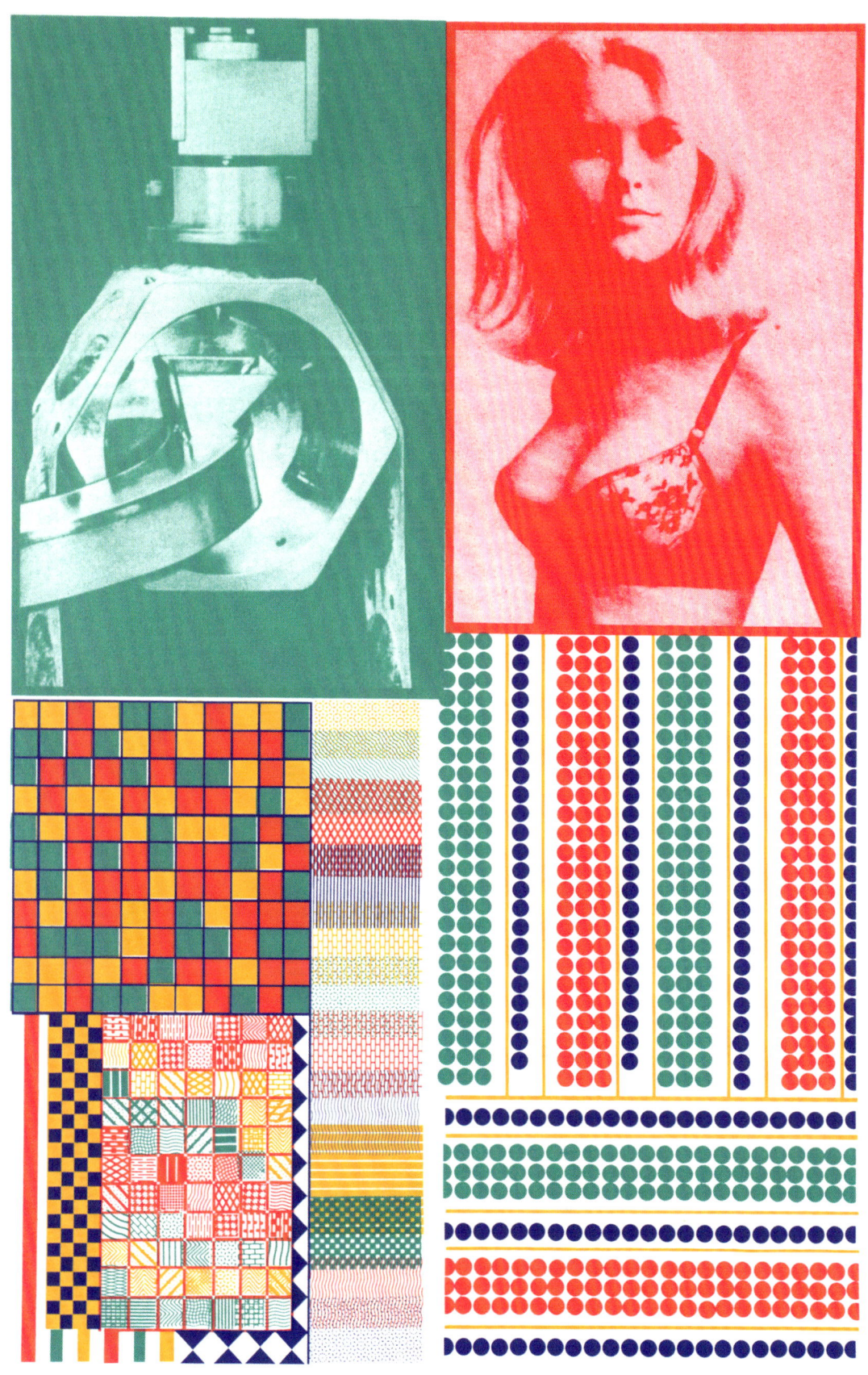

ABOVE: *Moonstrips Empire News* by Edoardo Paolozzi, 1967

OPPOSITE: Pomellato *Capri* collection in turquoise, coral, and diamonds

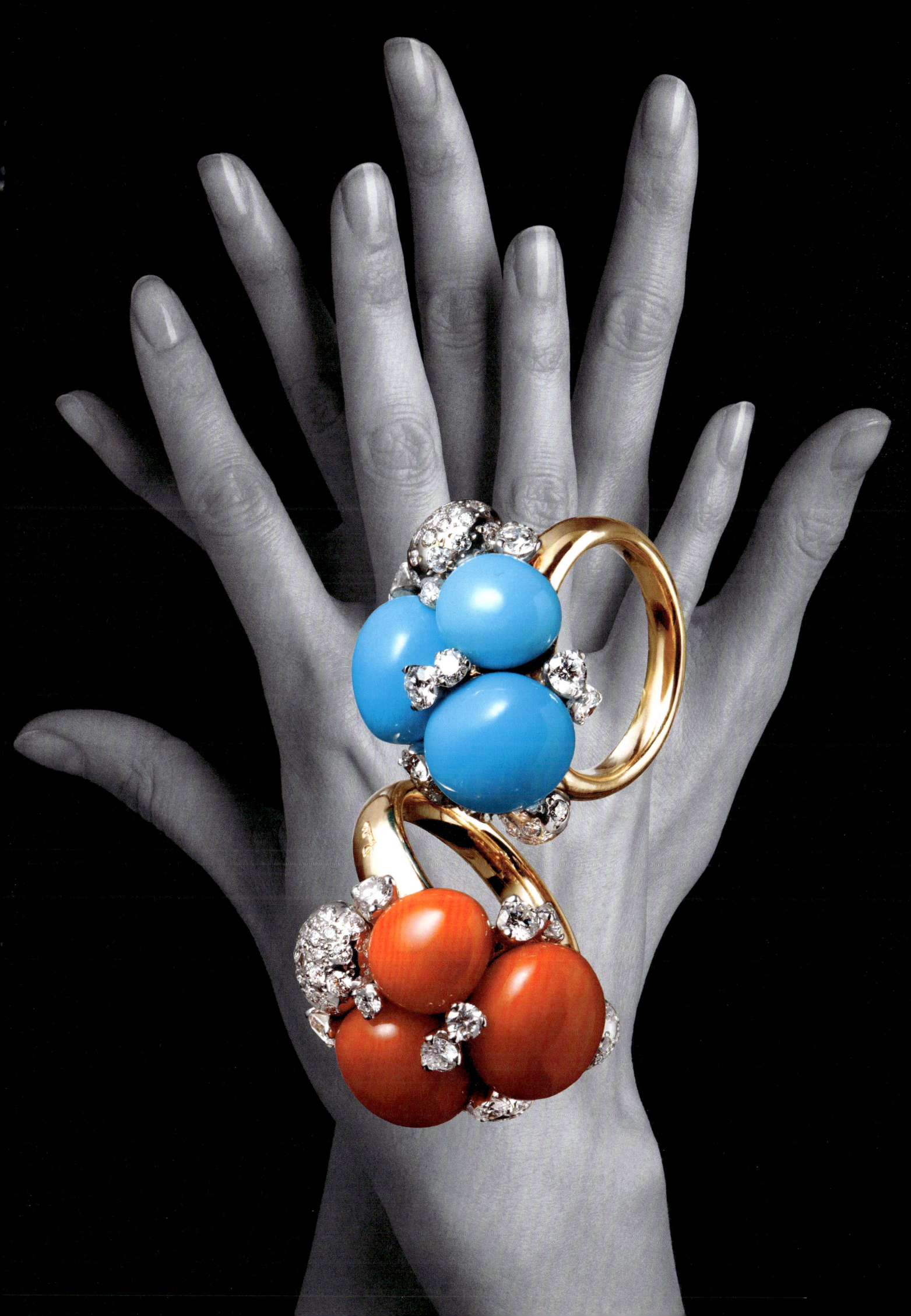

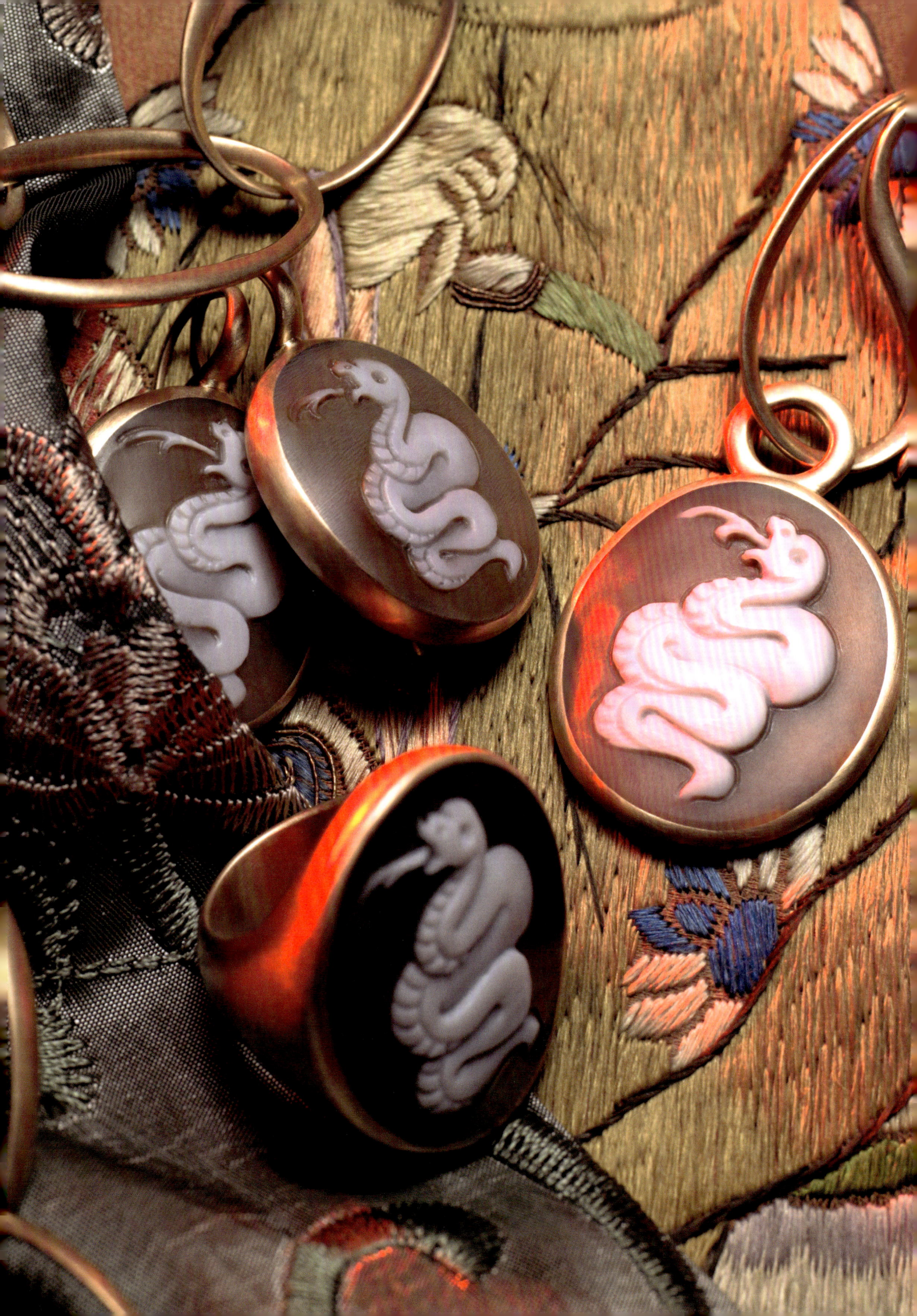

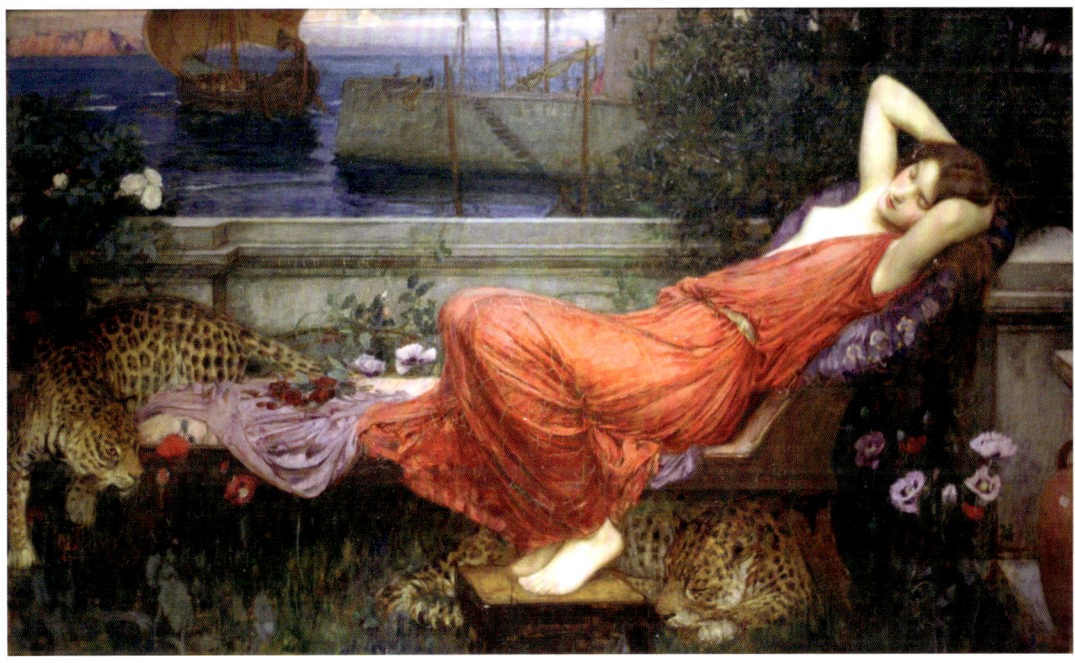

OPPOSITE: Sinful serpent, Pomellato *Eva* collection

ABOVE: *Battersea Bridge at Night* by John Atkinson Grimshaw (1836–1893). The flowing dresses and long hair found in Pre-Raphaelite paintings were a major source of inspiration for Biba's Barbara Hulanicki and the 1960s style she defined

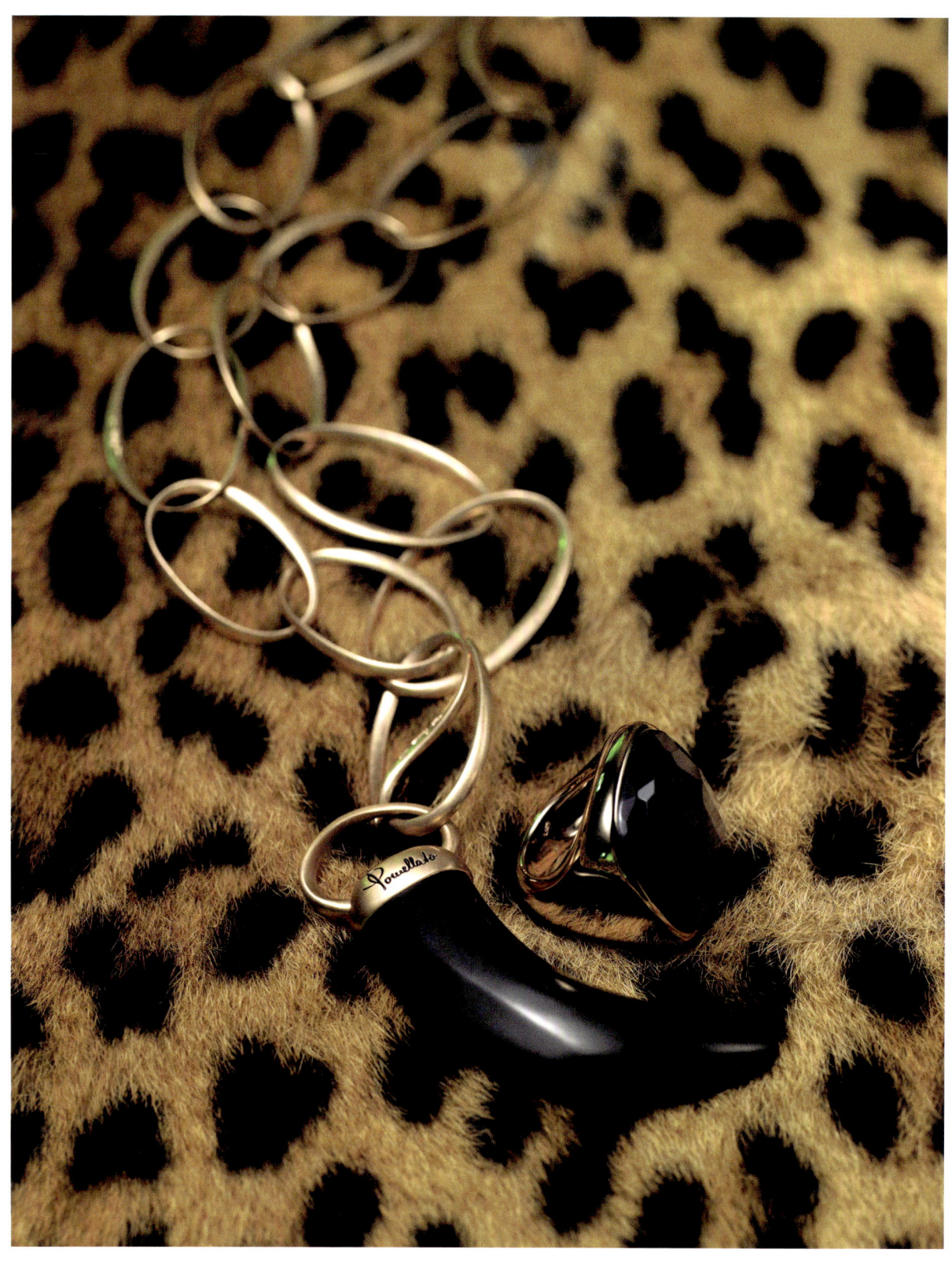

ABOVE: Pomellato *Victoria* collection in jet and gold

OPPOSITE: Free-spirited American singer Carly Simon shot by Jack Robinson for *Vogue*, 1971

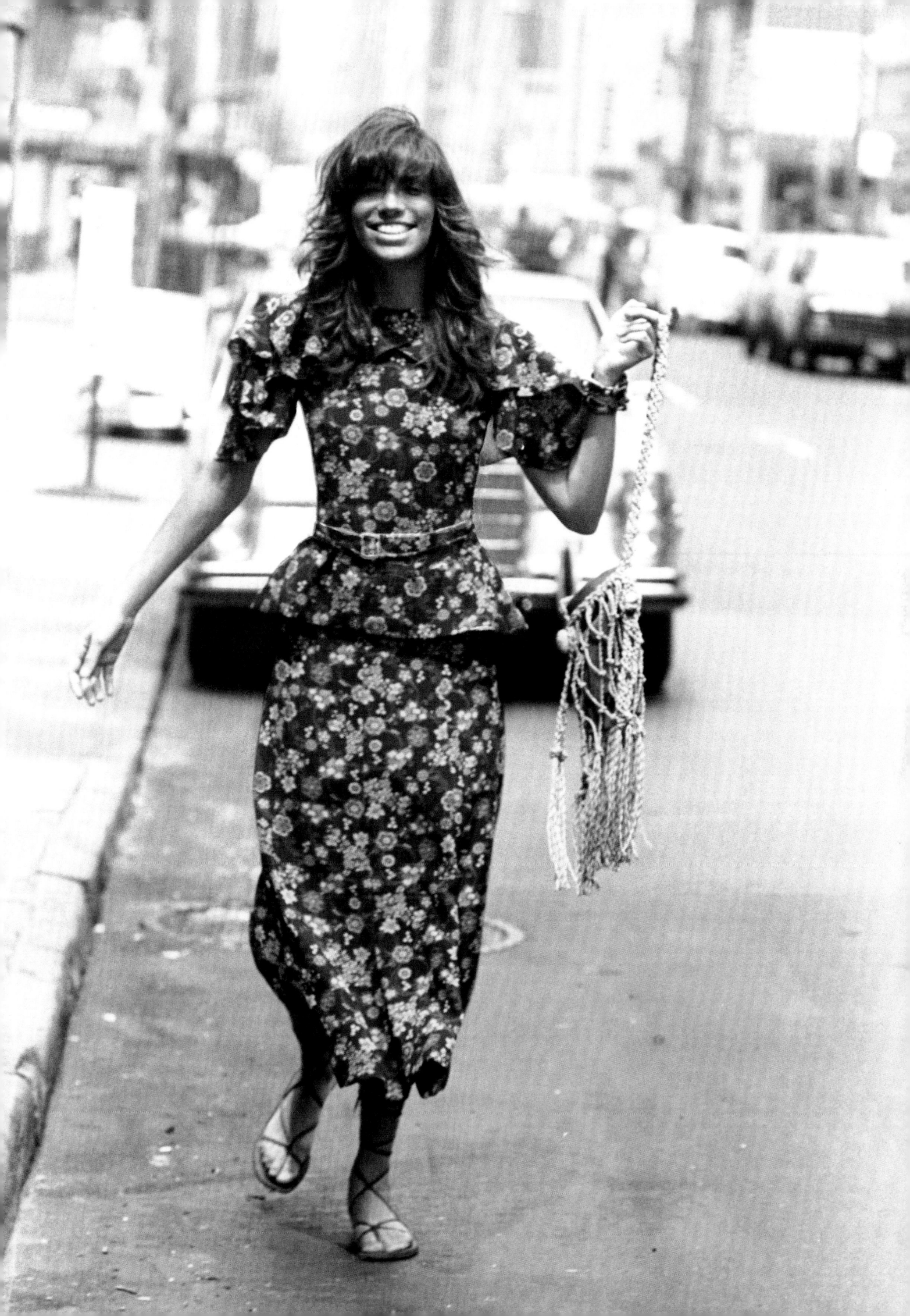

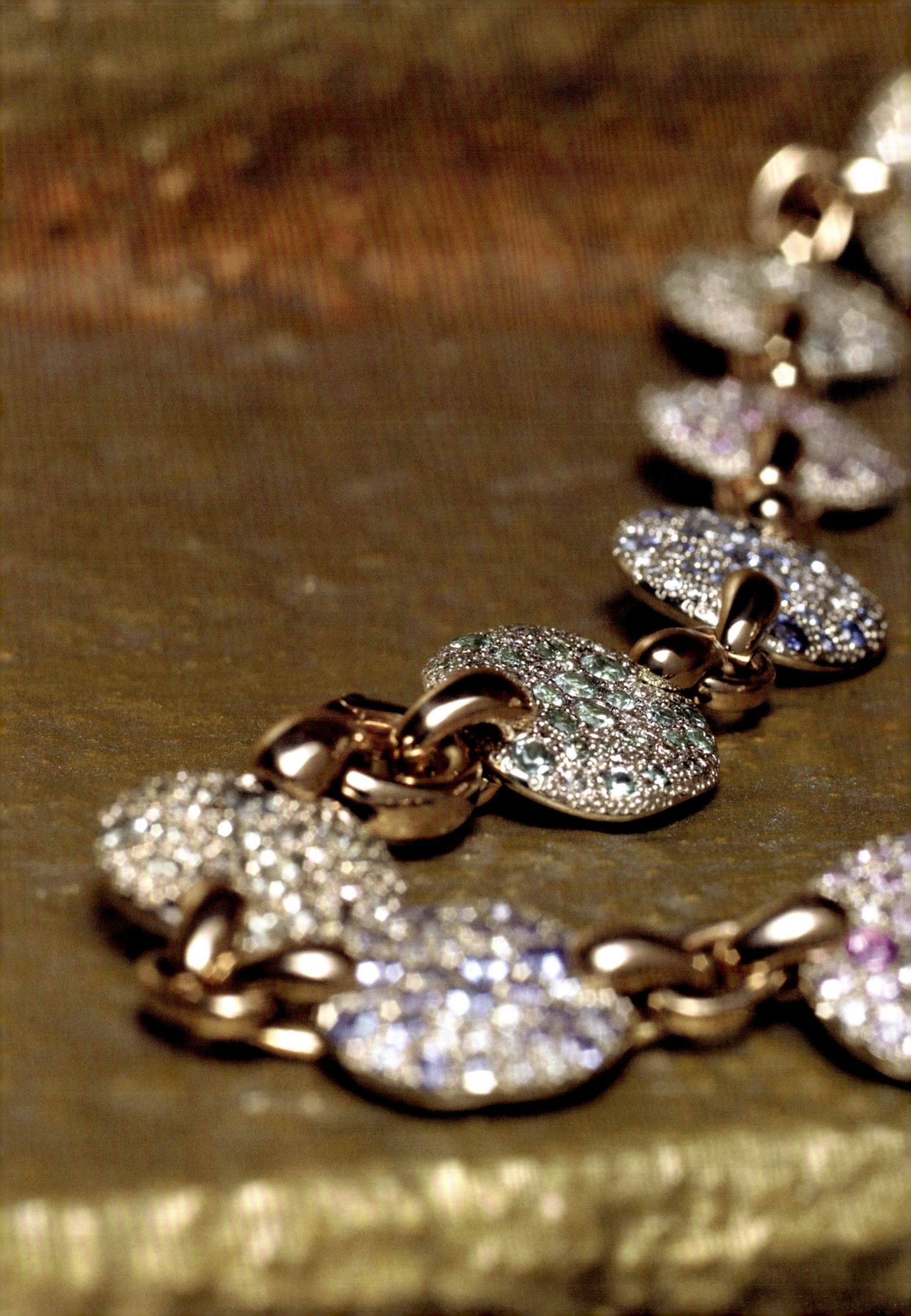

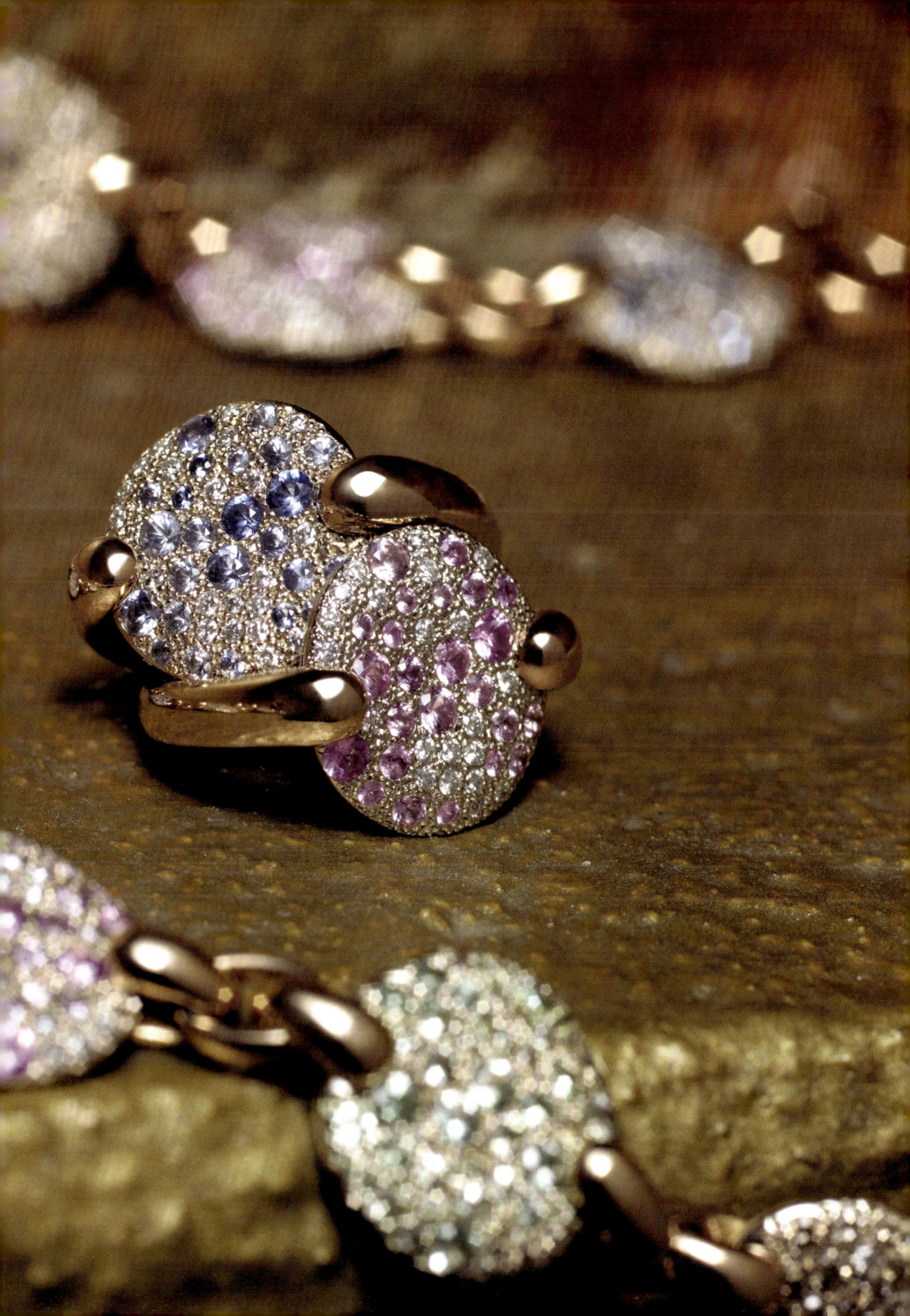

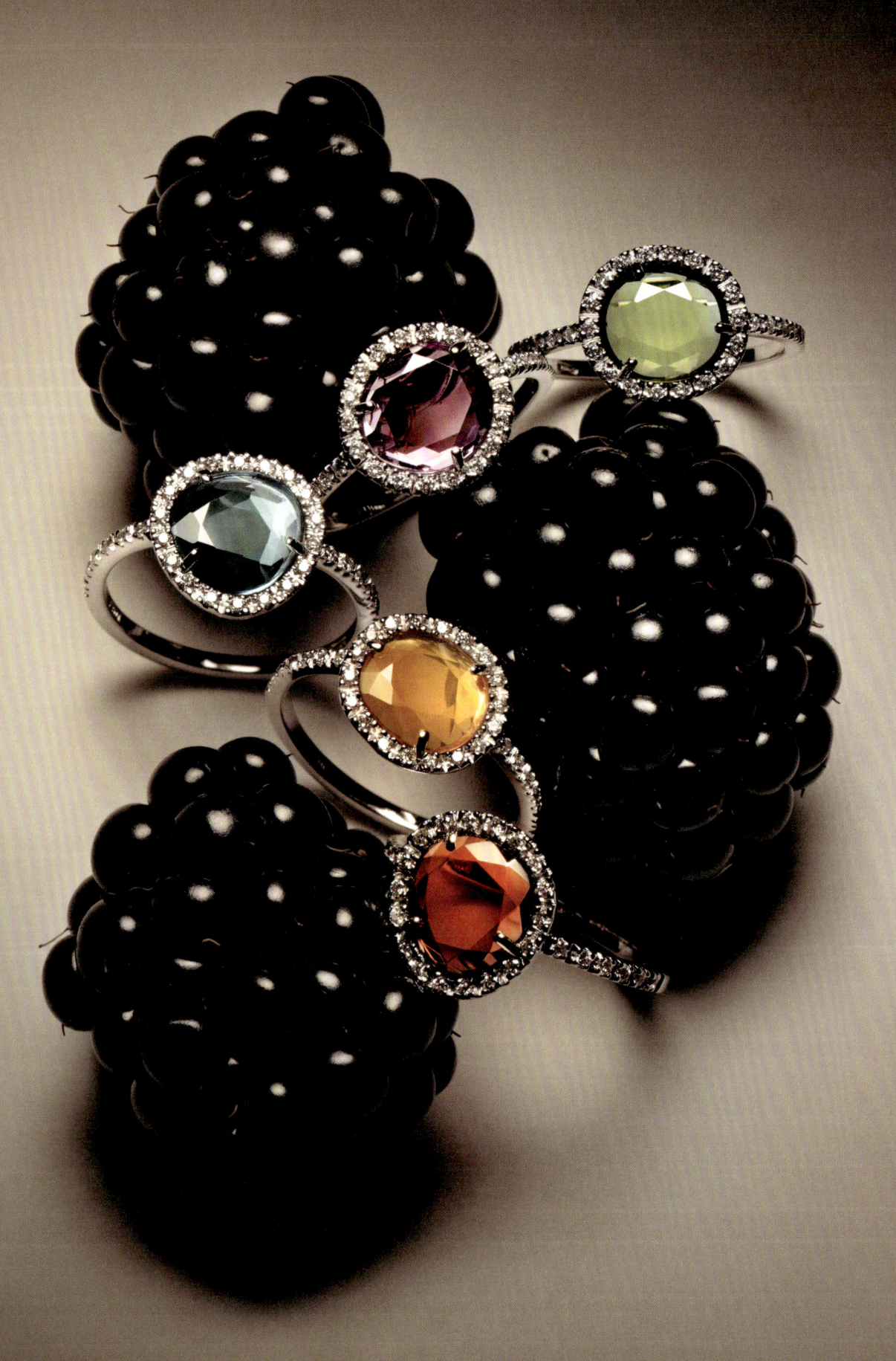

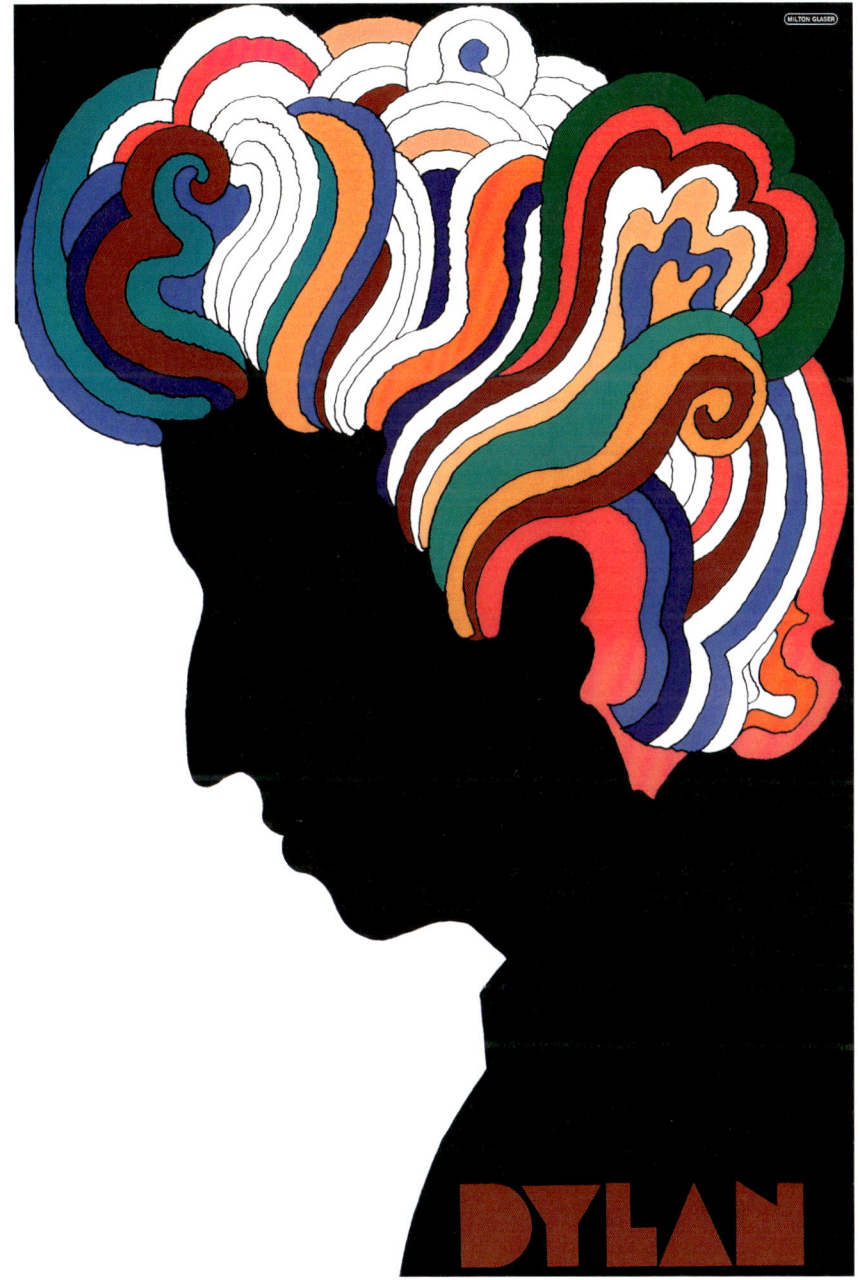

PREVIOUS SPREAD: Pomellato's diamond pavé collection, *Sabbia*

OPPOSITE: The juicy colors of the *Colpo di Fulmine* collection, photographed by Guido Mocafico

ABOVE: Bob Dylan by Milton Glaser, 1967

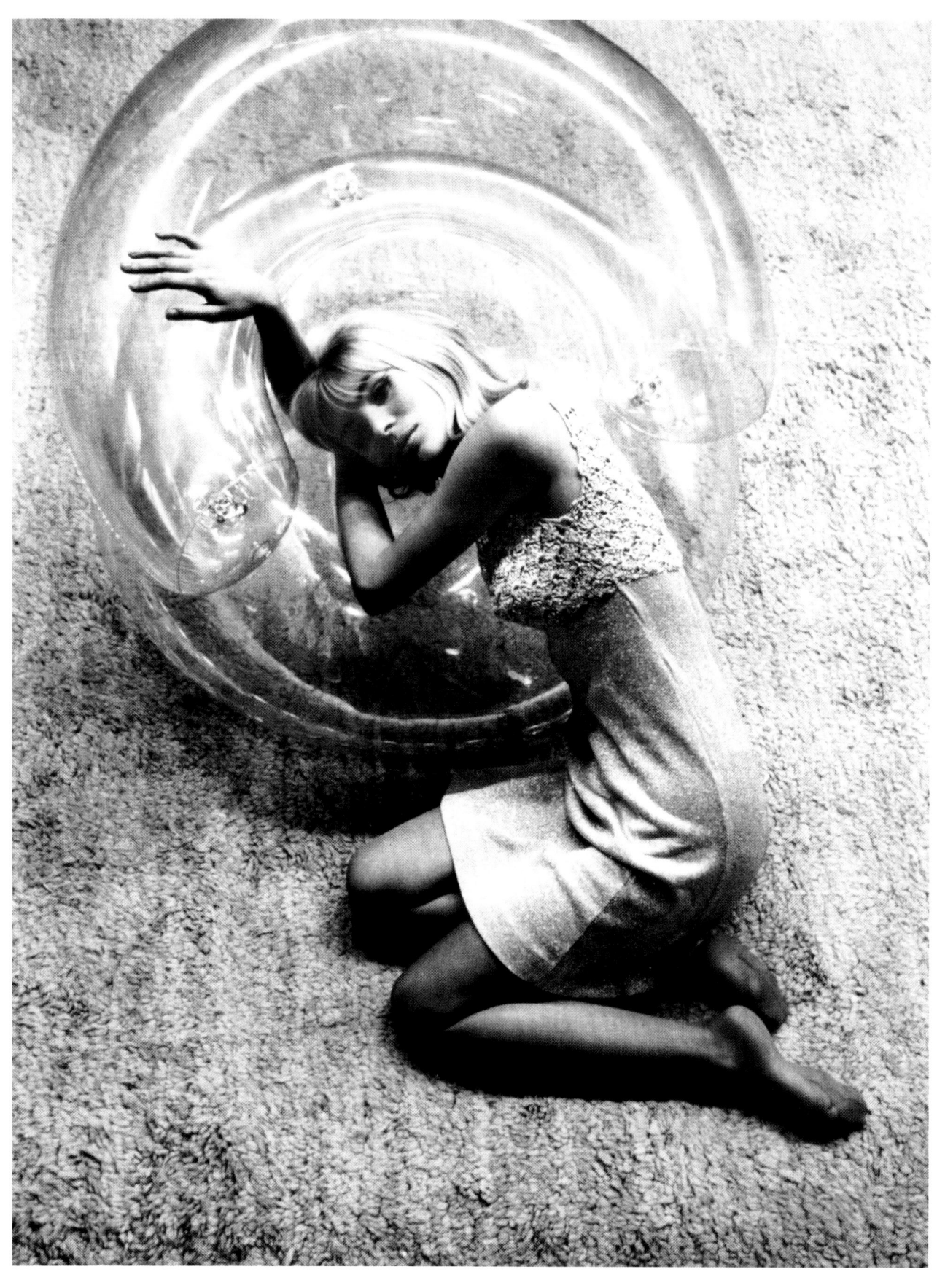

ABOVE: The iconoclast creator Quasar Khanh invented inflatable furniture

OPPOSITE: *Sabbia* collection rings in white, black, and brown diamonds

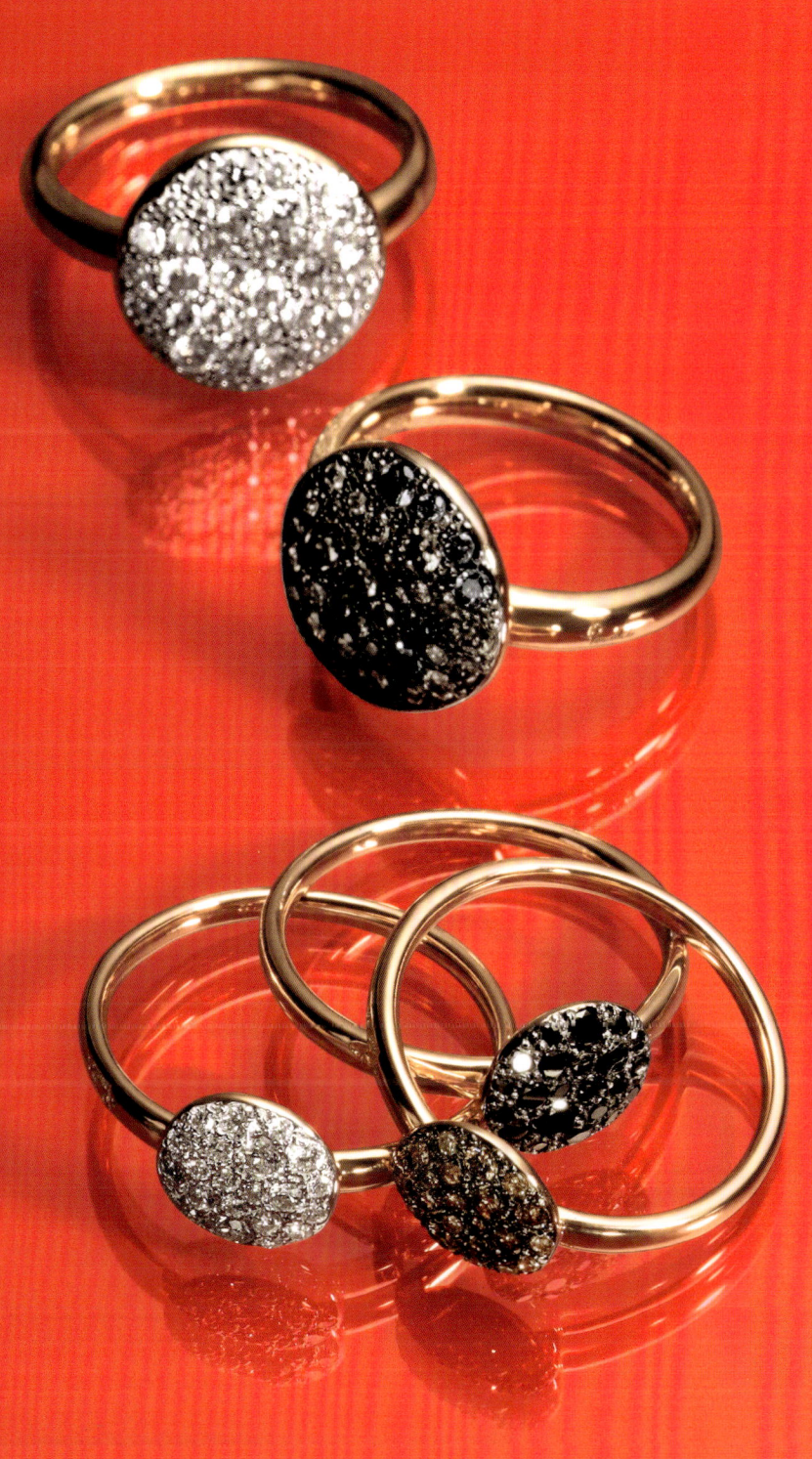

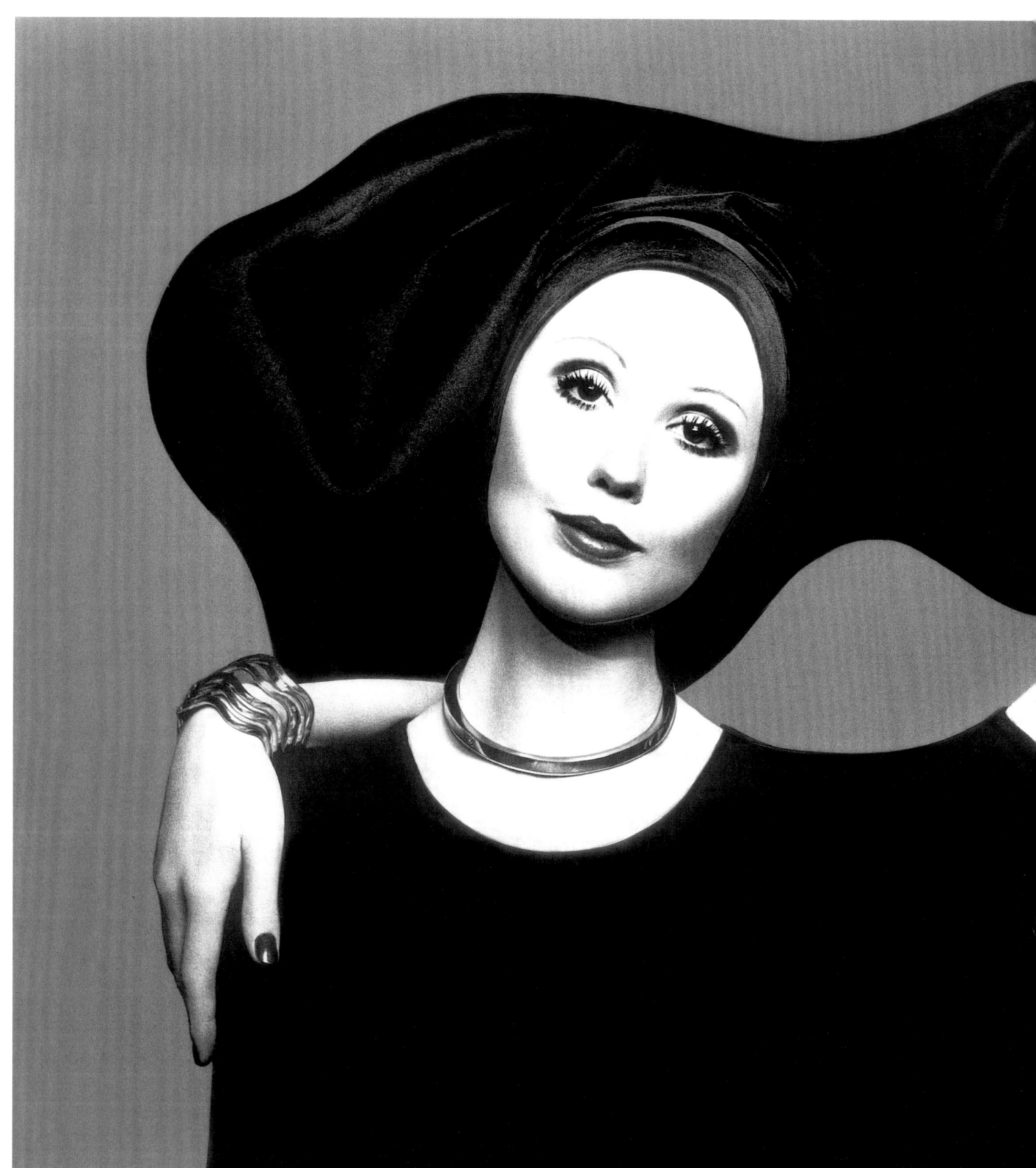

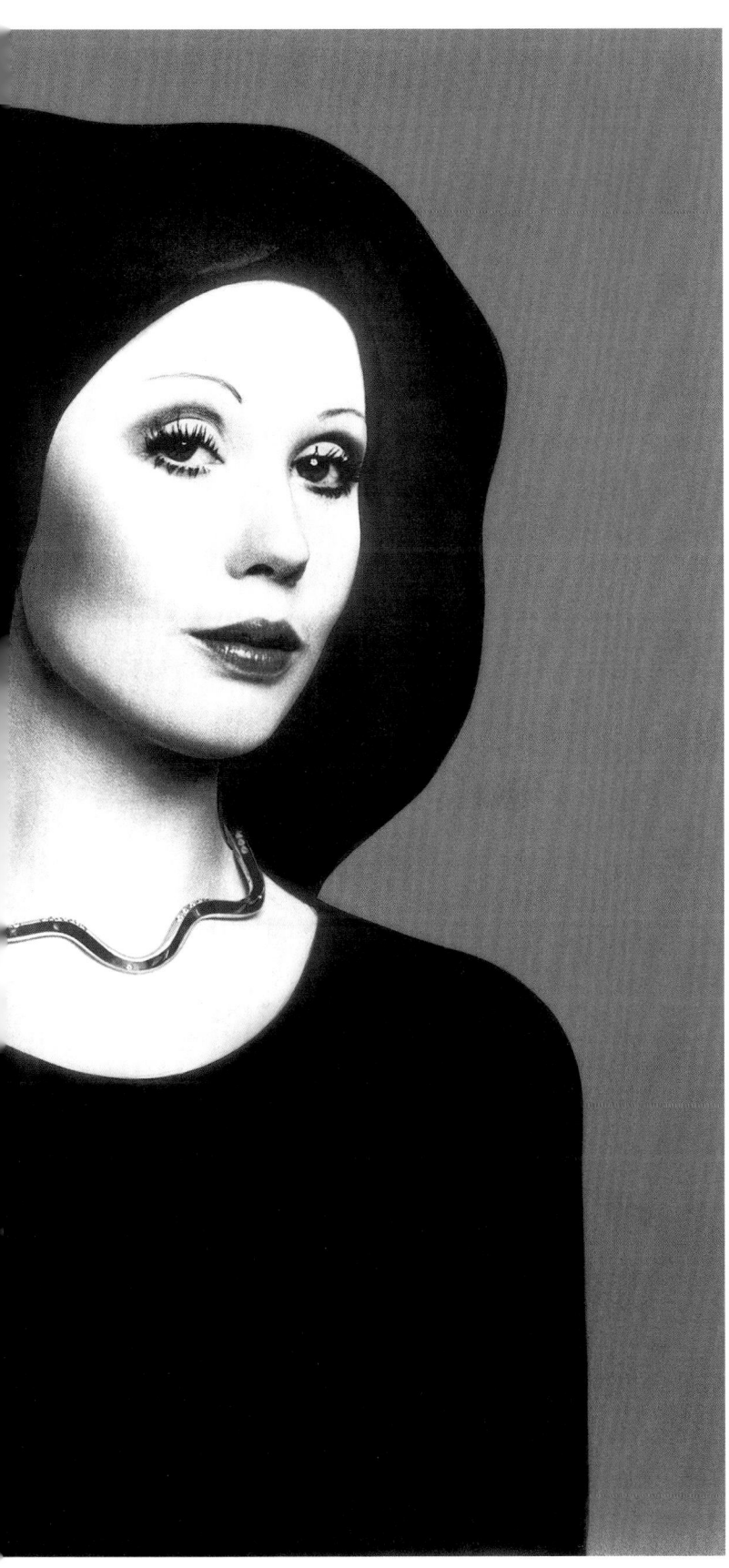

Pomellato advertising campaign by Gian Paolo Barbieri, 1971

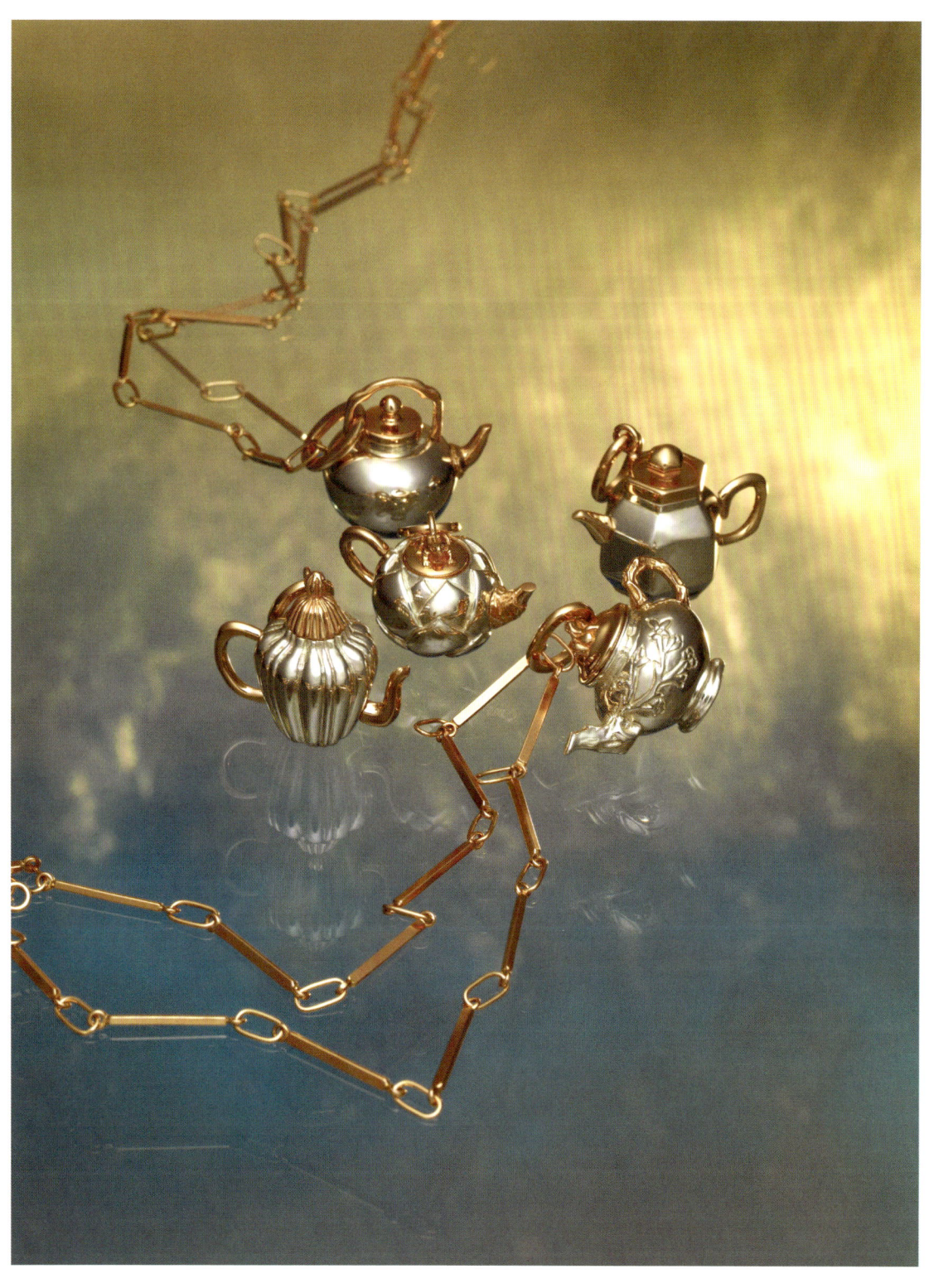

ABOVE: Pomellato's *Five O'Clock* teapot pendants in rose gold and silver

OPPOSITE: A fashionable commute in London, Brian Duffy, 1966

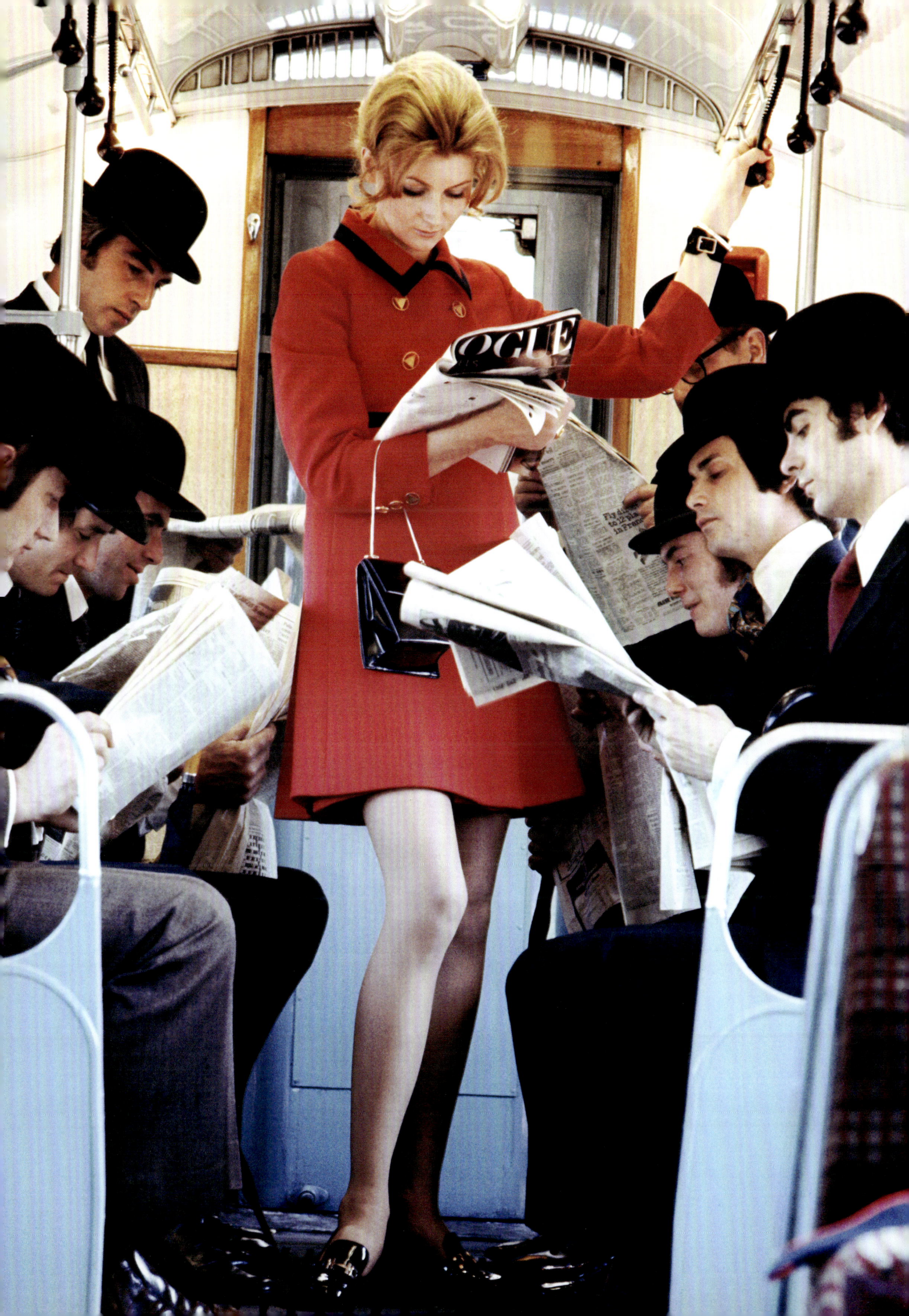

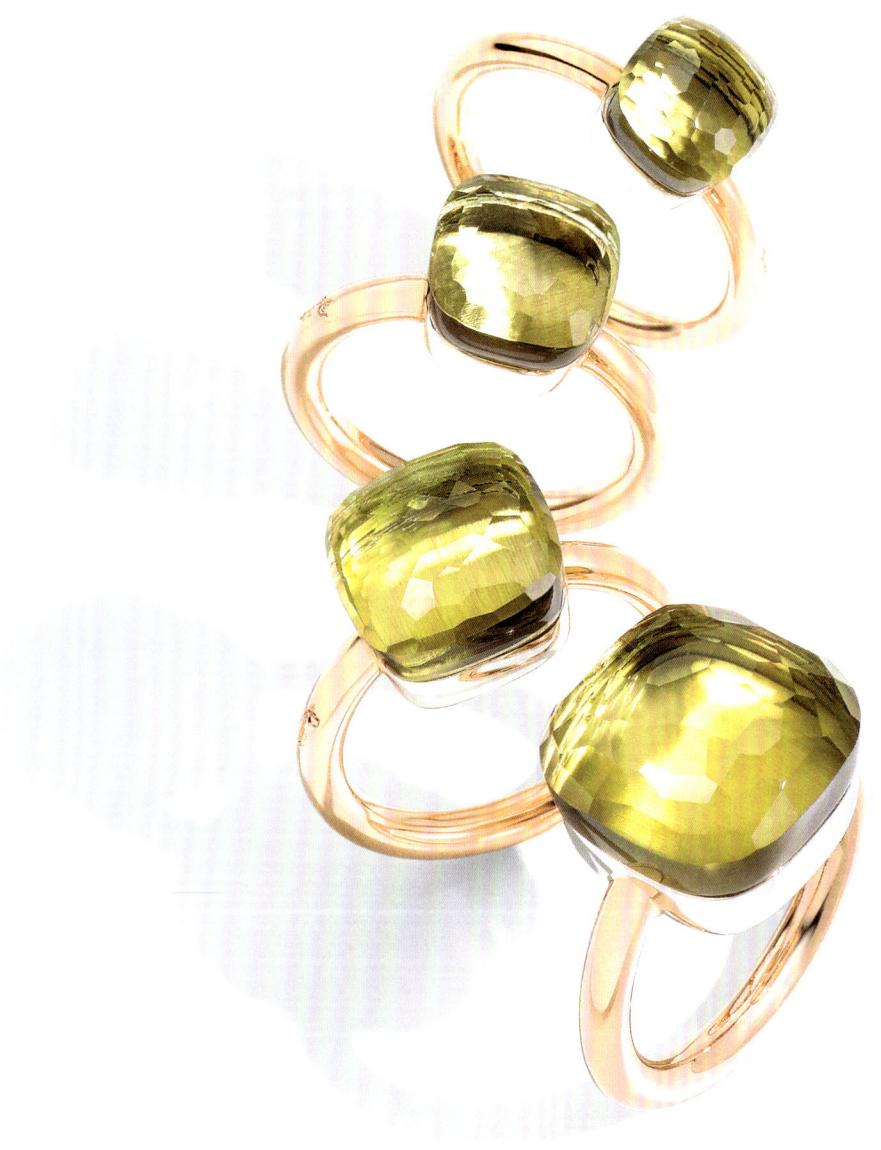

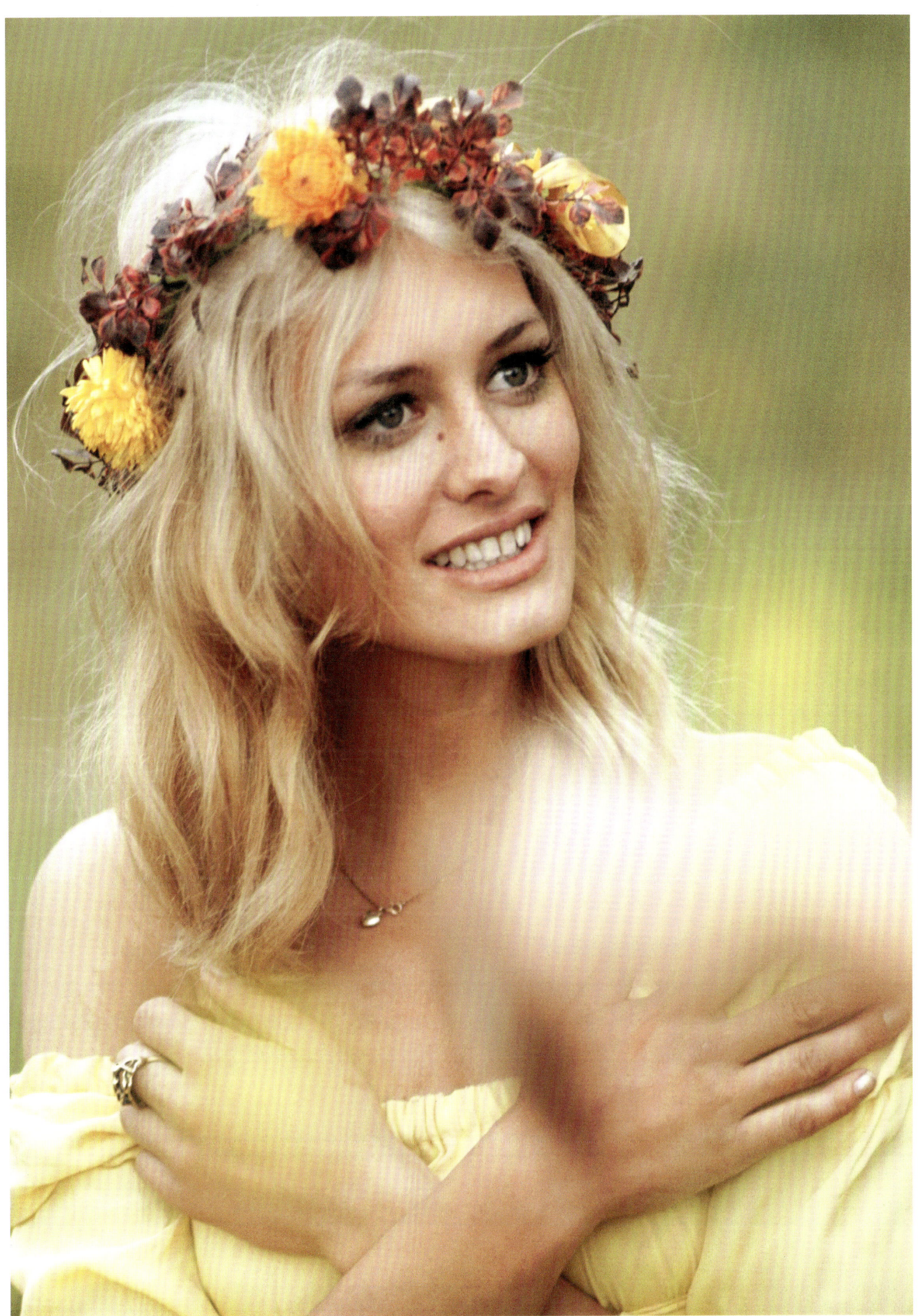

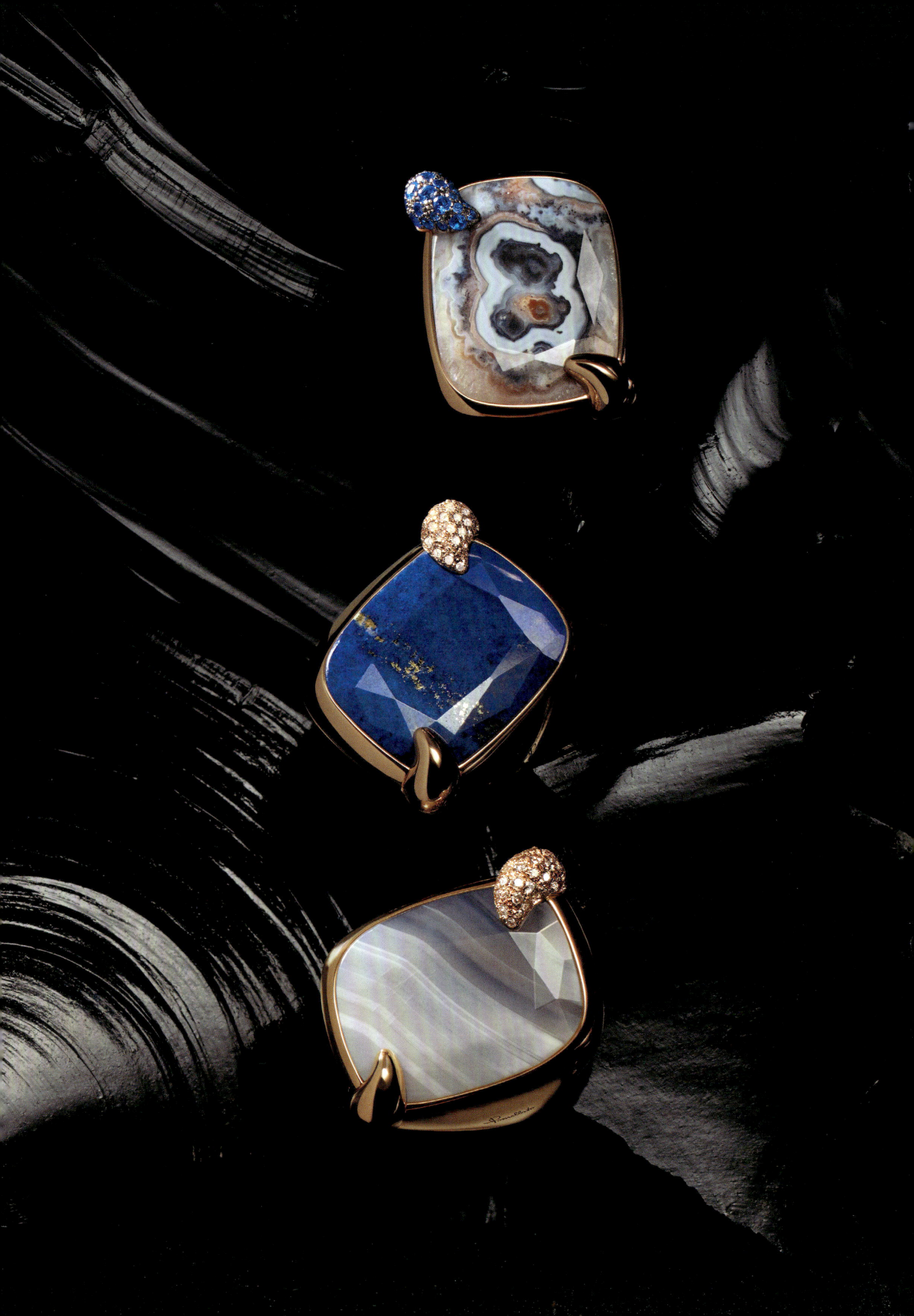

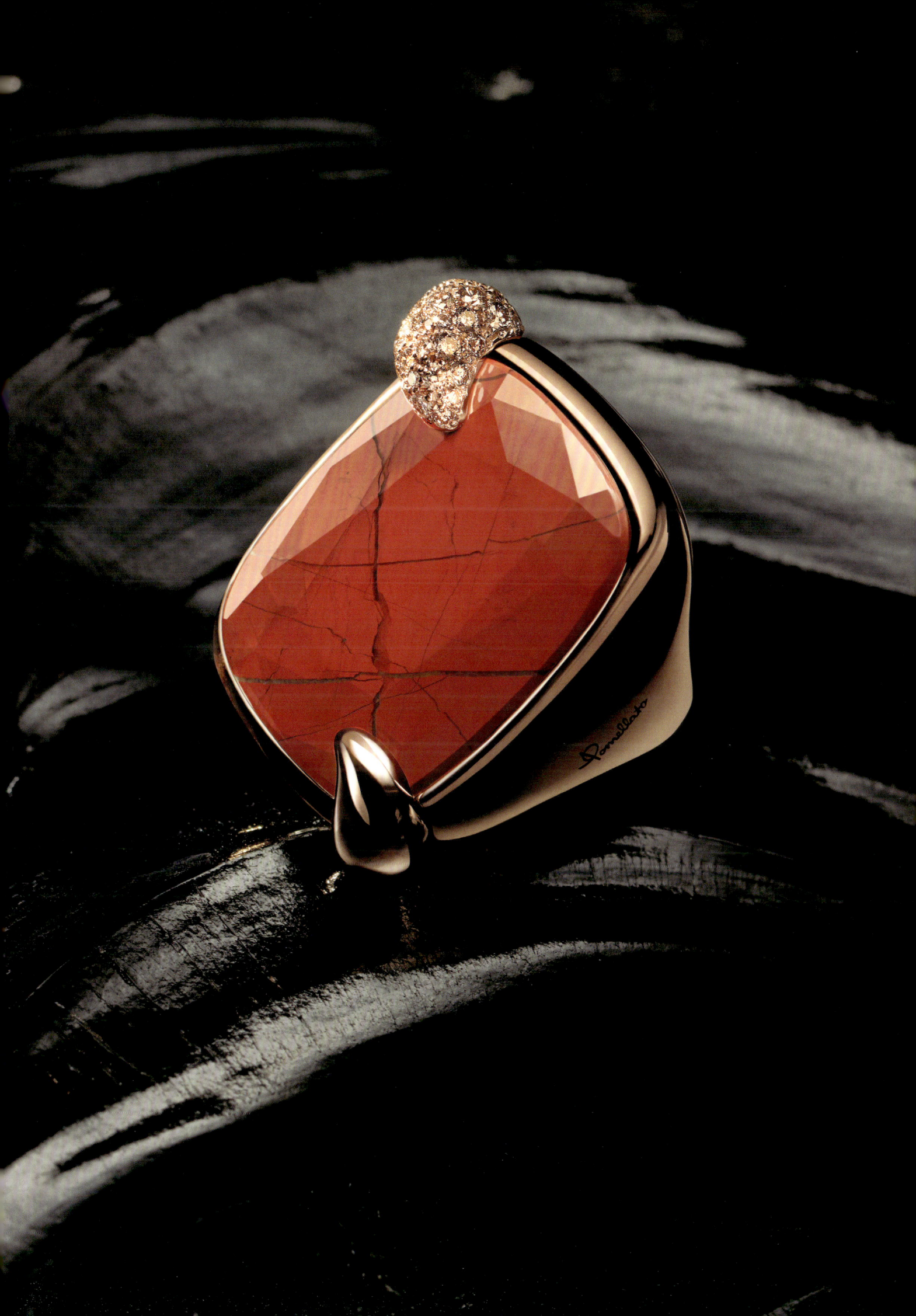

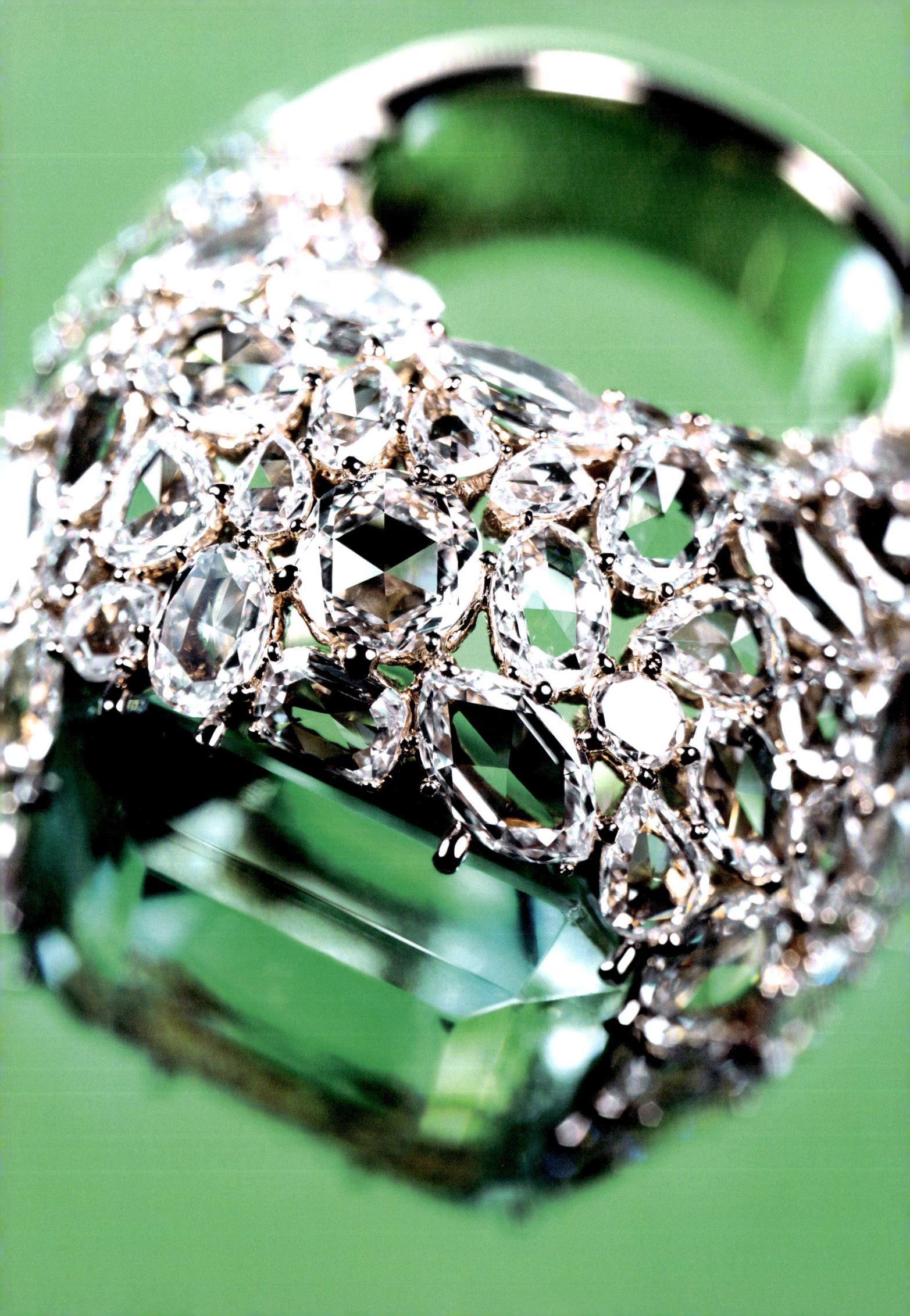

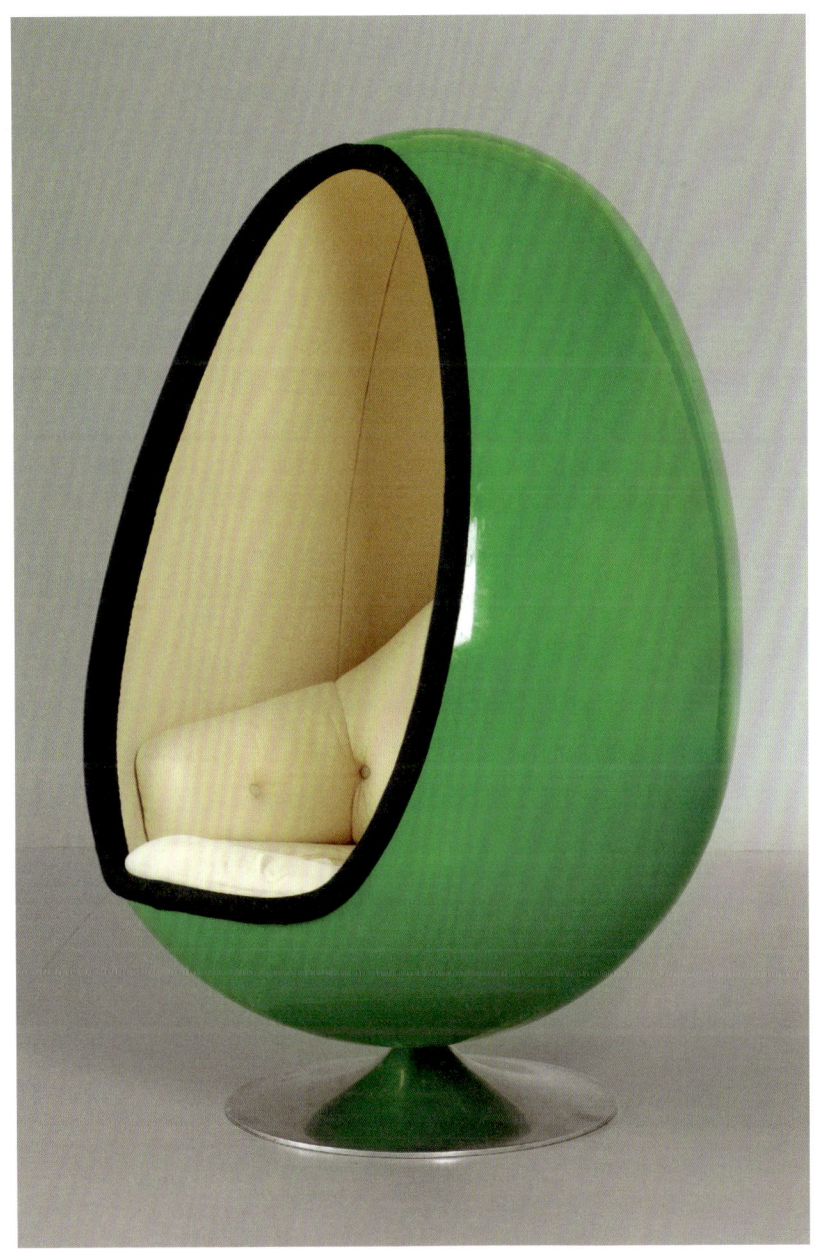

PREVIOUS SPREAD: Fifty unique hard stone creations in the *Ritratto* collection, to celebrate Pomellato's fiftieth anniversary

OPPOSITE: *Pom Pom* collection one-of-a-kind ring in white gold with a square faceted emerald and diamonds

ABOVE: *Ovalia* egg chair designed by Henrik Thor-Larsen, 1968

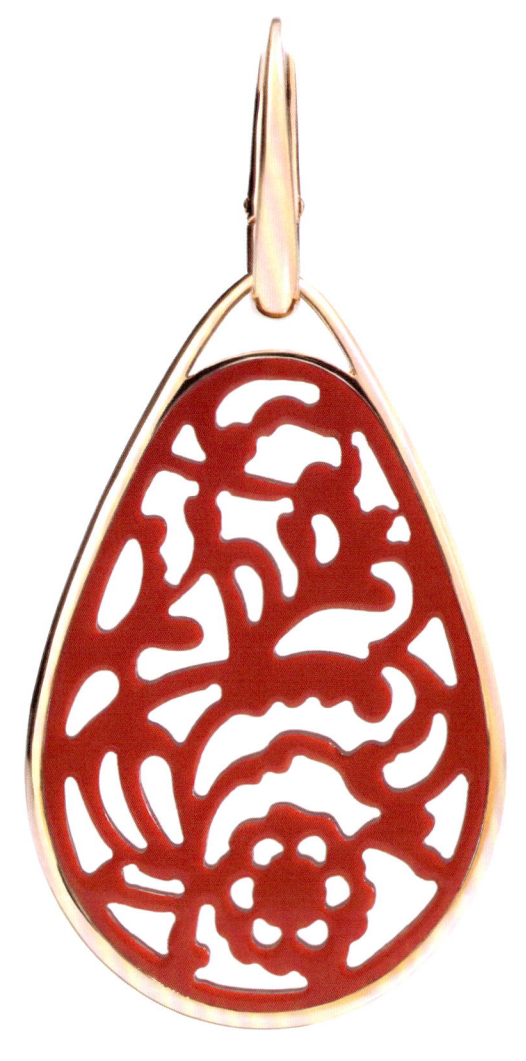
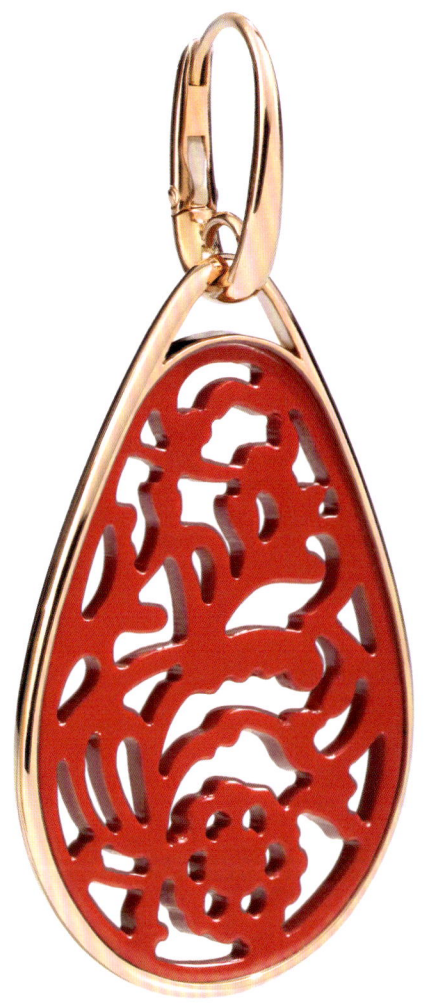

ABOVE: *Victoria* earrings in rose gold and lacquered red

OPPOSITE: Supermodel Twiggy embodied the free-spirited
playfulness of the 1960s, Jean-Claude Sauer, 1965

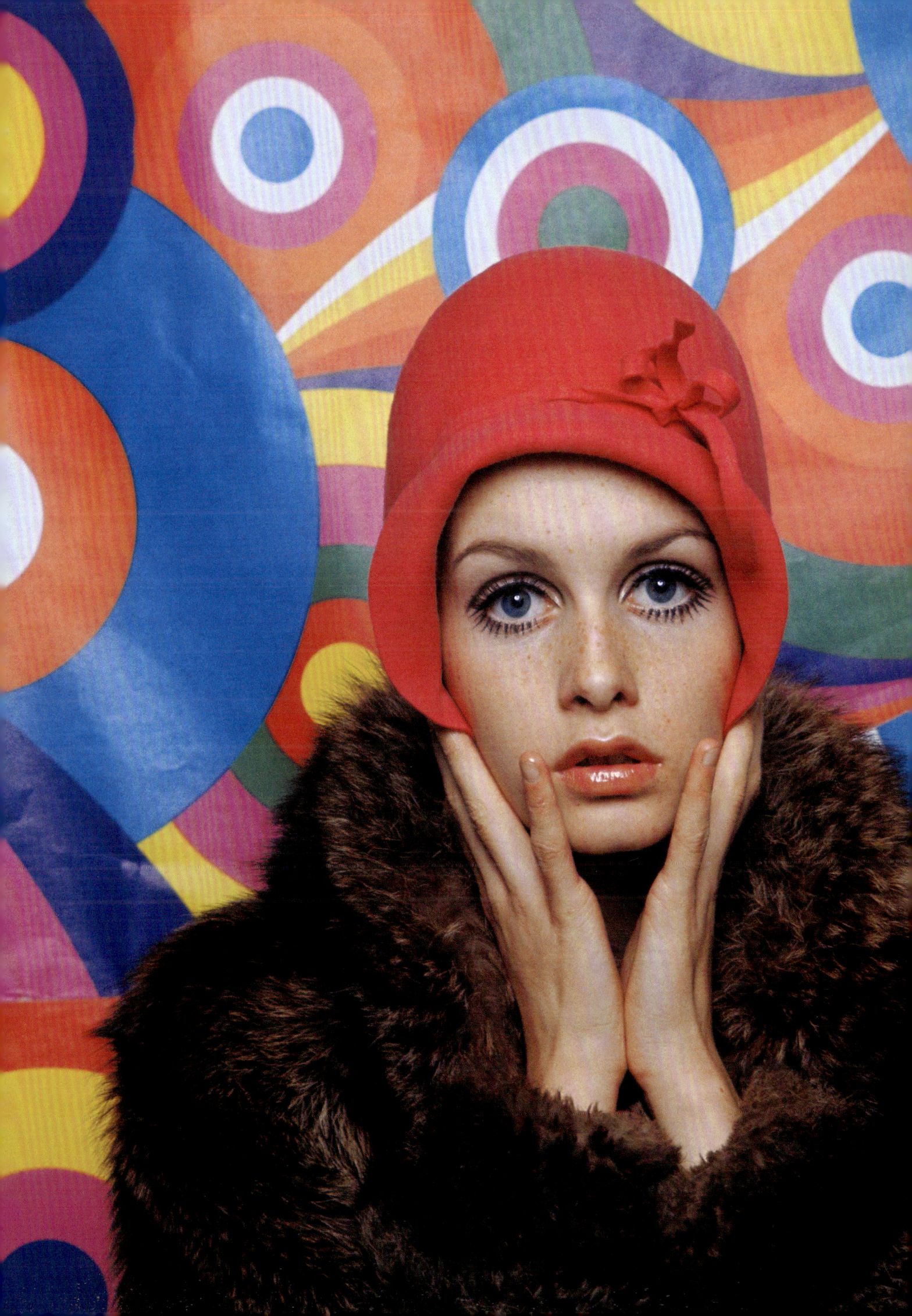

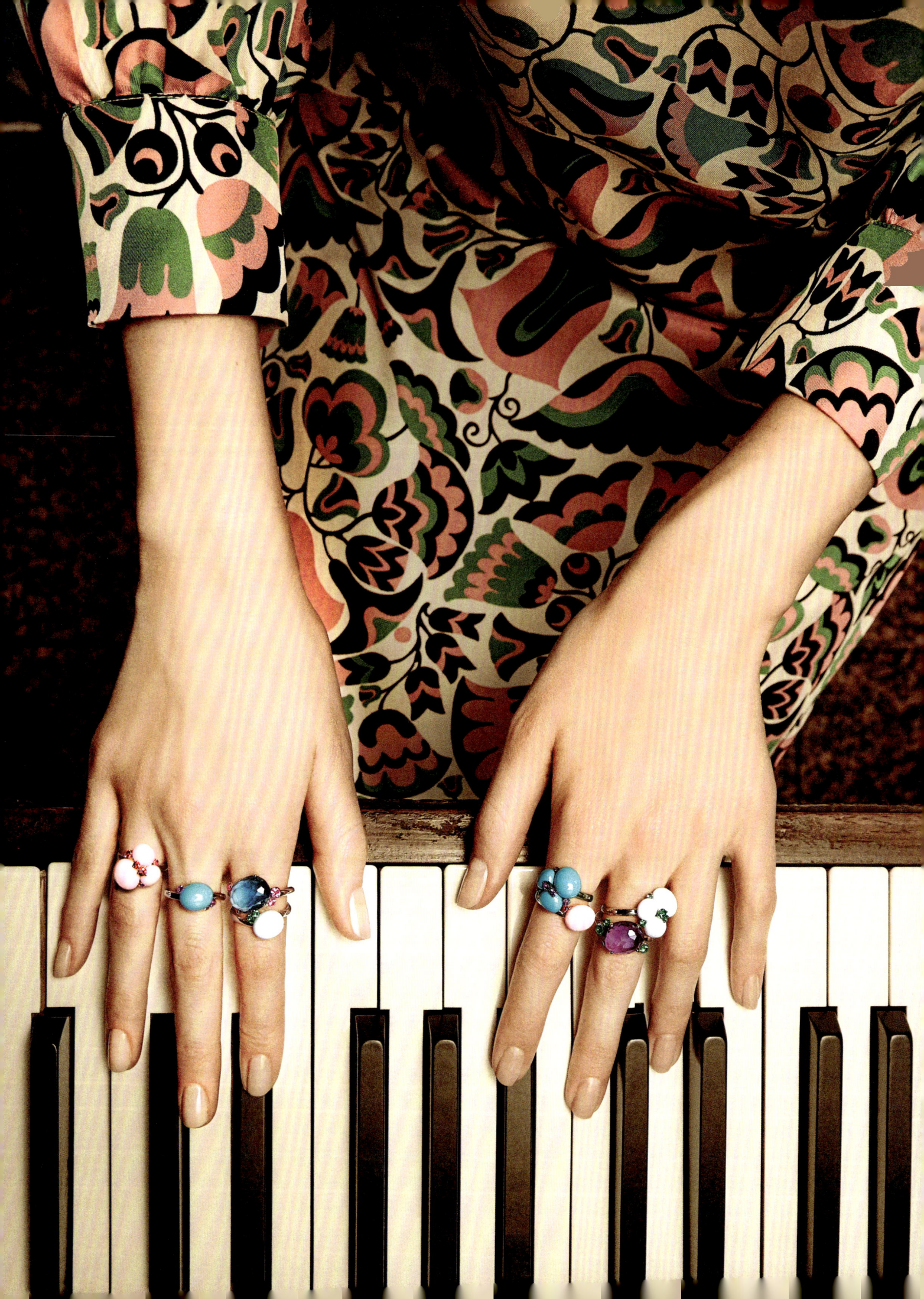

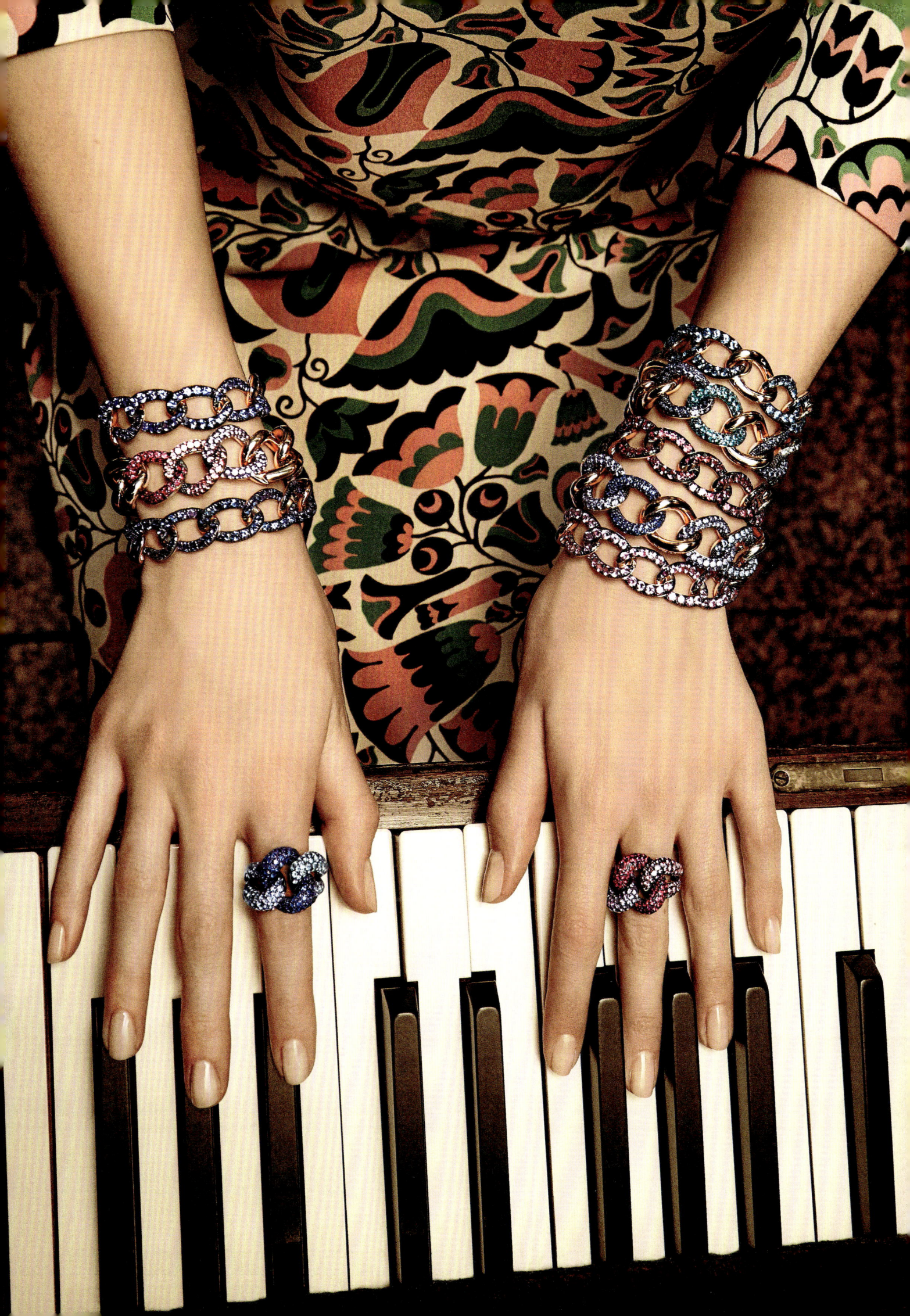

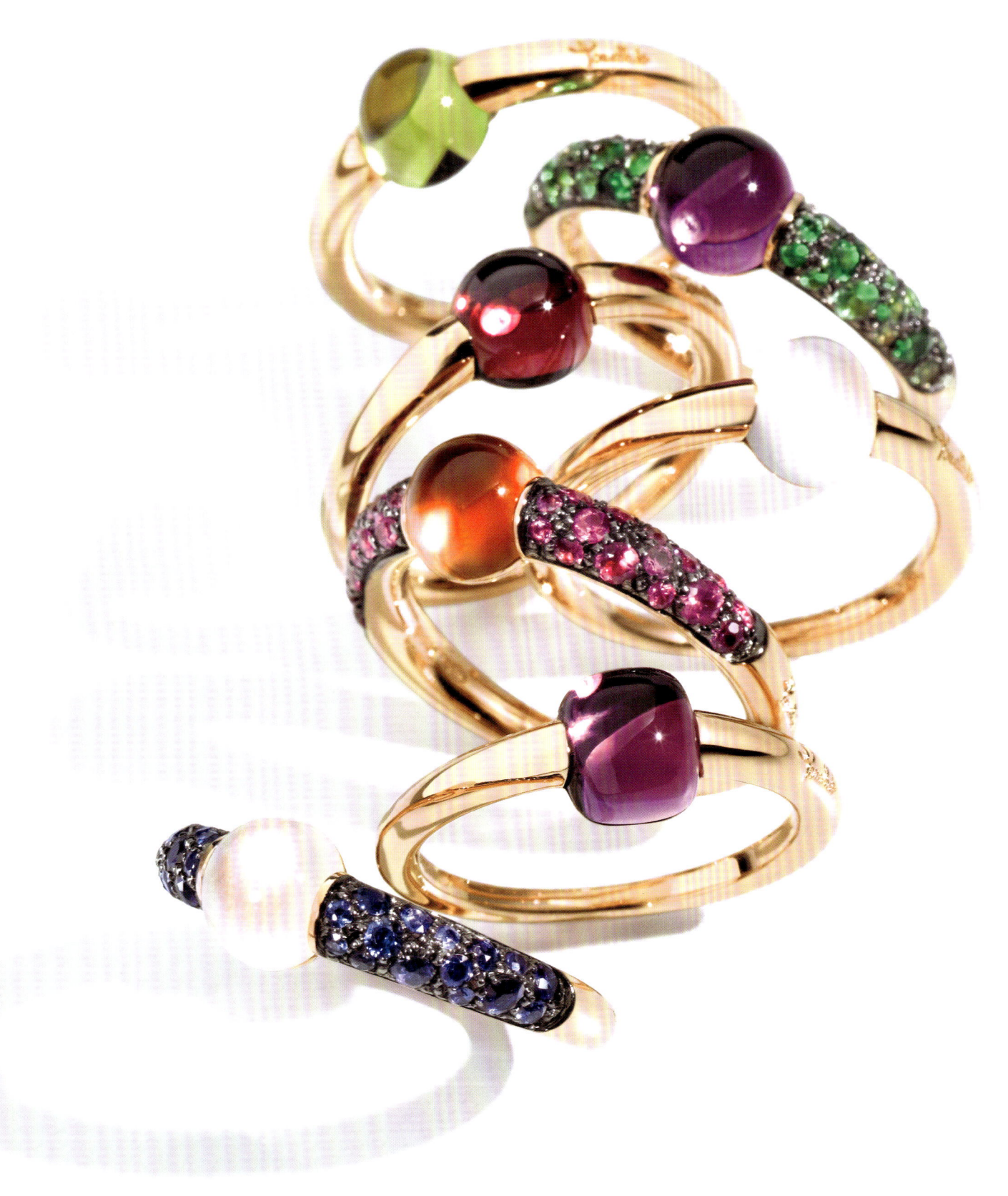

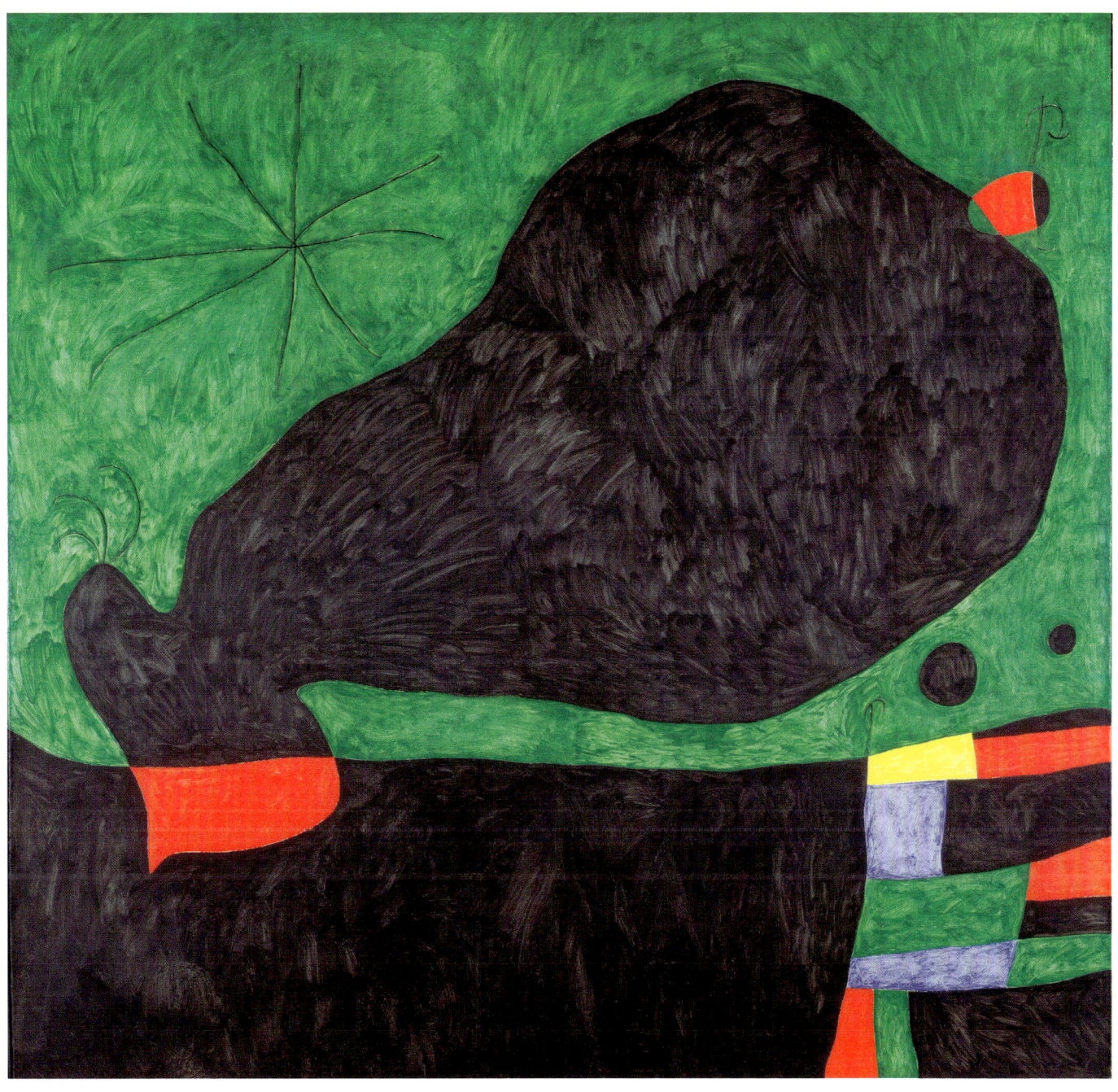

PREVIOUS SPREAD: Four-hand pianoforte. Pomellato
Capri, Bahia, and *Tango* bracelets and rings

OPPOSITE: Pomellato *M'ama non M'ama* collection

ABOVE: *Message from a Friend* by Joan Miró, 1964

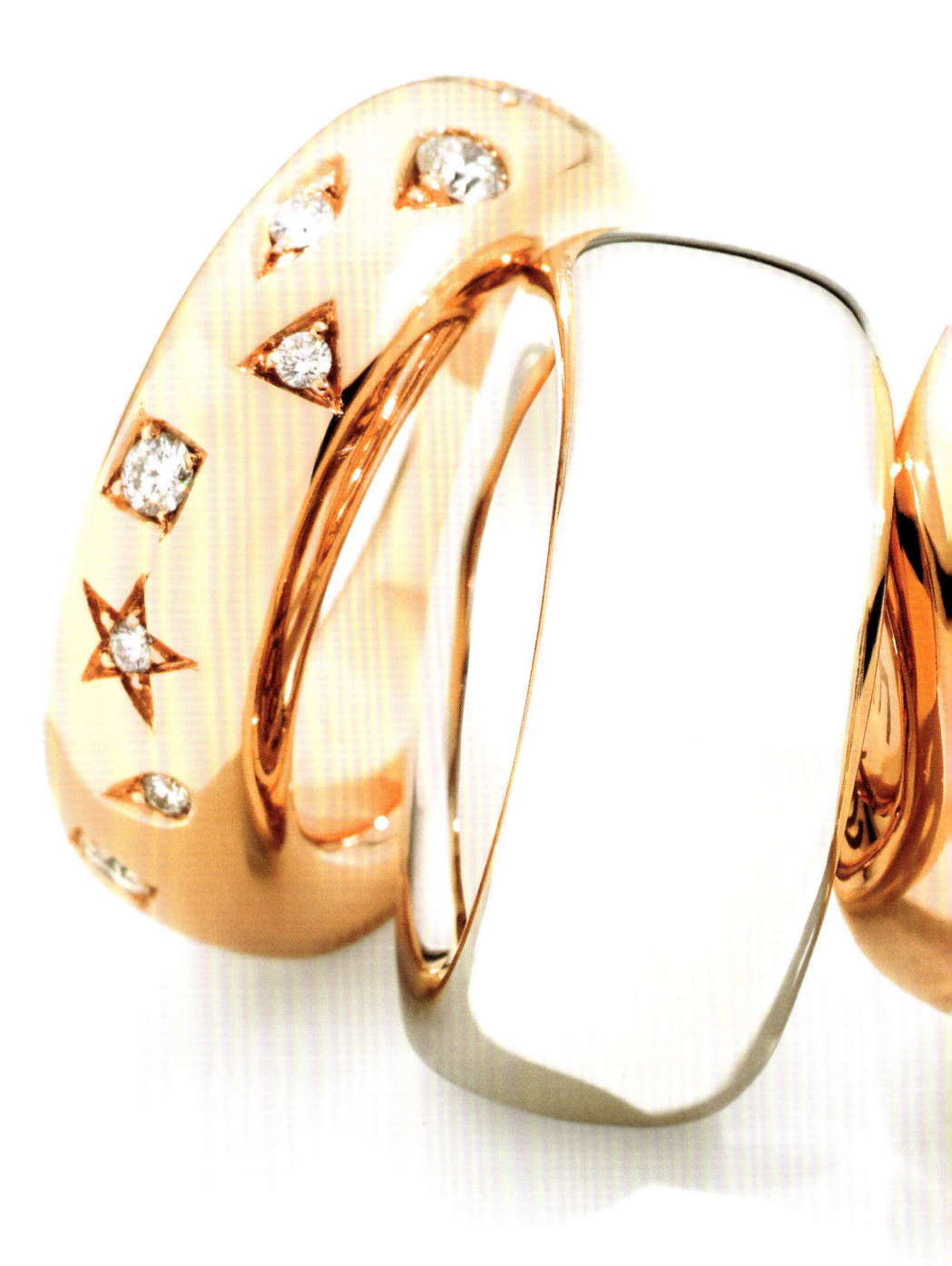

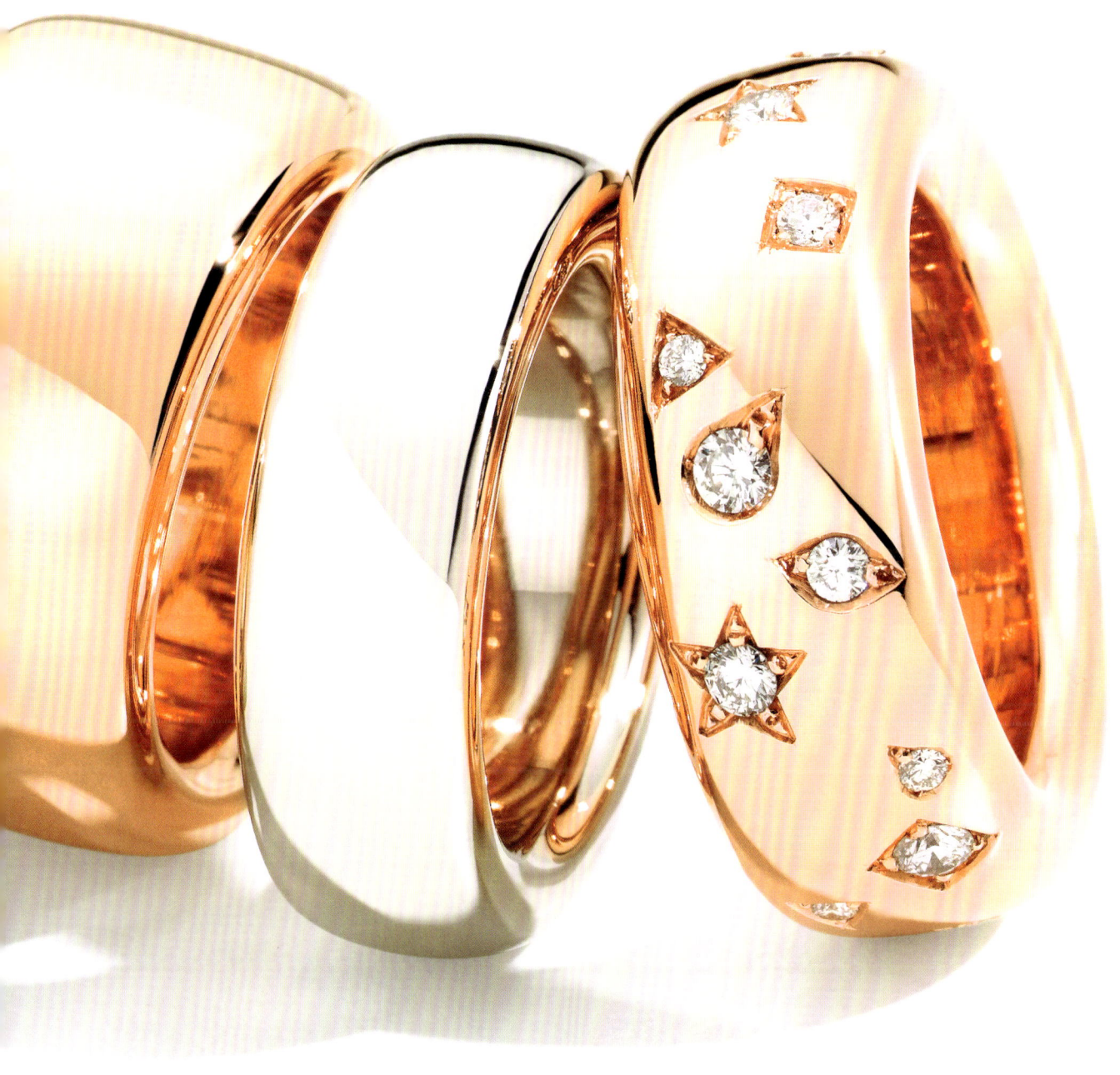

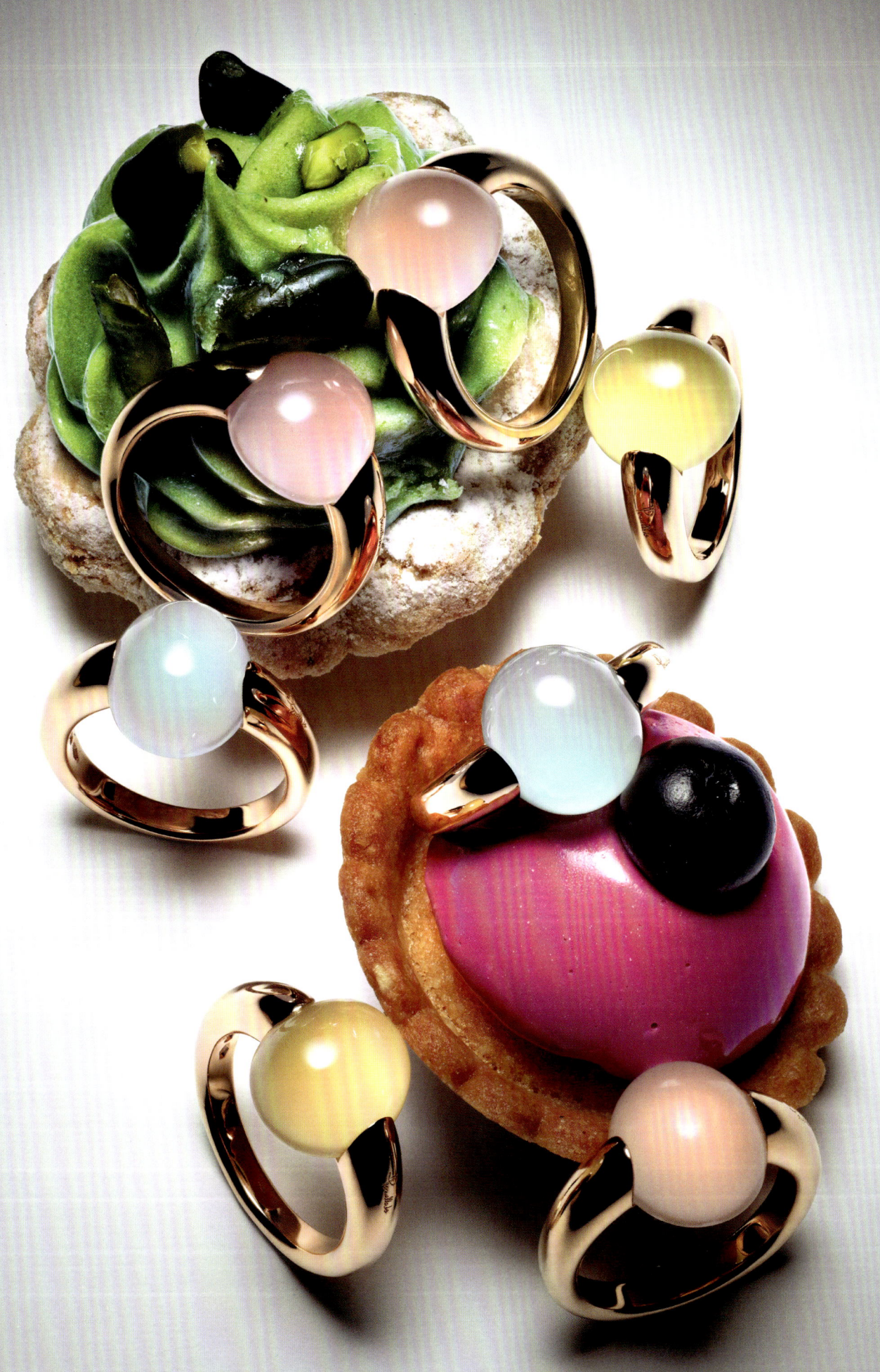

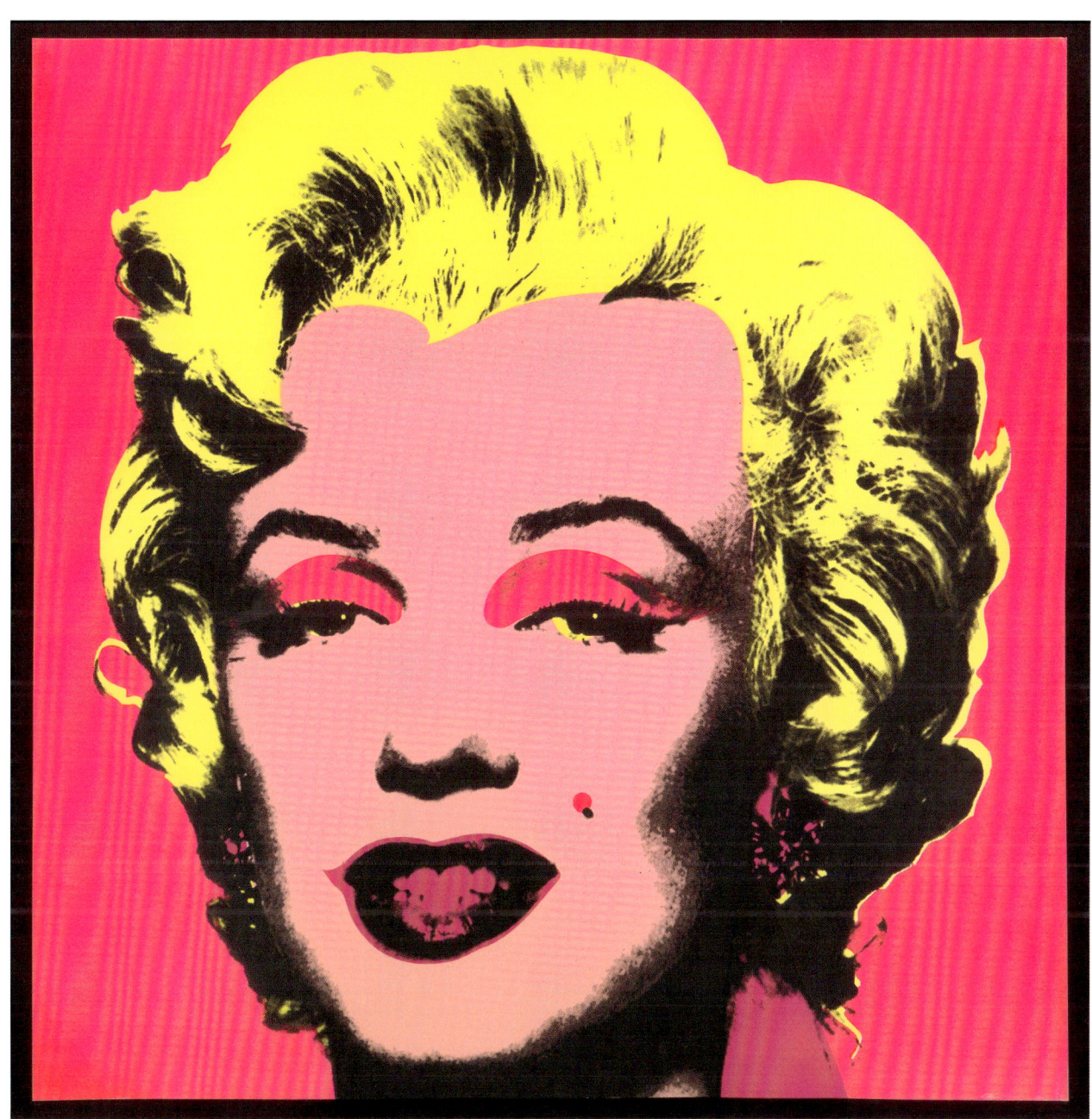

PREVIOUS SPREAD: *Iconica*, the new gold classic by Pomellato,
in rose gold, natural white gold, and diamonds, 2017

OPPOSITE: Pomellato *Luna* rings in rose quartz, lemon quartz, and aquamarine

ABOVE: *Untitled from Marilyn Monroe* by Andy Warhol, 1967

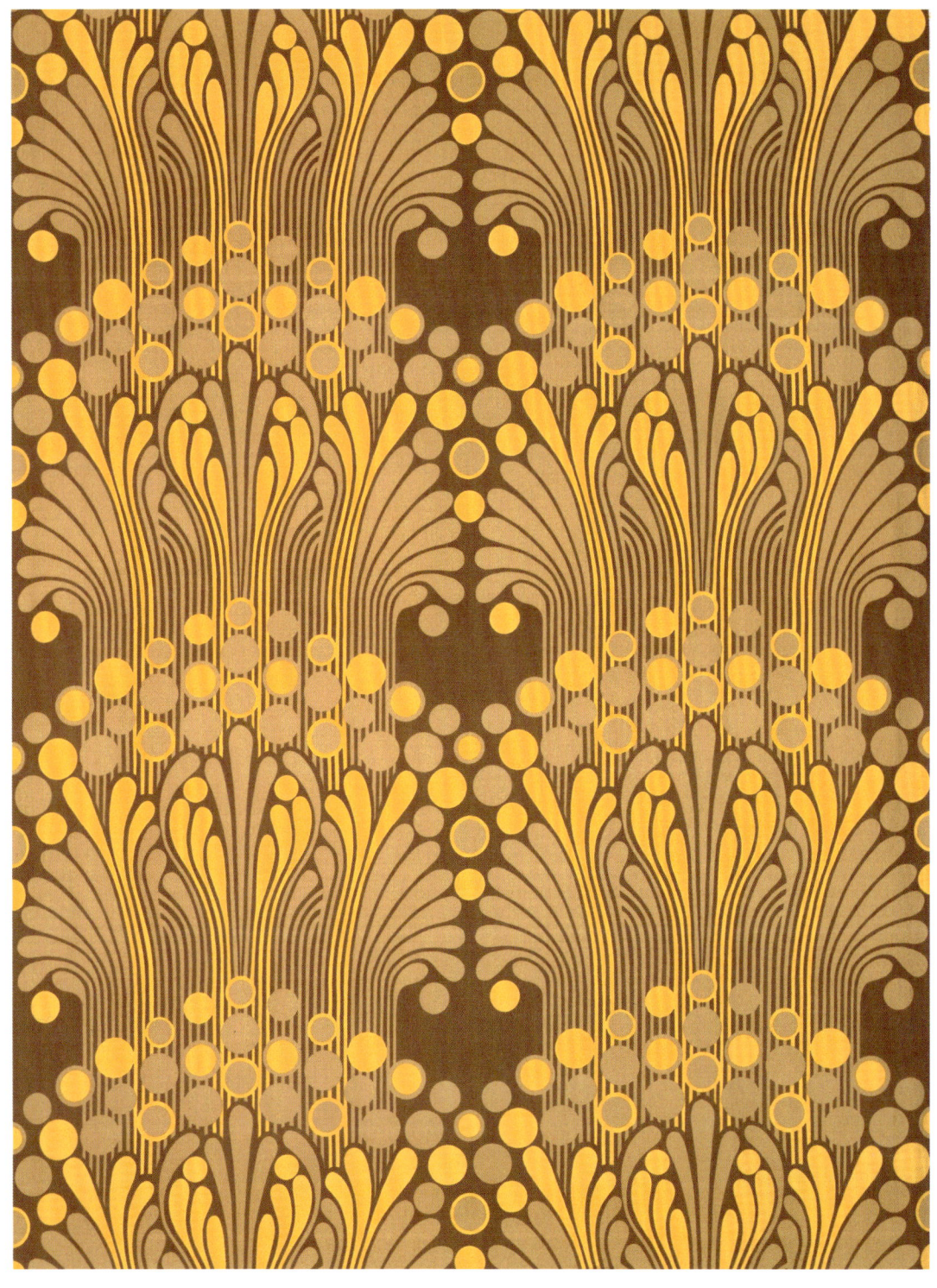

ABOVE: Tivoli fabric by Peter Hall

OPPOSITE: It takes two to *Tango:* bracelets in rose gold and diamonds

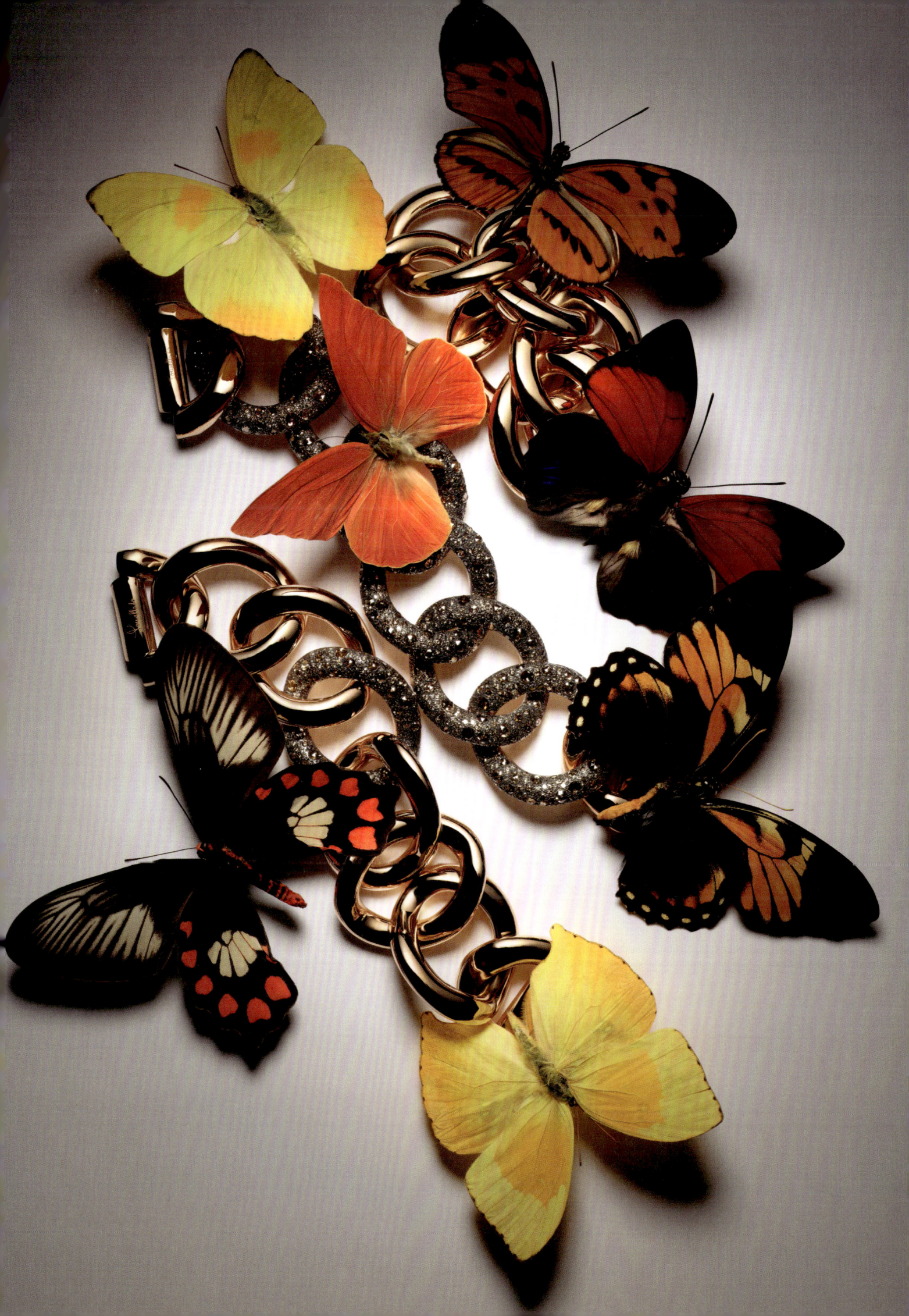

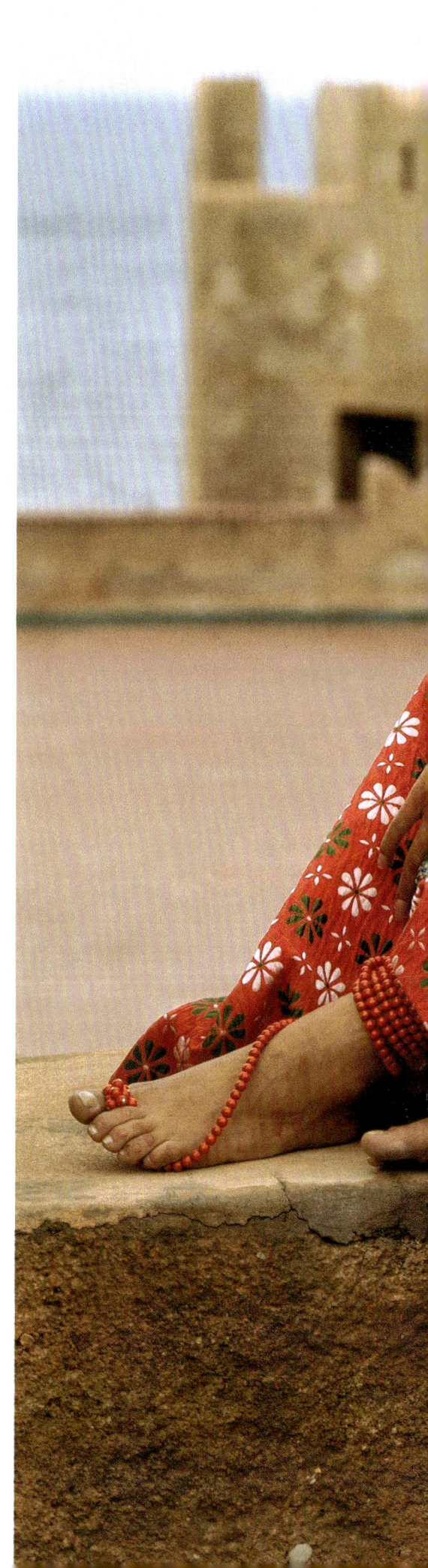

A red dress by Oscar de la Renta, Castello San Nicola, Palermo, Italy, 1967

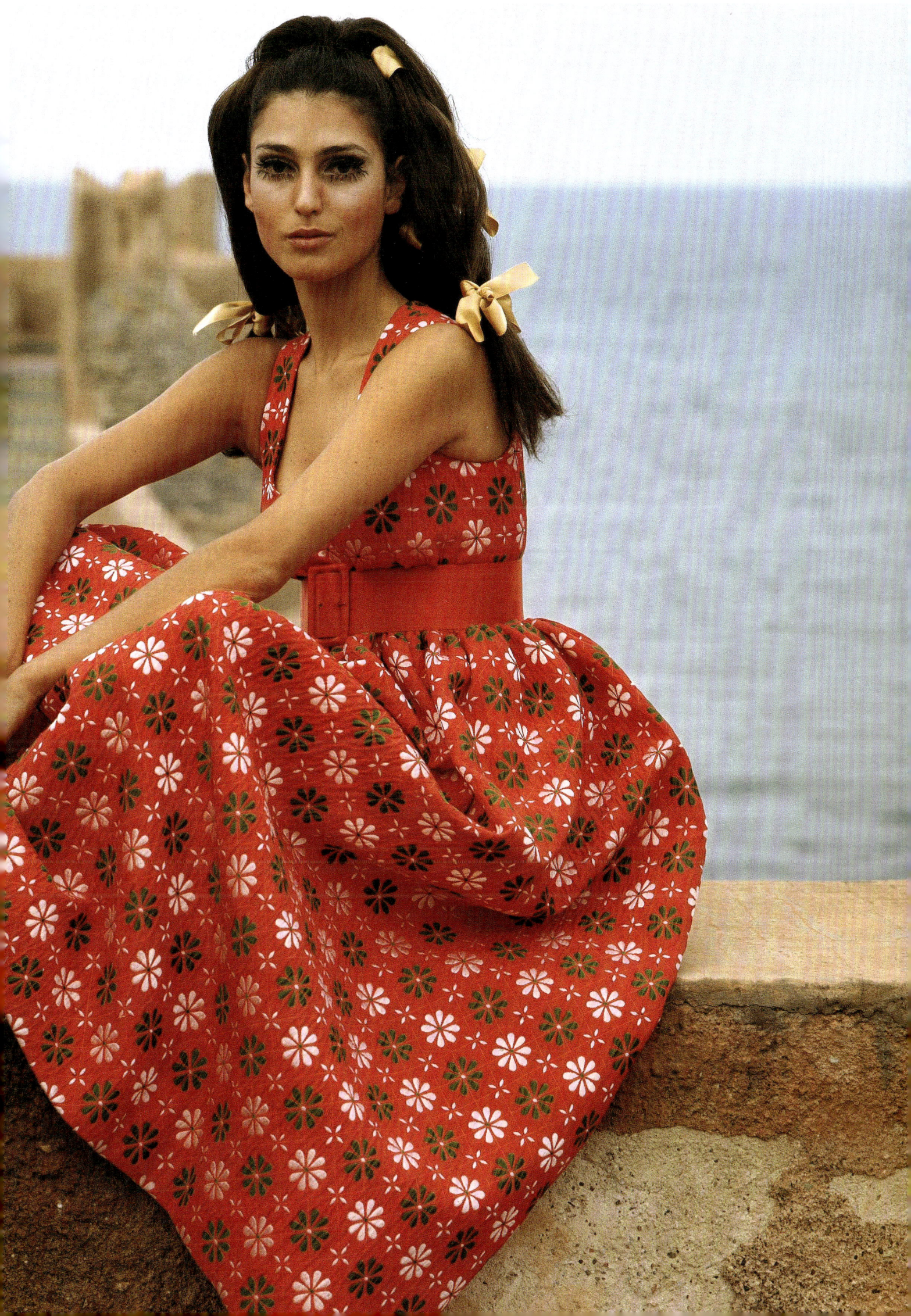

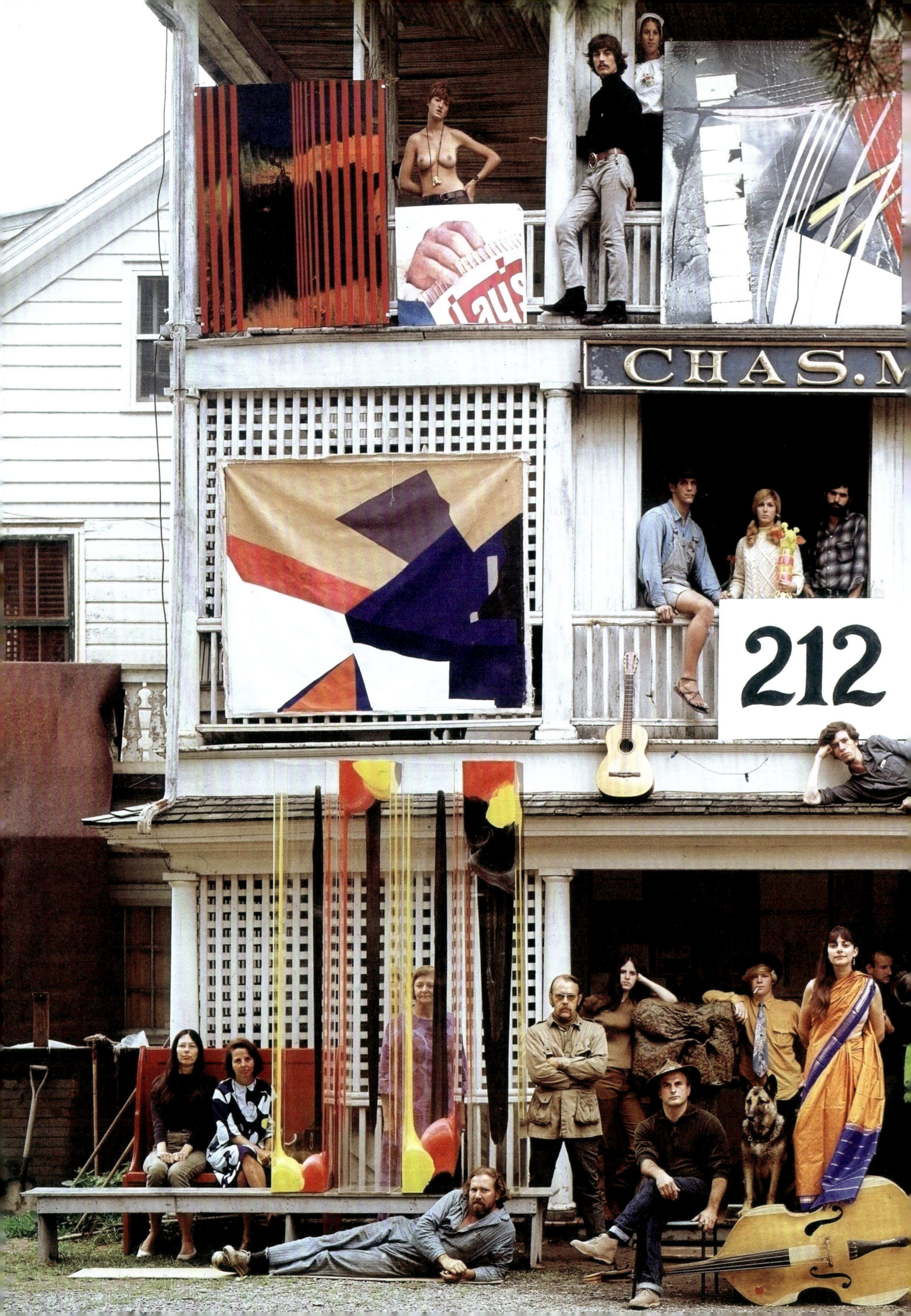

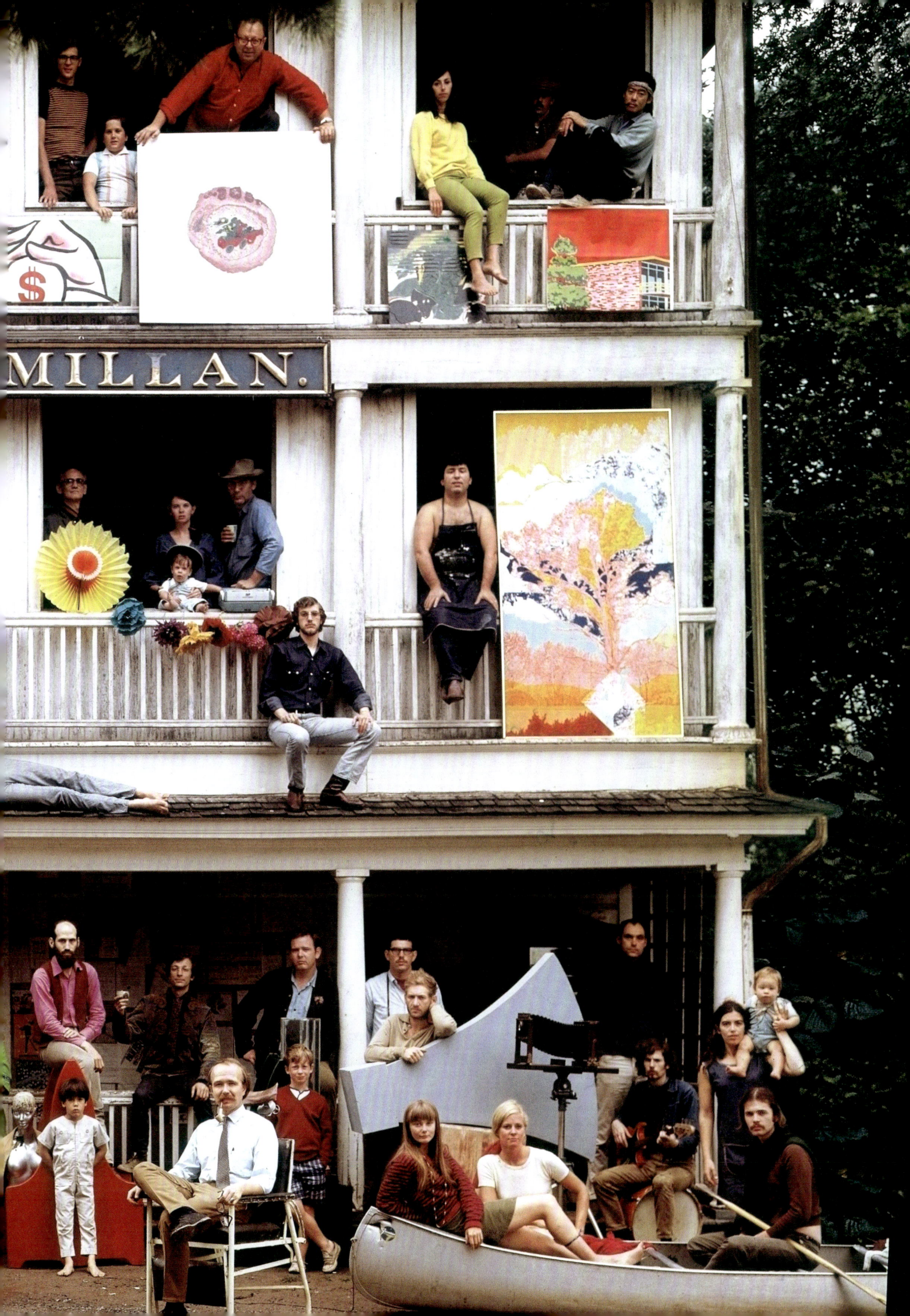

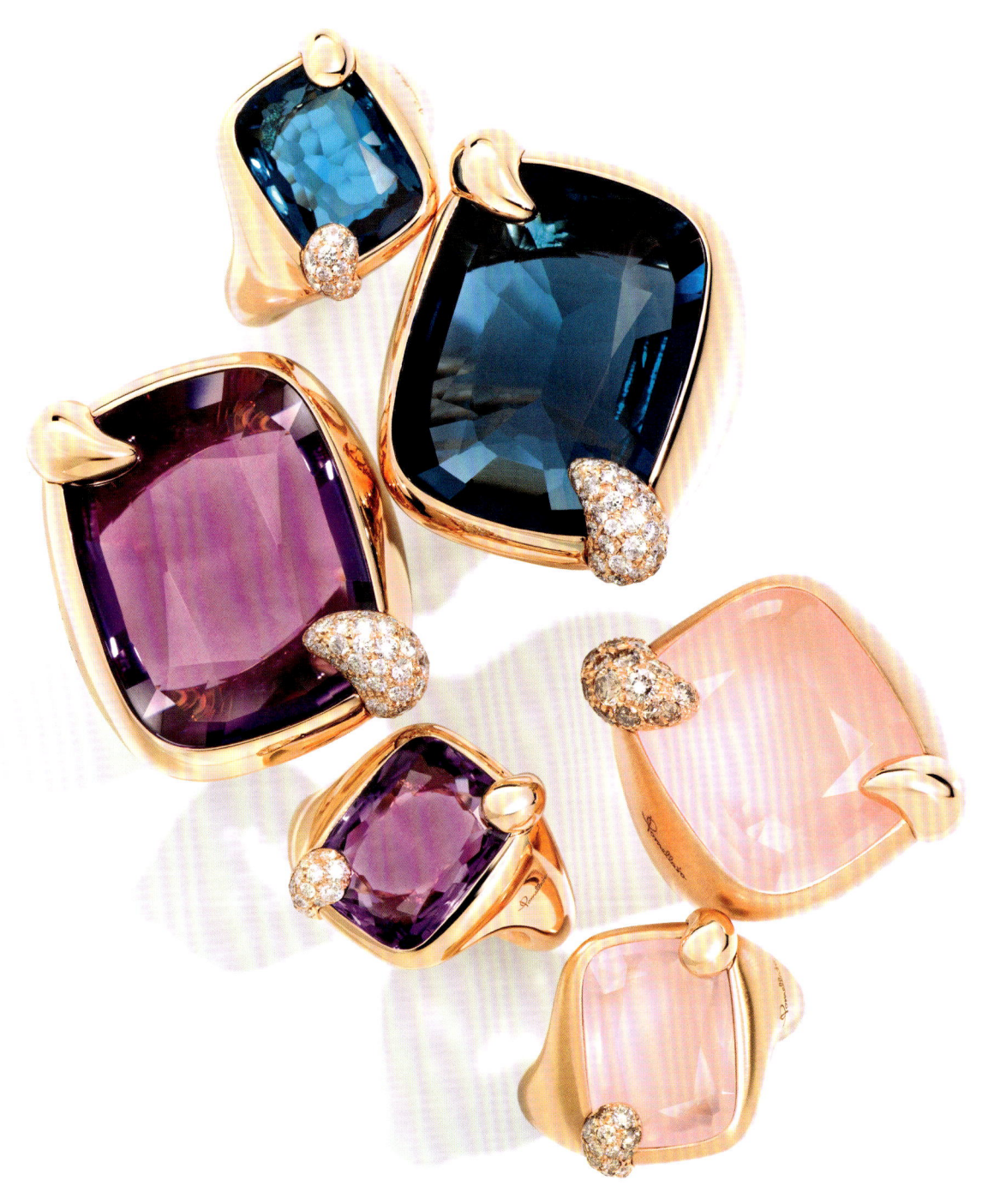

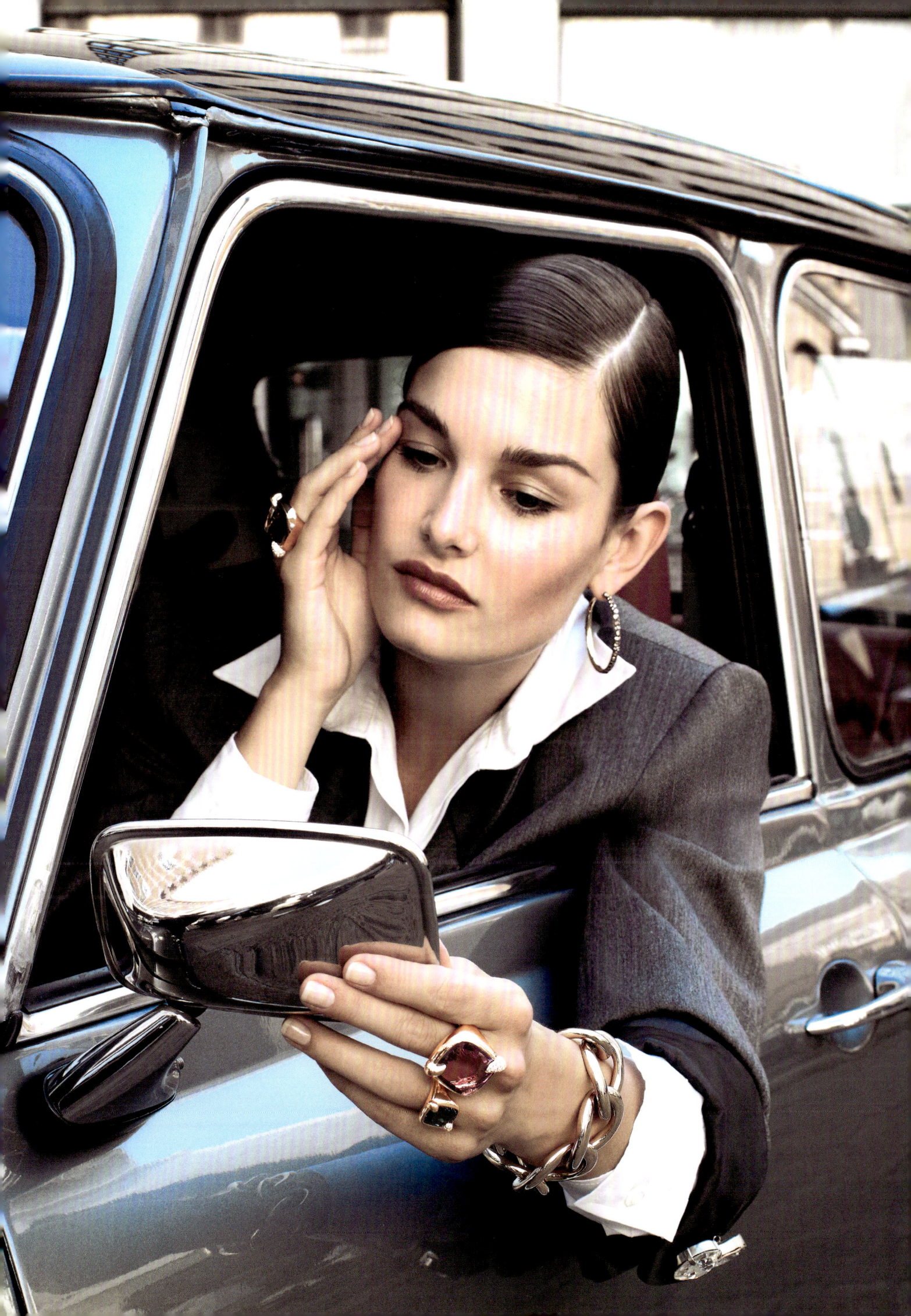

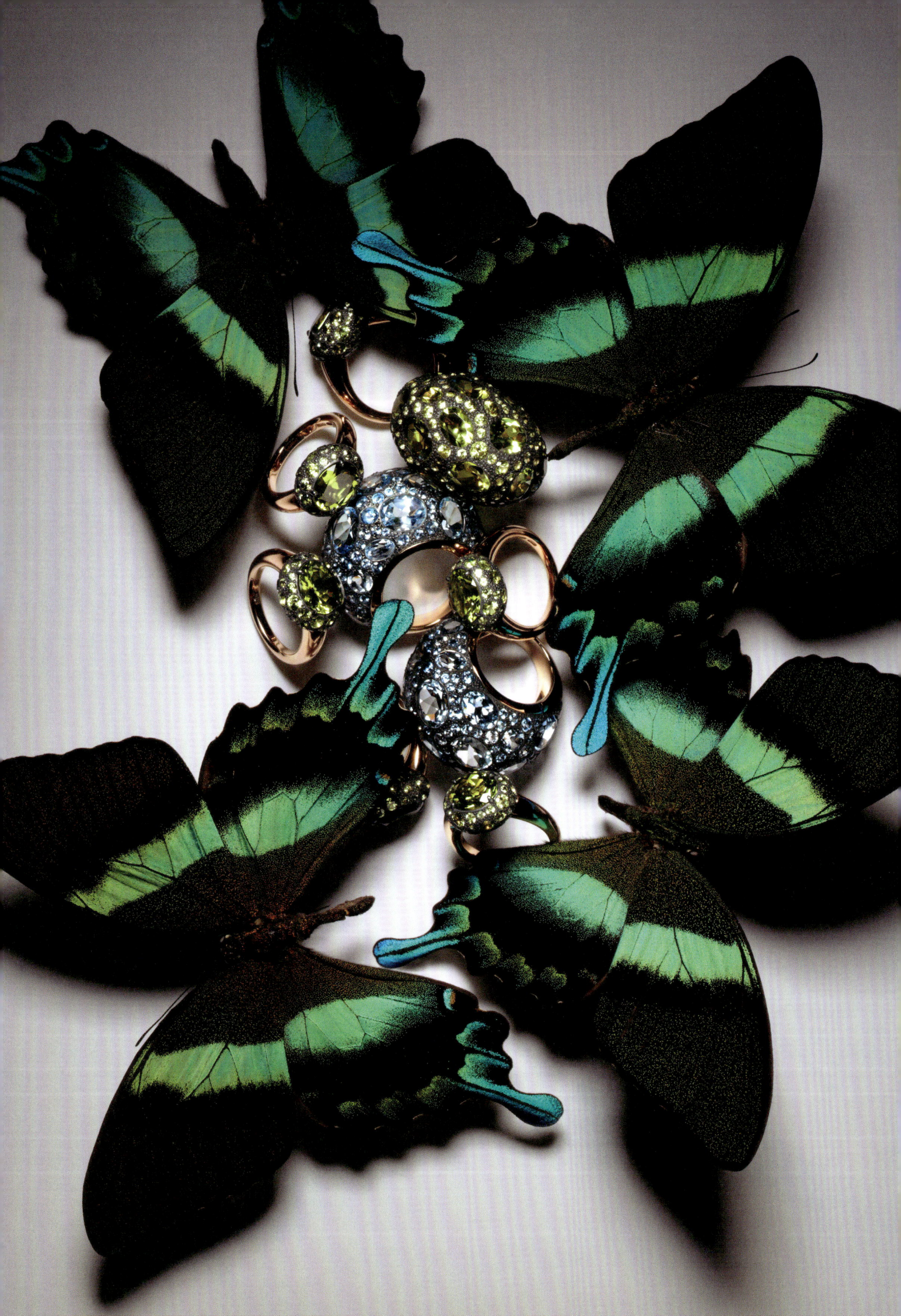

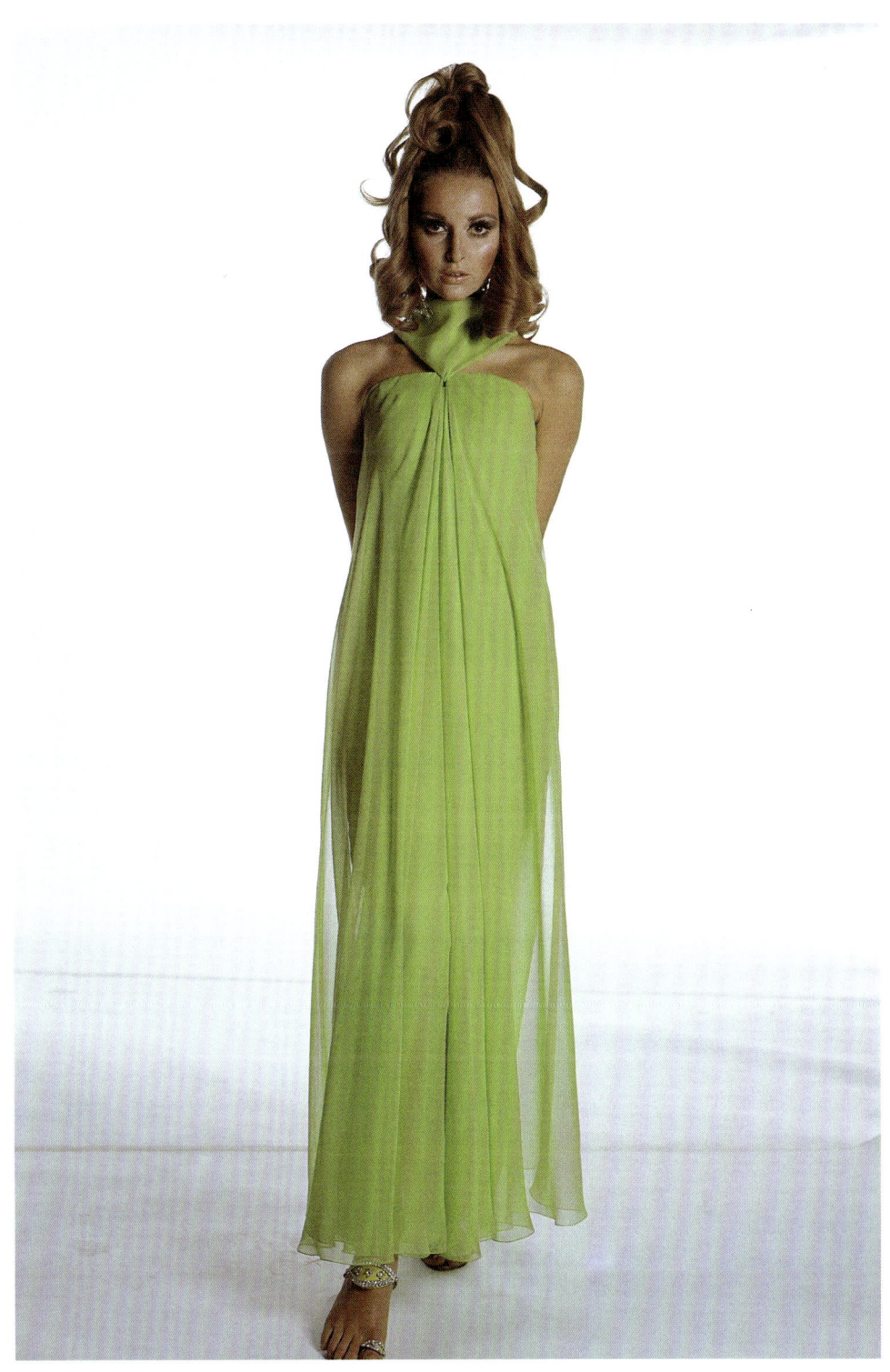

OPPOSITE: Pomellato *Tabou* rings in peridot and blue topaz

ABOVE: Color, please! Chiffon evening dress by Wilson
Folmar in *Vogue*, Bert Stern, 1967

Pomellato advertising campaign by Herb Ritts, 1990

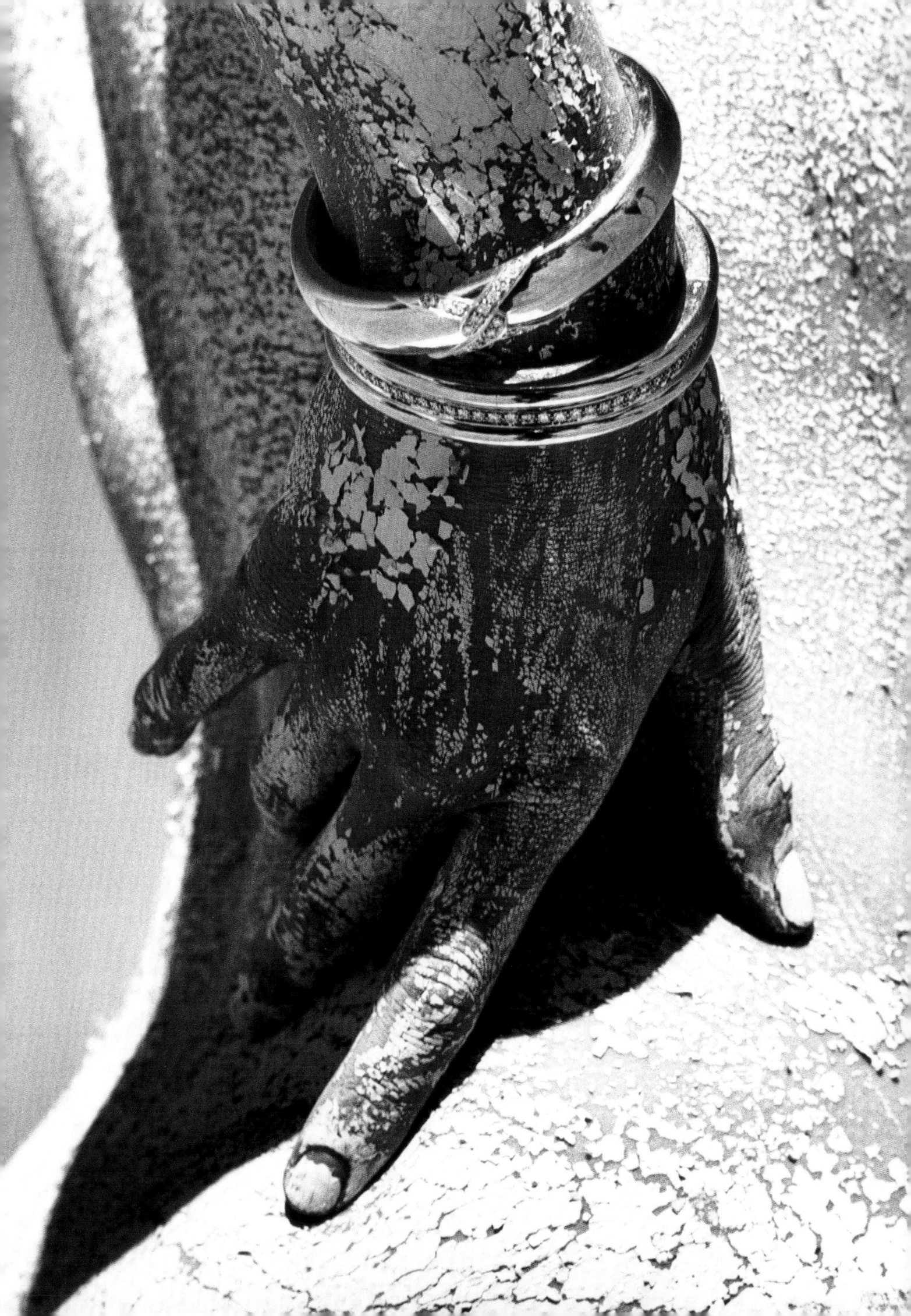

Pomellato *Nudo* rings in blue topaz

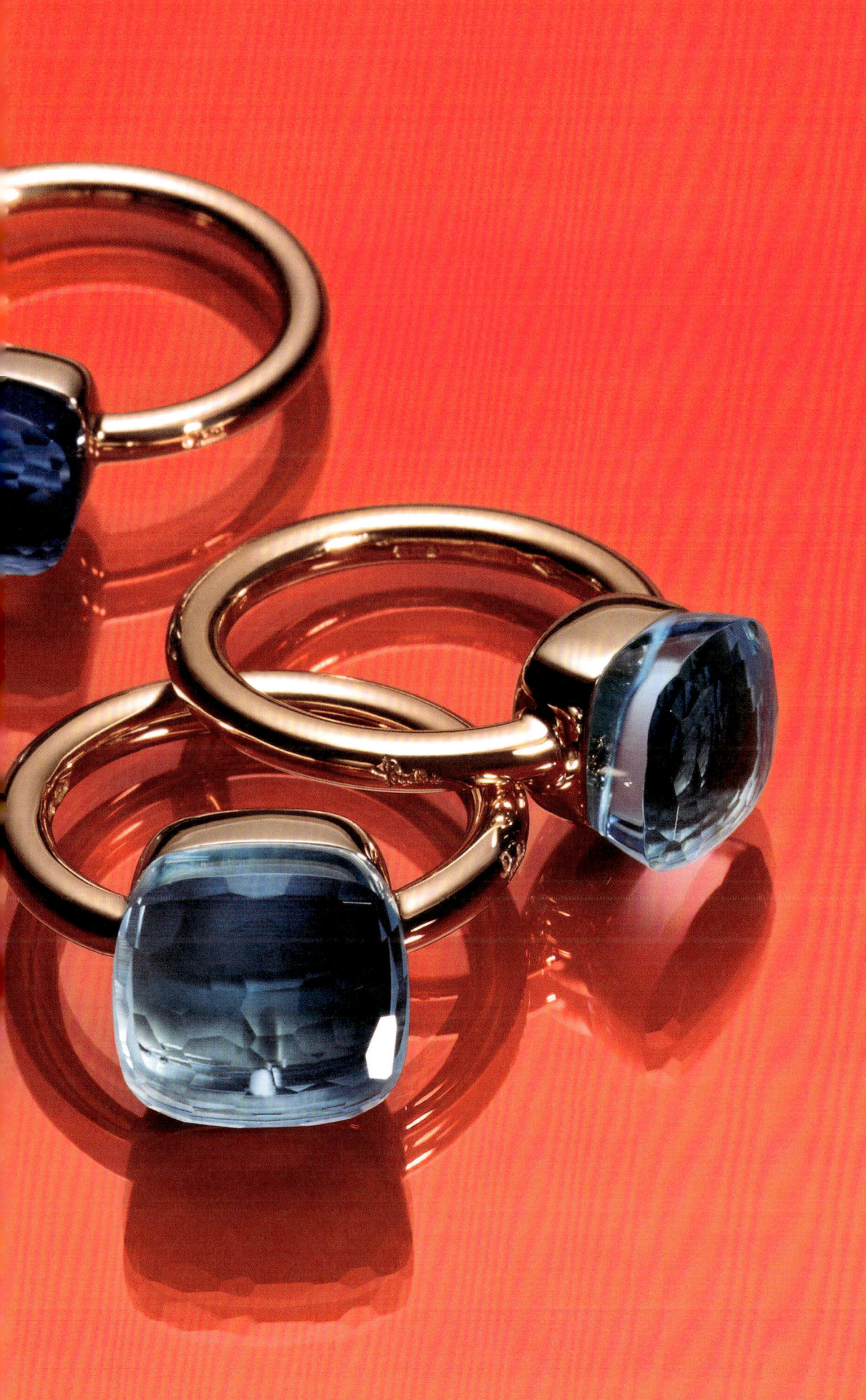

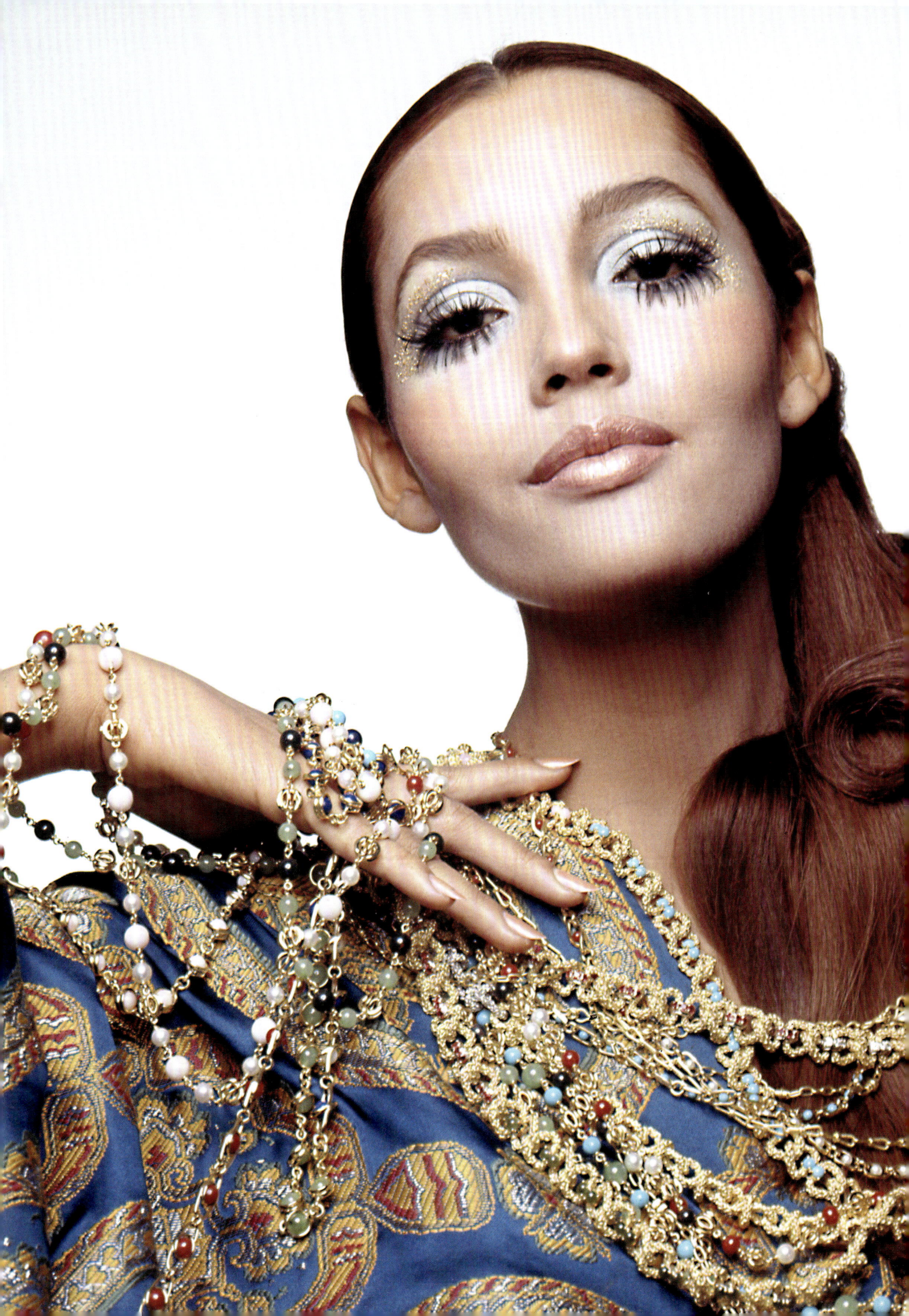

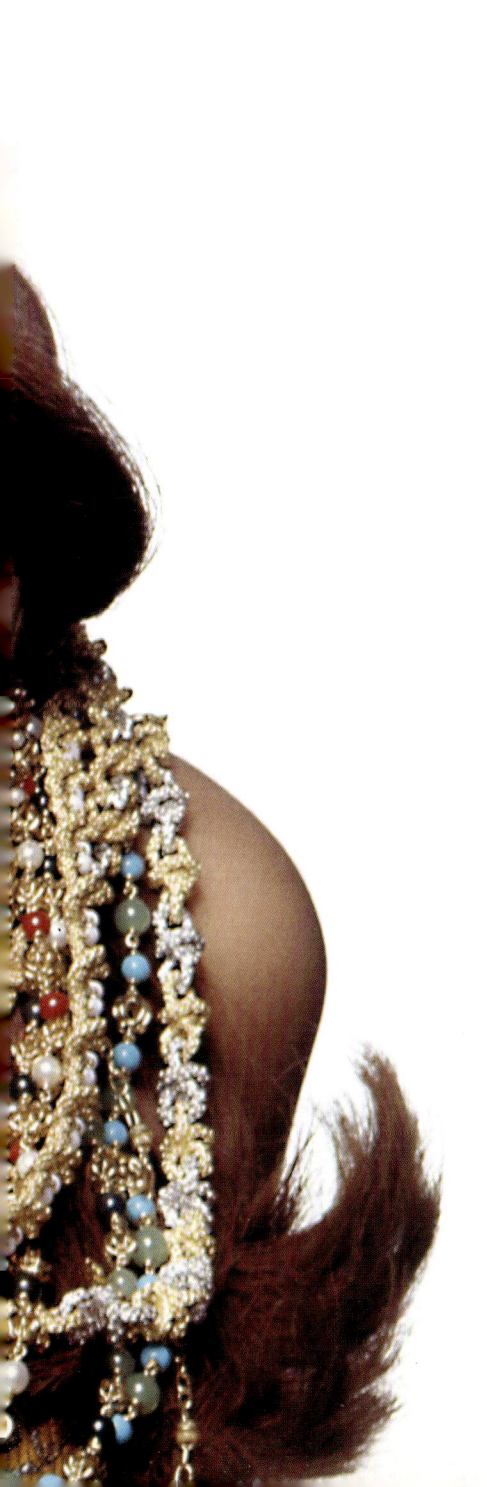

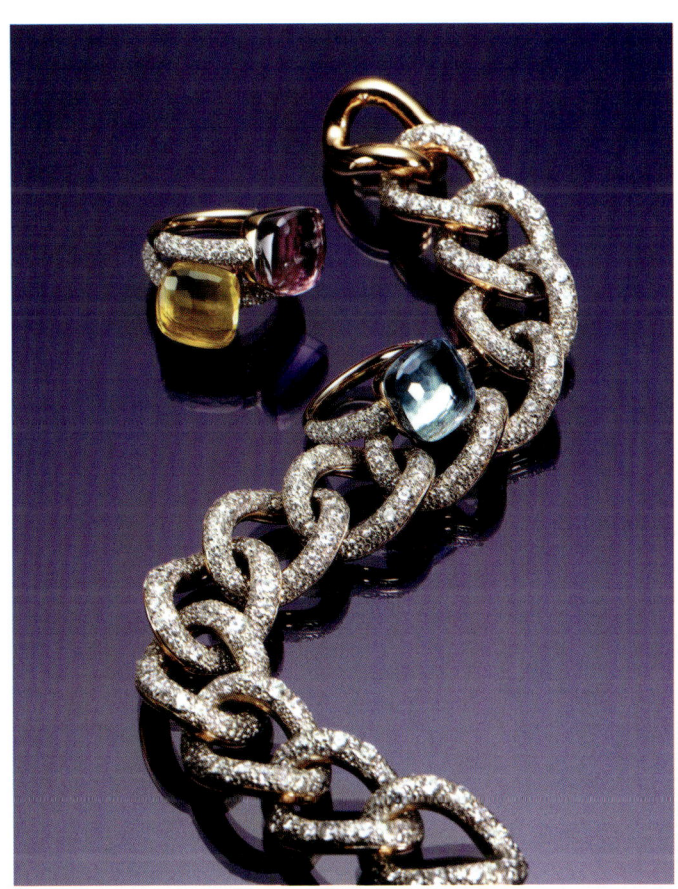

OPPOSITE: Layered Pomellato jewelry in a
Vogue Italia shot by Gian Paolo Barbieri, 1968

ABOVE: White diamond *Tango* bracelet and
stacked *Nudo* rings

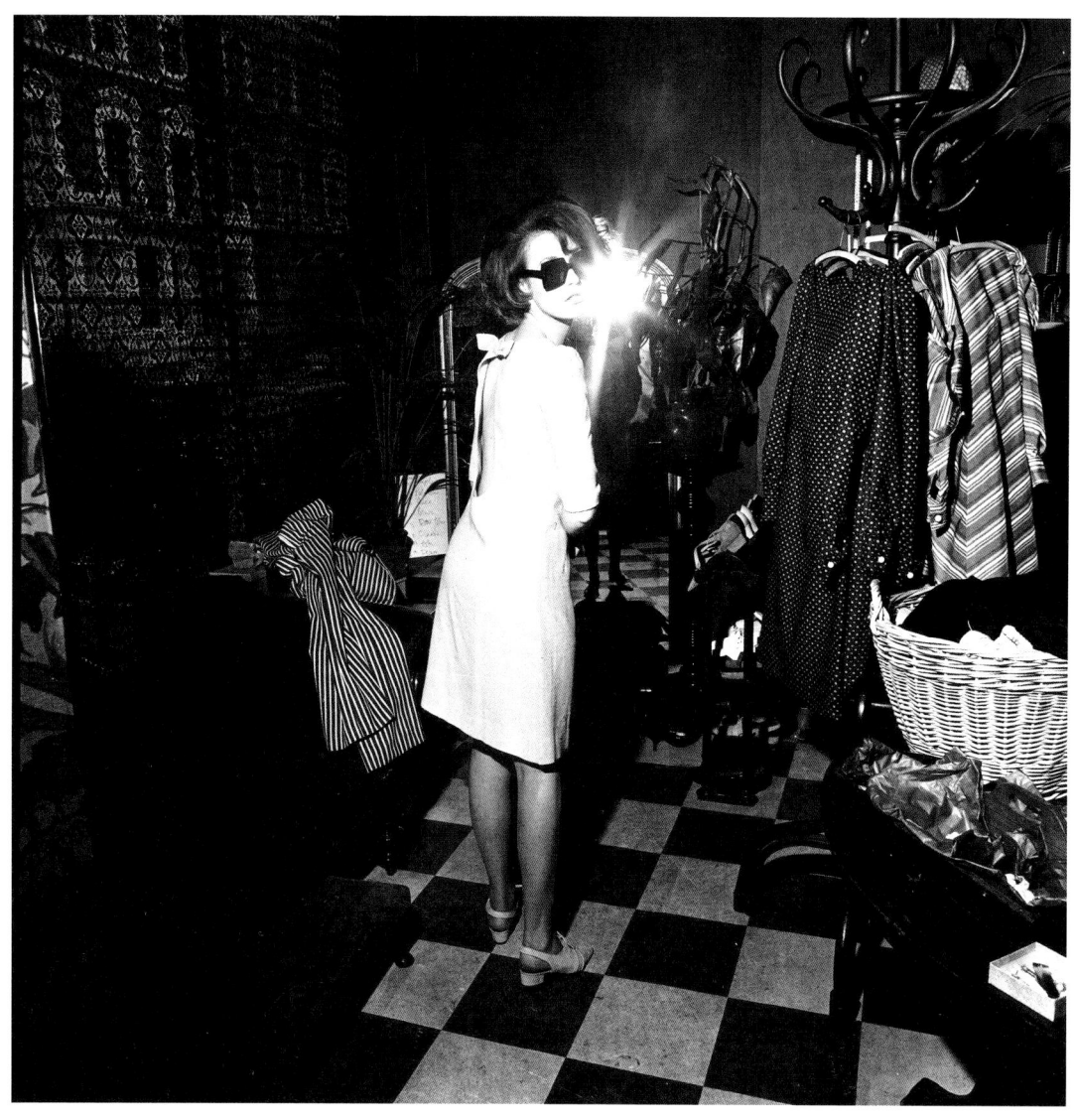

ABOVE: Instant stardom

OPPOSITE: The sophisticated simplicity of the *Milano* collection

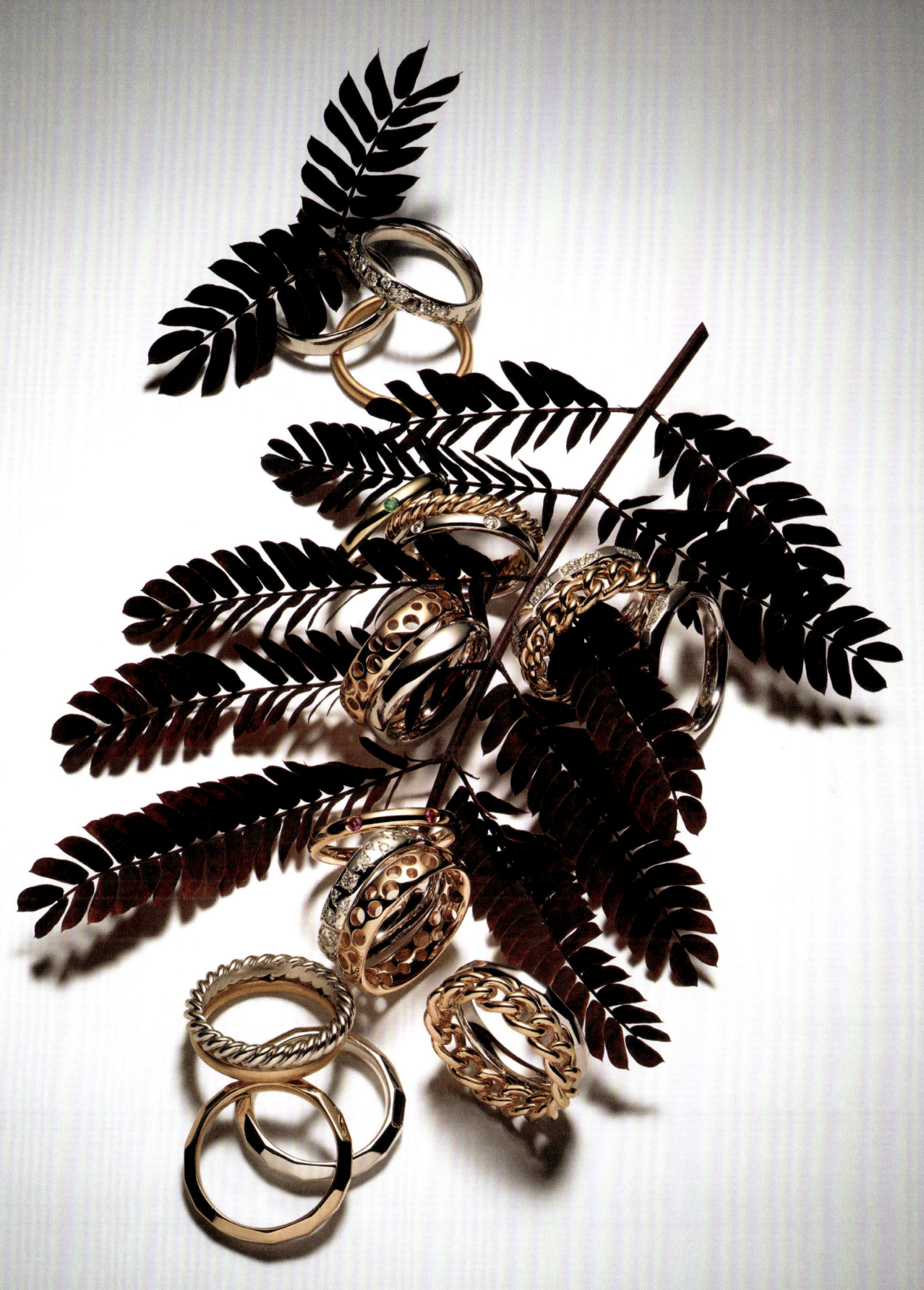

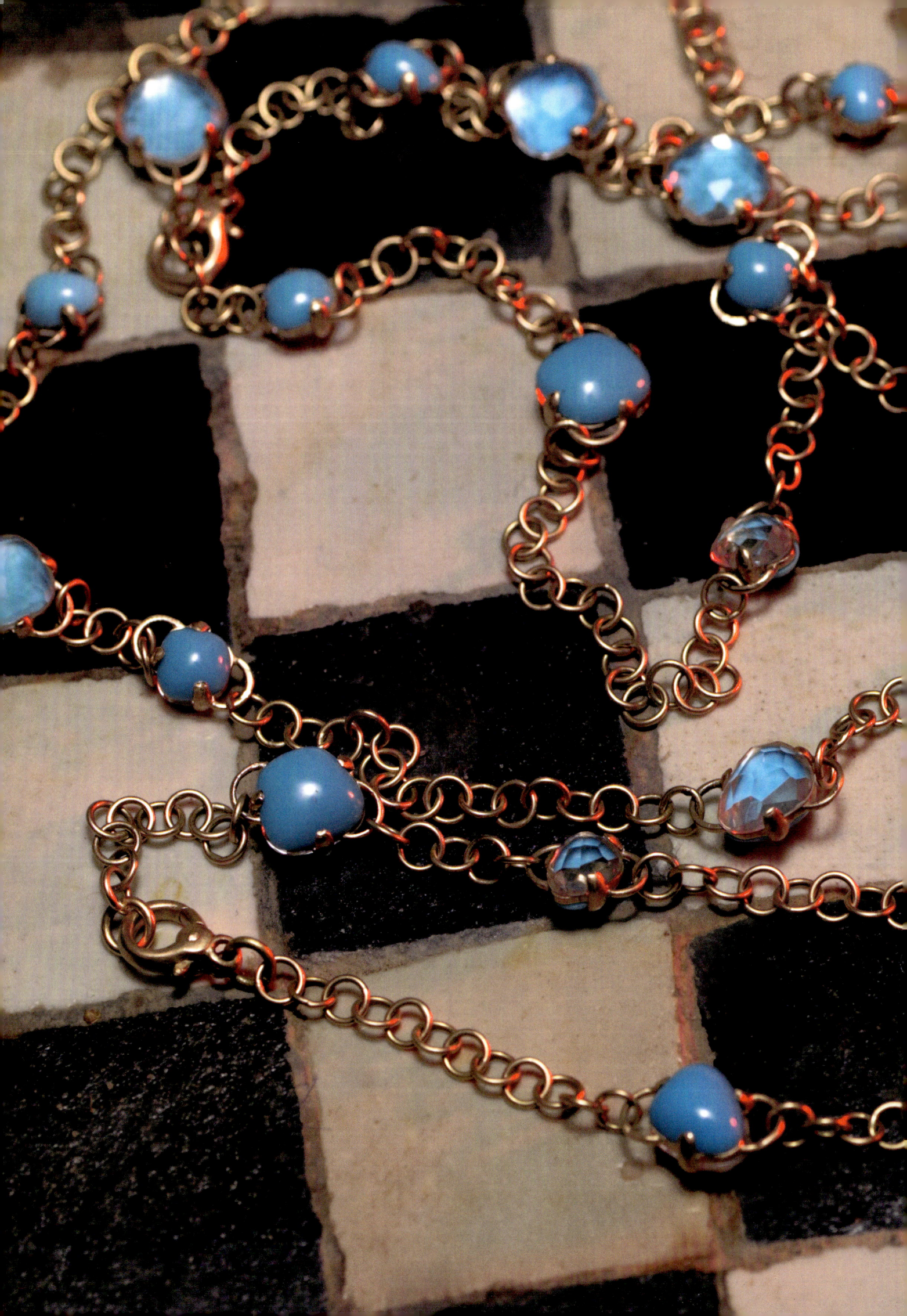

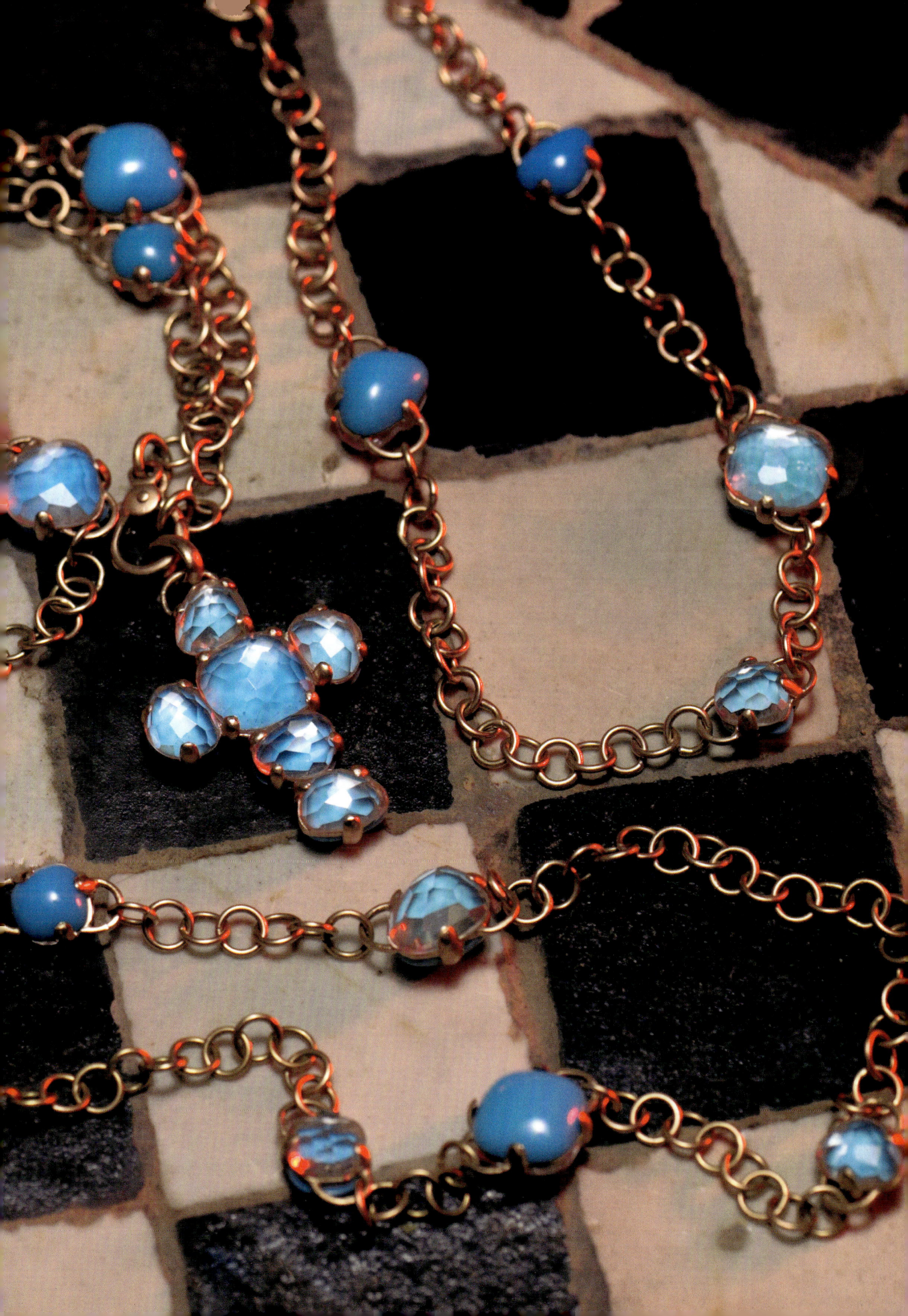

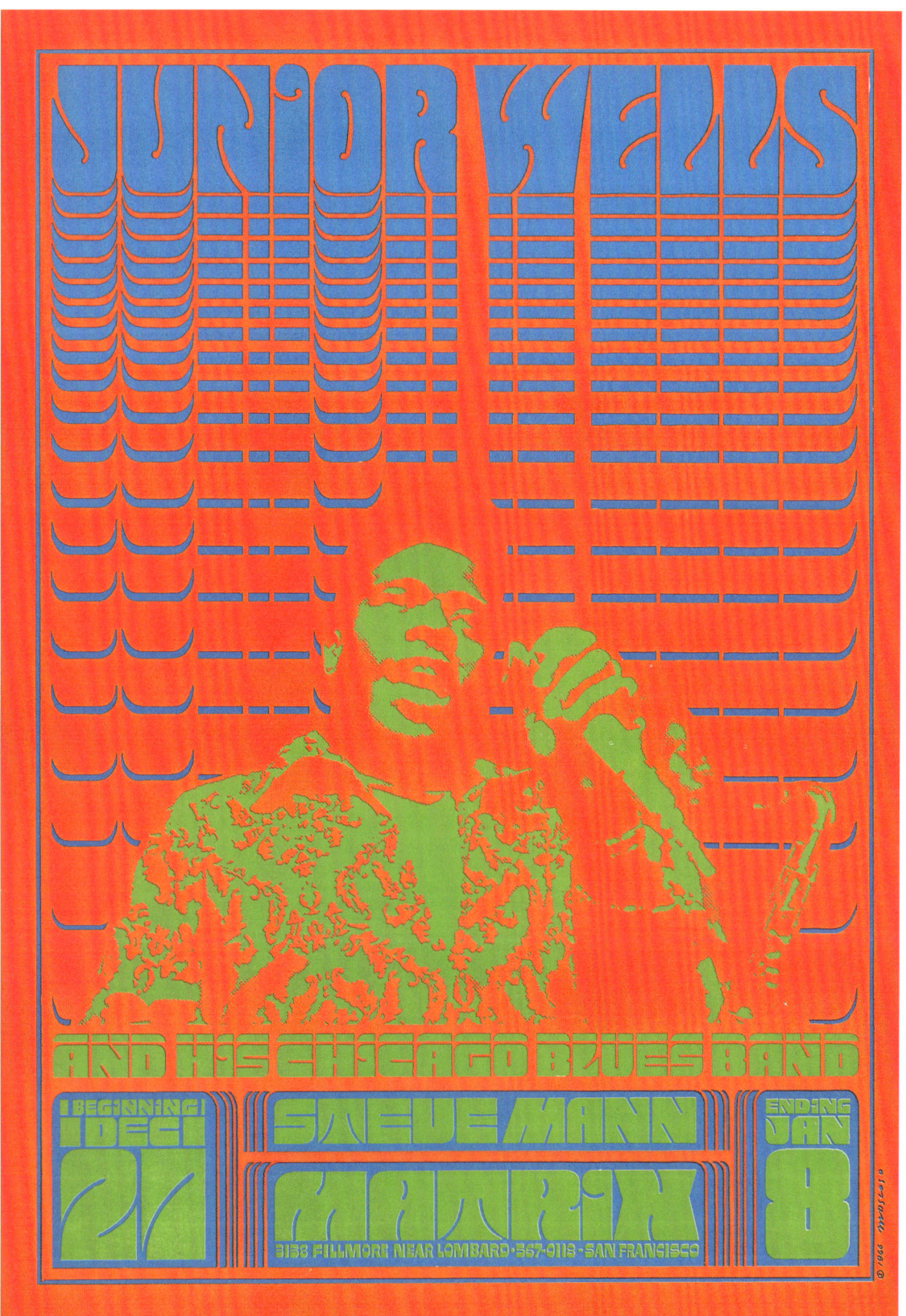

JUNIOR WELLS

AND HIS CHICAGO BLUES BAND

BEGINNING DEC 21   STEVE MANN   ENDING JAN 8

MATRIX

3138 FILLMORE NEAR LOMBARD · 567-0118 · SAN FRANCISCO

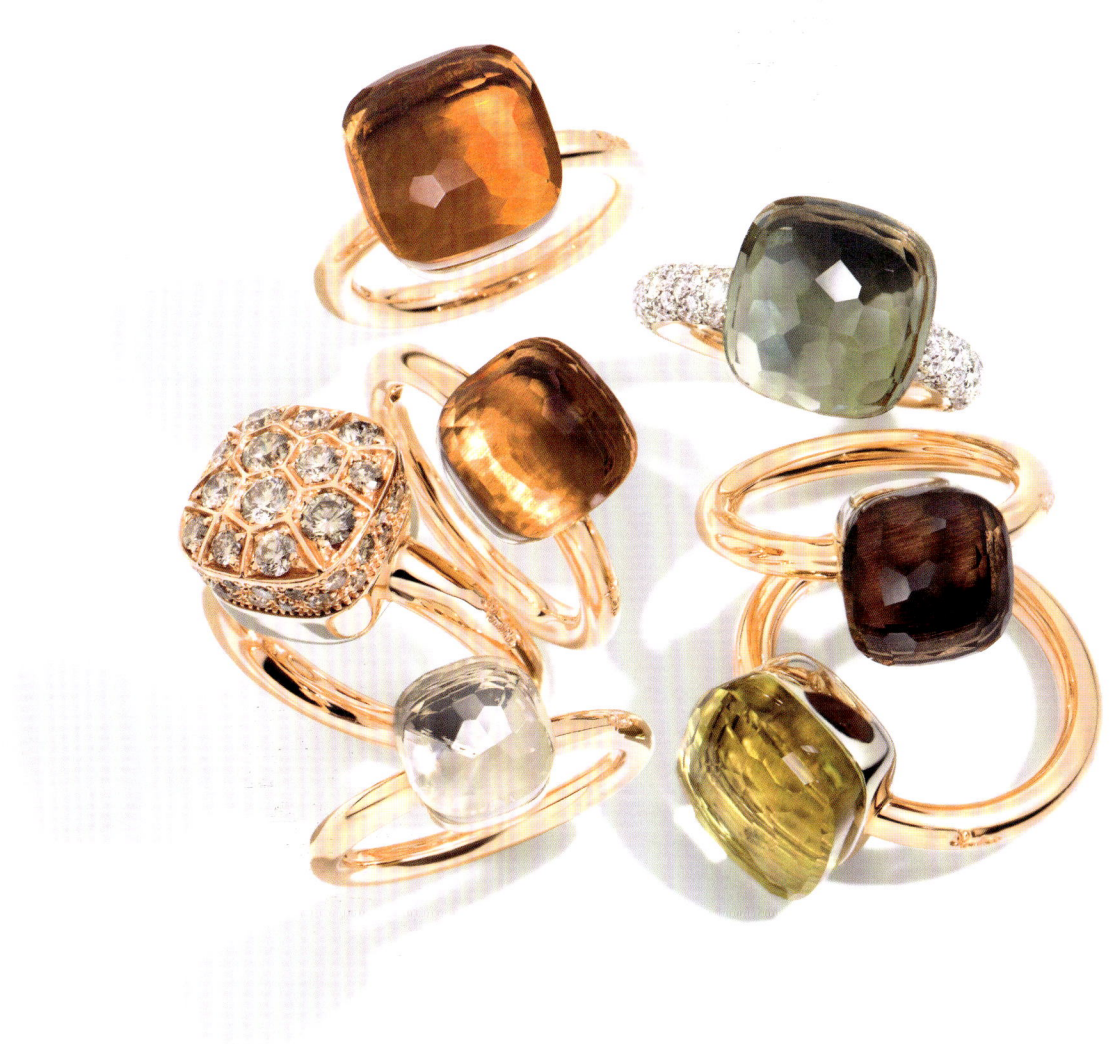

PREVIOUS SPREAD: Pomellato *Capri* necklaces and pendant in turquoise and rock crystal

OPPOSITE: *Neon Rose #1* by Victor Moscoso, 1967

ABOVE: *Nudo* collection rings in warm, autumnal hues and colors

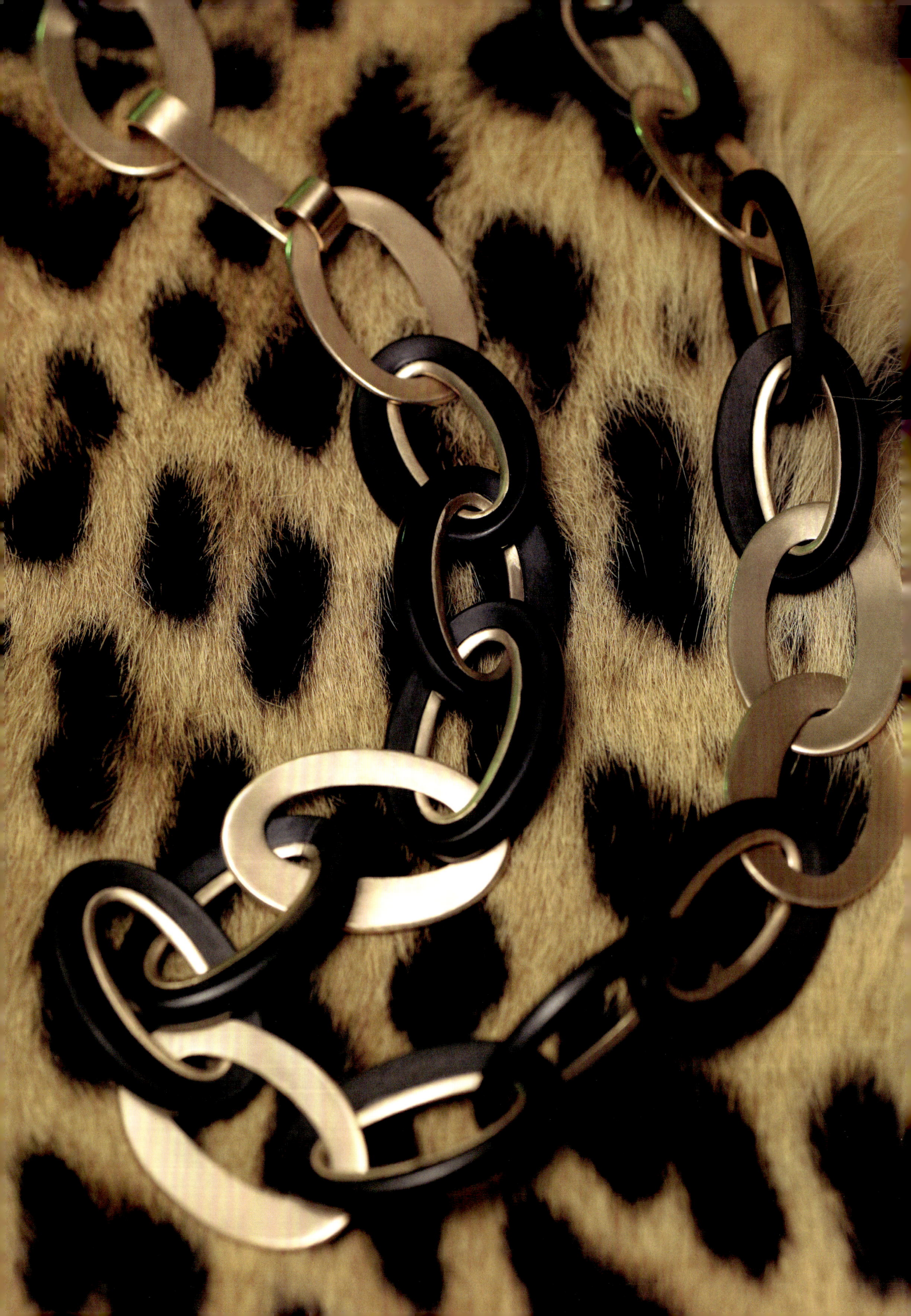

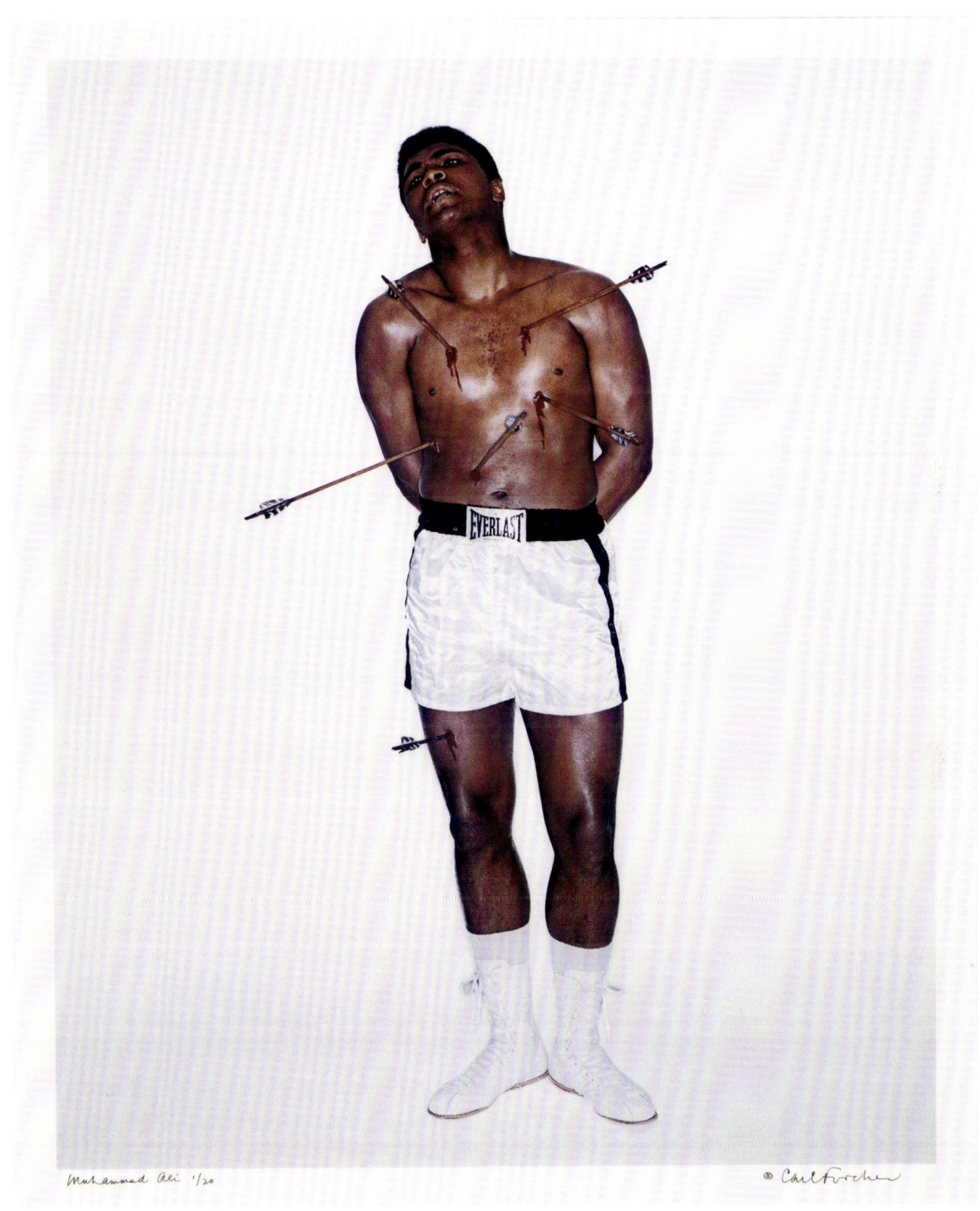

Muhammad Ali ¹/₂₀   © Carl Fischer

OPPOSITE: *Victoria* necklace

ABOVE: Muhammad Ali as Saint Sebastian, commissioned
by American *Esquire* magazine, Carl Fischer, 1967

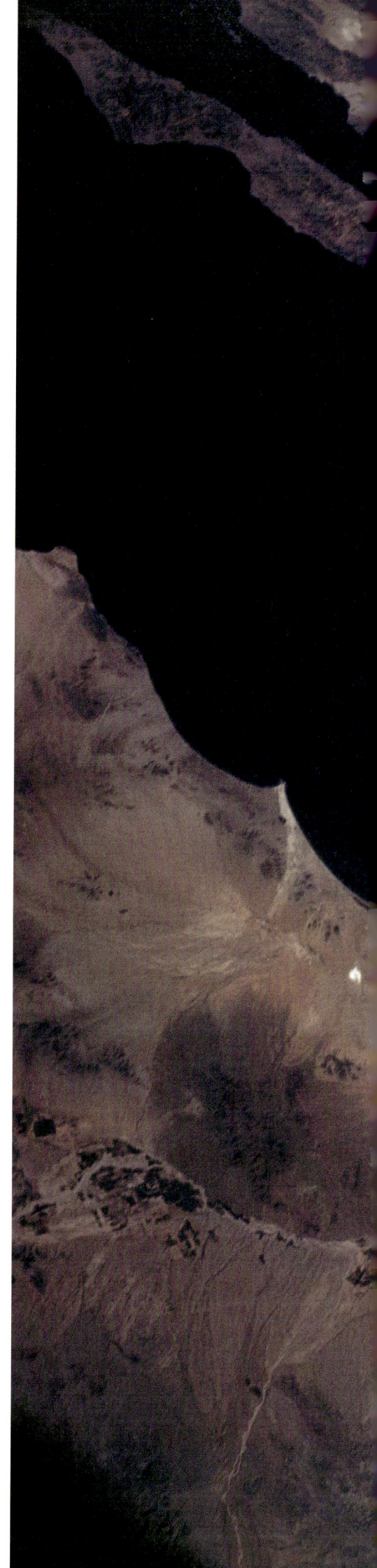

The 1968 space conquest. The spent S-IVB third stage of a Saturn V
rocket, after the launch of Apollo 7 in 1968. Apollo 7 was the first
manned flight to test the Apollo command module in earth's orbit

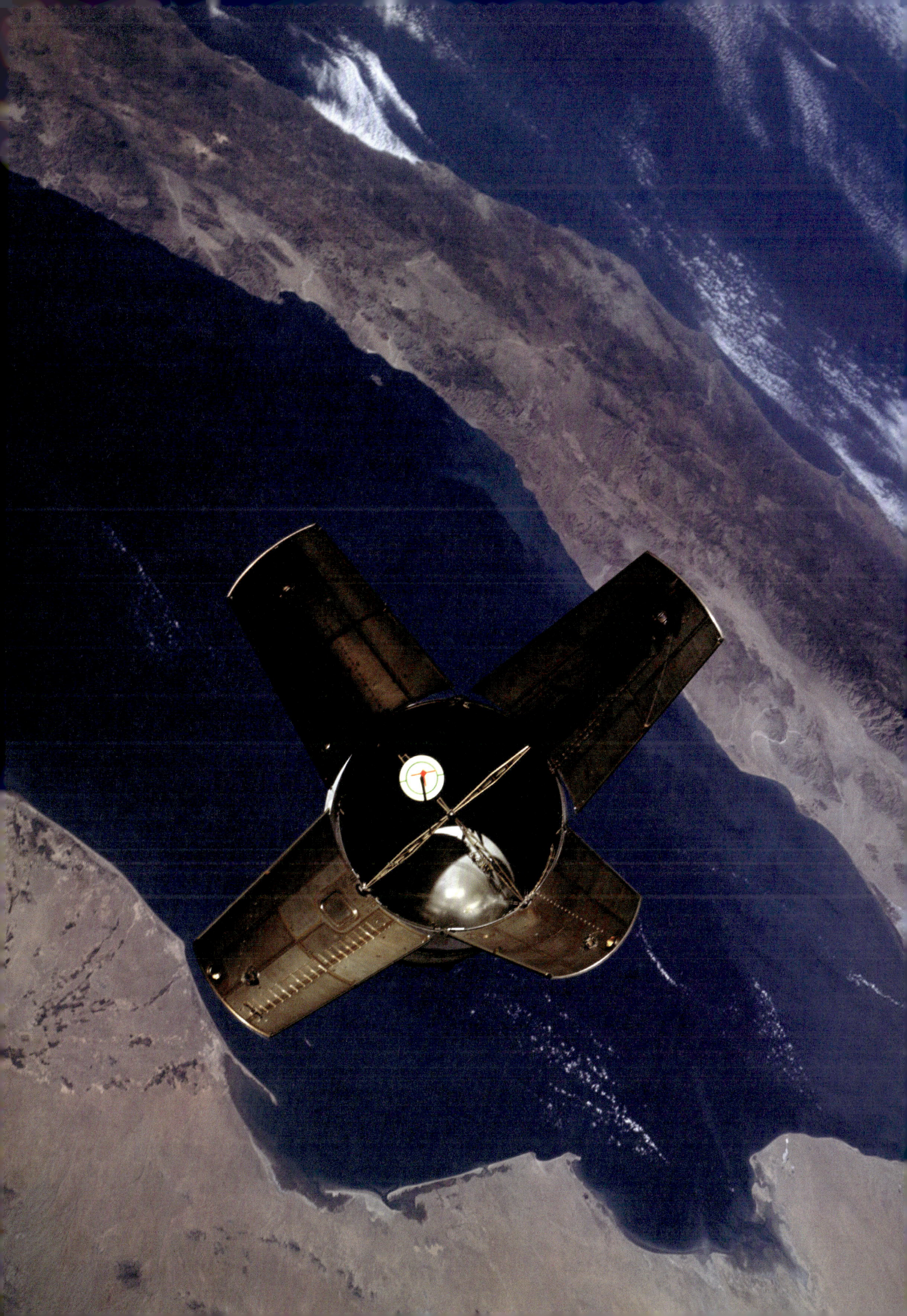

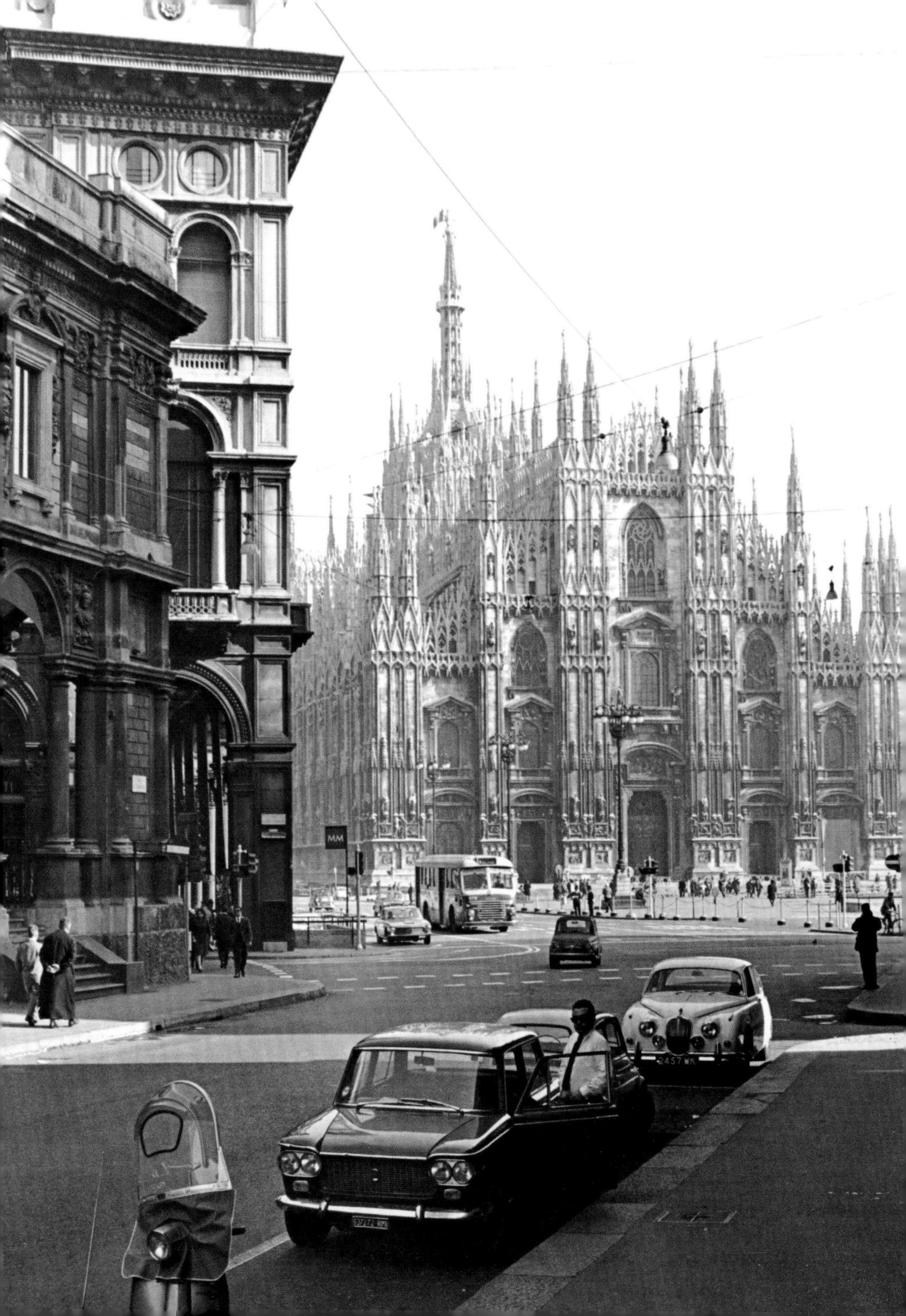

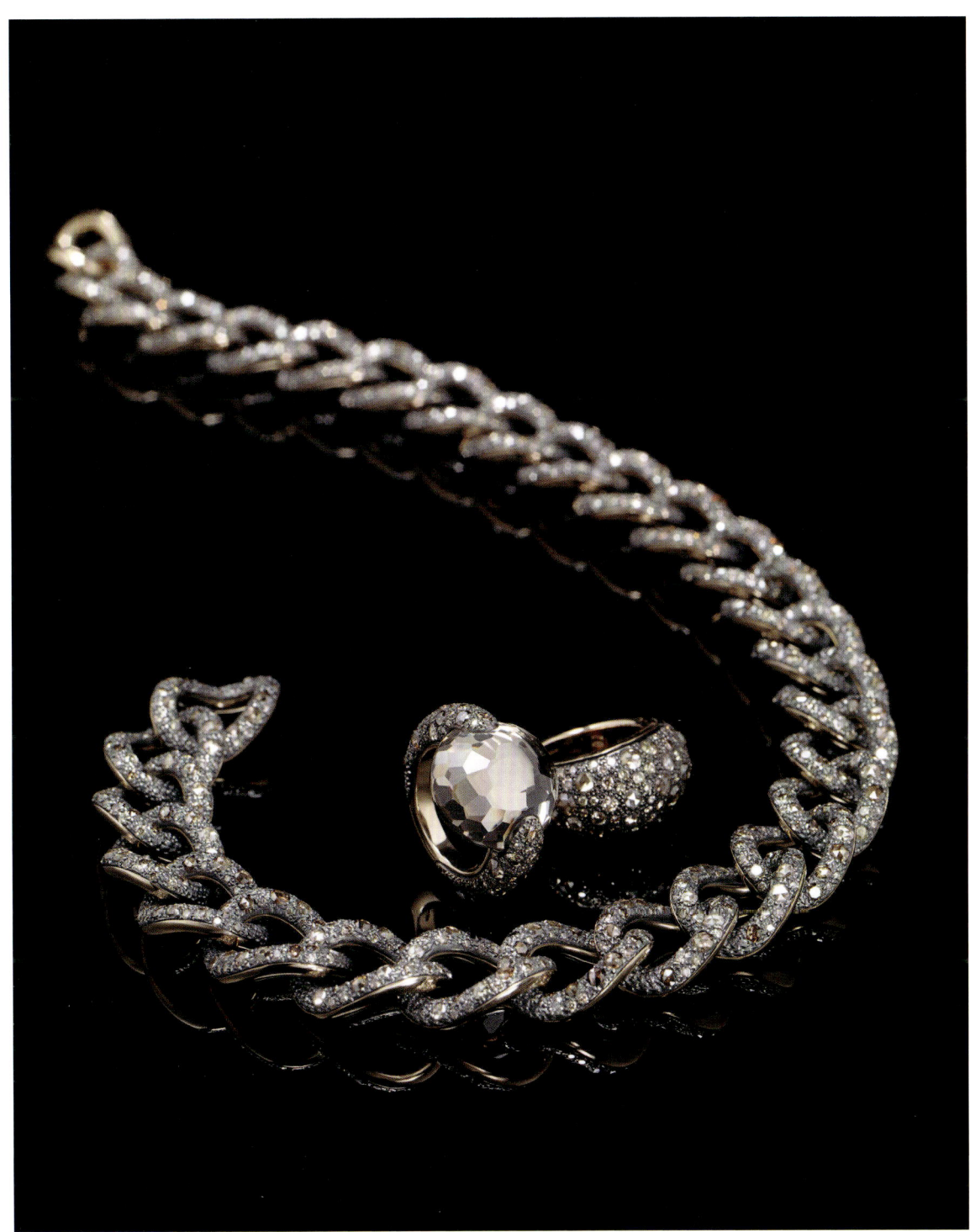

OPPOSITE: Milan's Duomo in the 1960s

ABOVE: *Tango* collection rings and necklace
embellished with brown diamonds

FOLLOWING SPREAD: Signature chains and bracelets
in rose gold reflecting the spirit of Milanese design

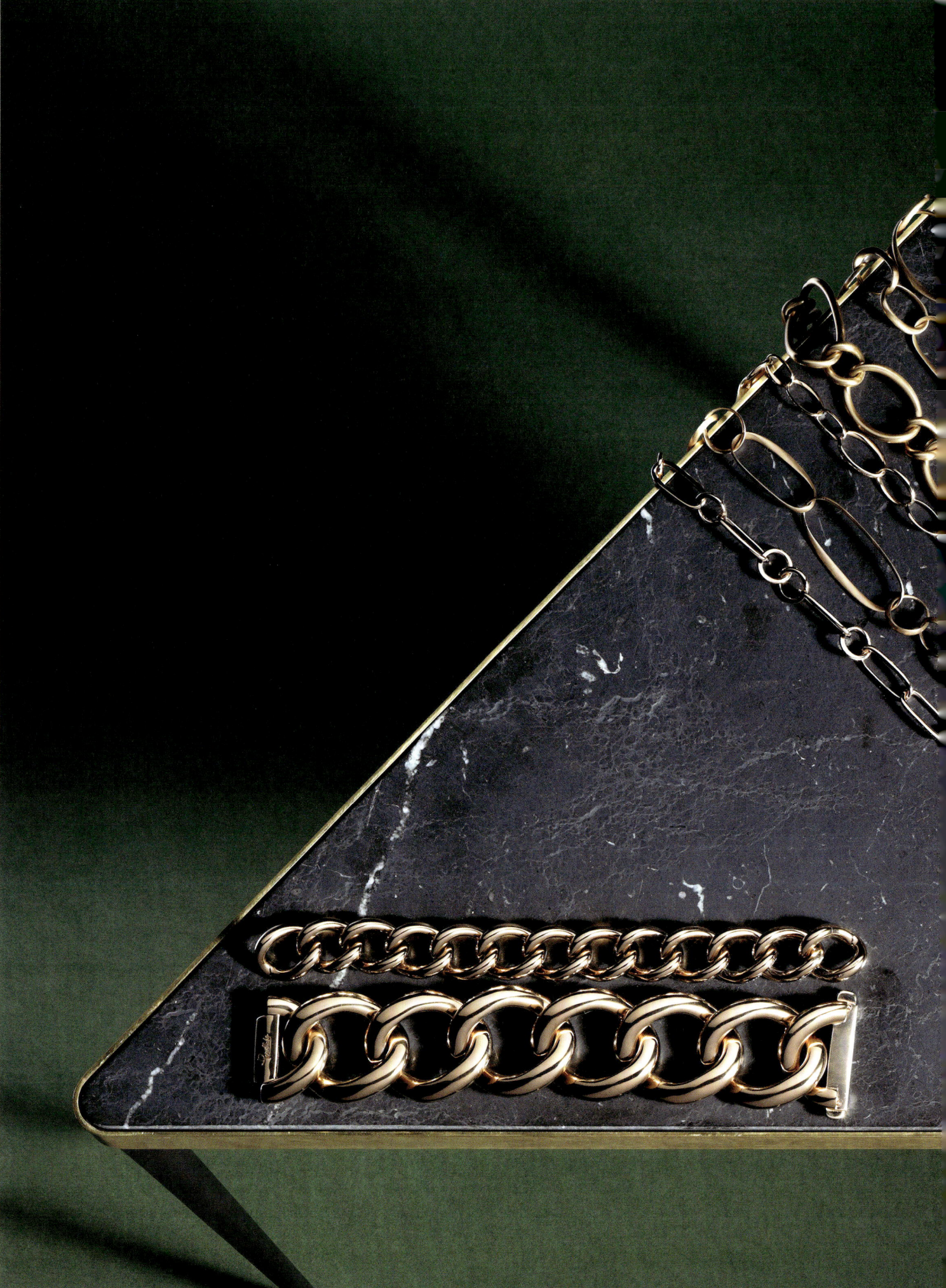

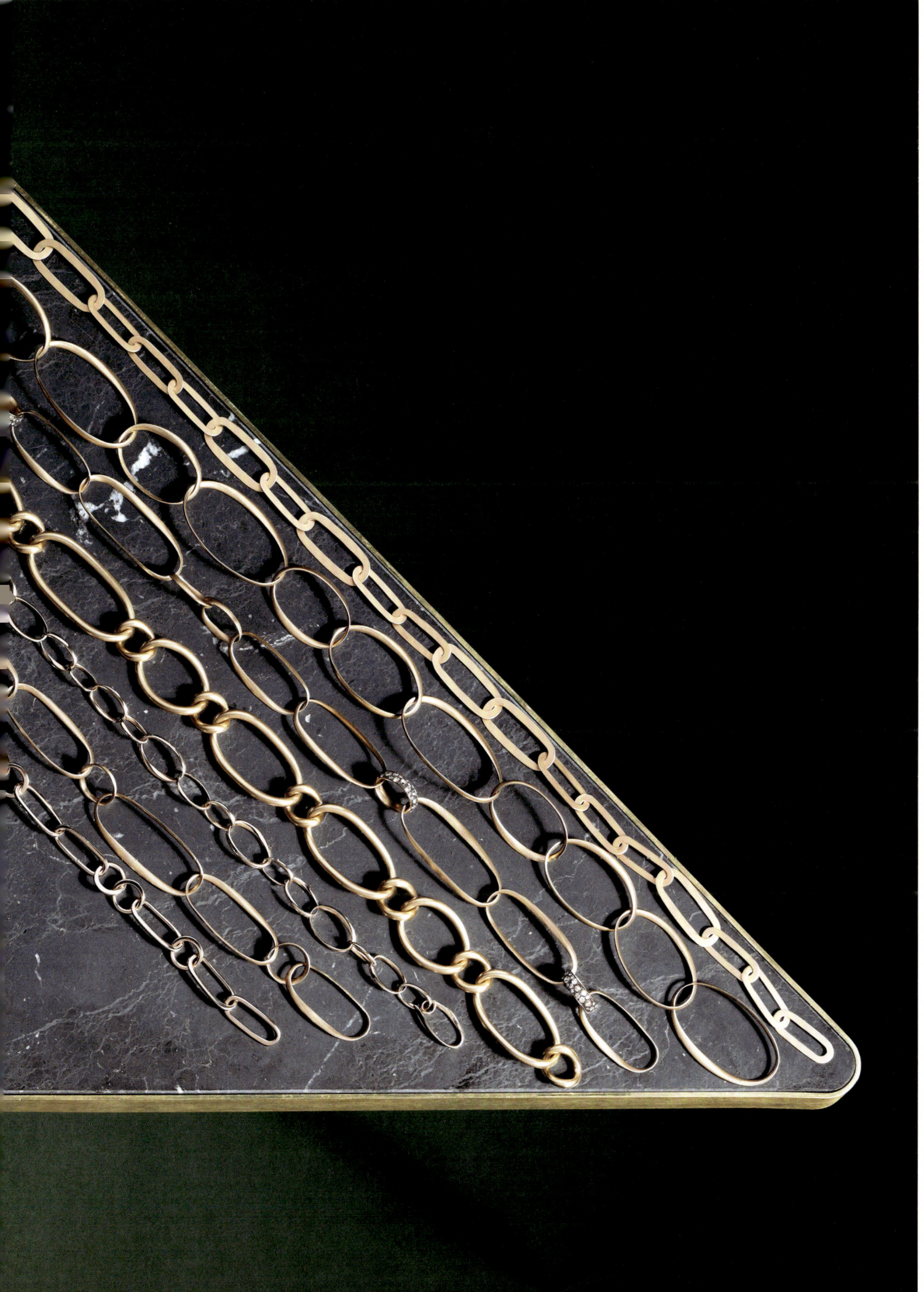

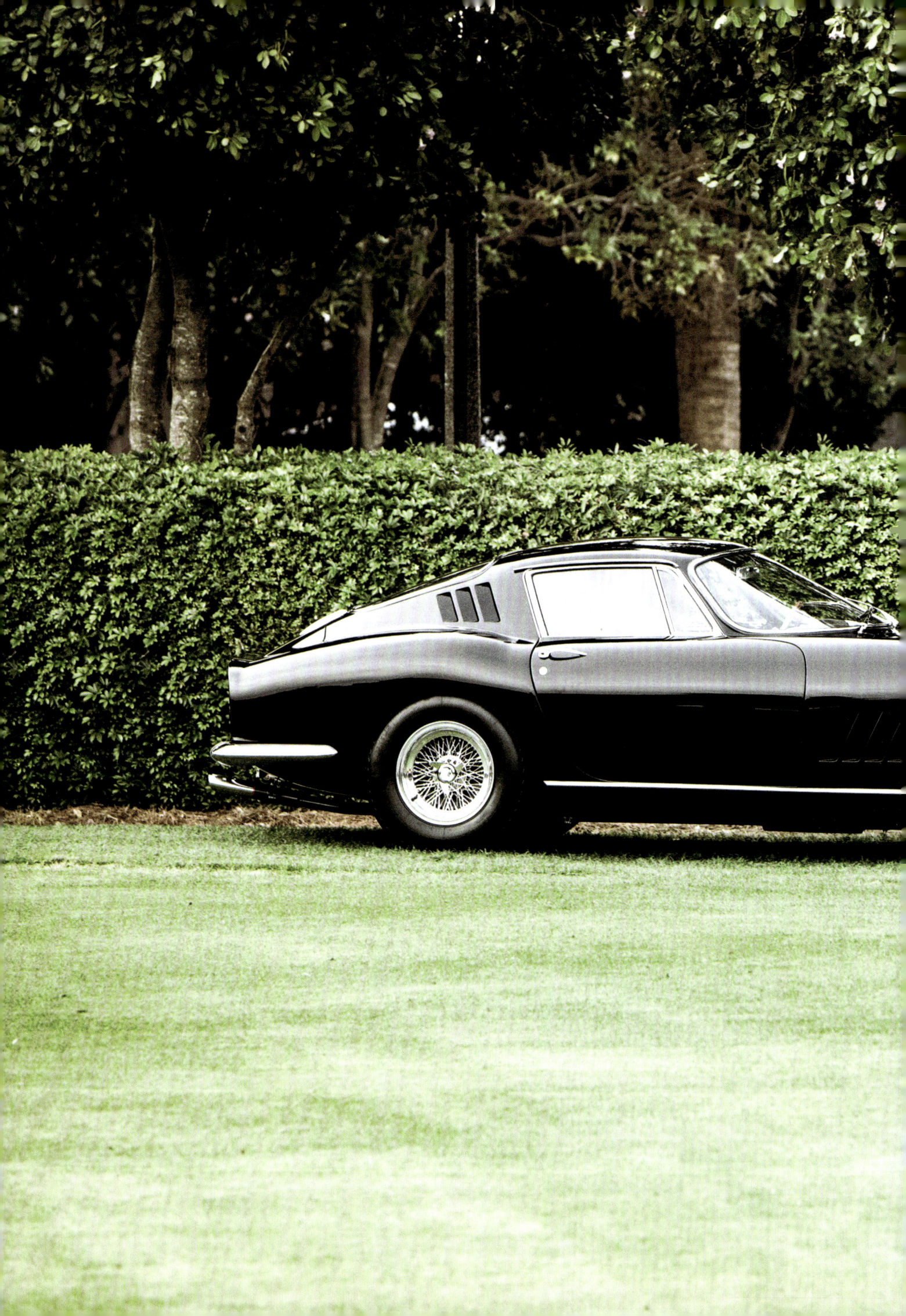

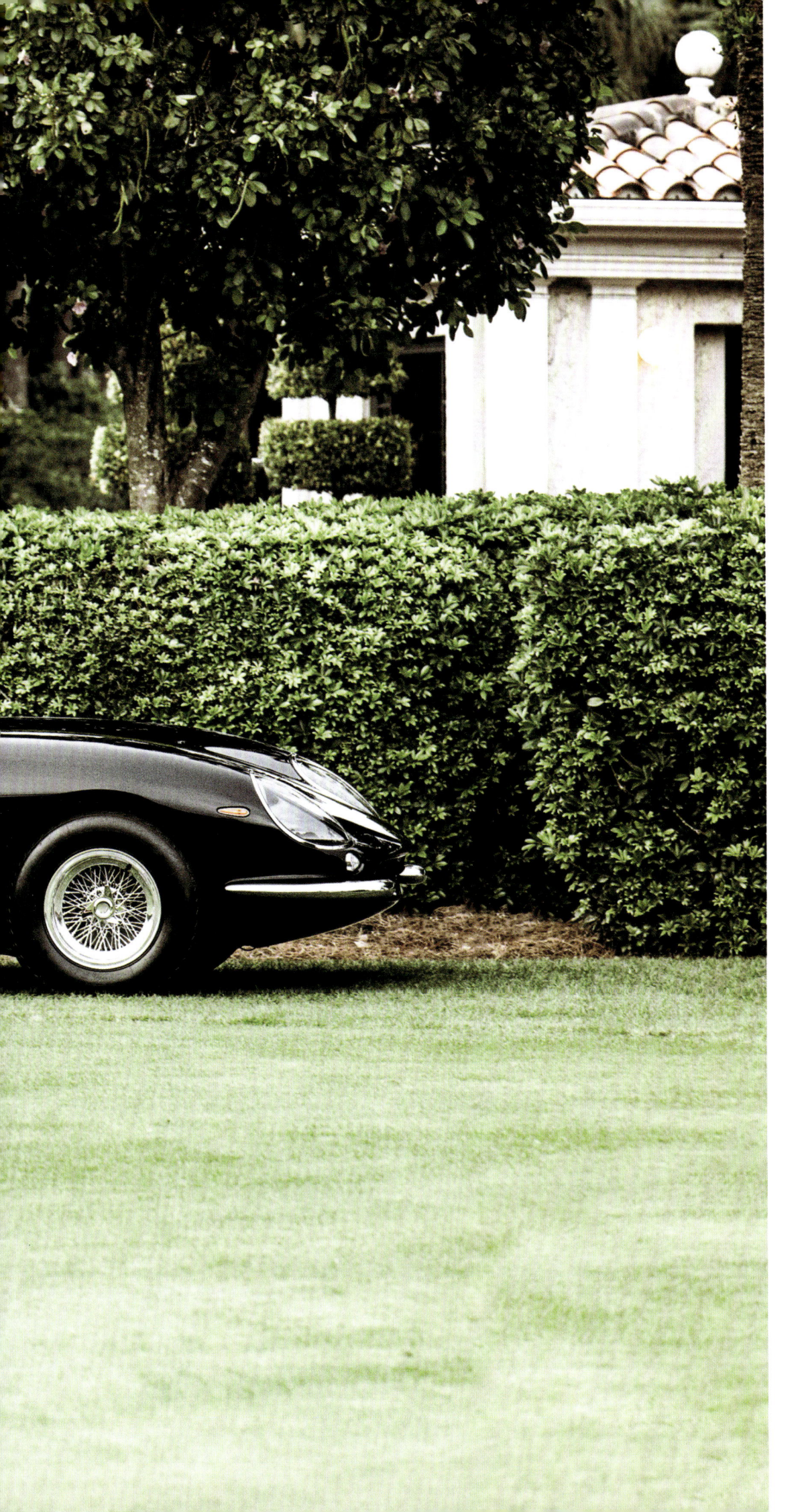

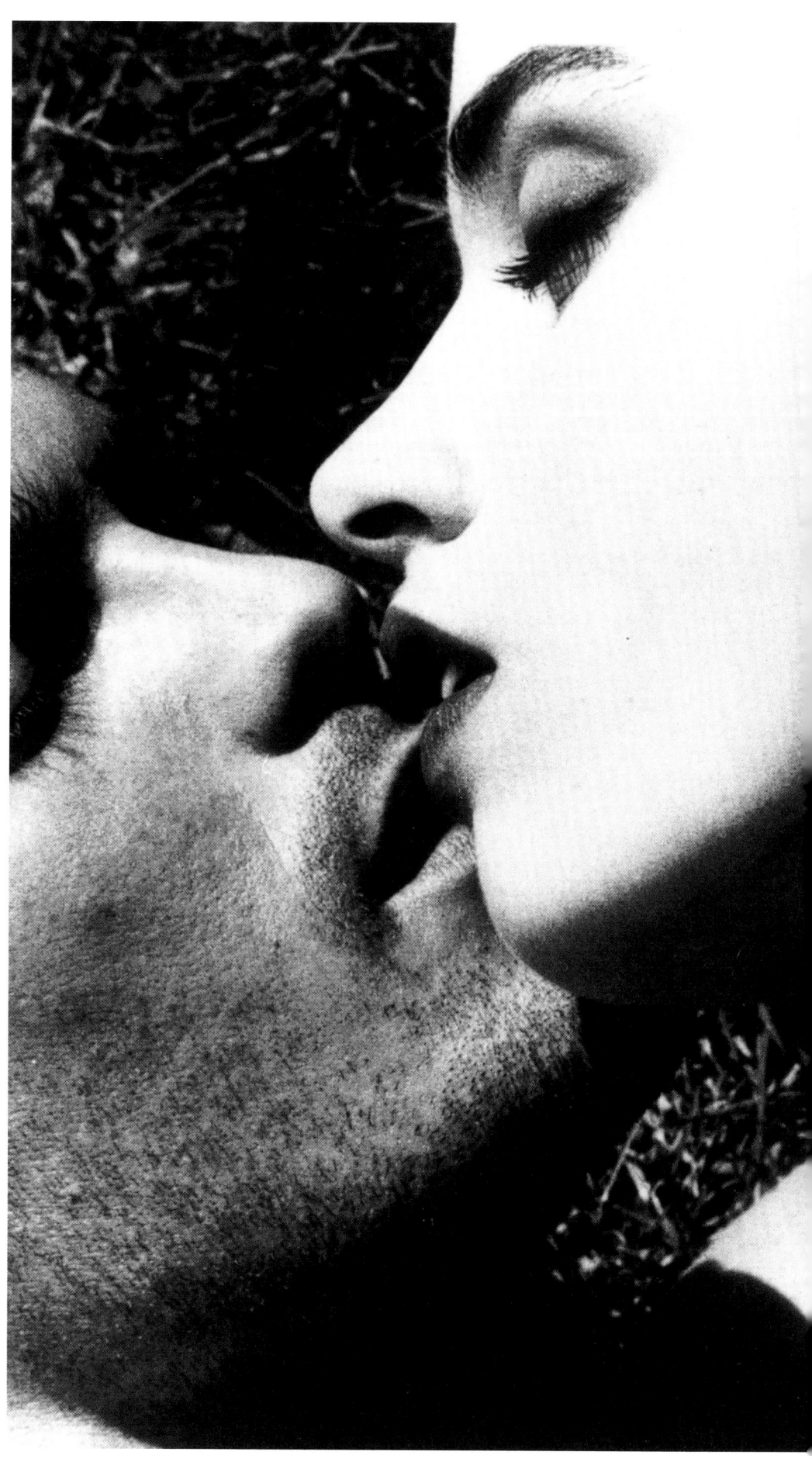

PREVIOUS SPREAD: The 1967 Ferrari 275
GTB/4, a Gran Tourismo for the ages,
and one of the greatest Ferraris ever built.
Pininfarina crafted the graceful lines, and the
Colombo V12 provided smooth yet
stirring power

OPPOSITE: Chains and the *Iconica* ring
in a Pomellato advertising campaign
by Helmut Newton, 1983

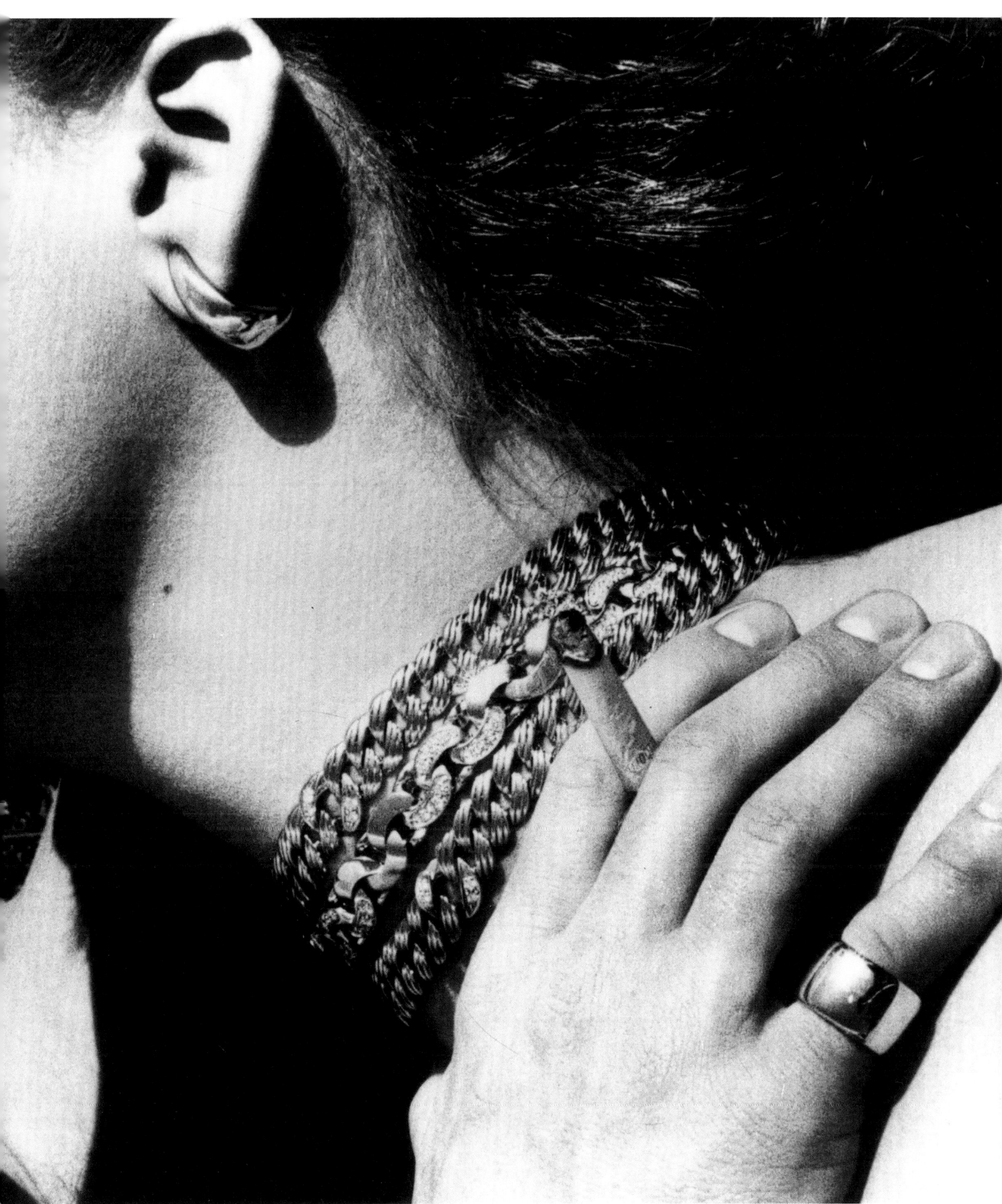

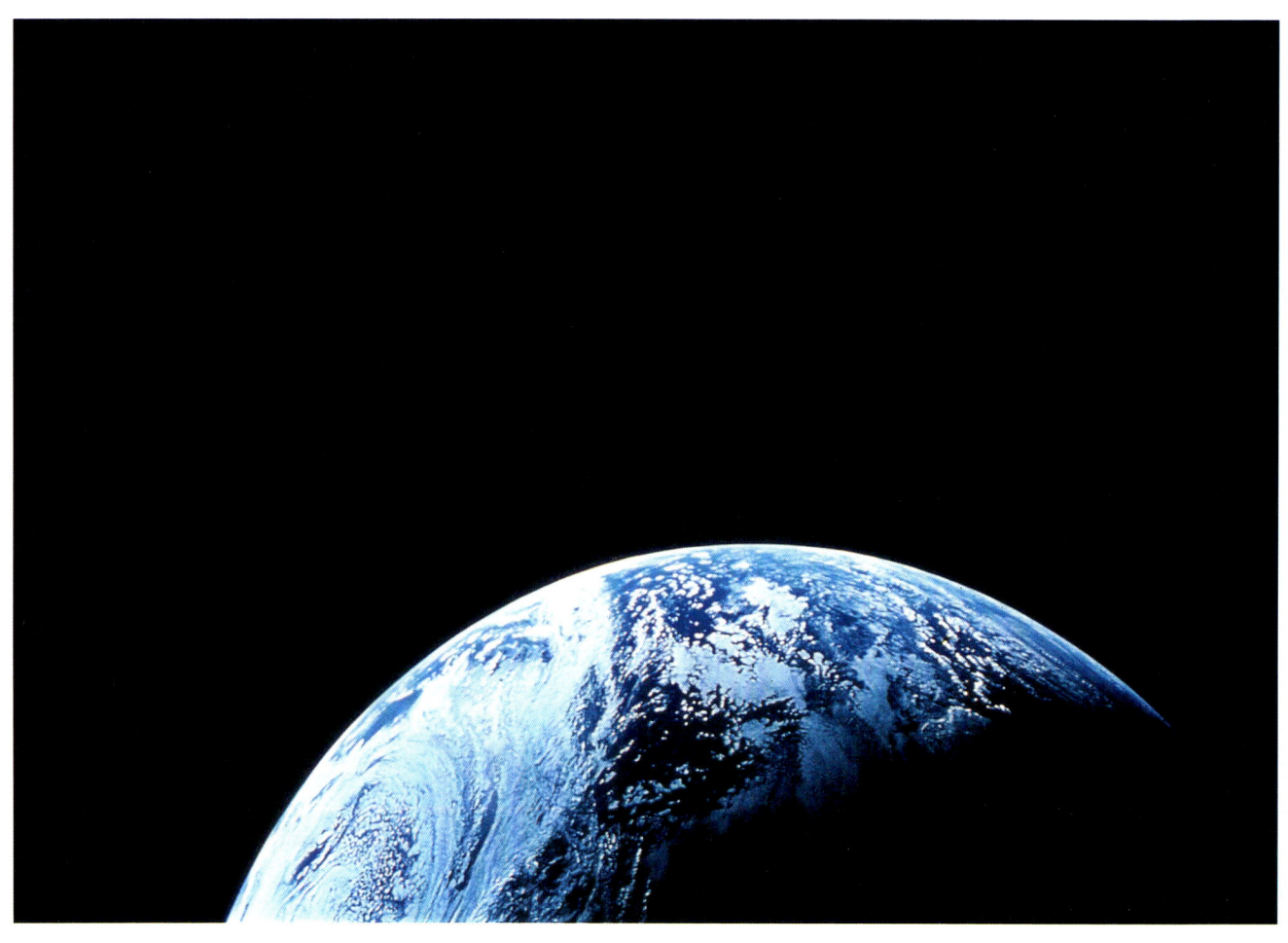

ABOVE: A view of the earth from space during the Apollo 4 unmanned mission with coastal Brazil, the Atlantic Ocean, West Africa, and the Sahara visible, November 9, 1967

OPPOSITE: *Capri* collection rings in turquoise with rubies and onyx with black diamonds.

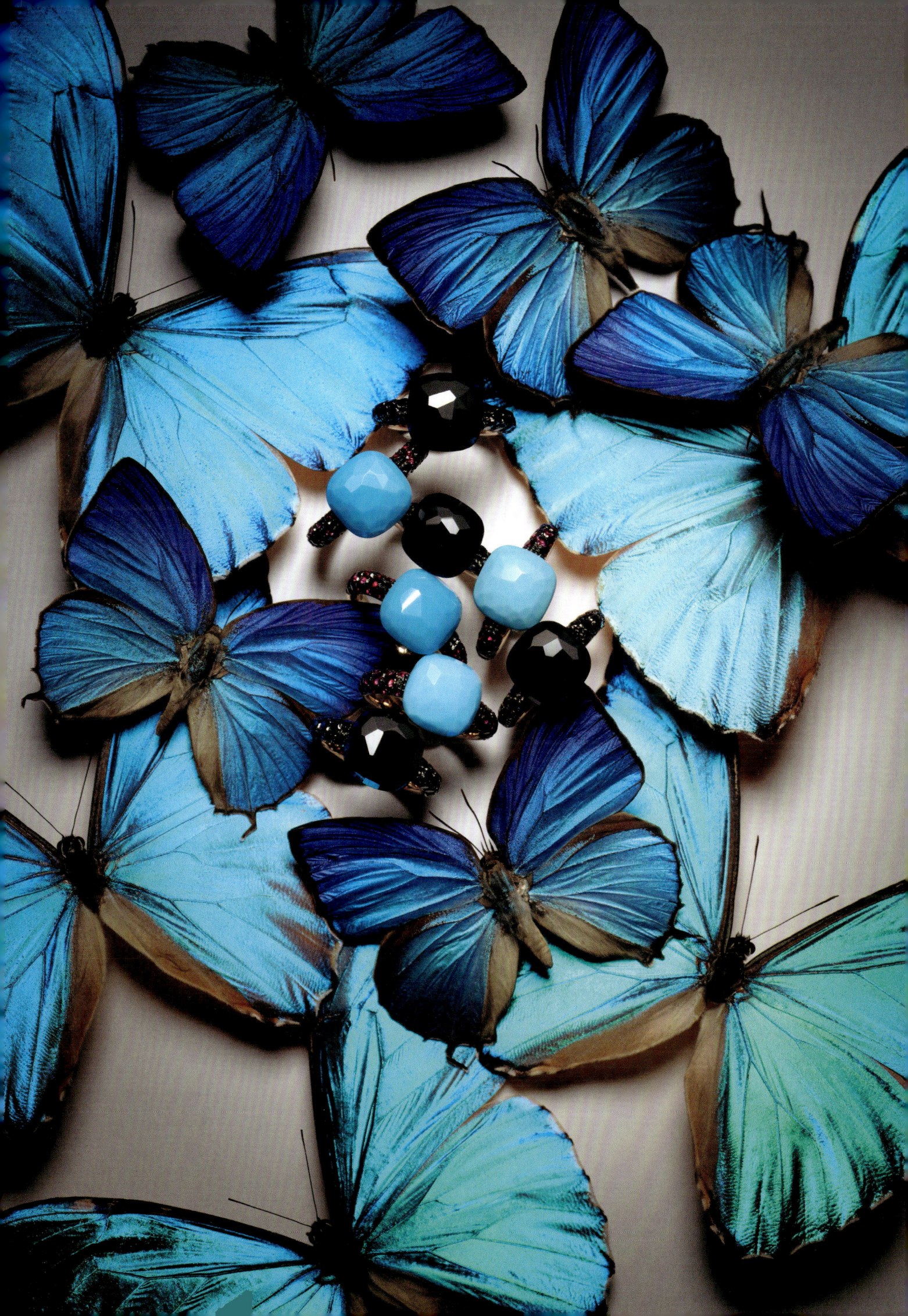

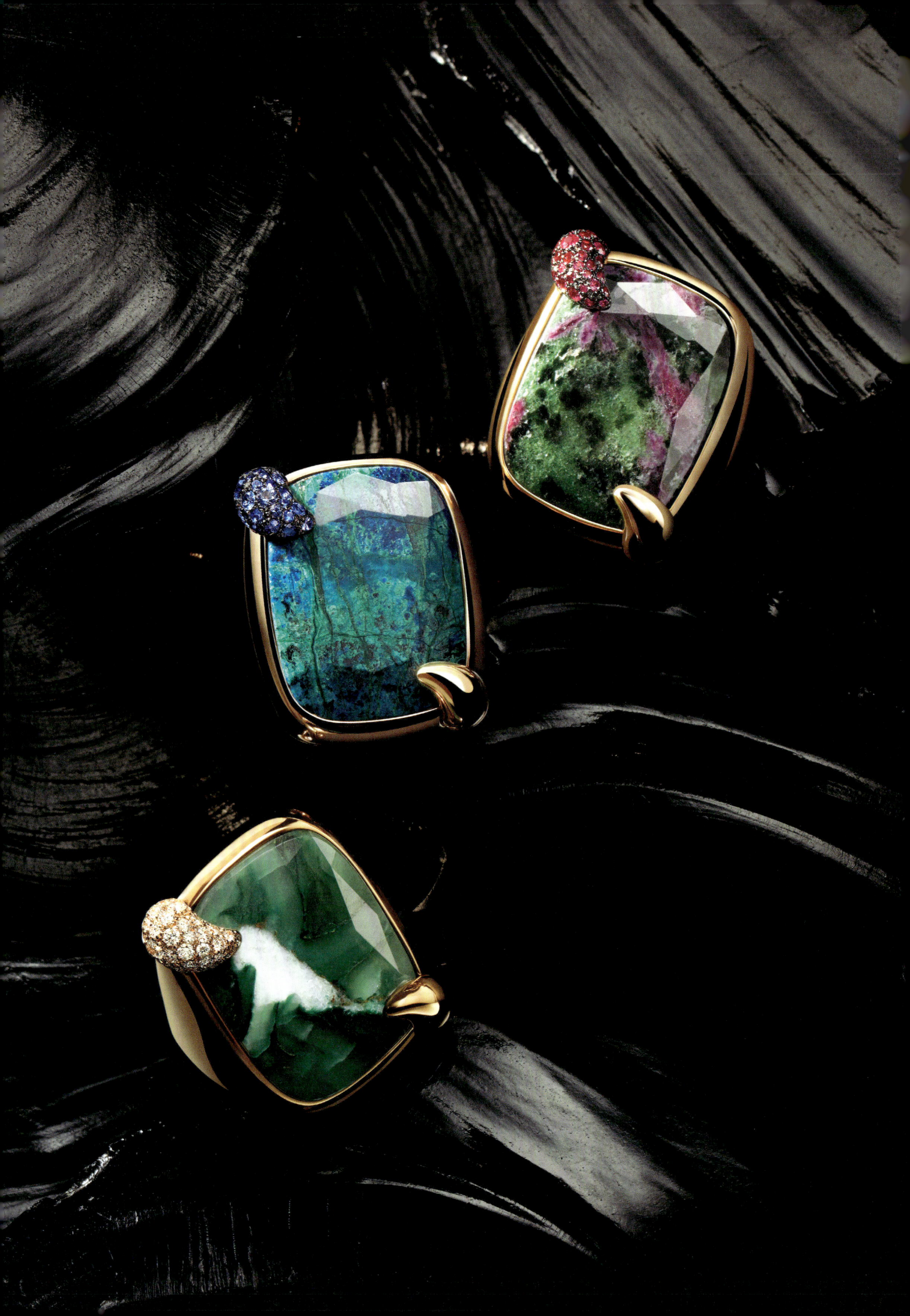

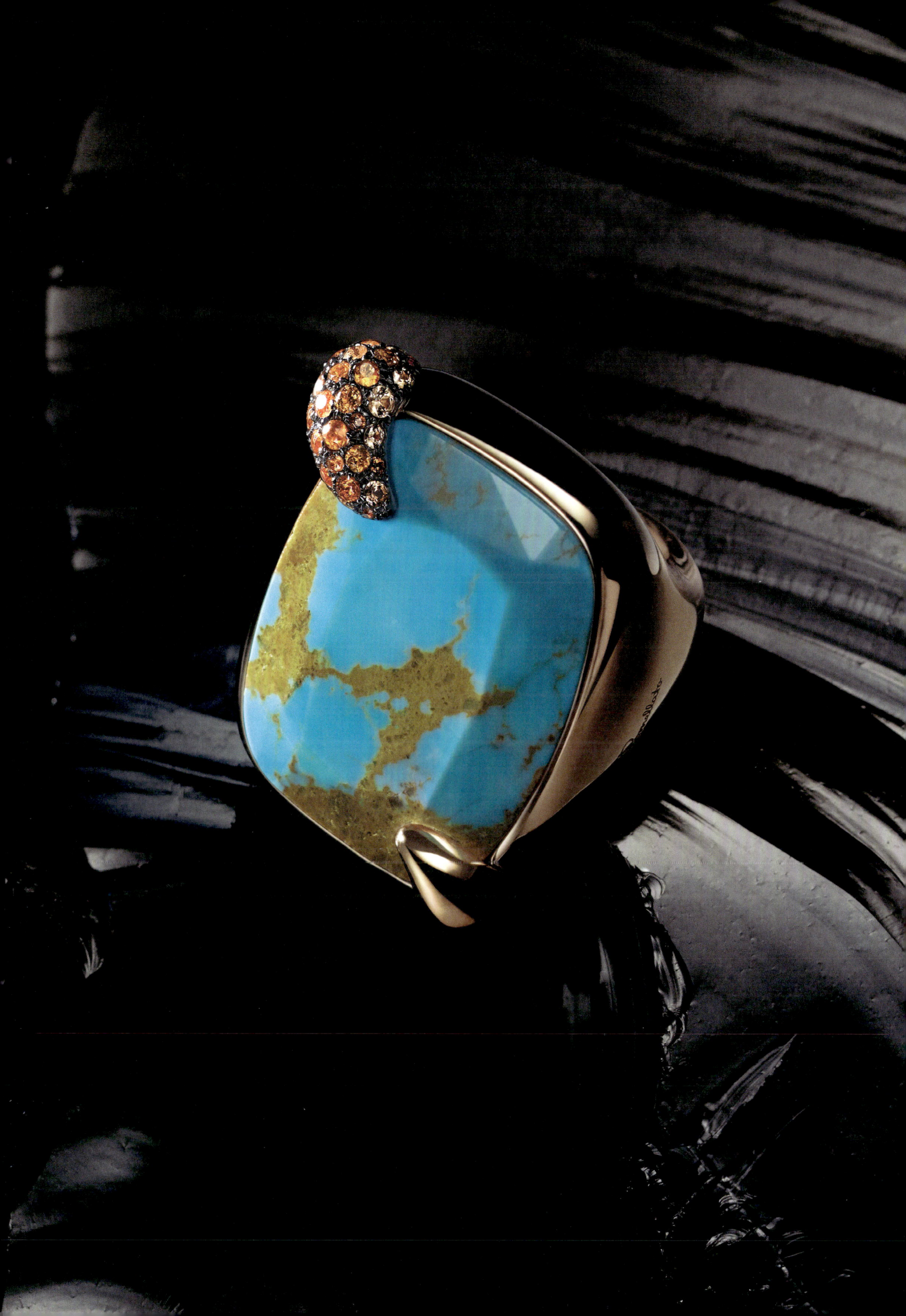

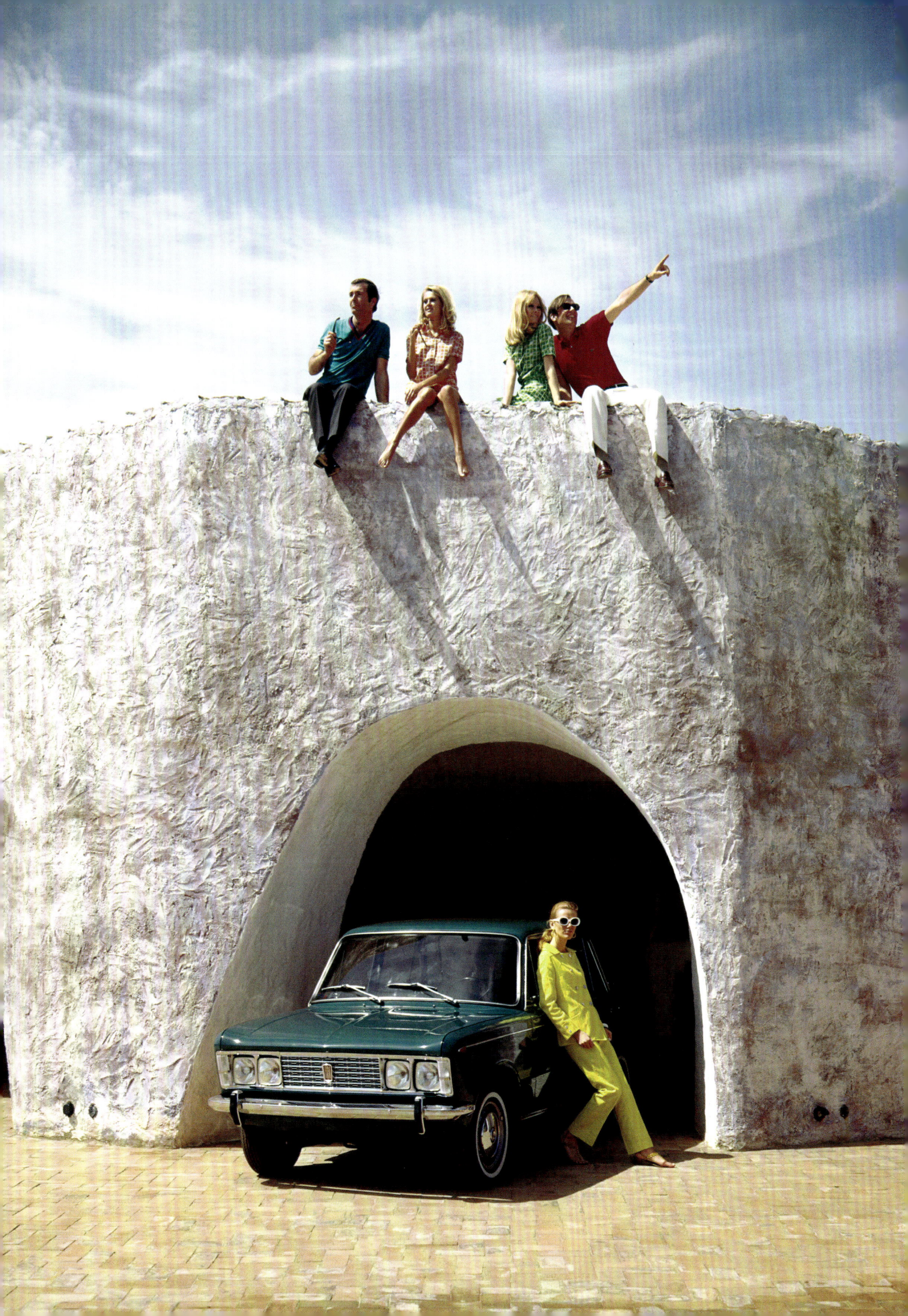

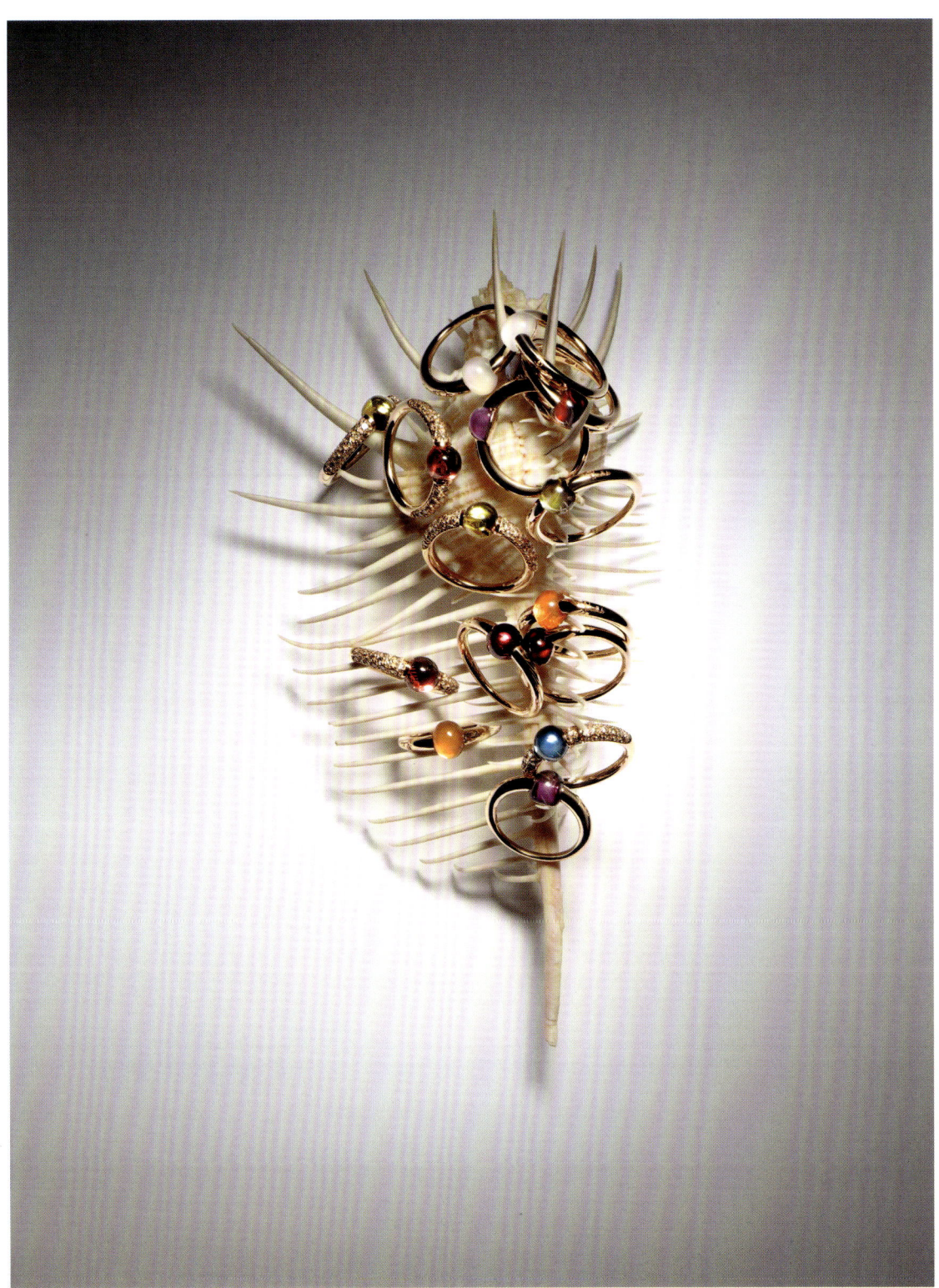

PREVIOUS SPREAD: The art of Mother Nature in the shape of a ring: *Ritratto* anniversary collection rings in zoisite with rubies, chrysocolla with blue sapphires, verdite with white diamonds, and turquoise with mandarin garnets

OPPOSITE: Square and organic: a Fiat 125 parked in one of the typical buildings of the hotel Cala di Volpe, Porto Cervo, Italy, Giorgio Lotti, 1967

ABOVE: Pomellato *M'ama non M'ama* rings in colorful stones

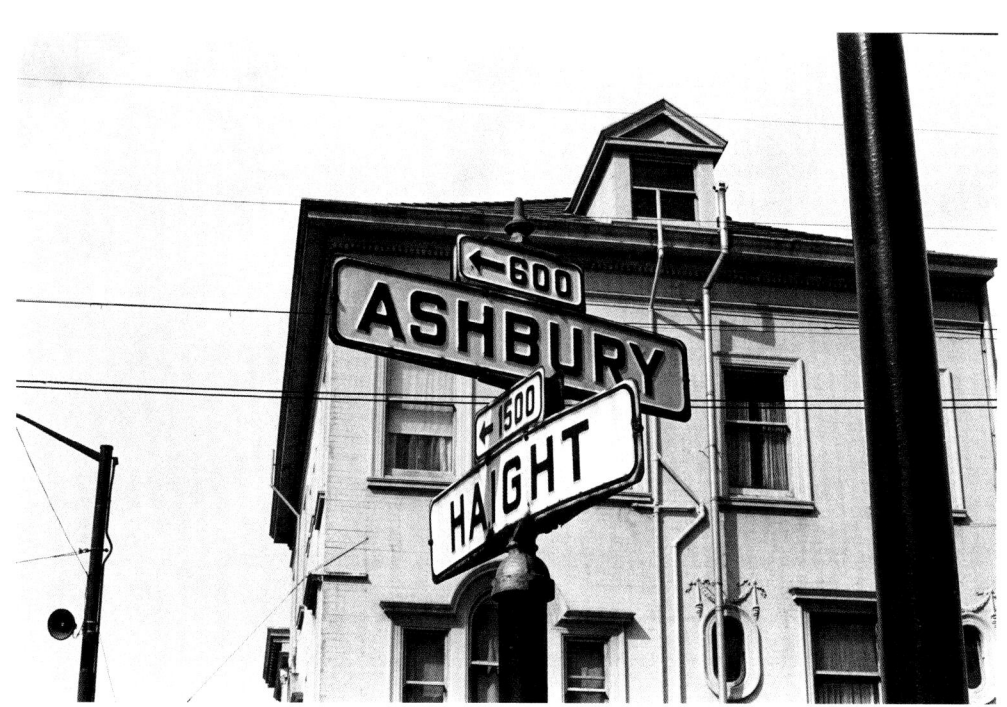

ABOVE: The intersection of Haight and Ashbury Streets was a beacon for thousands of thrill-seekers during the Summer of Love in San Francisco

OPPOSITE: Activist, journalist, and leader of the feminist movement Gloria Steinem attends a fundraiser and rally for the California State Senate candidate Catherine O'Neill in 1972

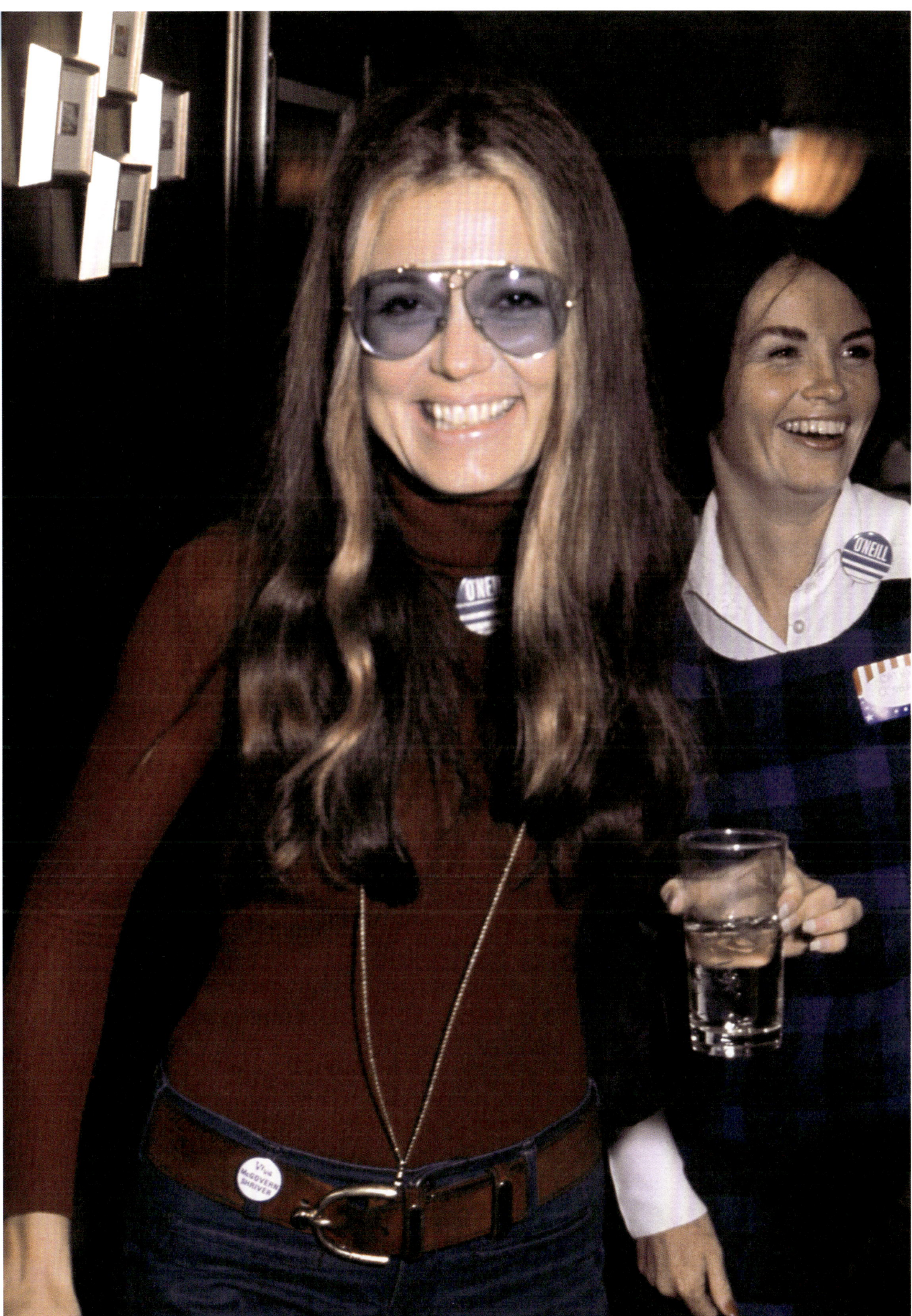

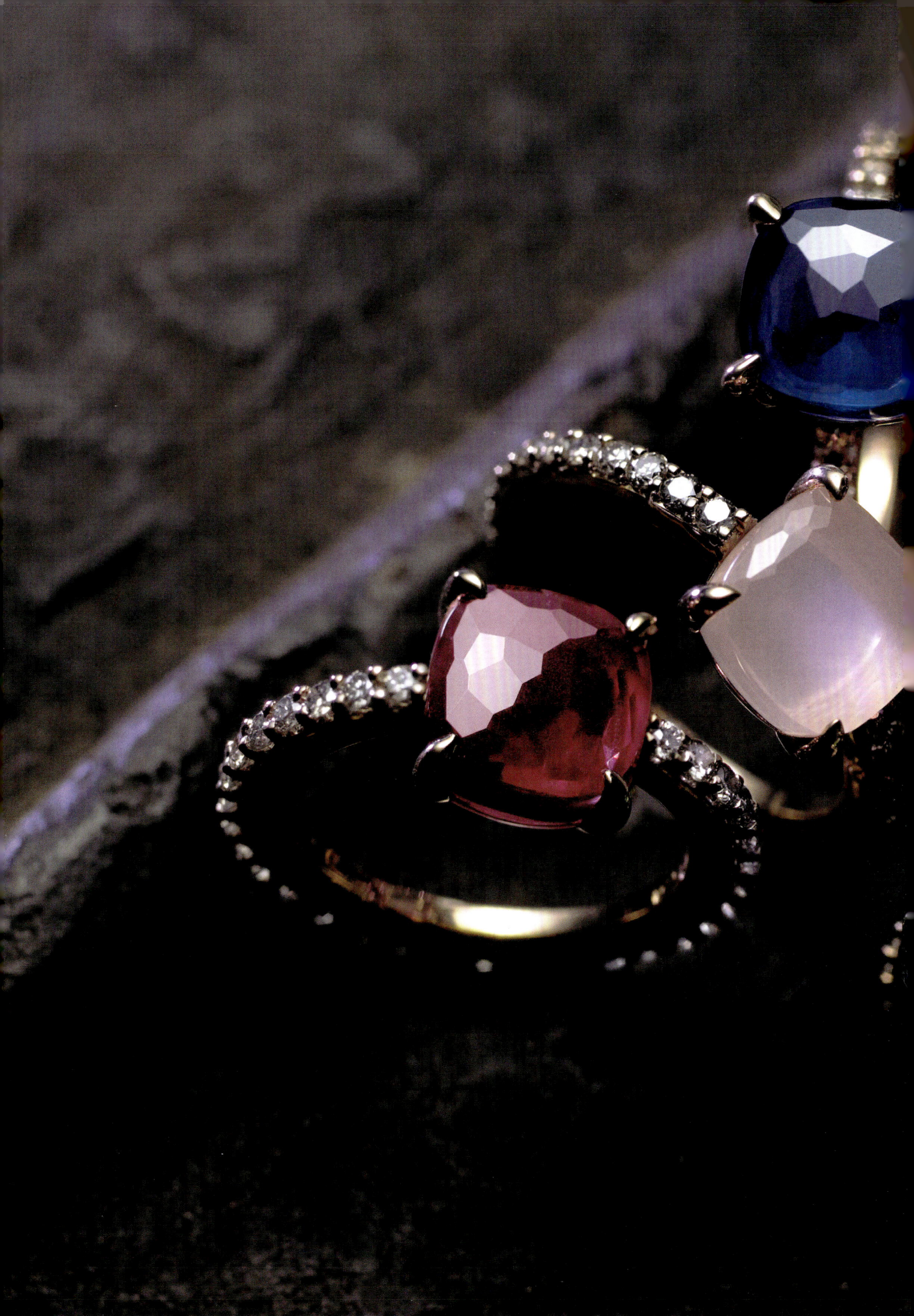

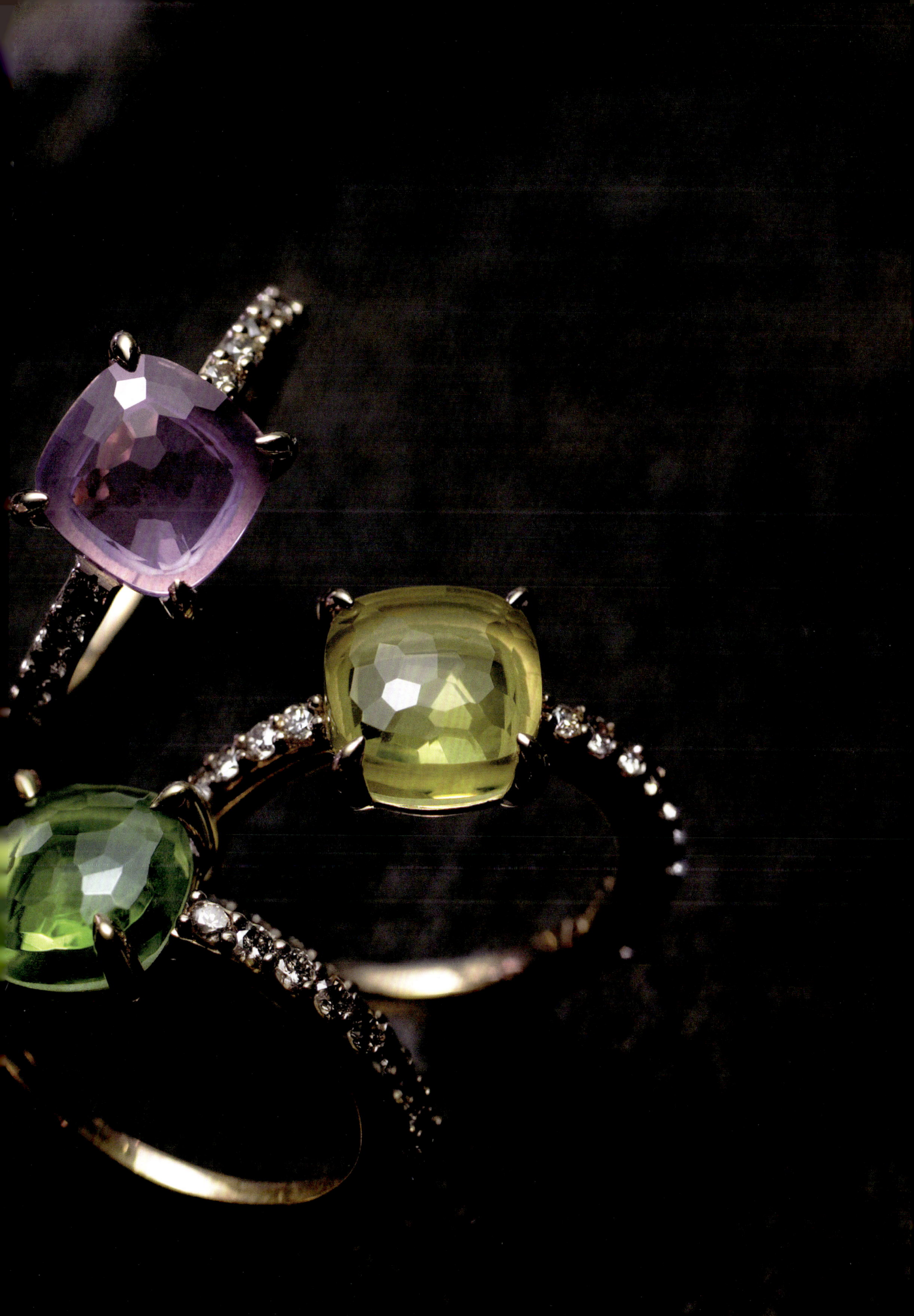

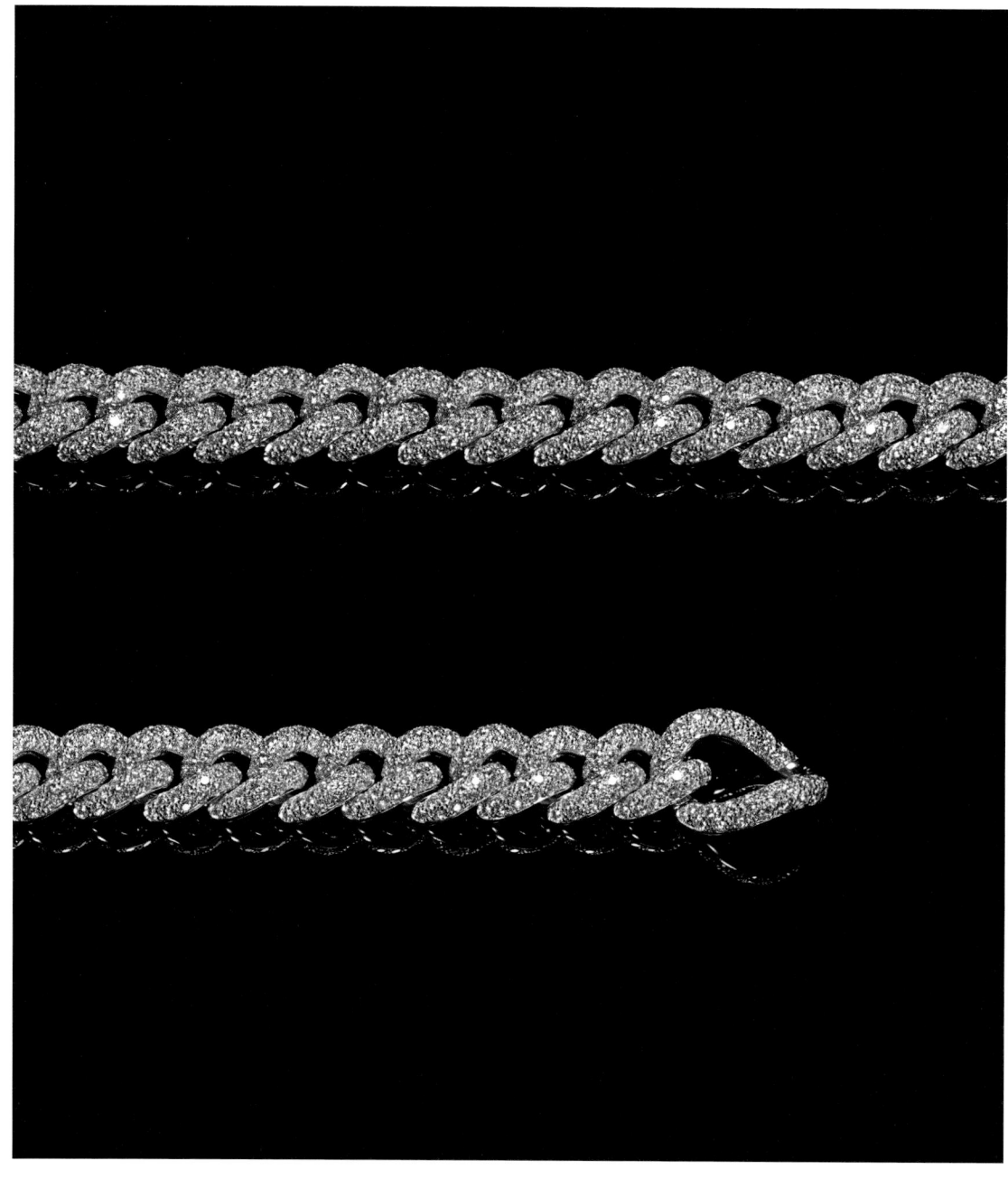

PREVIOUS SPREAD: The bright, watercolor essence of the *Baby* collection

ABOVE: *Gourmette* chain necklace with white diamonds

OPPOSITE: Pomellato advertising campaign by Albert Watson, 1984

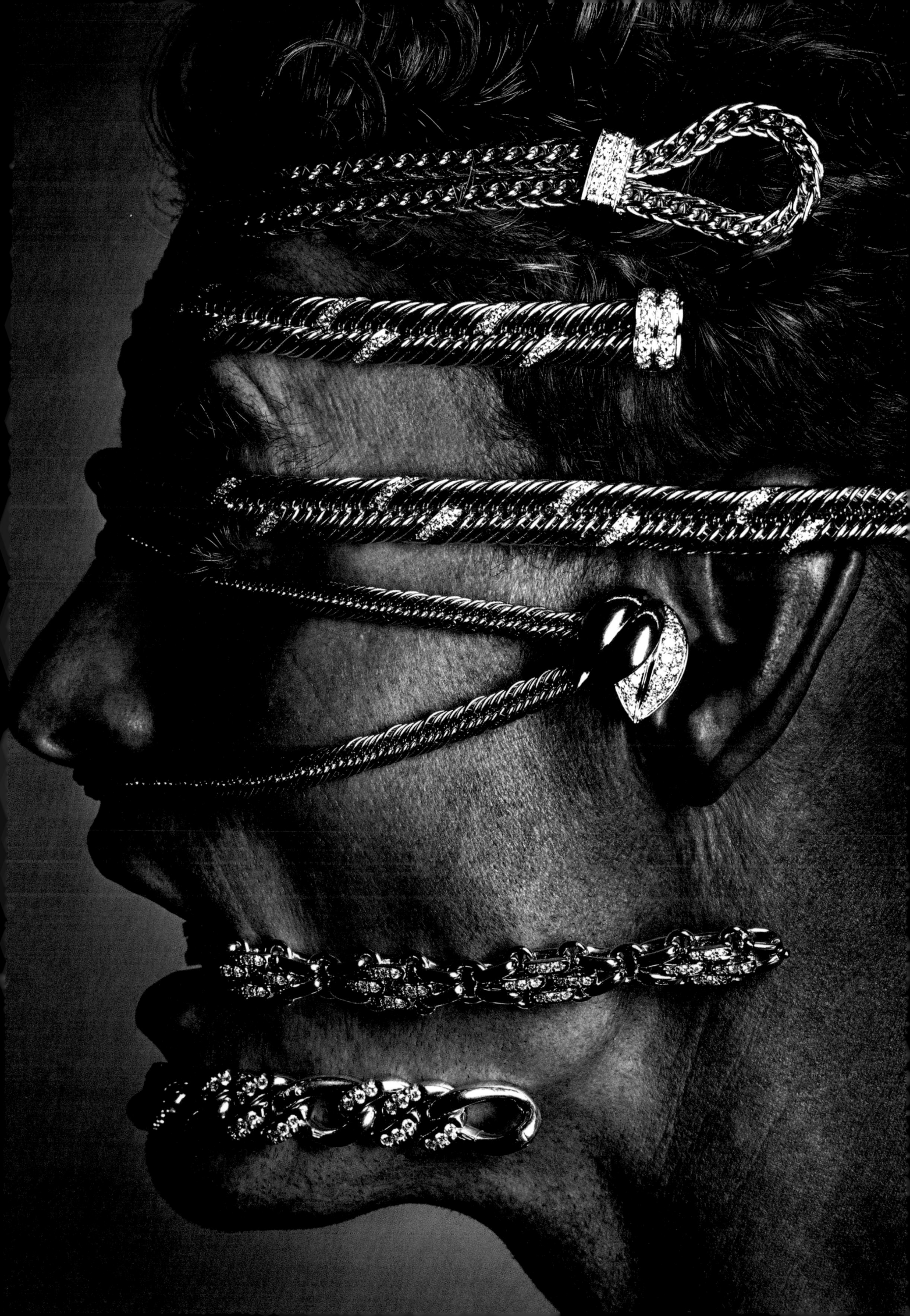

ABOVE: *Untitled* by Mark Rothko, 1967

OPPOSITE: *Capri* collection shot by Guido Mocafico

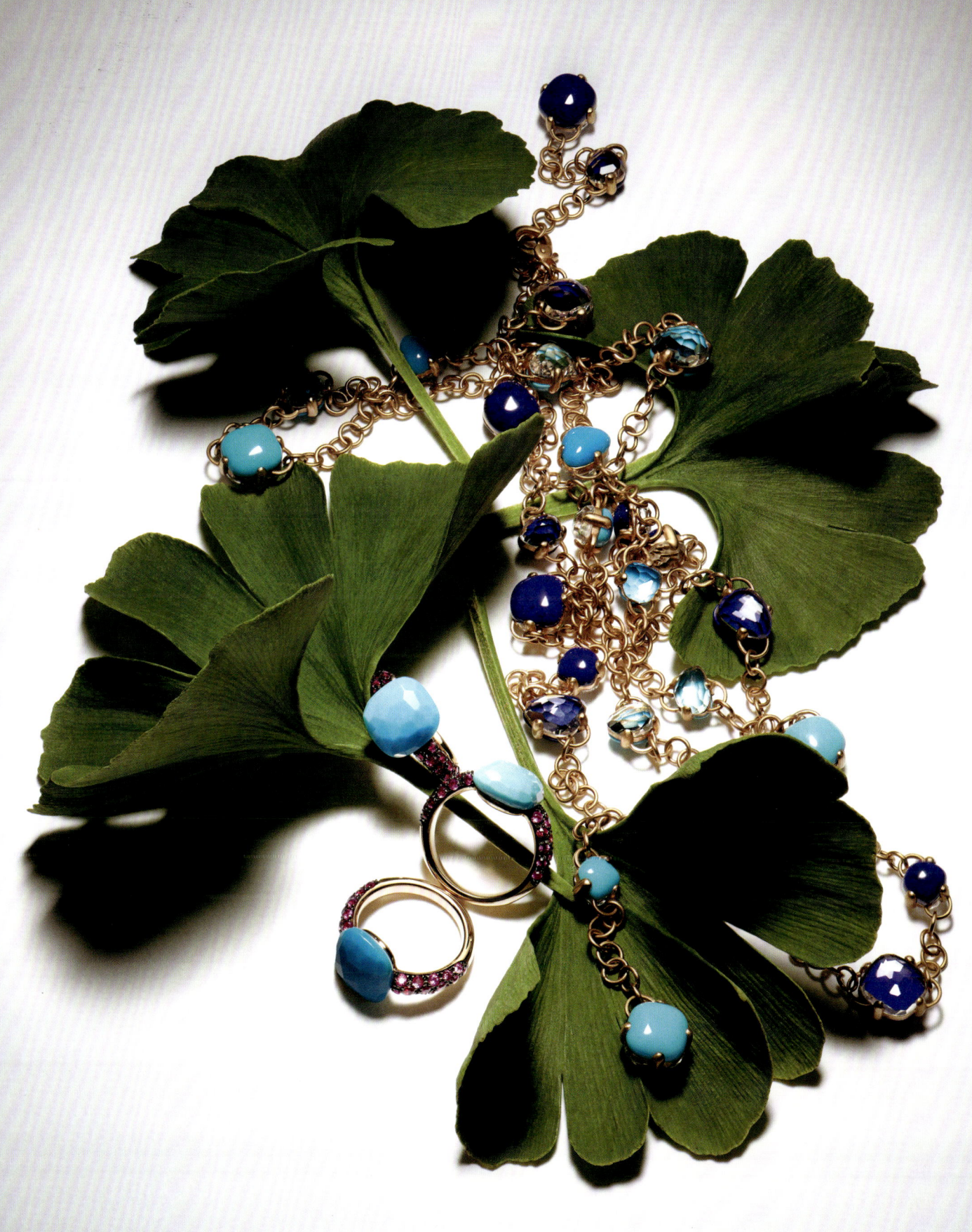

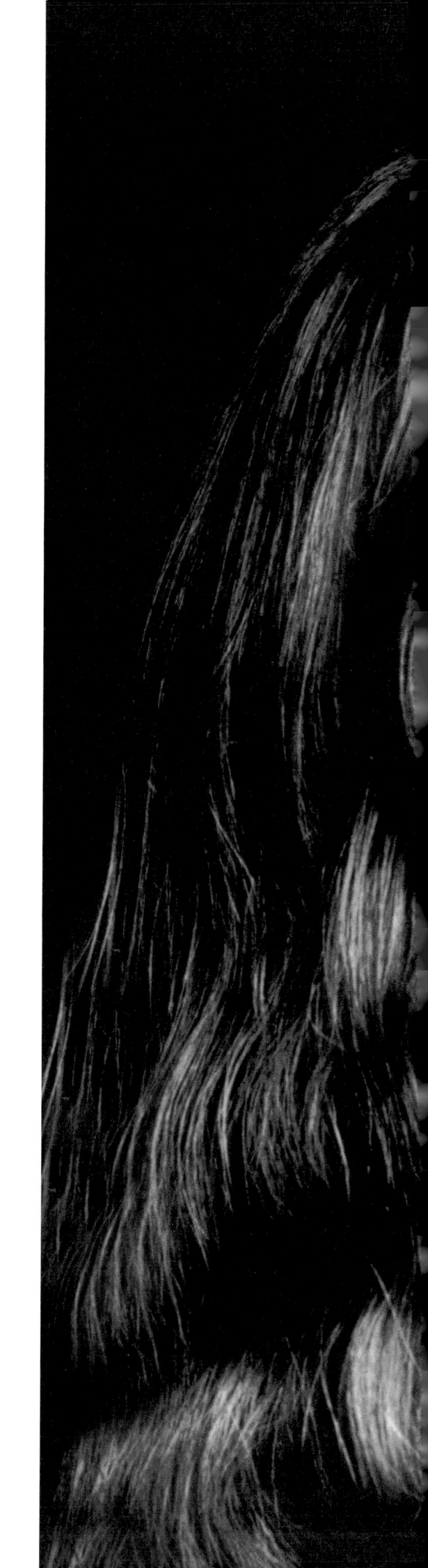

Pomellato advertising campaign by Lord Snowdon, 1992

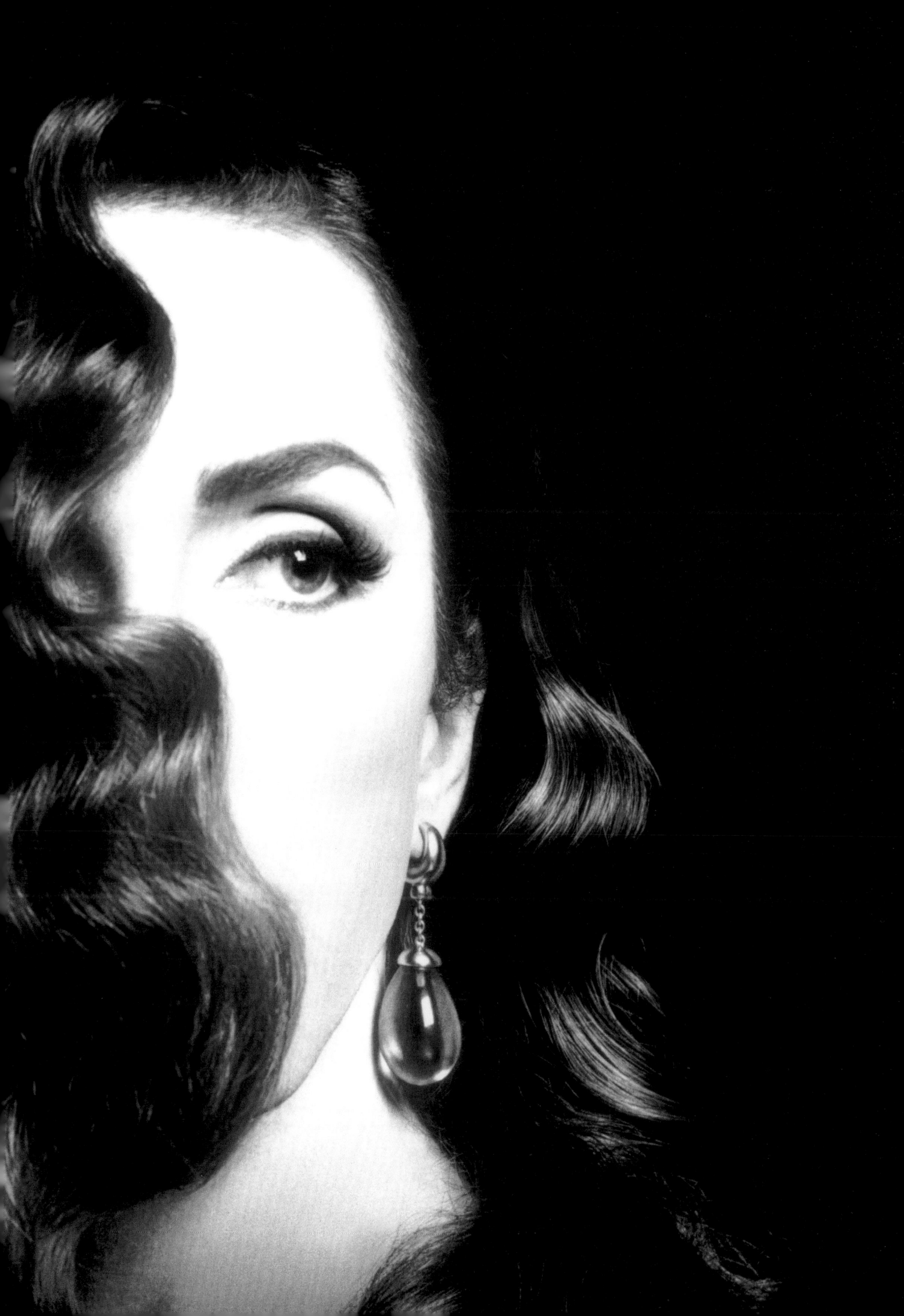

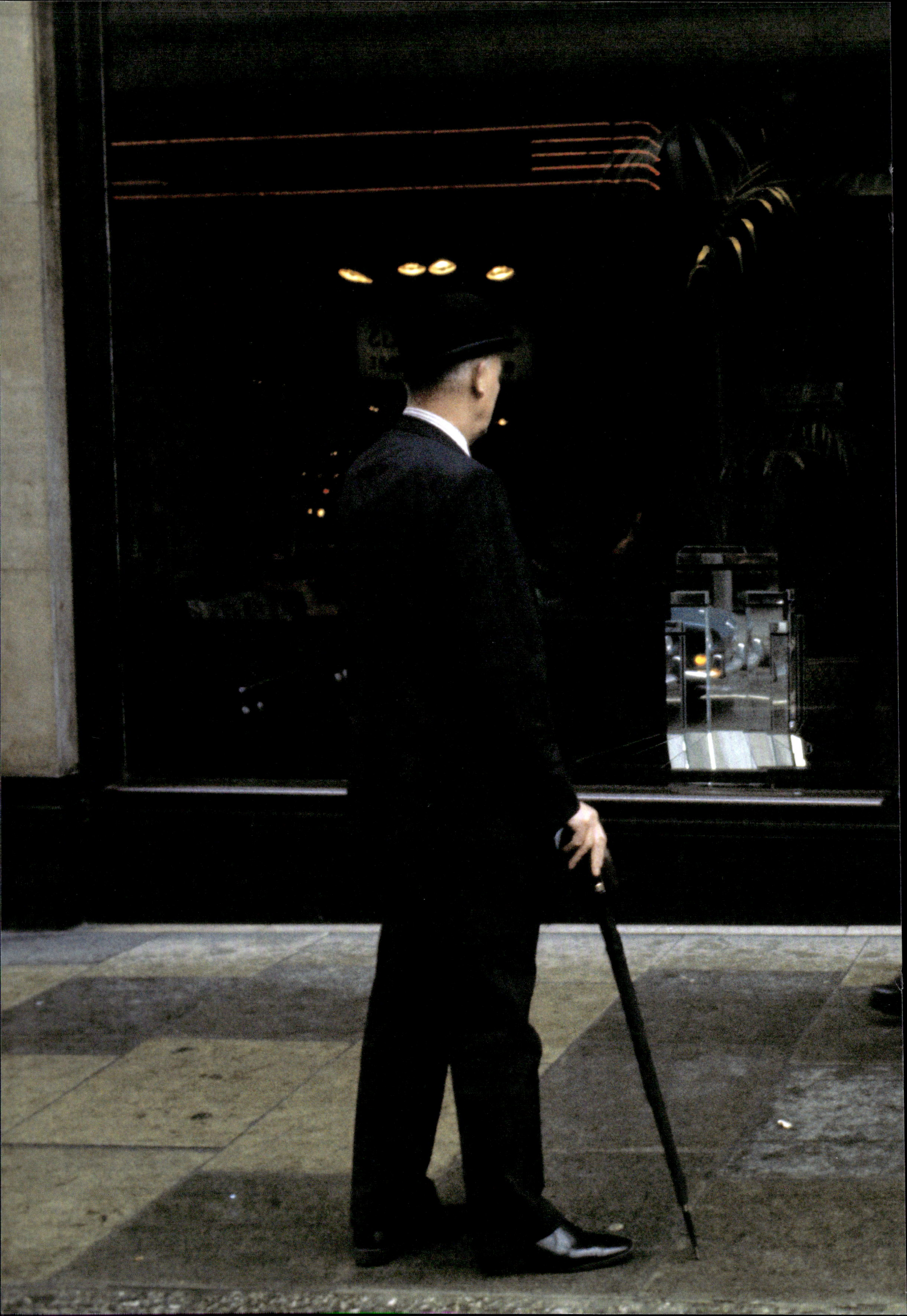

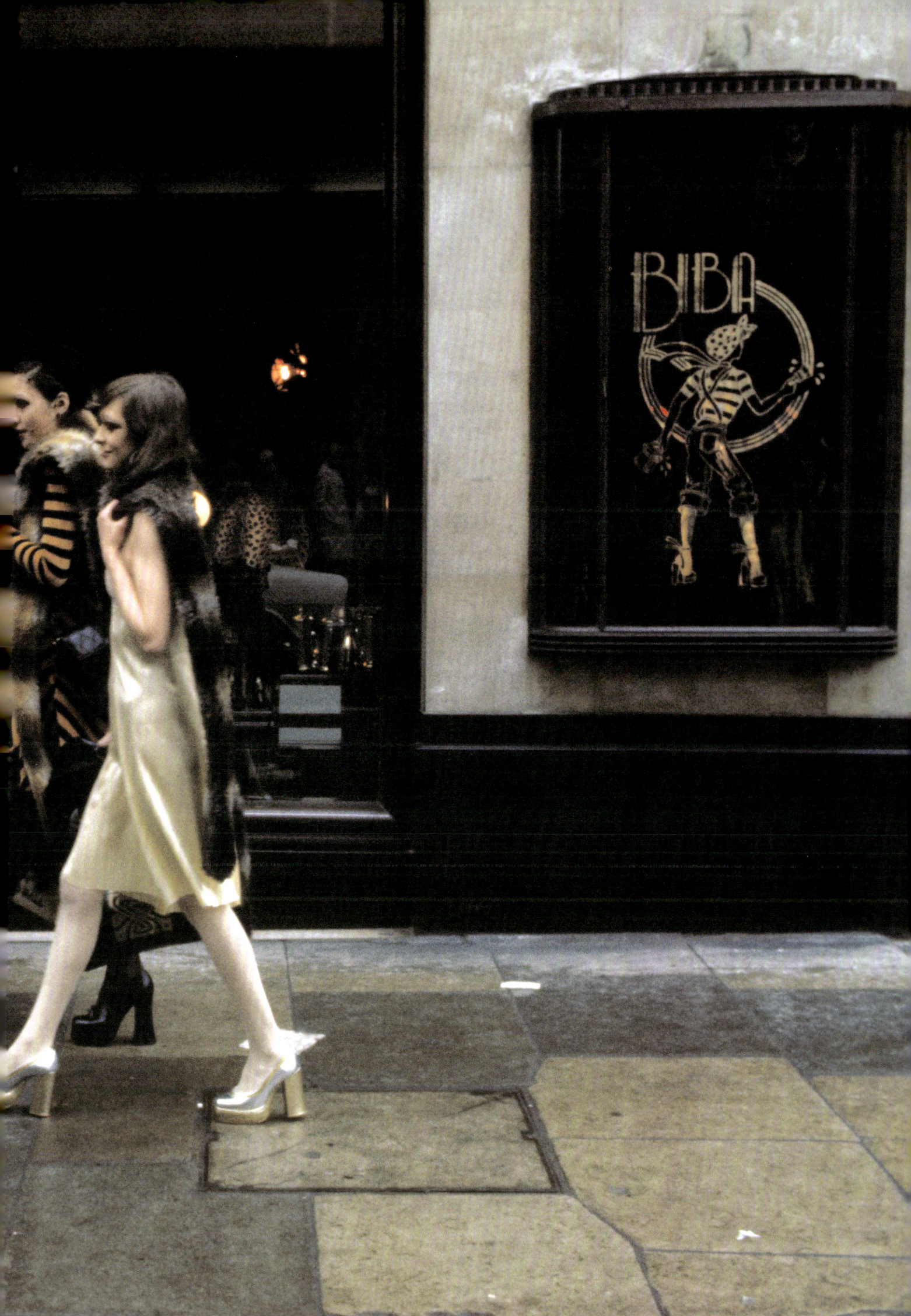

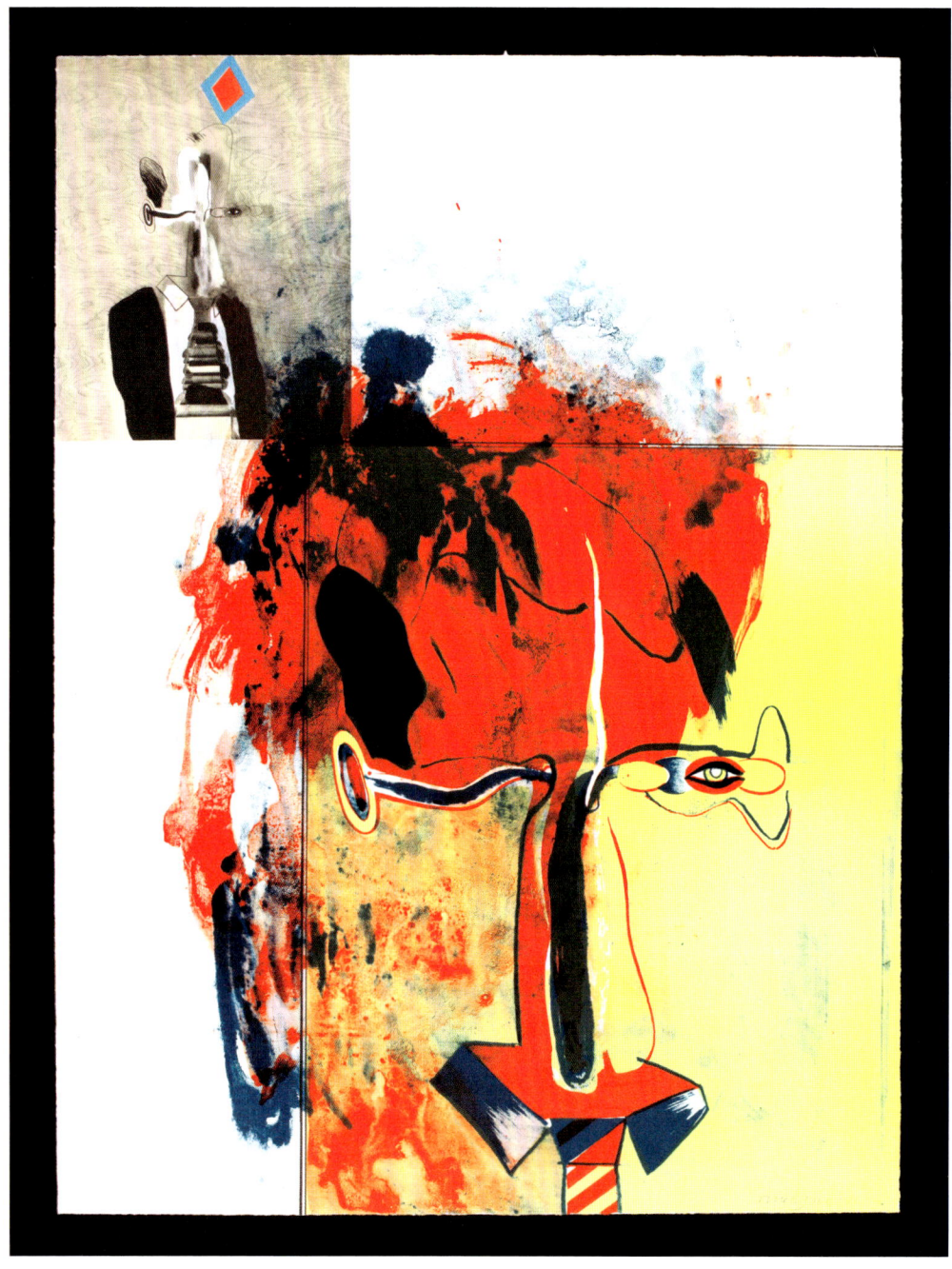

PREVIOUS SPREAD: Self-assured in front of conservative London, Barbara Hulanicki's iconic store Biba in 1973

ABOVE: One plate from the suite of seven plates entitled *Album* by pop artist Allen Jones, 1971

OPPOSITE: Inspired by the beauty of nature, the inner spirit of the *Sabbia* collection is revealed through its irregular pavé in white, brown, and black diamonds

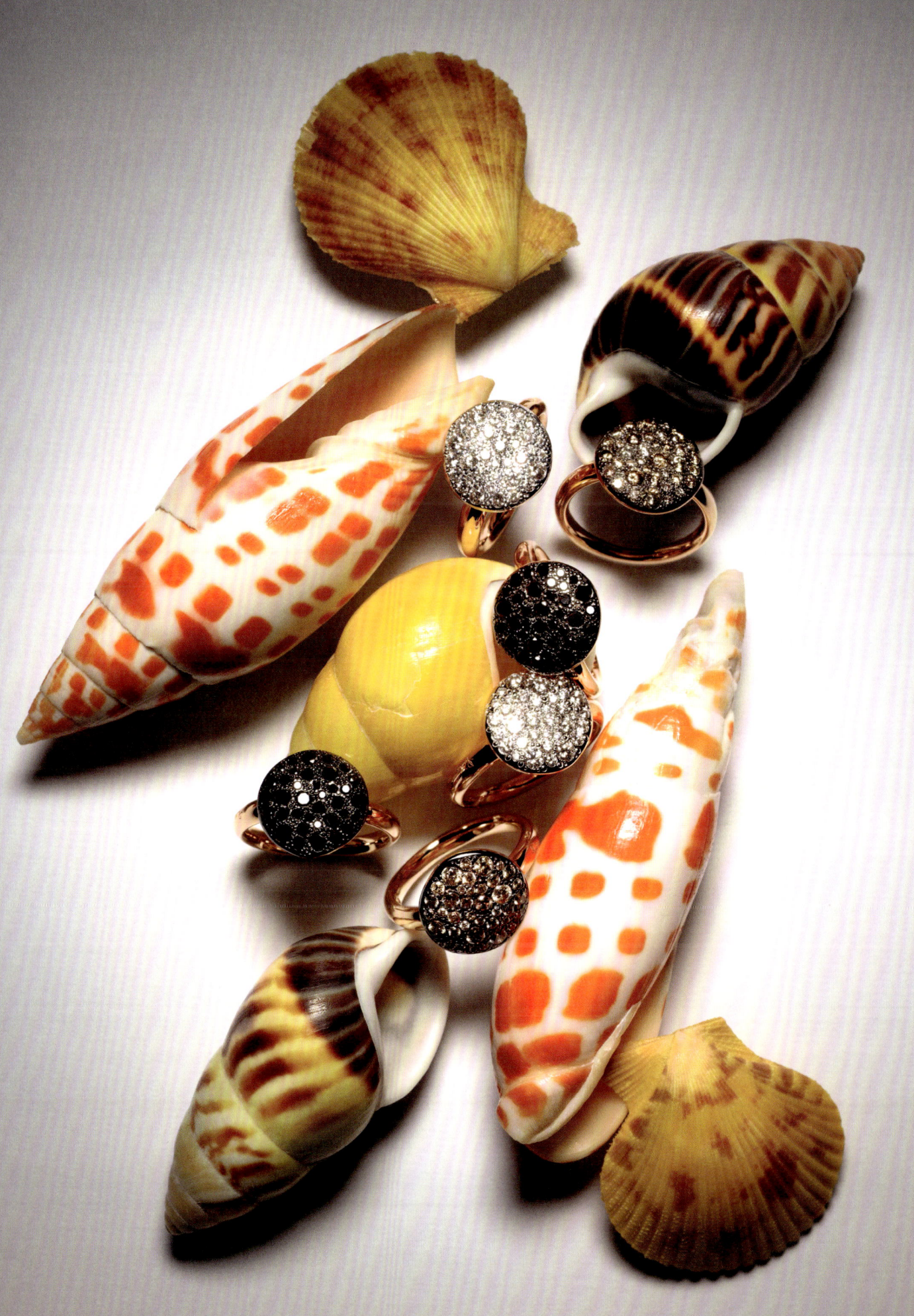

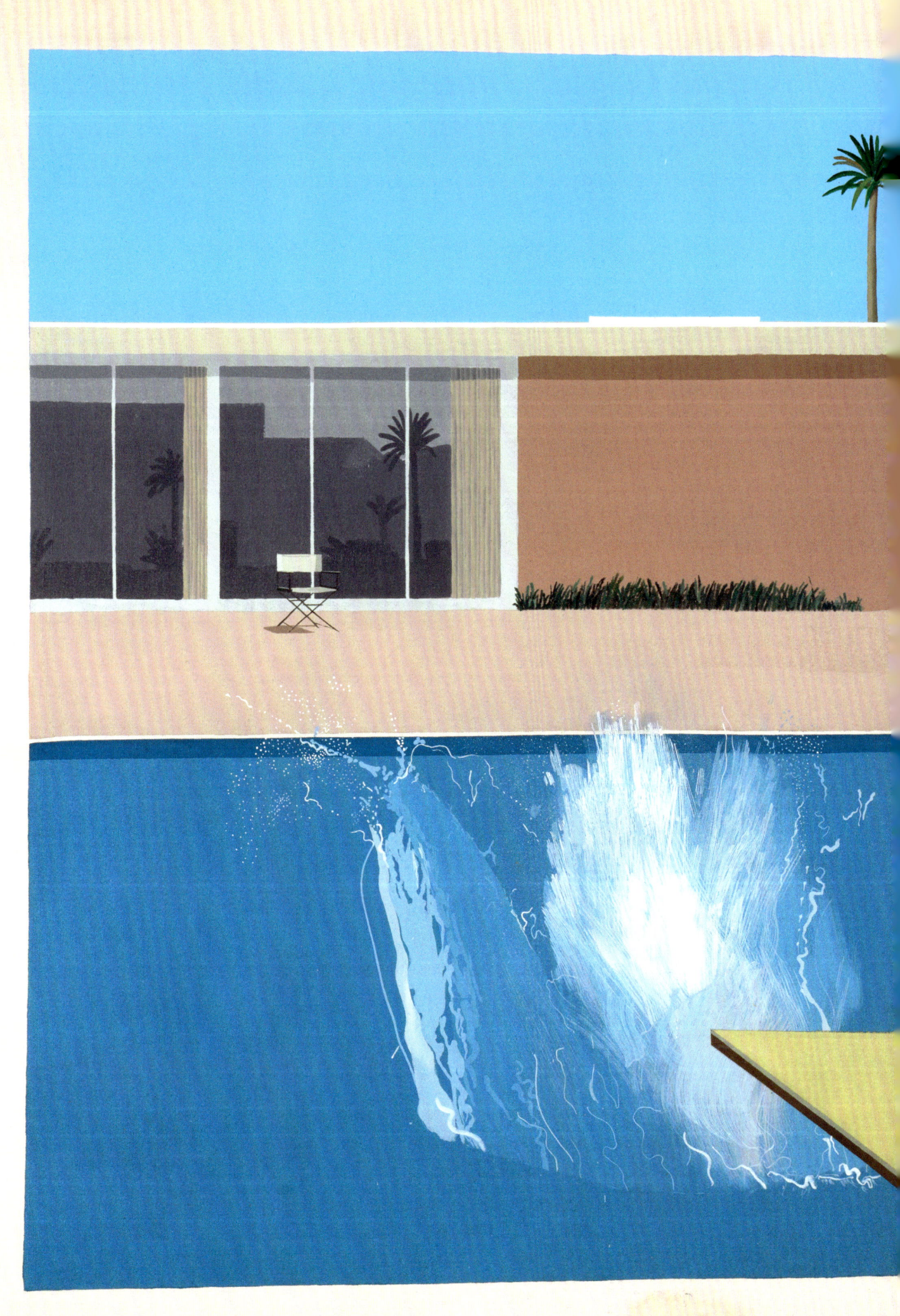

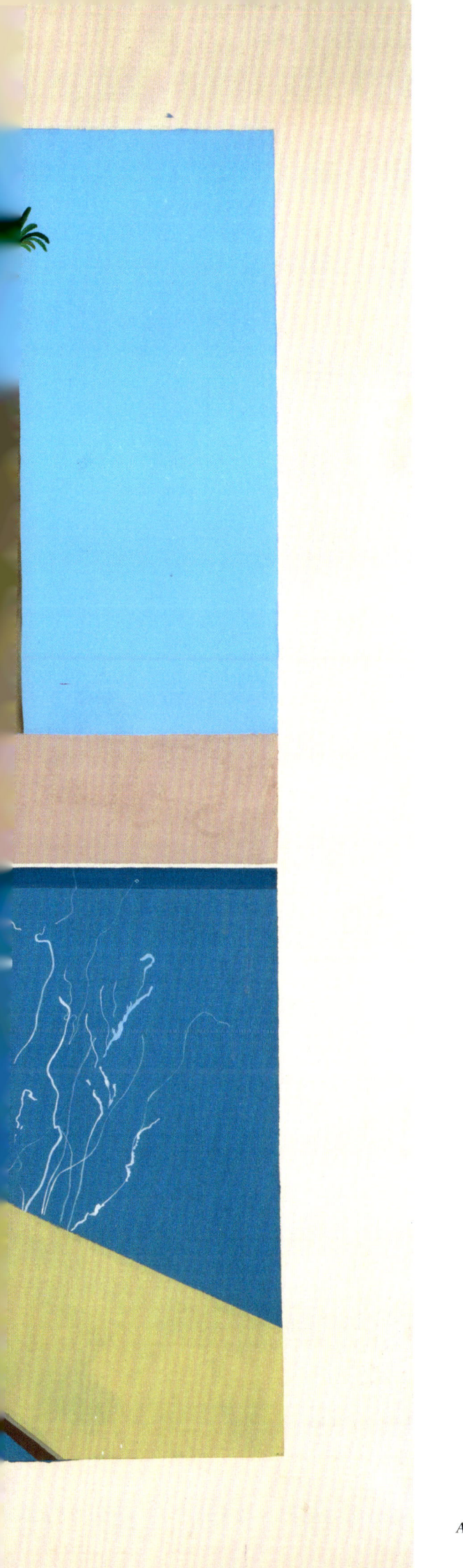

A Bigger Splash by David Hockney, 1967

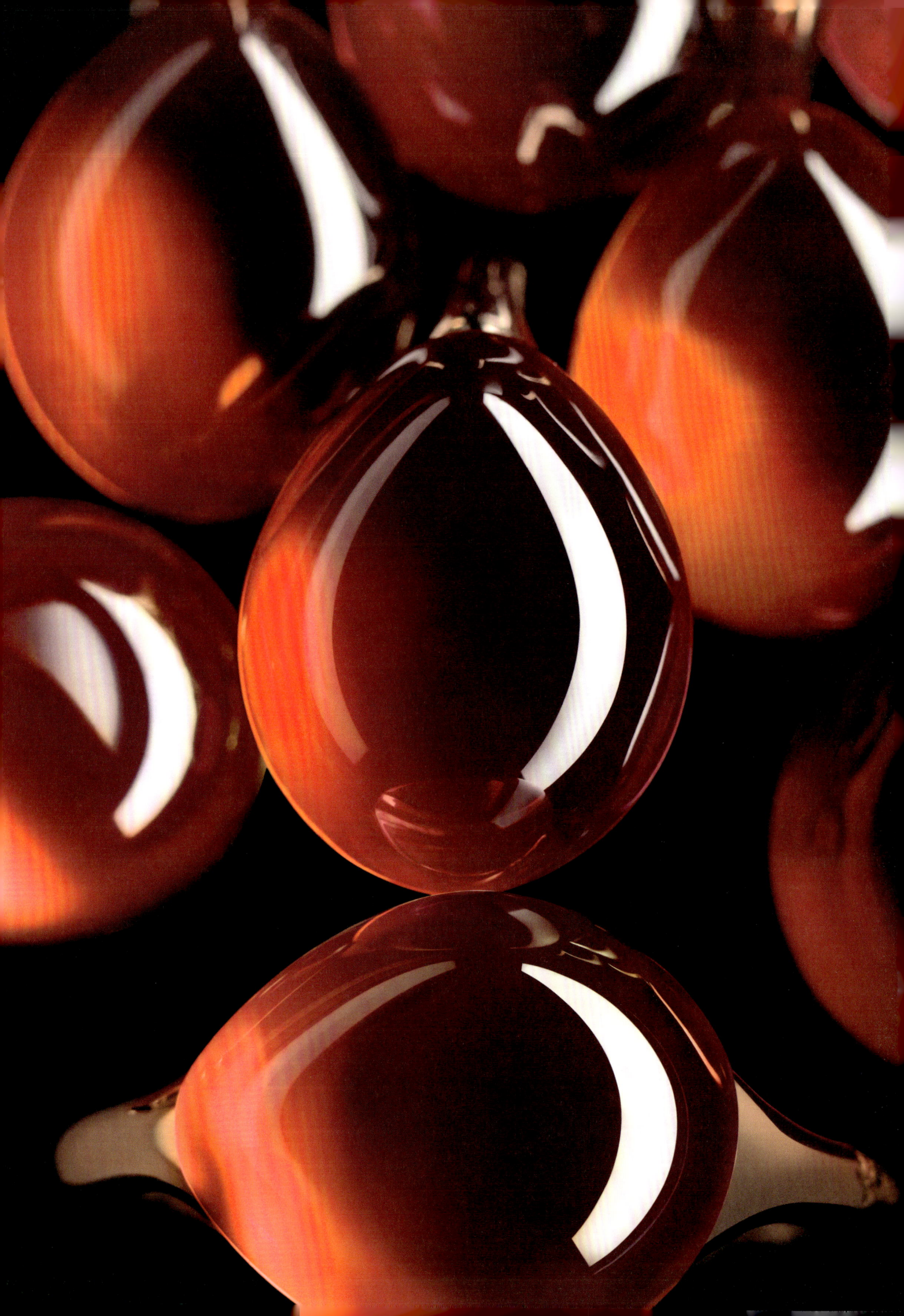

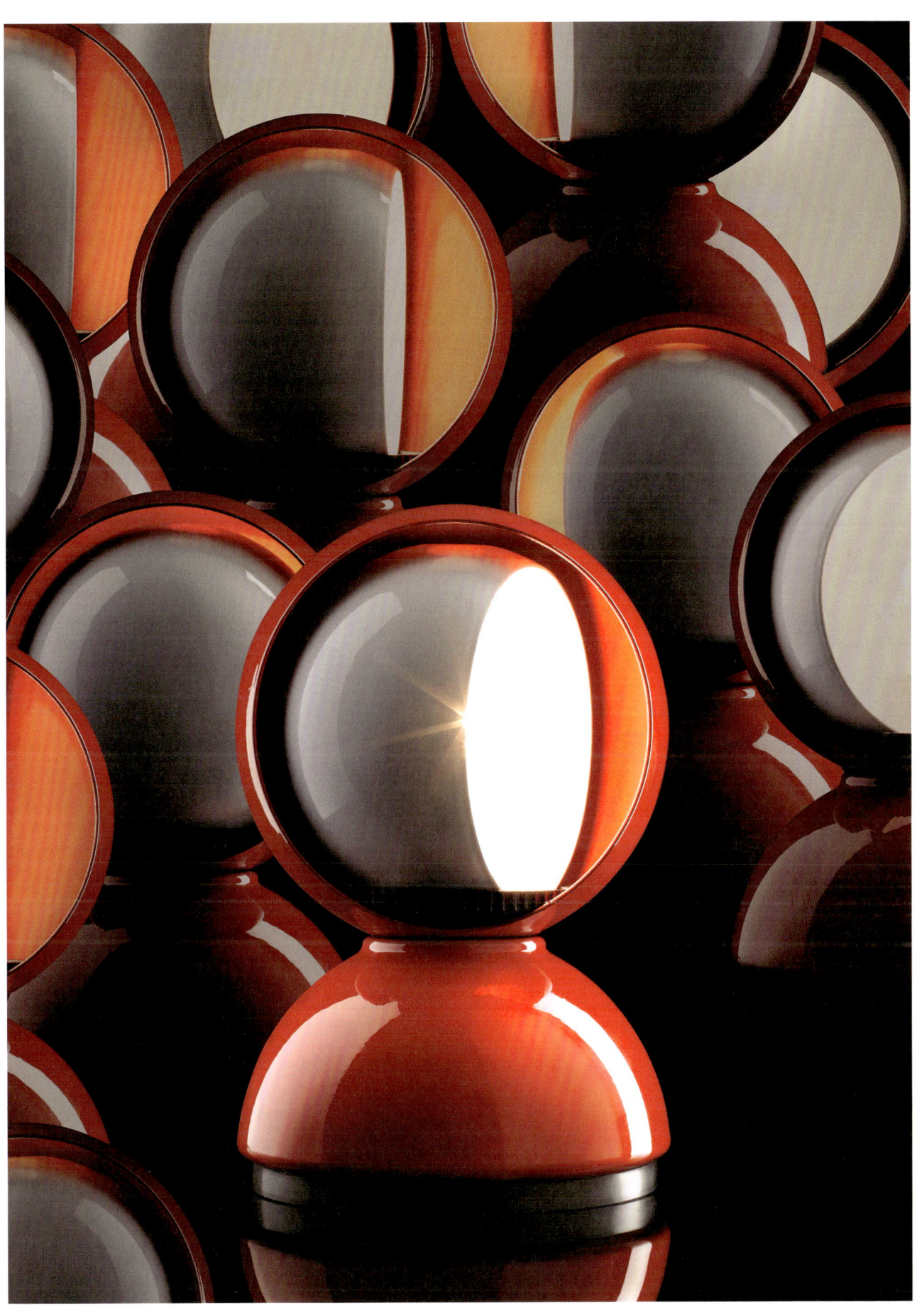

OPPOSITE: Colorful drops of synthetic cabochon
rubies of the *Rouge Passion* collection

ABOVE: *Eclisse* table lamp designed by Vico
Magistretti for Artemide in 1967

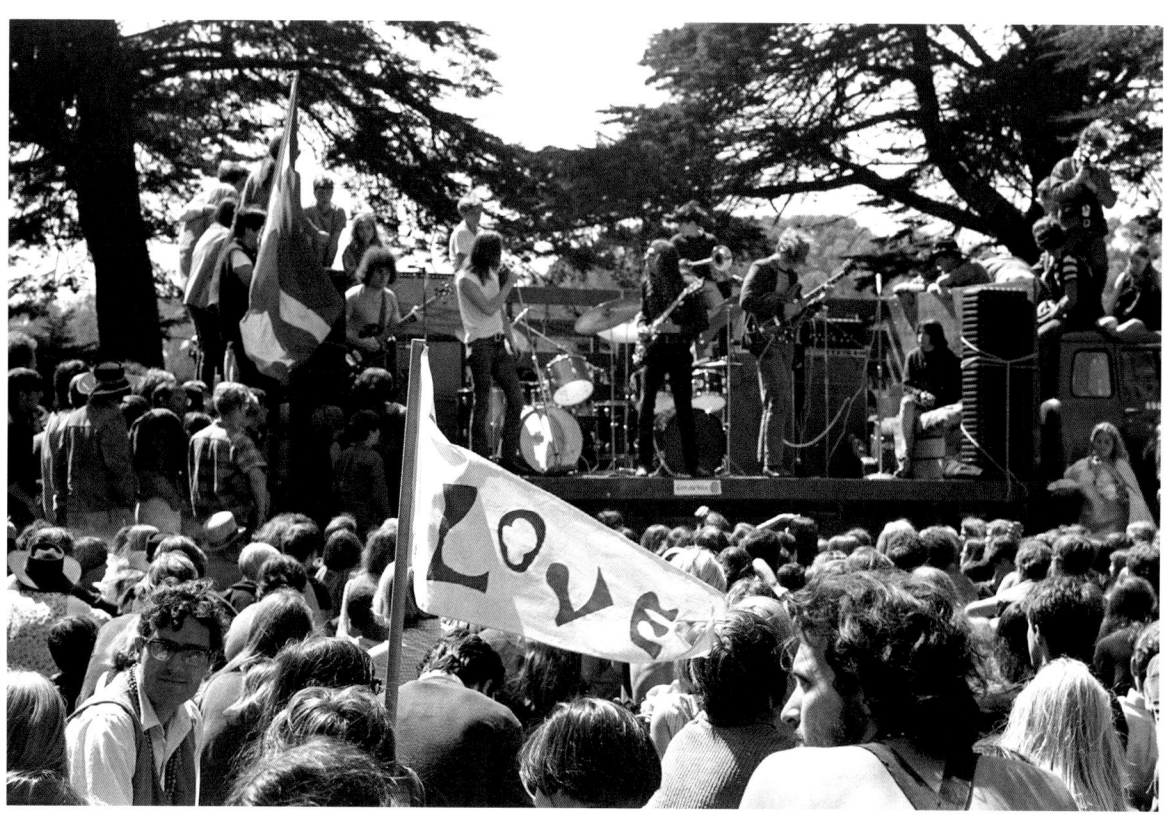

ABOVE: Hippie crowd at a summer solstice celebration,
Golden Gate Park, San Francisco, 1967

OPPOSITE: *Narciso* drop earrings and rings in prasiolite
and smoky quartz

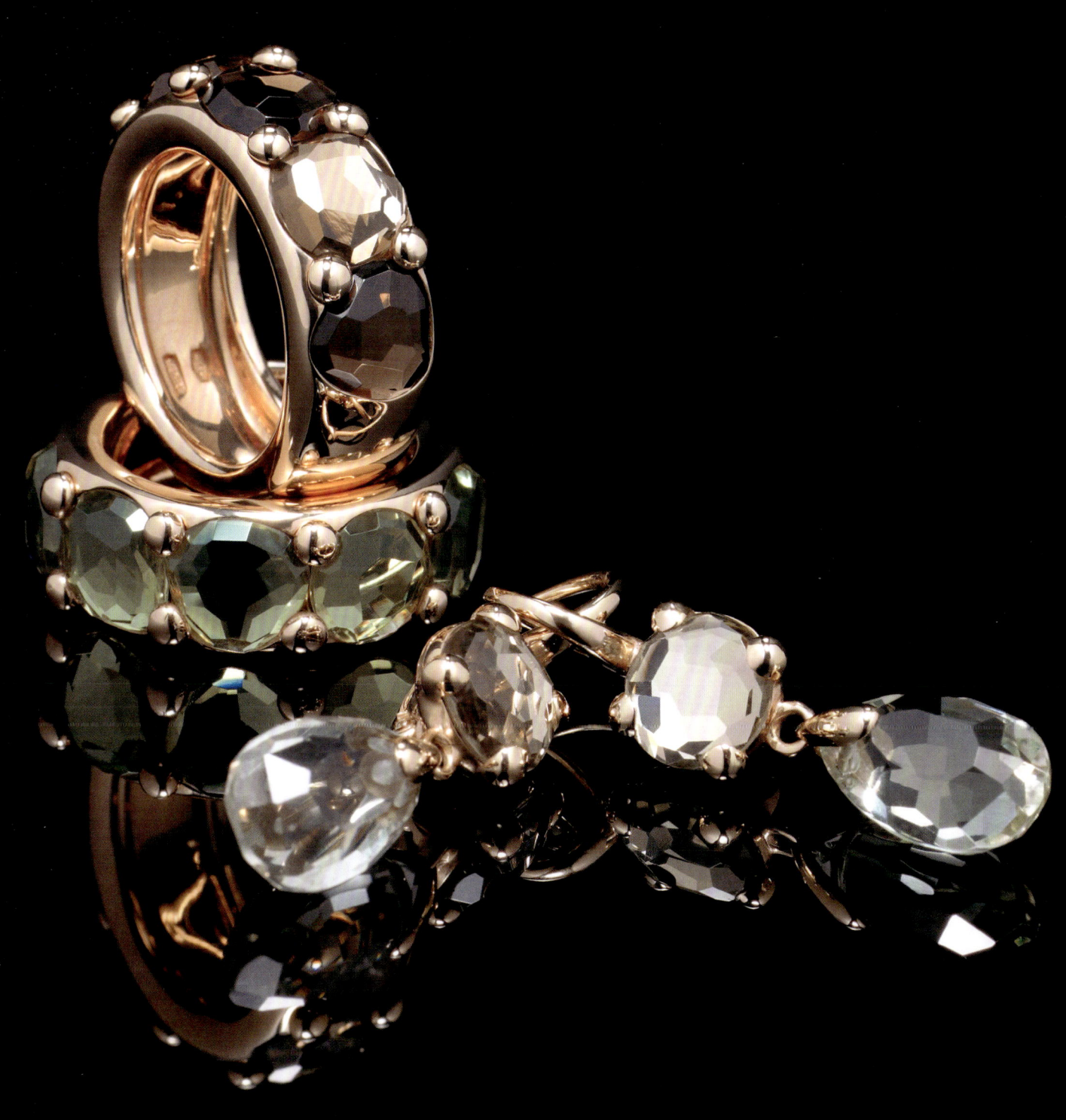

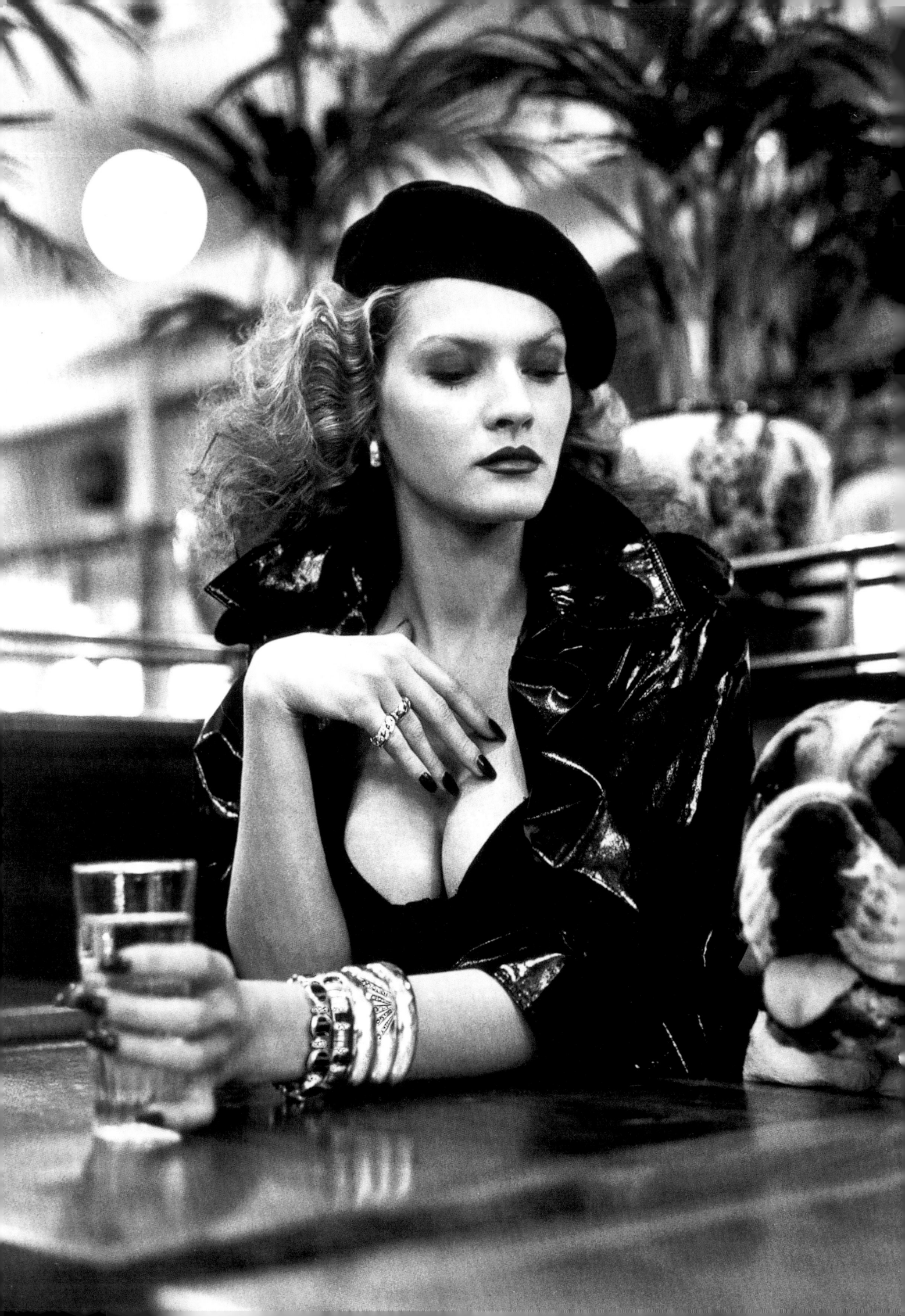

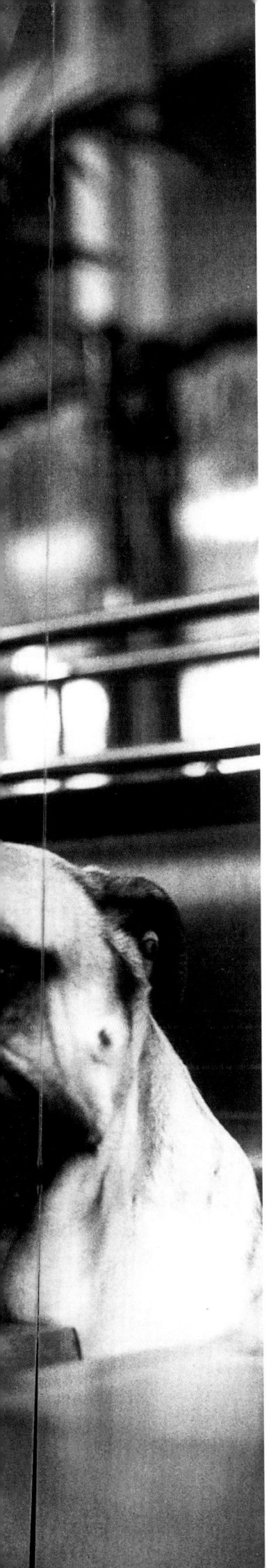

Pomellato advertising campaign by Helmut Newton, 1982

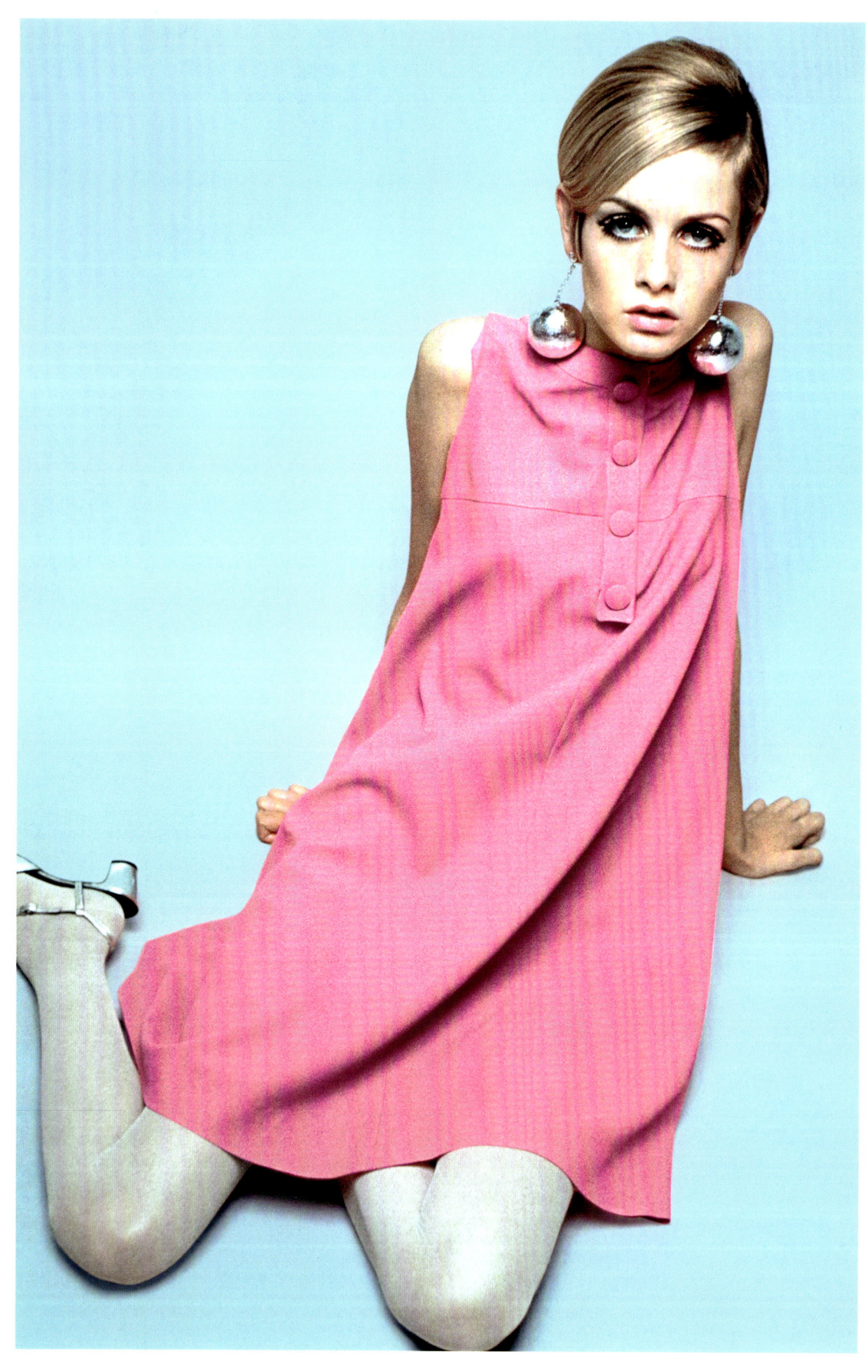

ABOVE: Fashion icon Twiggy wearing a pink A-line dress in 1966

OPPOSITE: *Ritratto* collection ring in amethyst with a white diamond claw

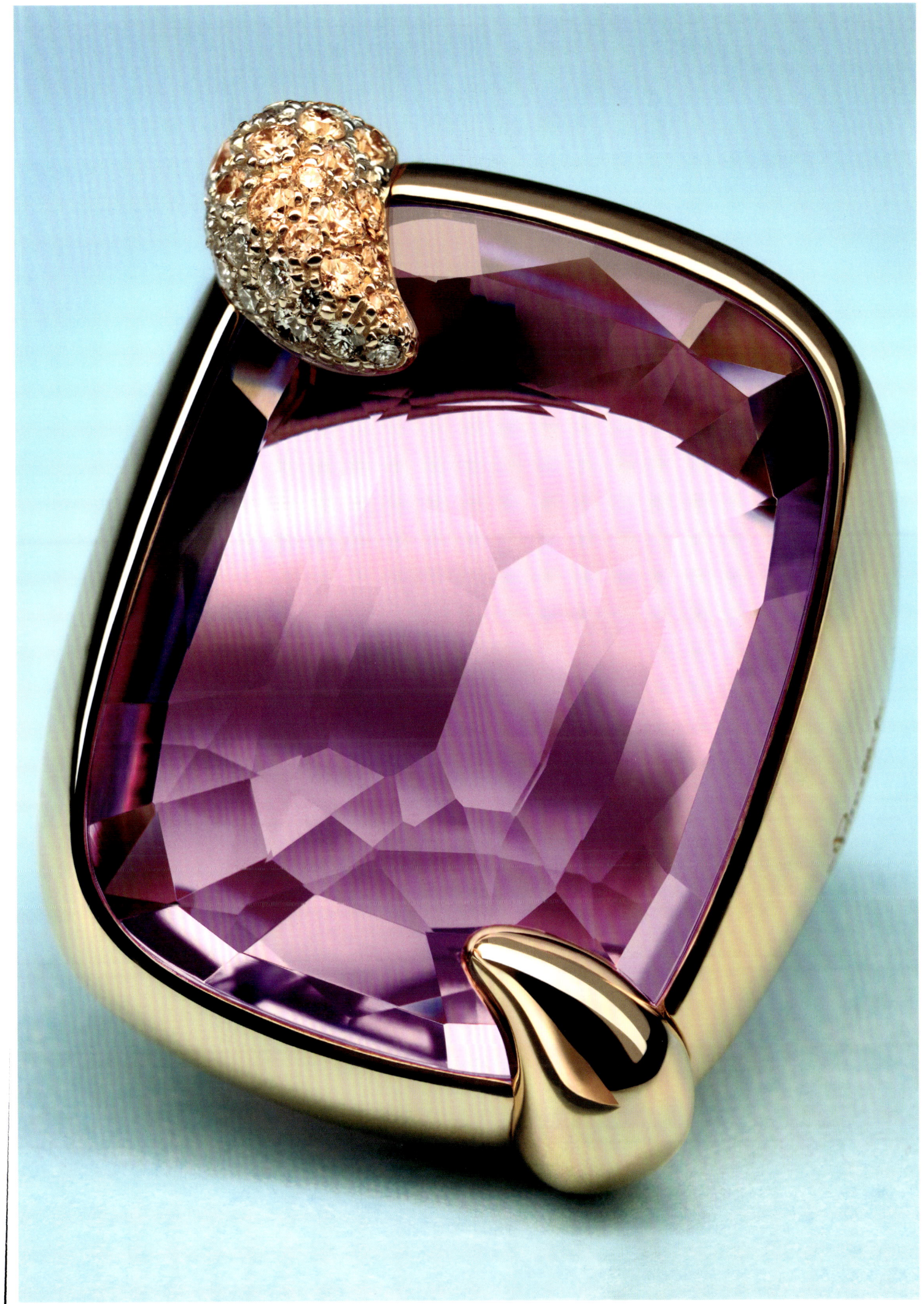

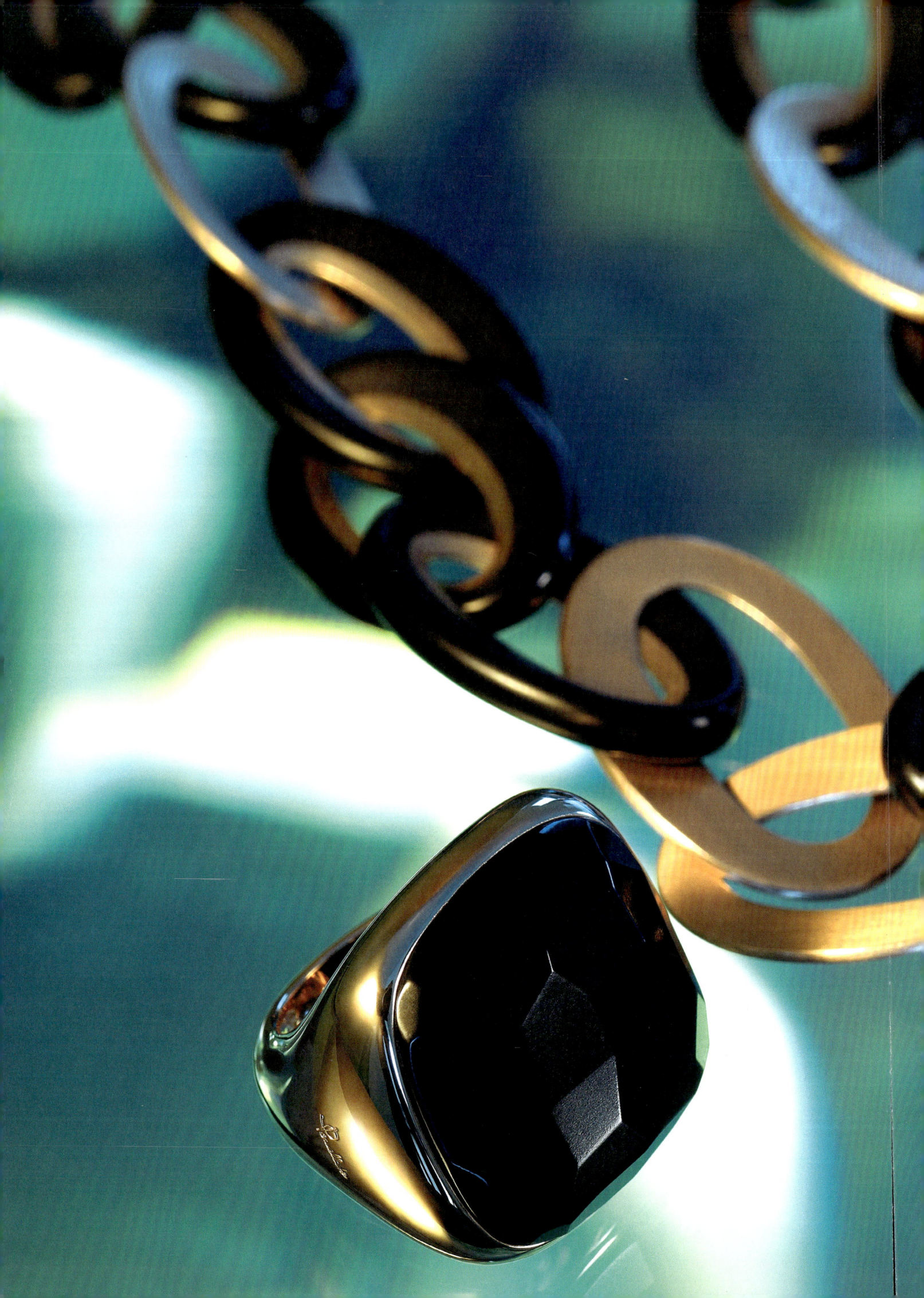

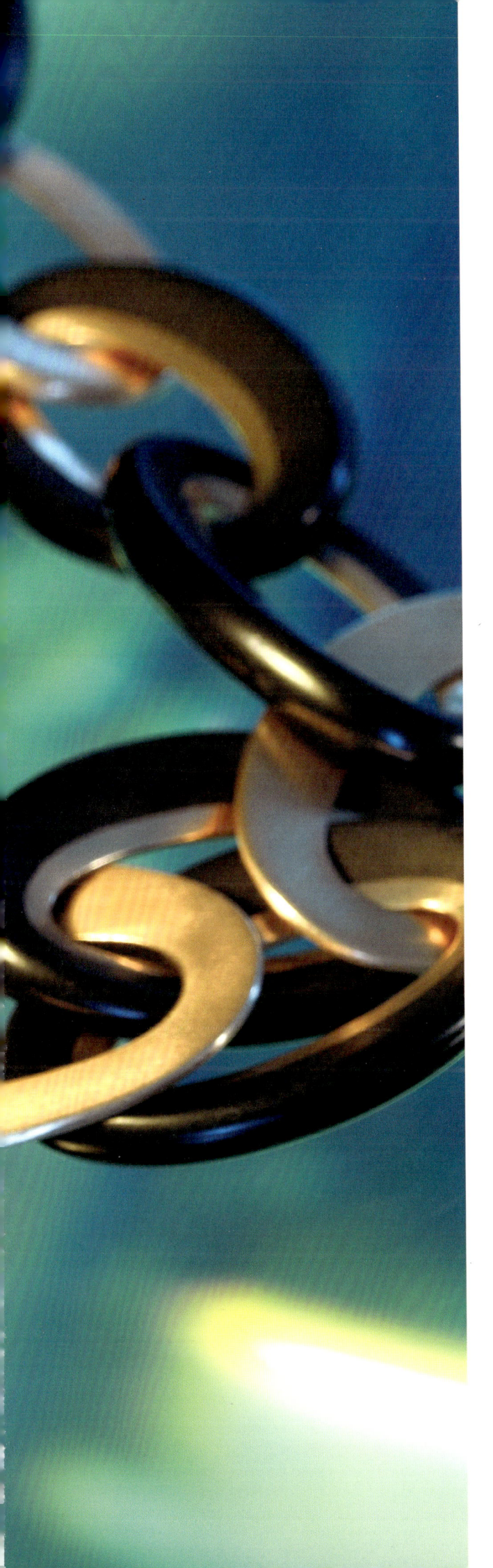

Ring and necklace in jet from the *Victoria* collection

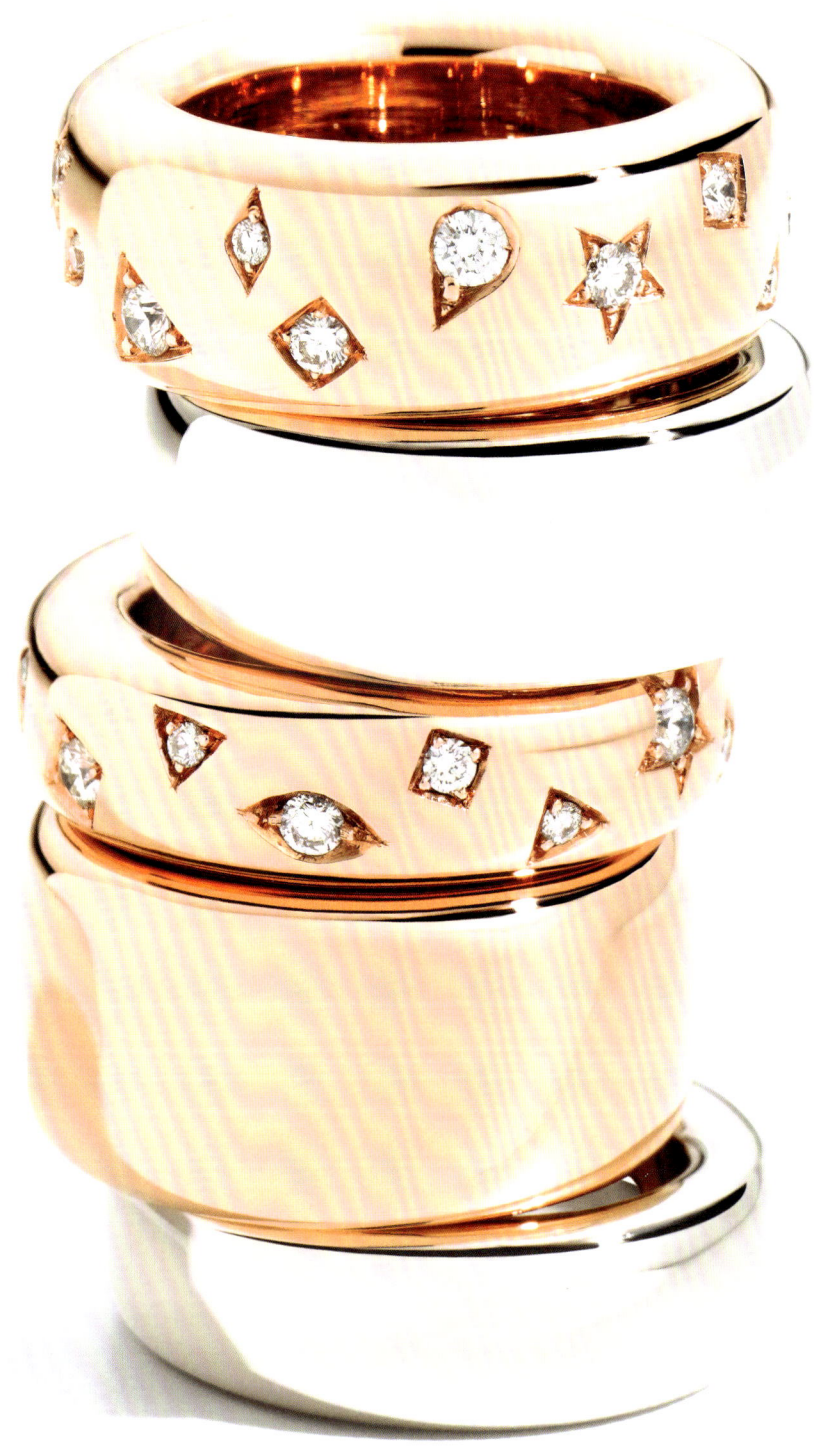

ABOVE: Pomellato *Iconica* collection in rose gold, natural white gold, and diamonds

OPPOSITE: *Capri* collection captures the essence of fresh femininity

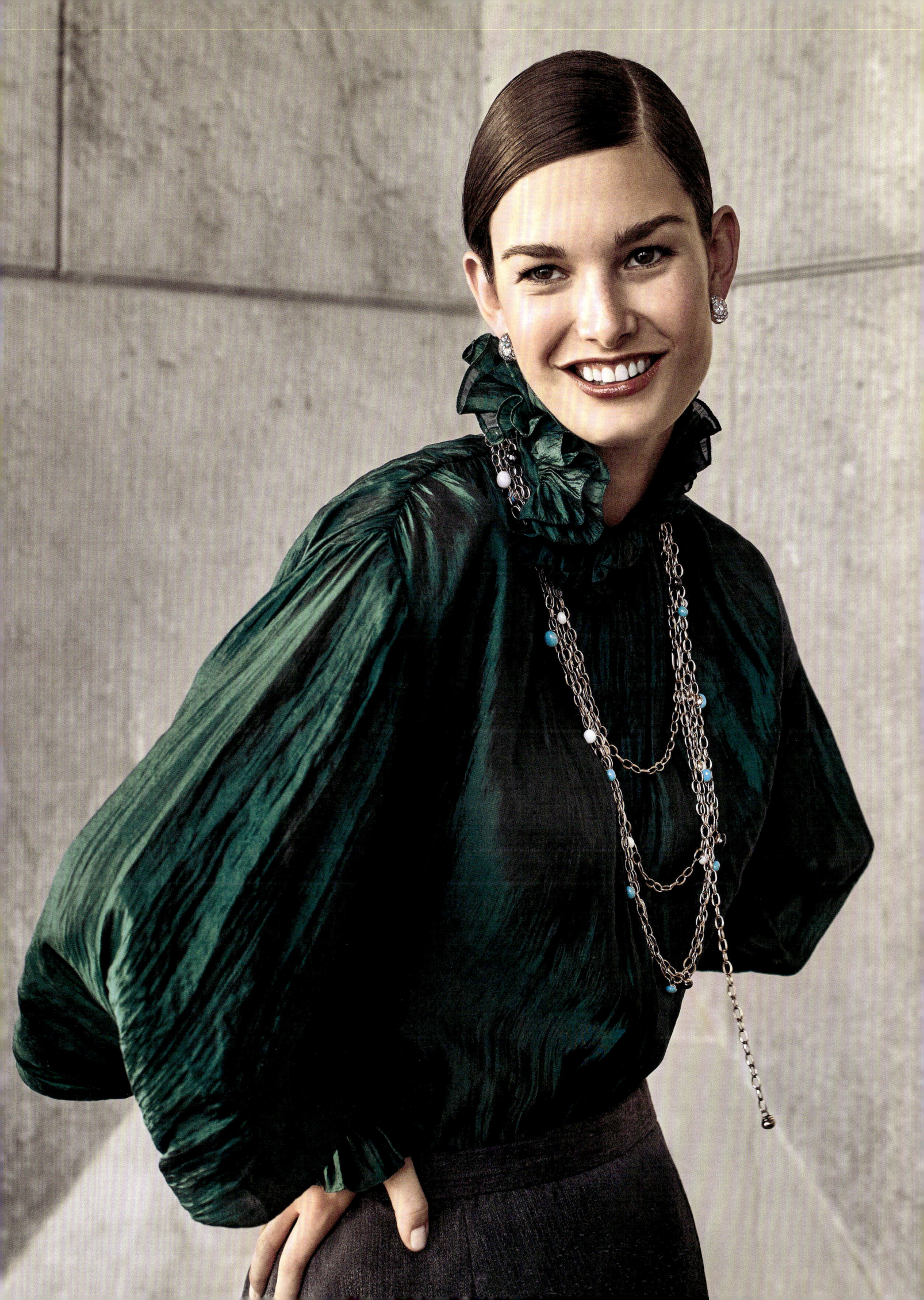

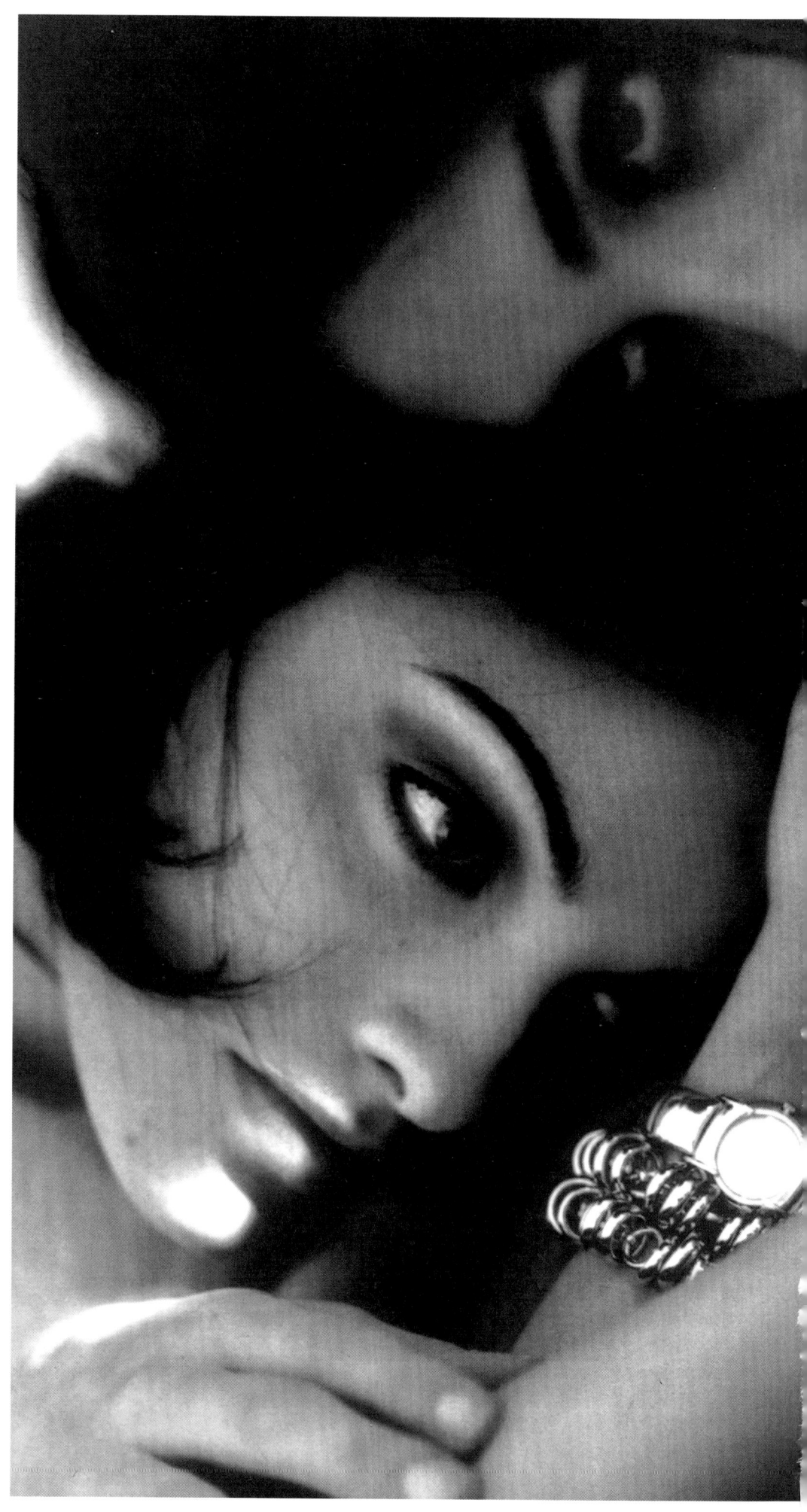

Pomellato advertising campaign featuring
Iconica rings, Javier Vallhonrat, 1993

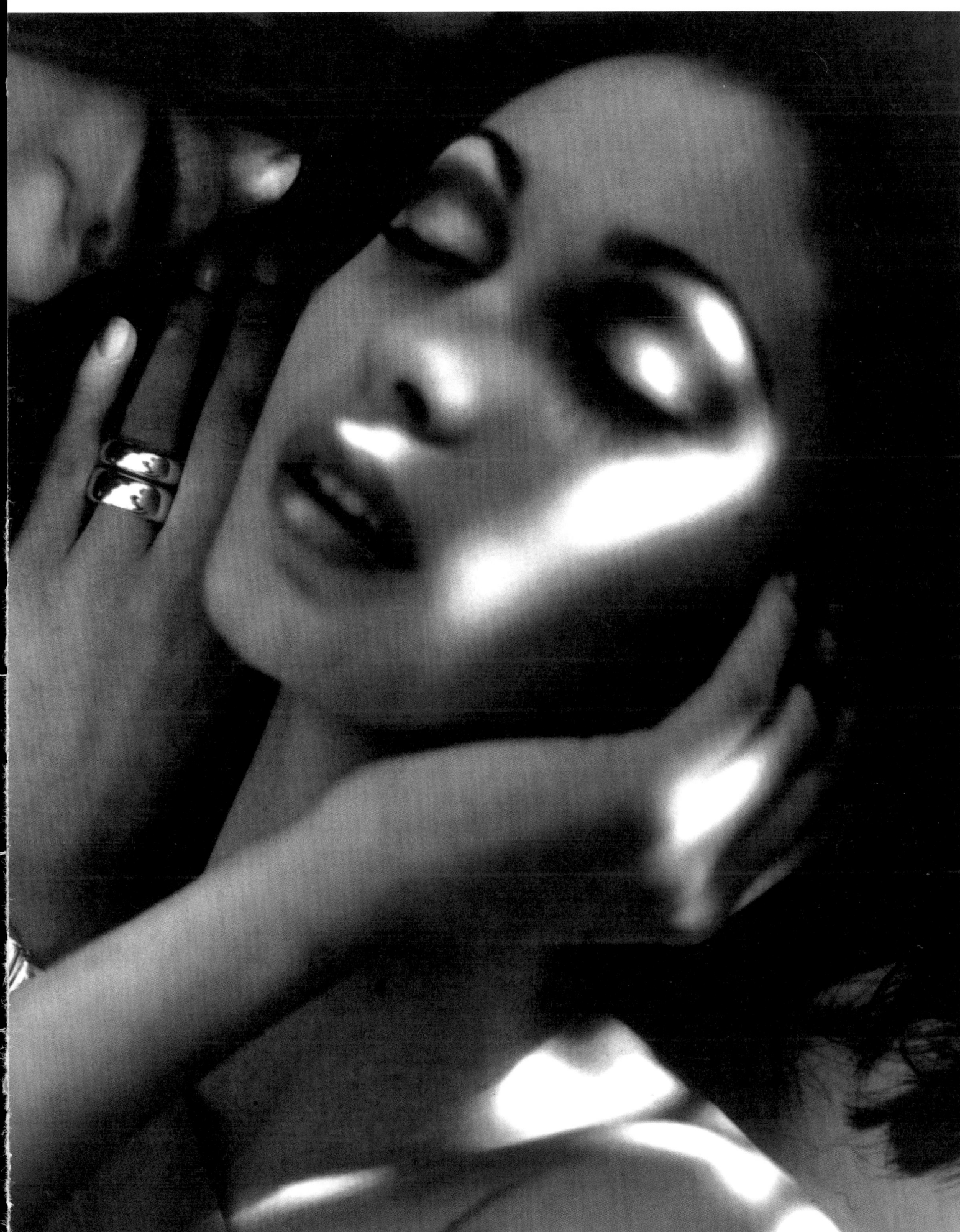

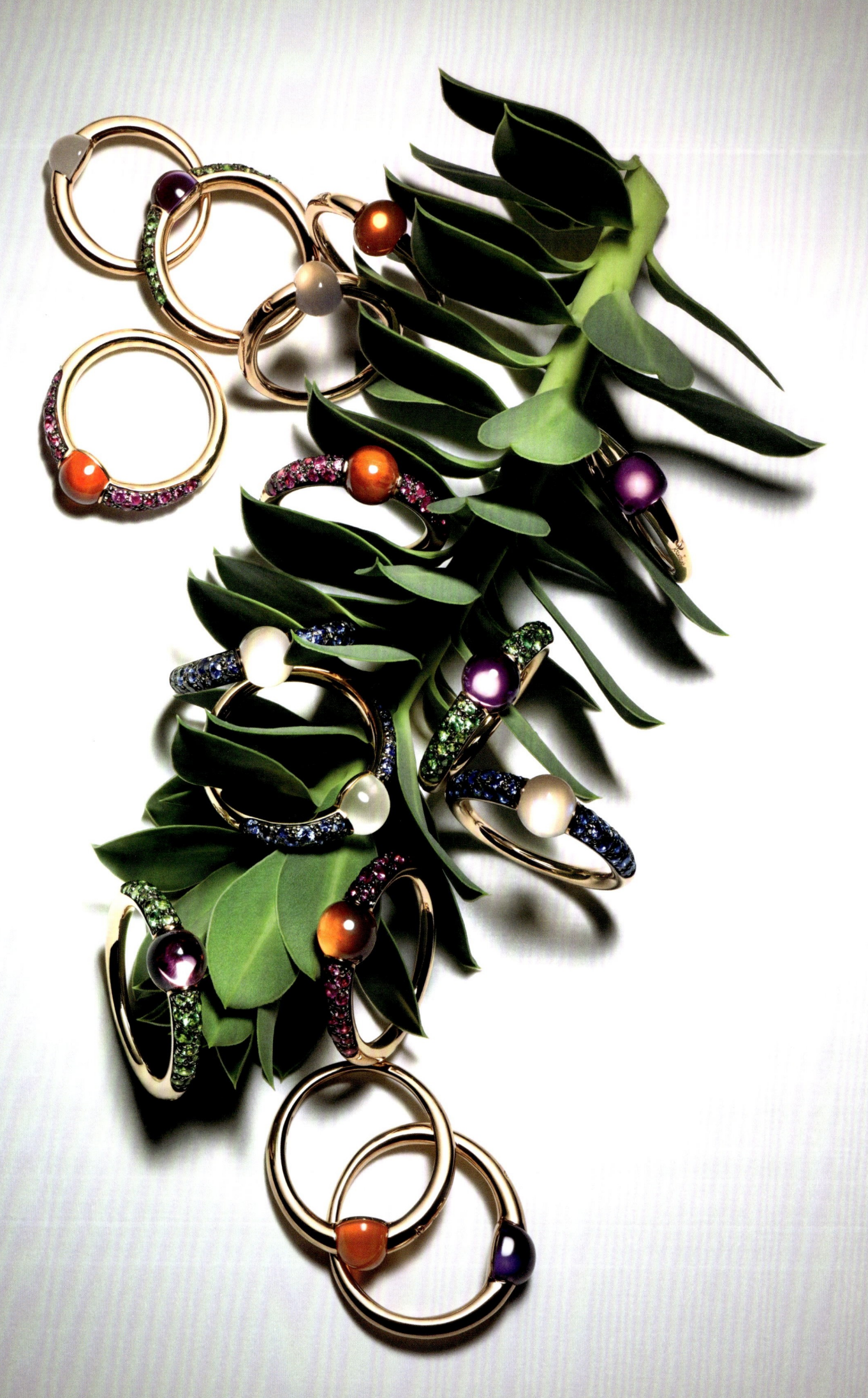

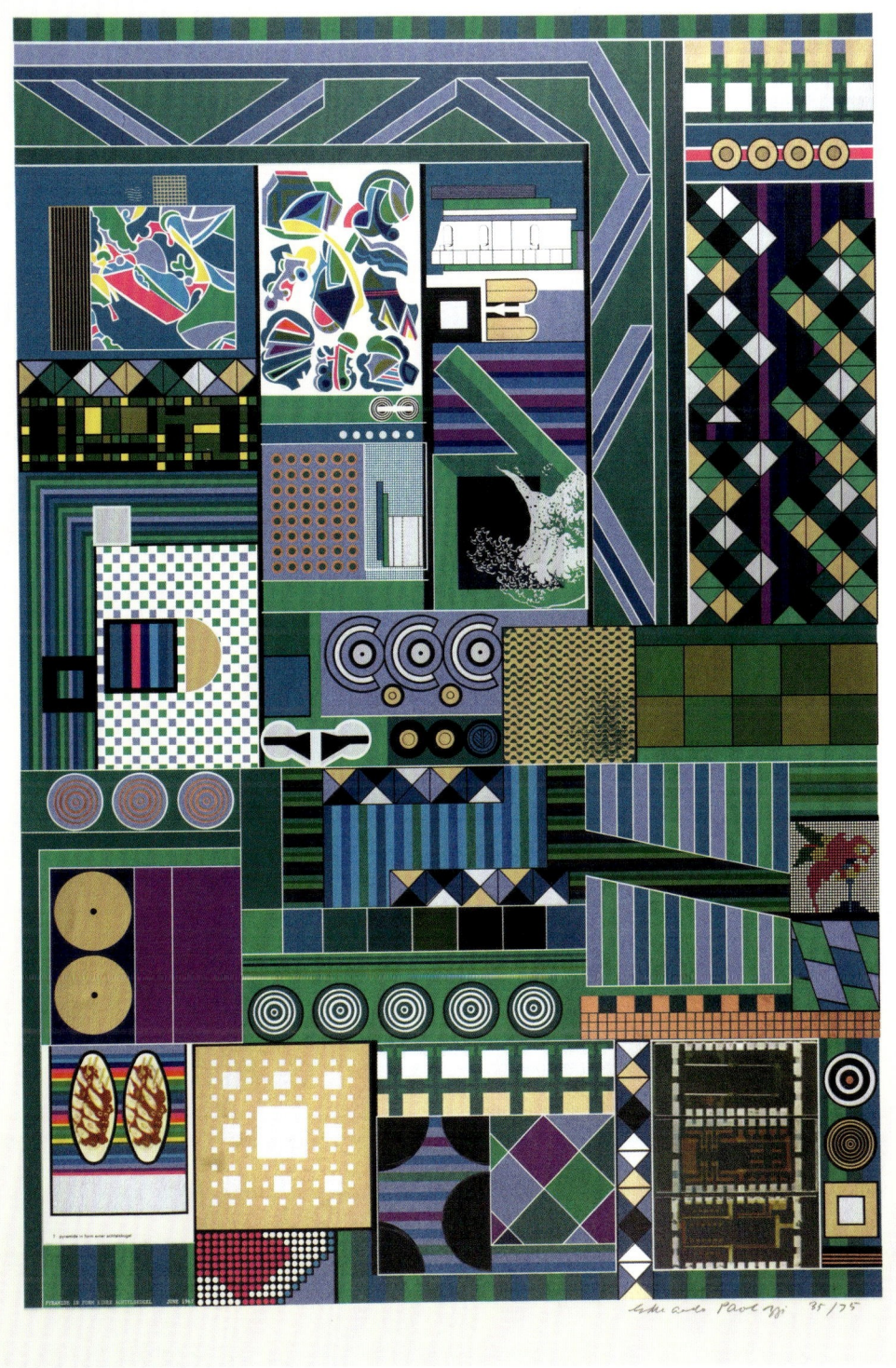

OPPOSITE: *M'ama non M'ama* collection rings with colorful
combinations by Guido Mocafico

ABOVE: *Universal Electronic Vacuum* by Edoardo Paolozzi, 1967

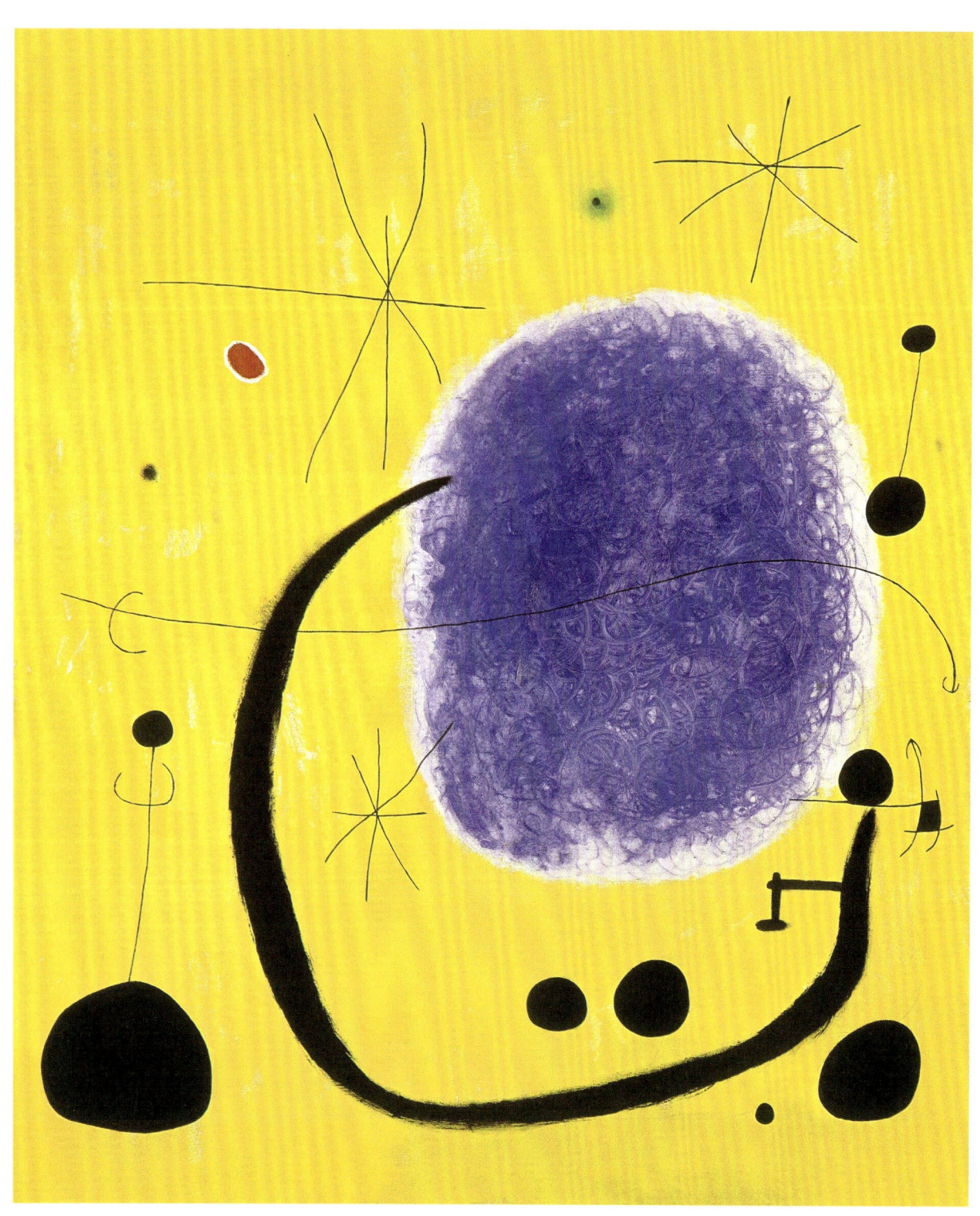

ABOVE: *The Gold of the Azure* by Joan Miró, 1967

OPPOSITE: The deepest shade of blue for the *Nudo* ring in London blue topaz

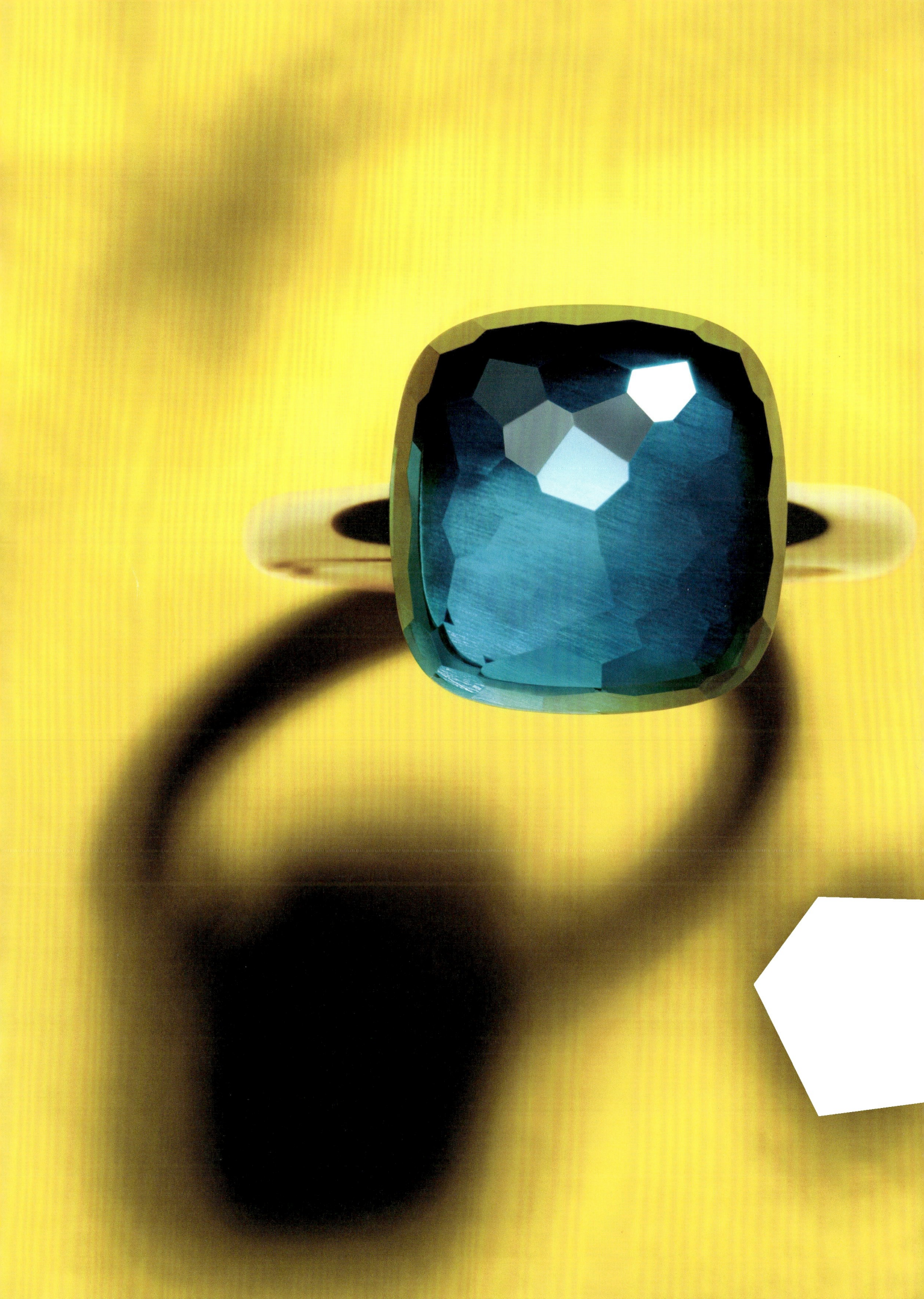

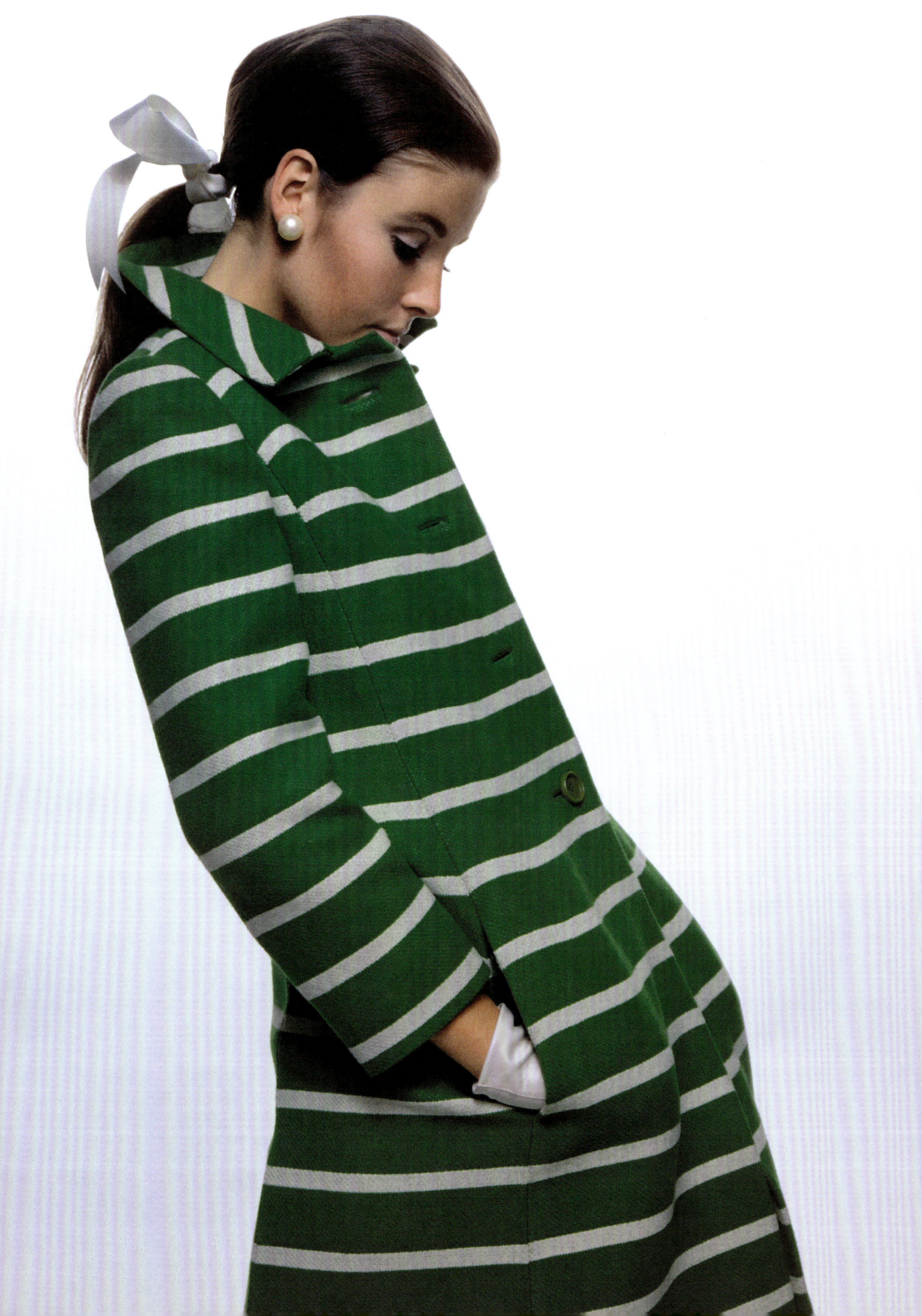

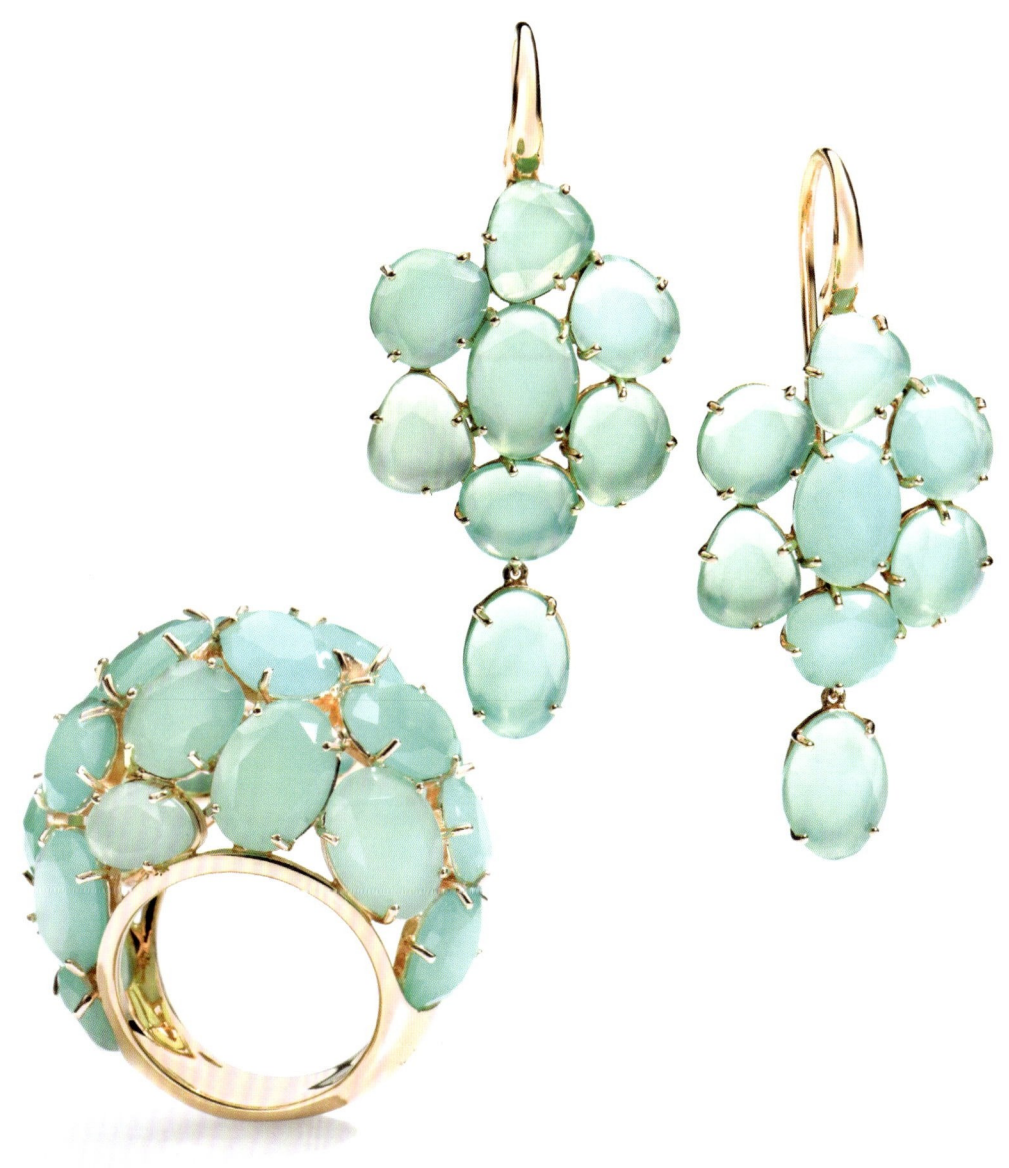

ABOVE: Ring and drop earrings in chrysoprase and rock crystal

OPPOSITE: A model wearing a green and white striped Shetland wool coat by Ginala

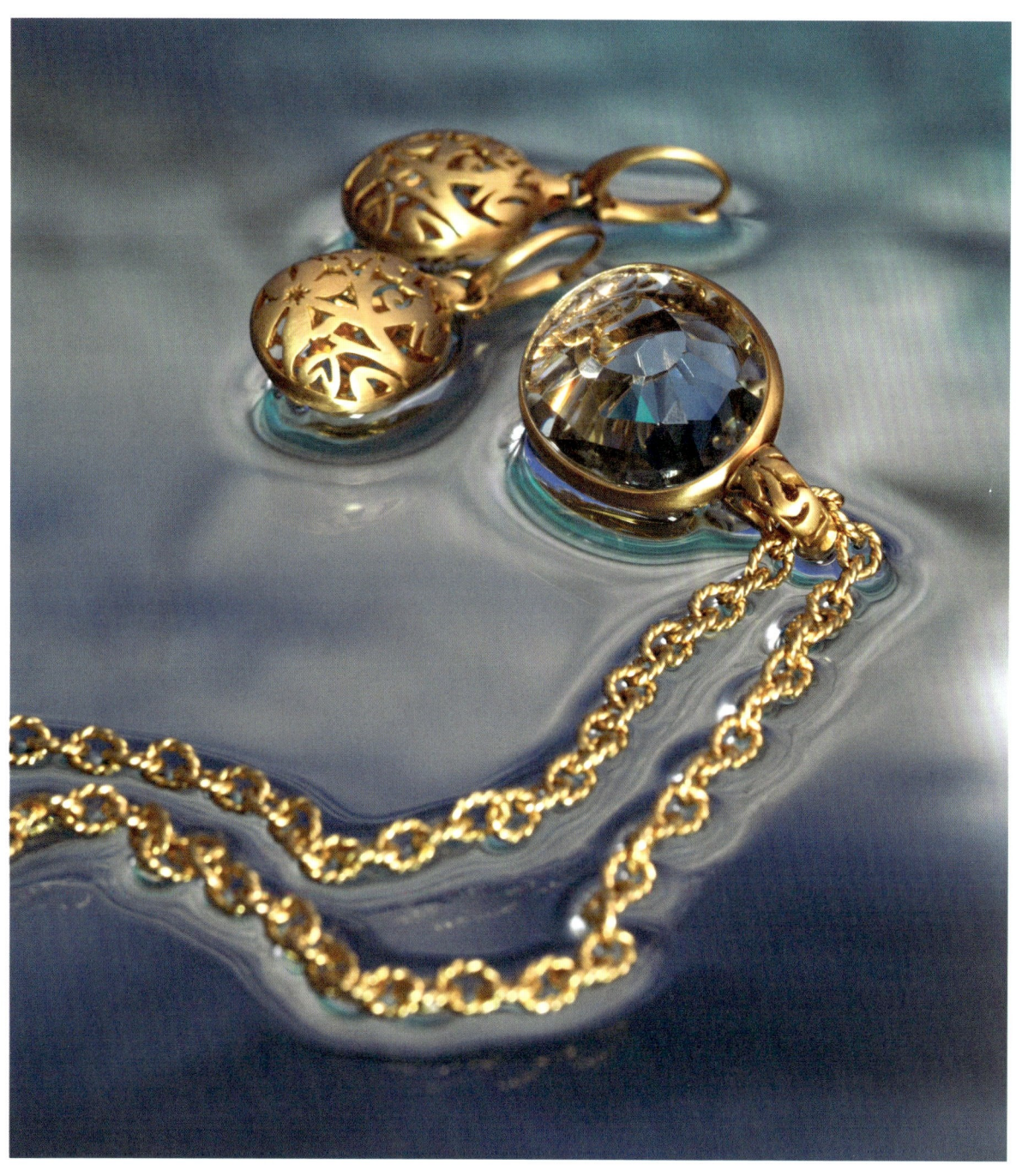

ABOVE: The magical see-through effect of the mysteriously oriental *Arabesque* collection

OPPOSITE: Channeling peace and love by wearing oriental artifacts, Elysian Park, Los Angeles, 1967

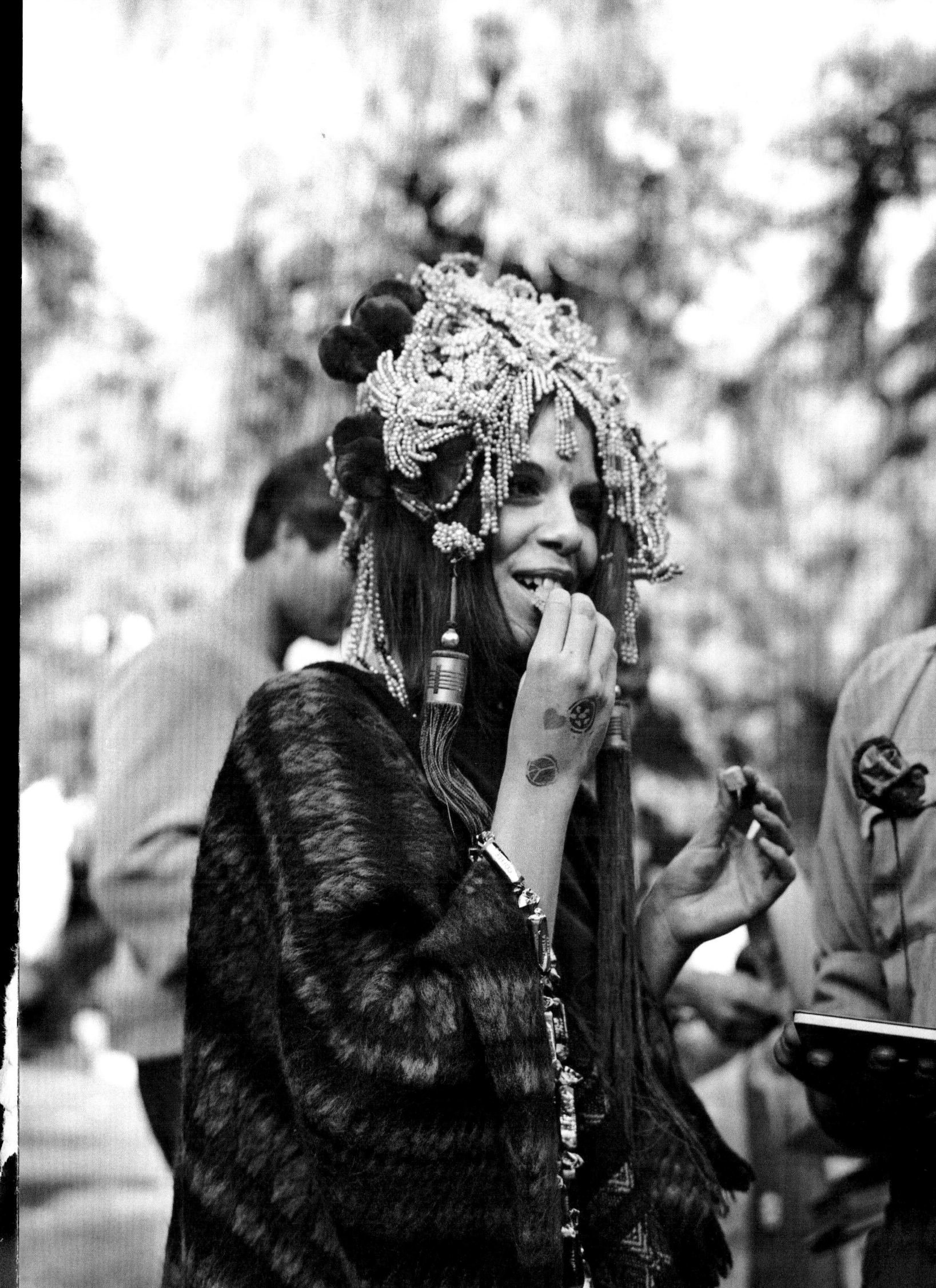

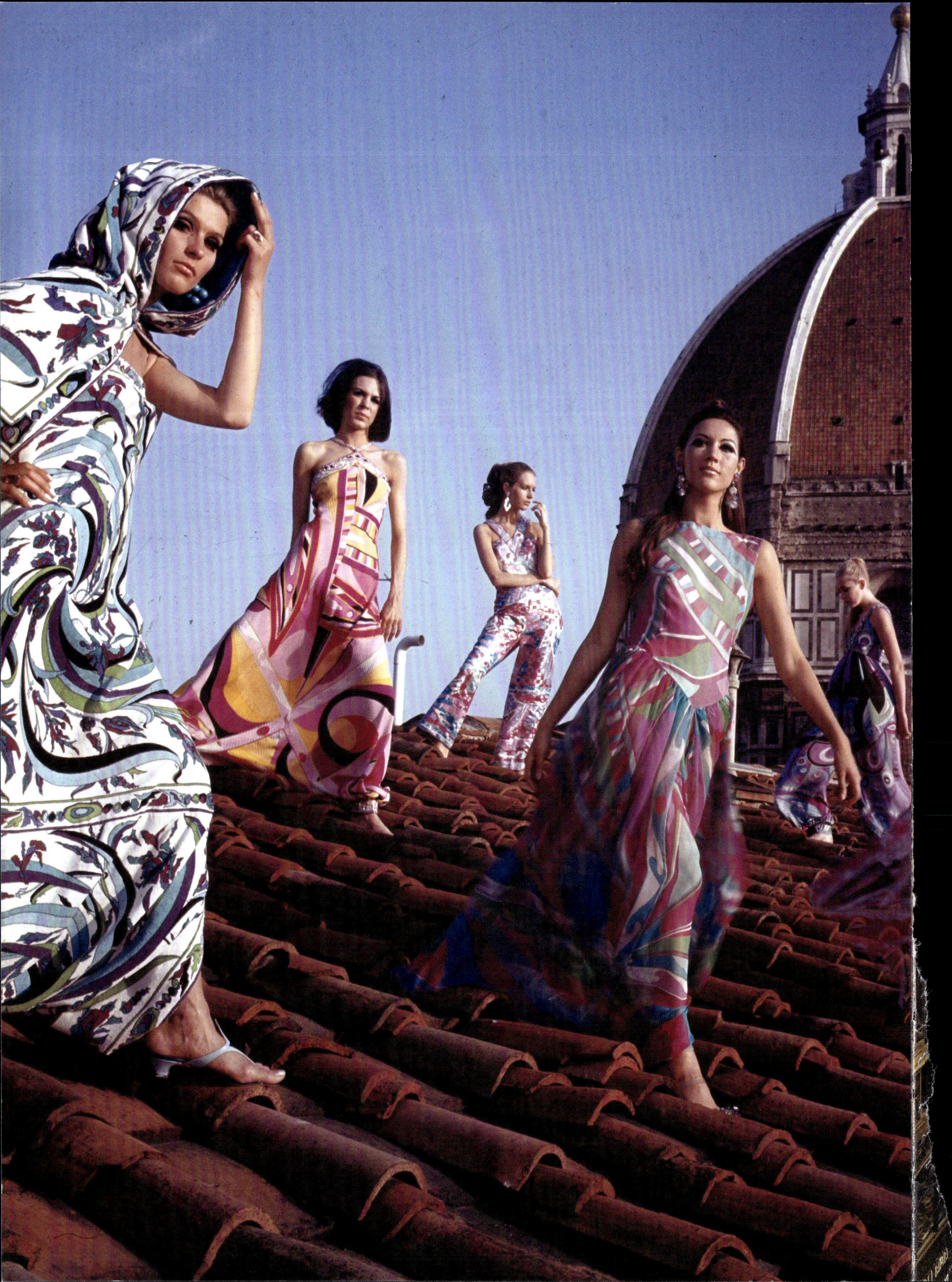

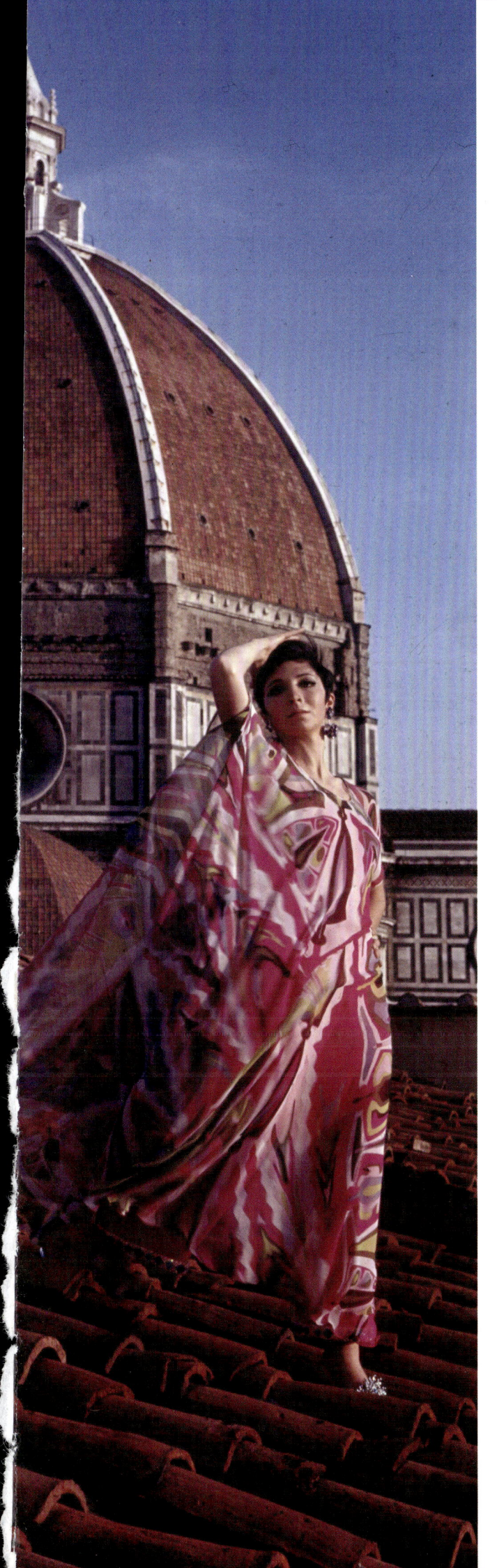

OPPOSITE: Emilio Pucci shoot on a roof in front of the cathedral of Santa Maria del Fiore in Florence, 1967

FOLLOWING SPREAD, LEFT TO RIGHT: Far side of the moon, Apollo 16 mission, 1972; the lunar pavé of this *Sabbia* collection pendant highlights its delicate artisanal work

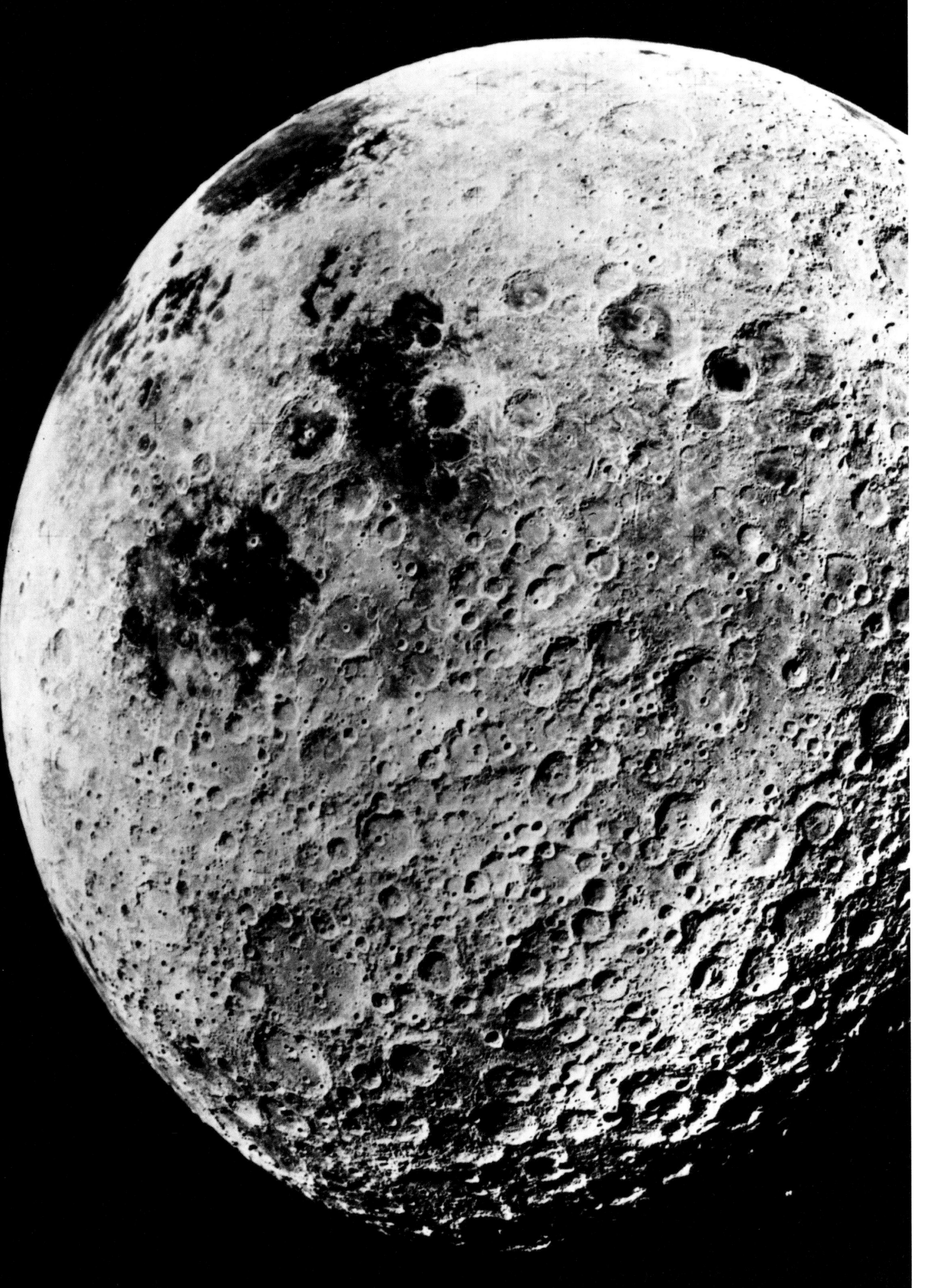

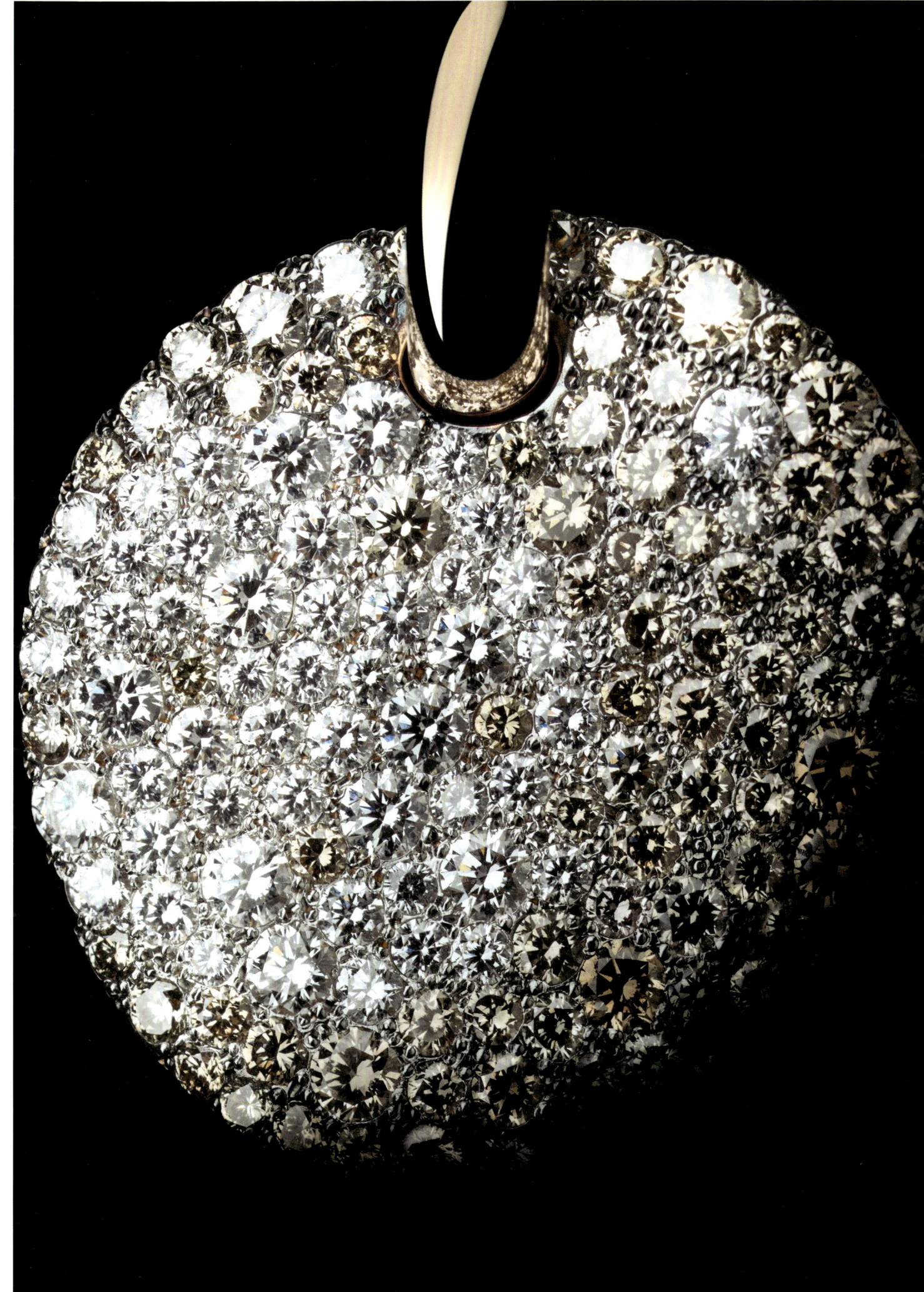

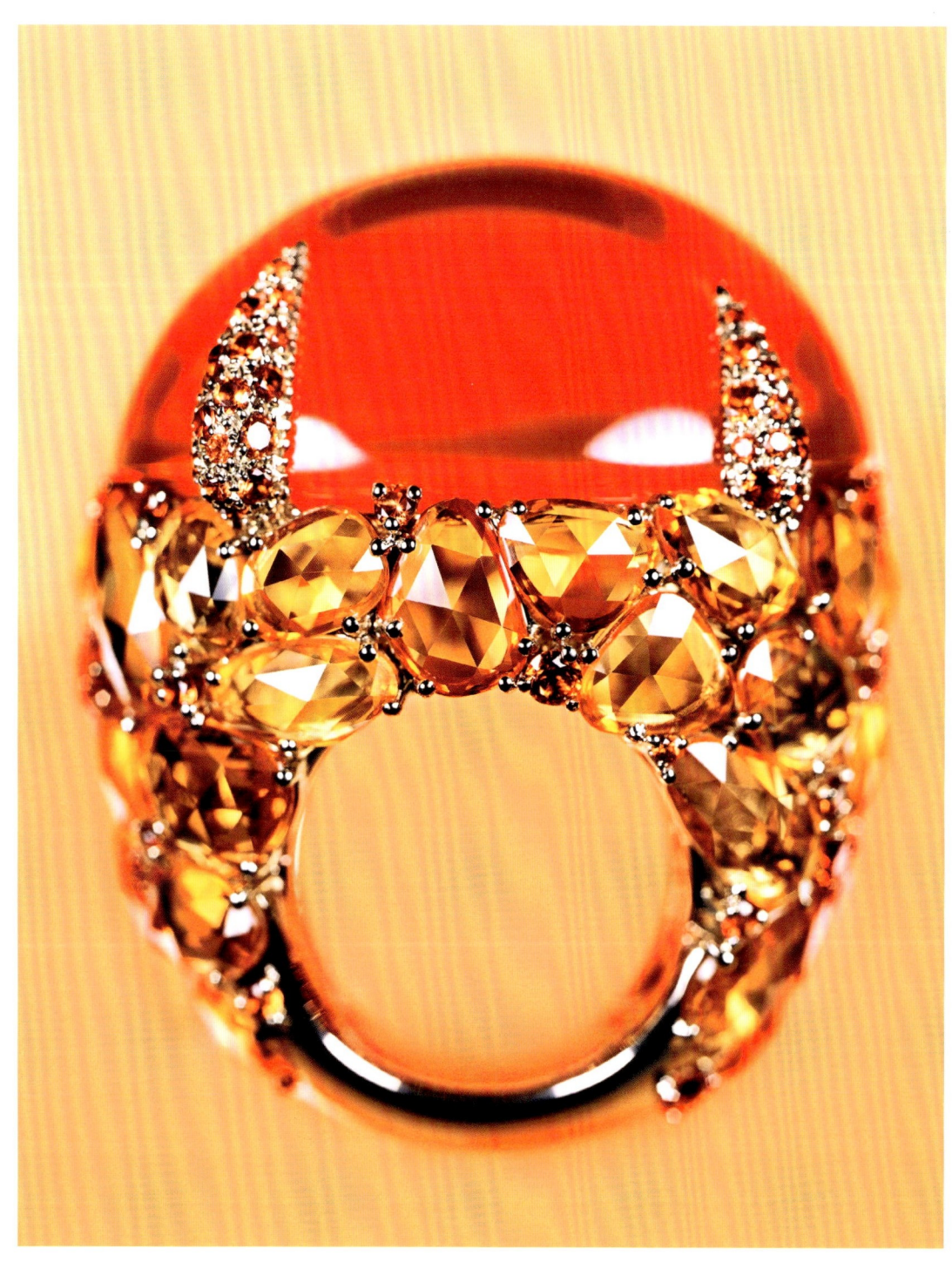

ABOVE: A *Pom Pom* ring under its brightest light: fire opal and orange sapphires

OPPOSITE: An Italian *ragazza* opening the door of a Fiat 500L, Giorgio Lotti, 1968

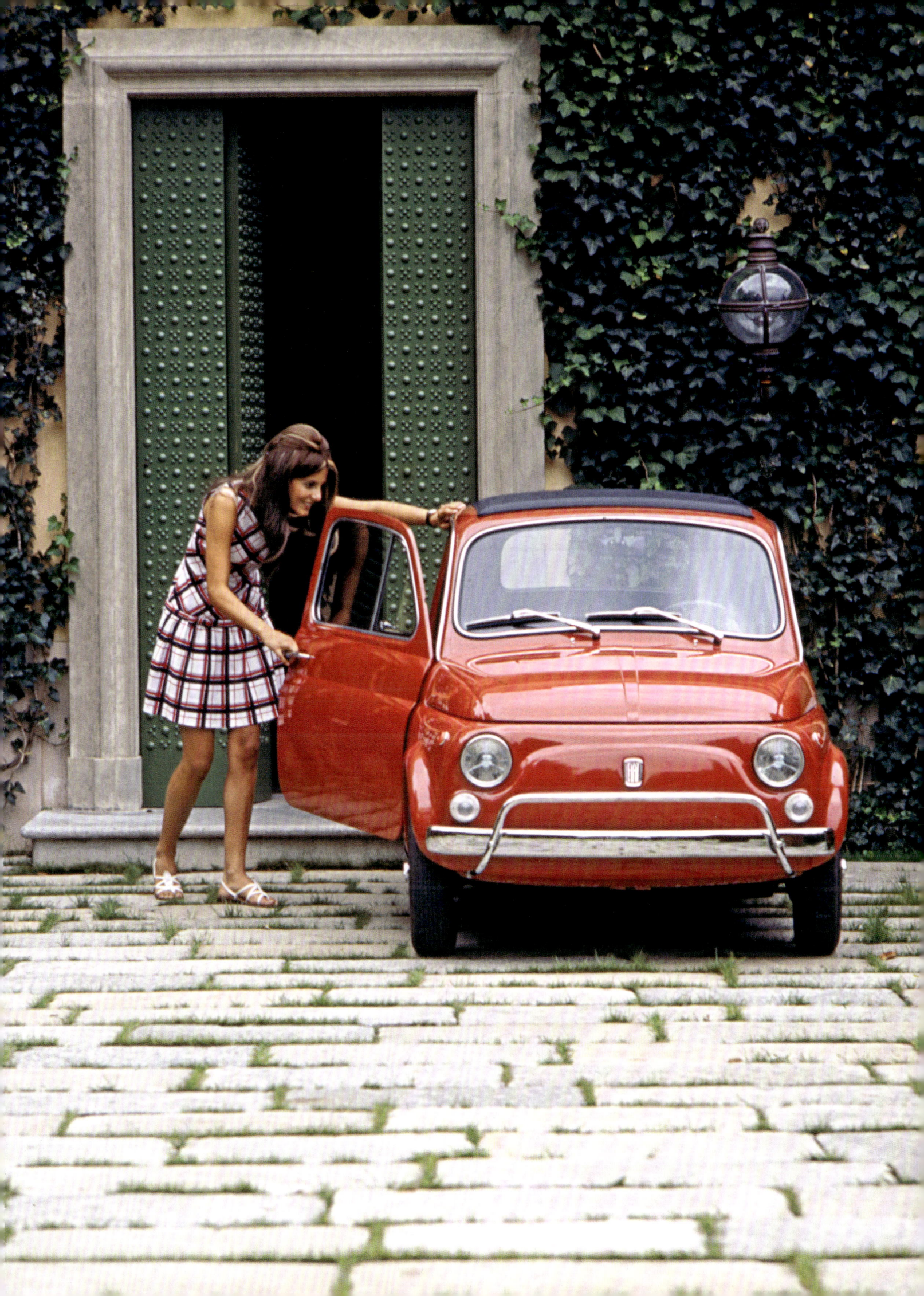

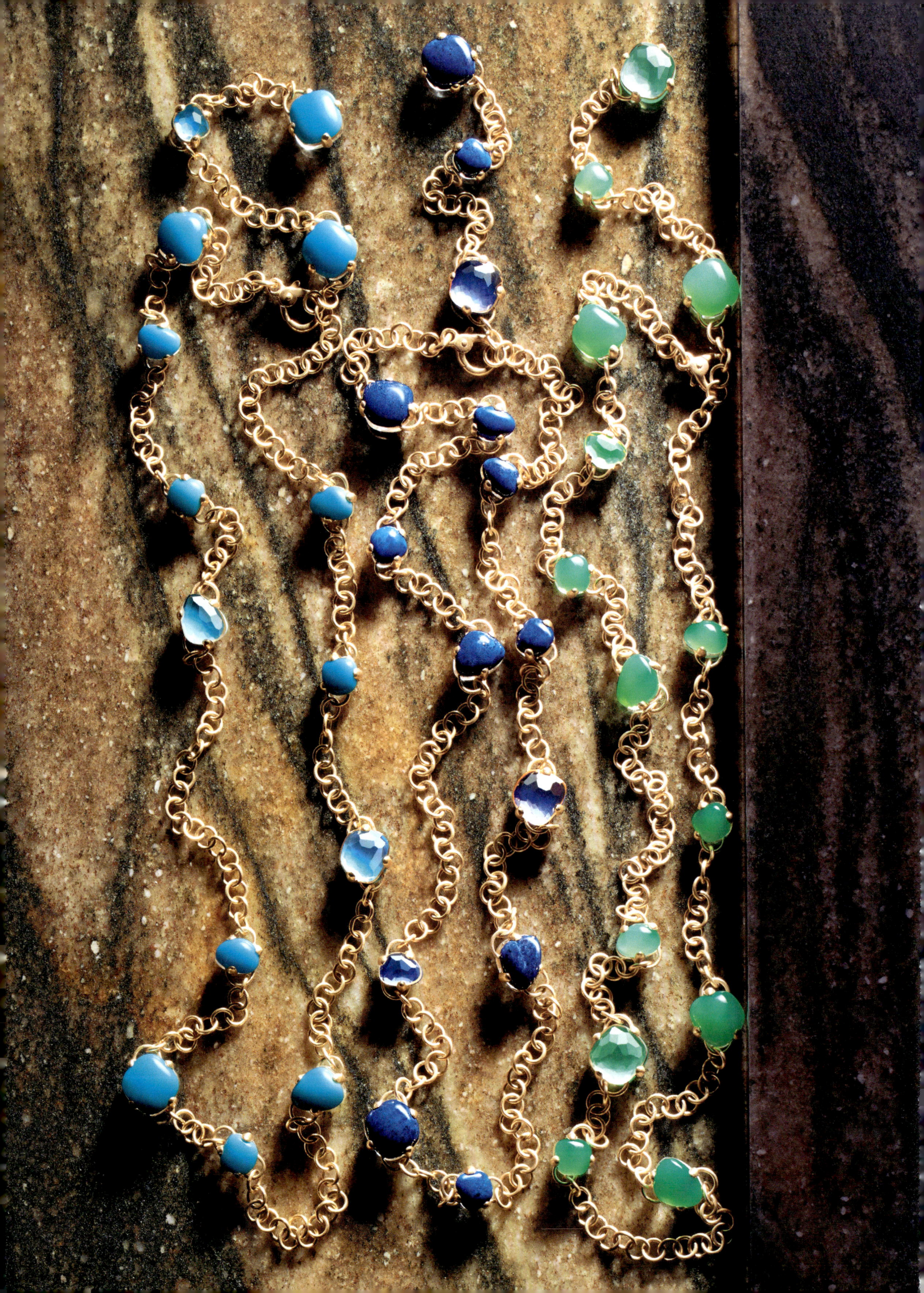

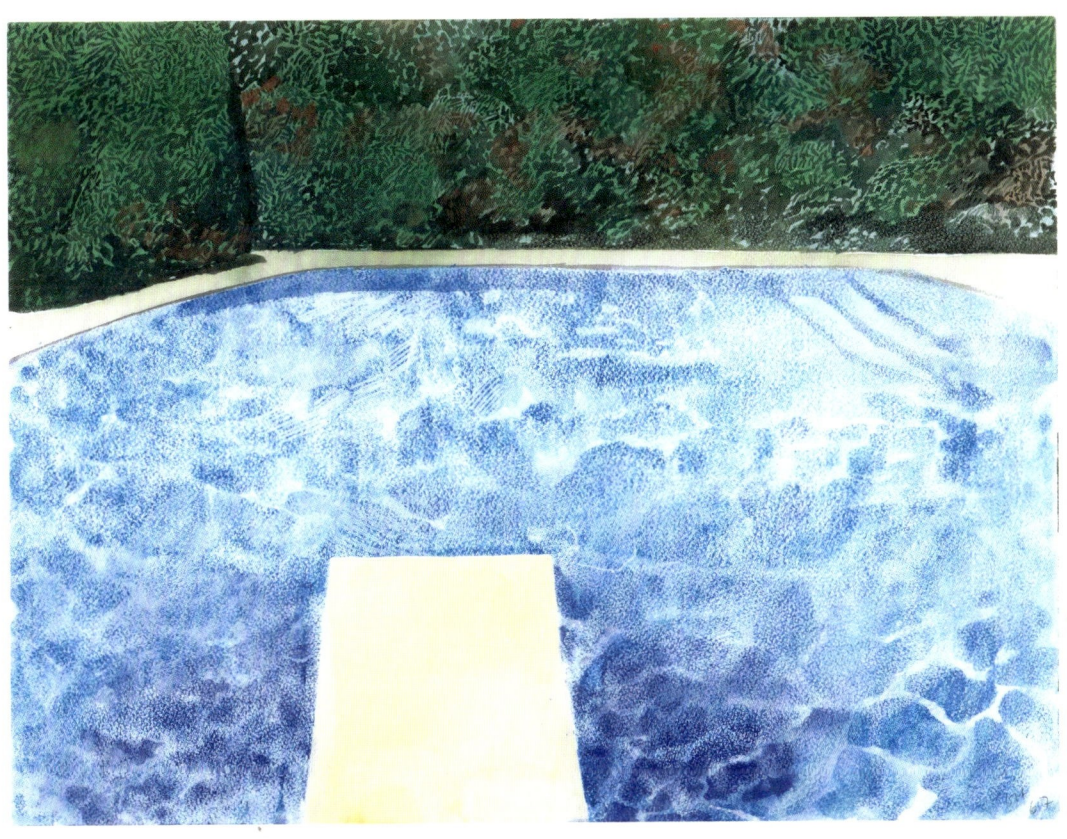

OPPOSITE: *Capri* collection necklaces in turquoise, lapis, and chrysoprase with rock crystal

ABOVE: *Untitled Study for a Painting* by David Hockney, 1967

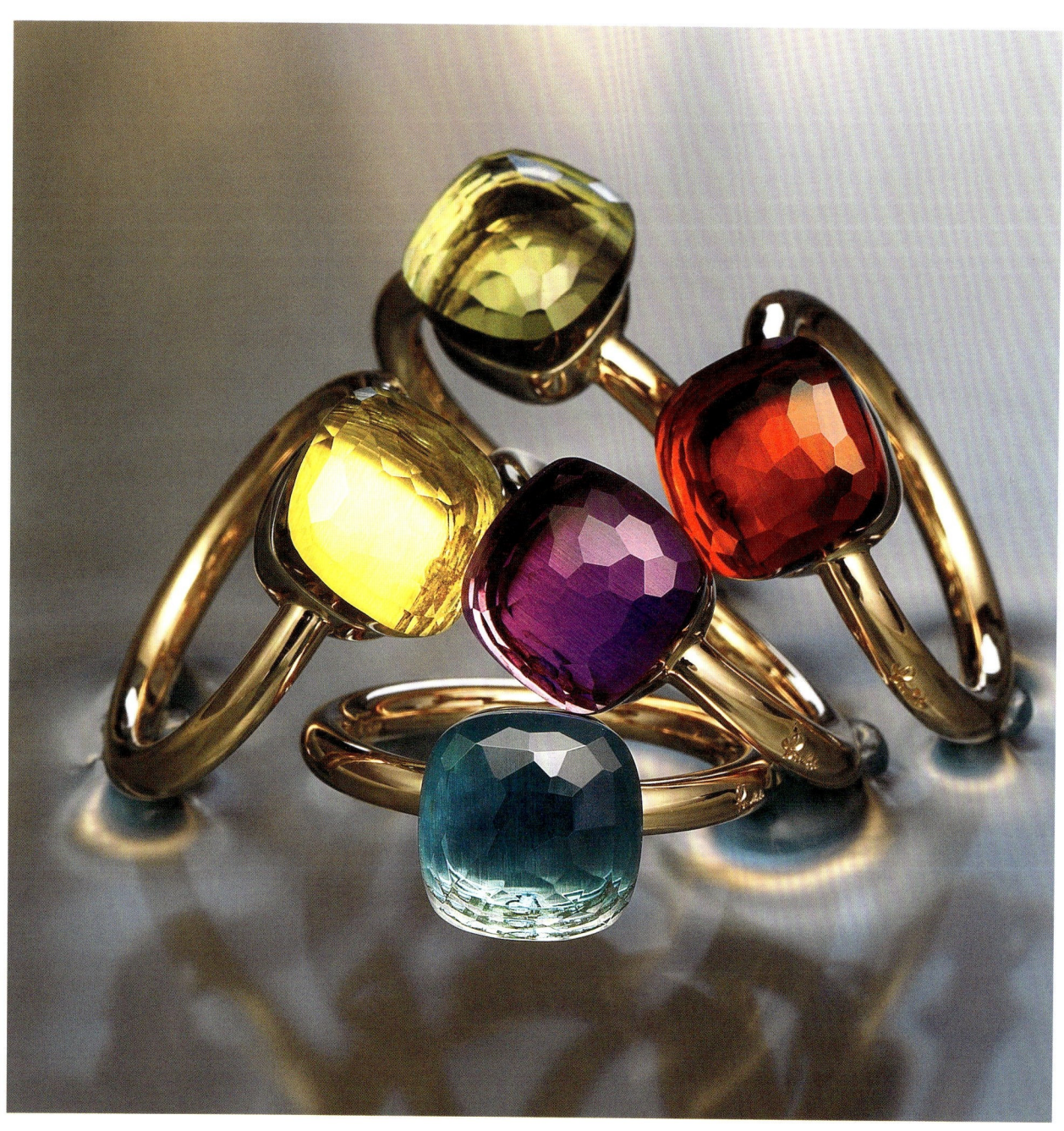

ABOVE: This is *Nudo*: Milanese heritage combined with the purest design

OPPOSITE: A view looking down Milan's Galleria Vittorio Emanuele II. Opened in 1890, the covered arcade is on the northern side of the Piazza del Duomo, Slim Aarons, 1960

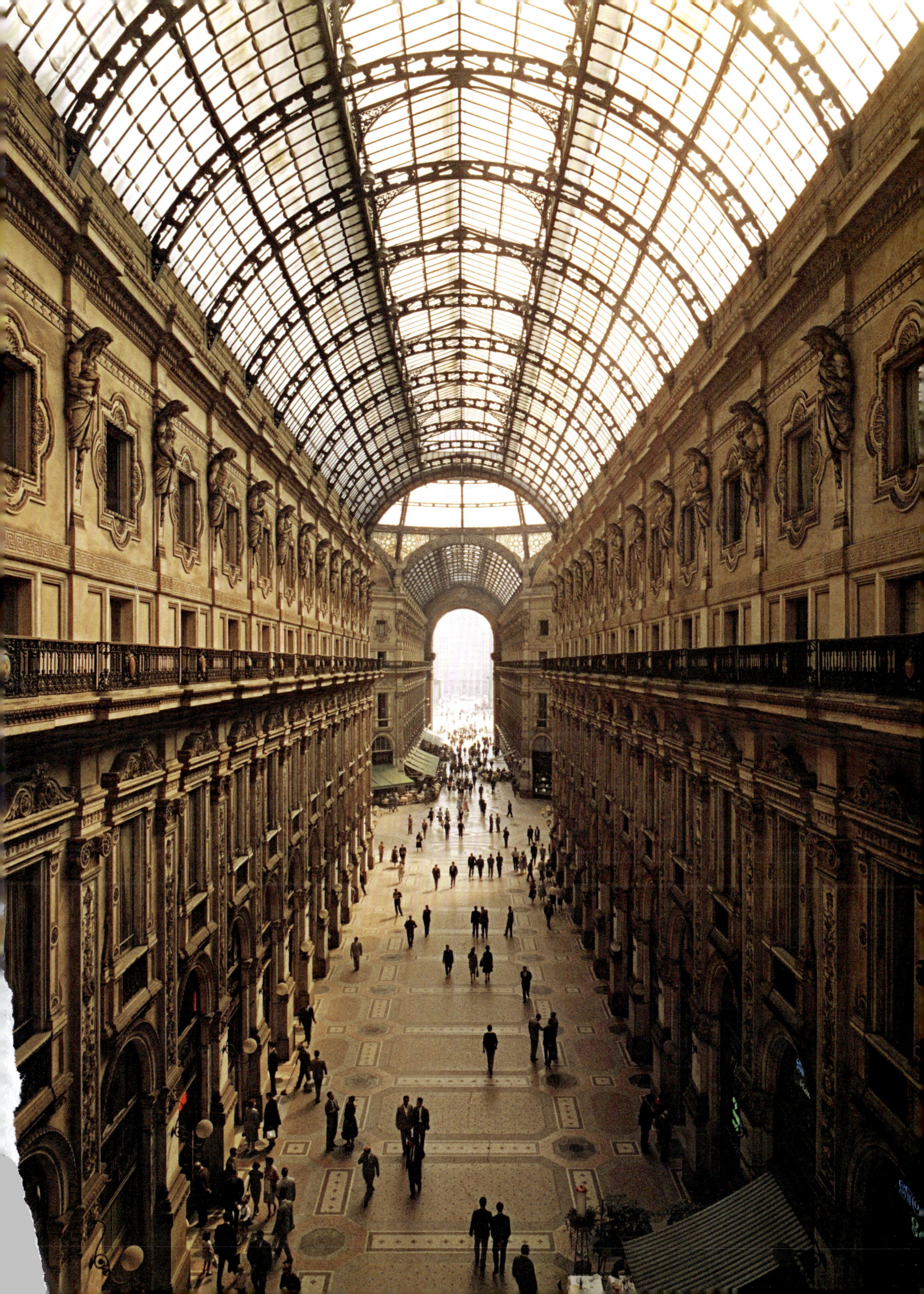

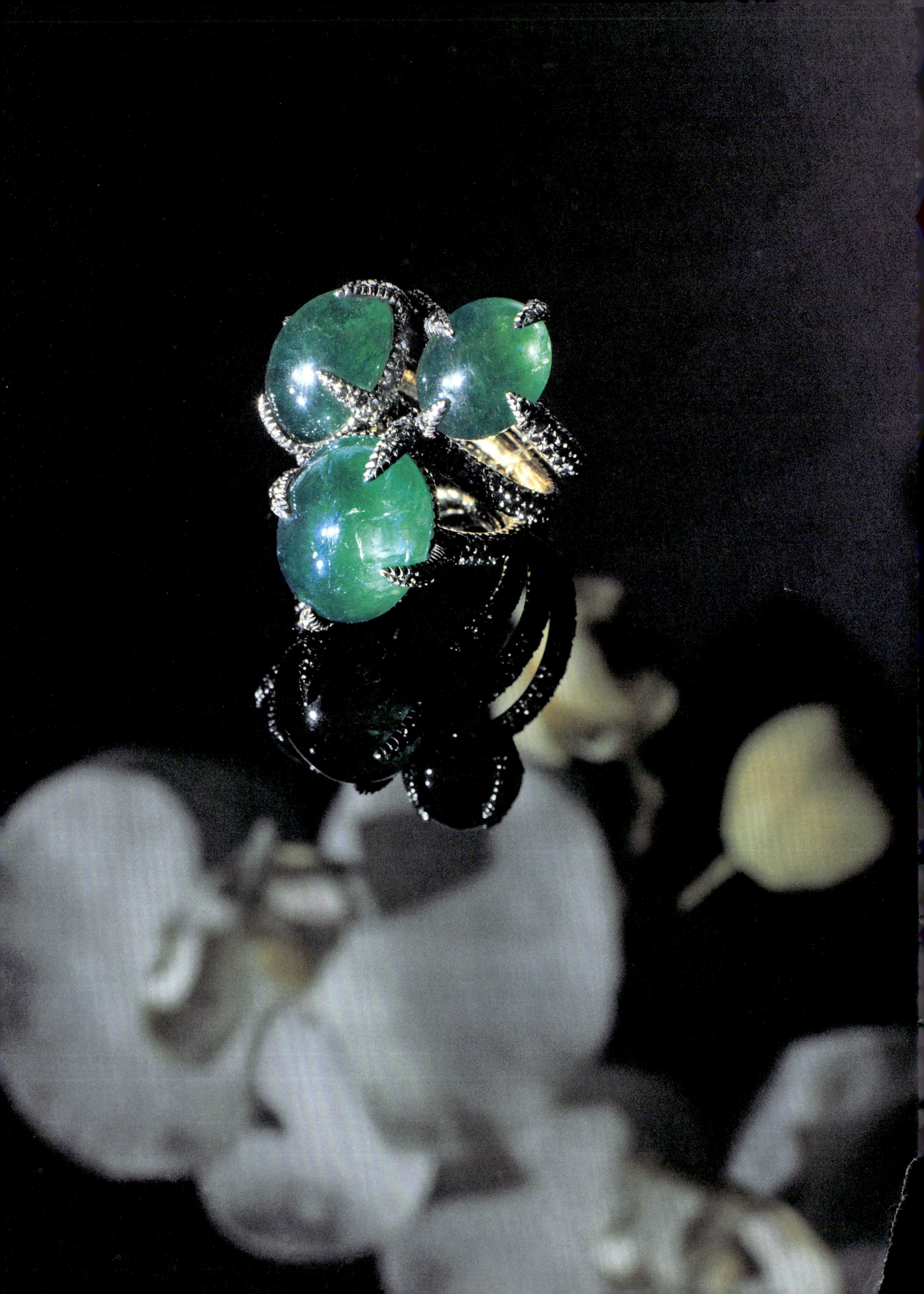

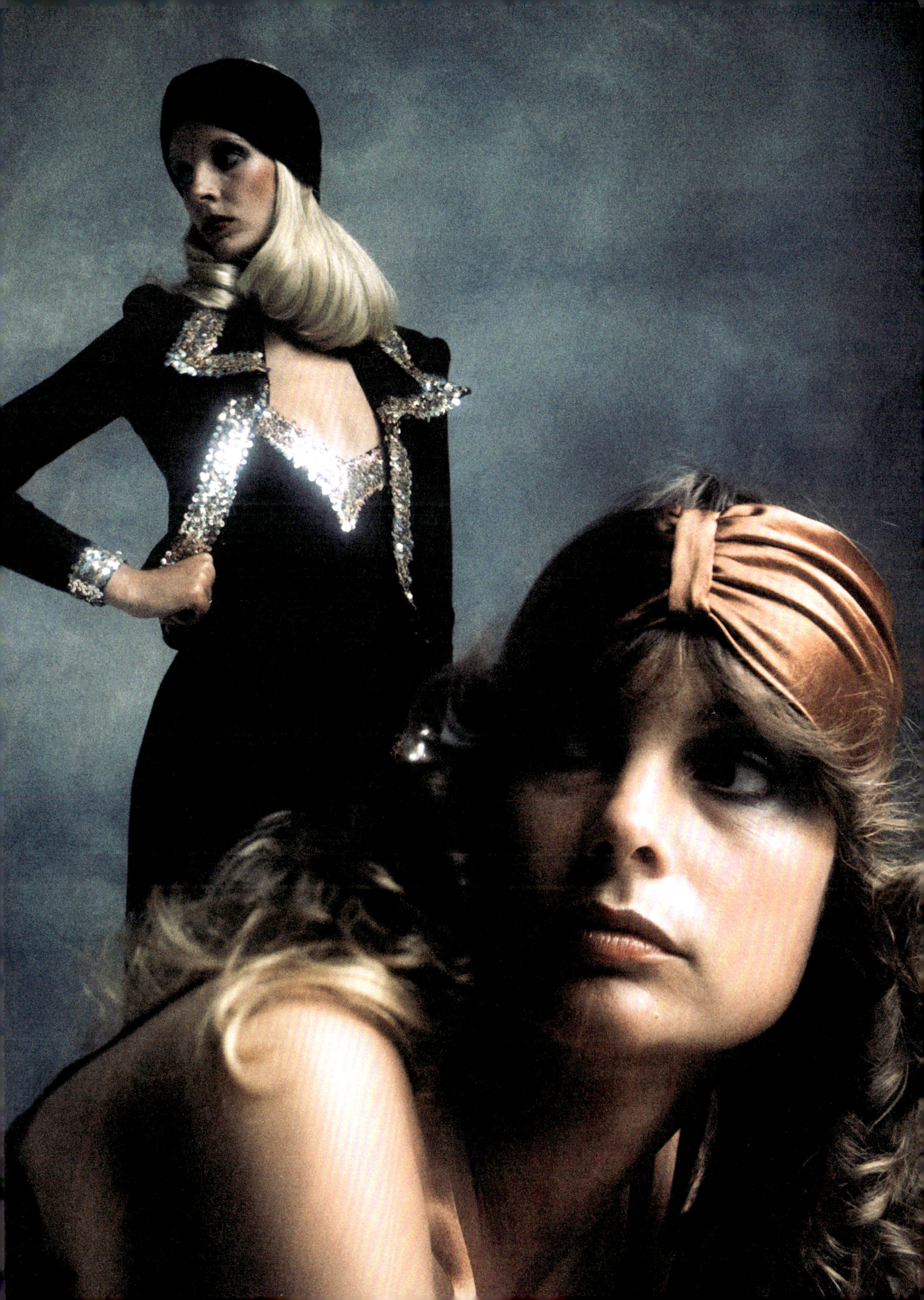

PREVIOUS SPREAD, LEFT TO RIGHT: The adventurous spirit of *Pom Pom* rings in emeralds and black diamonds; models wearing Biba in a photoshoot for *The Daily Telegraph*, Brian Duffy, circa 1970

RIGHT: The tempting colors of the Pomellato *Nudo* collection

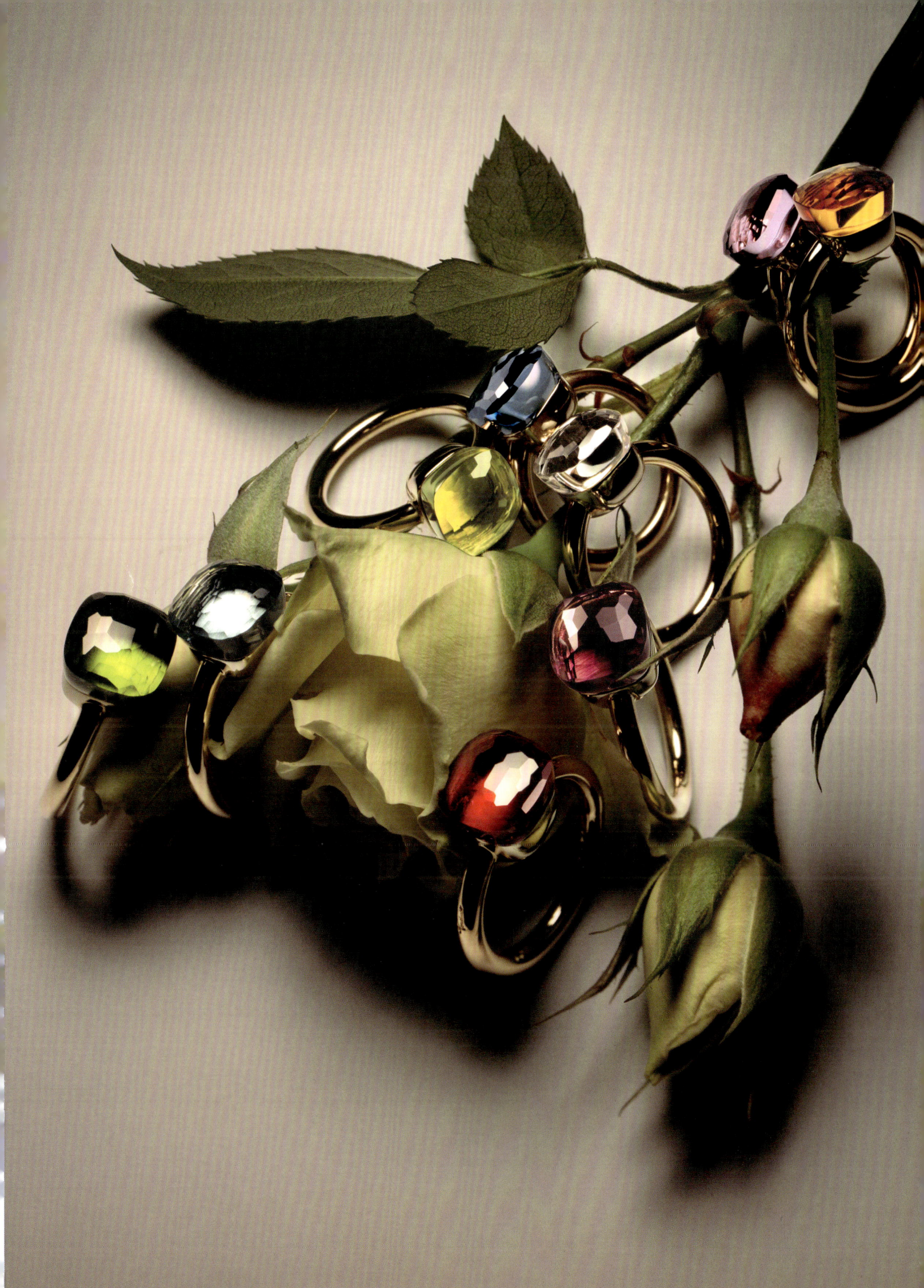

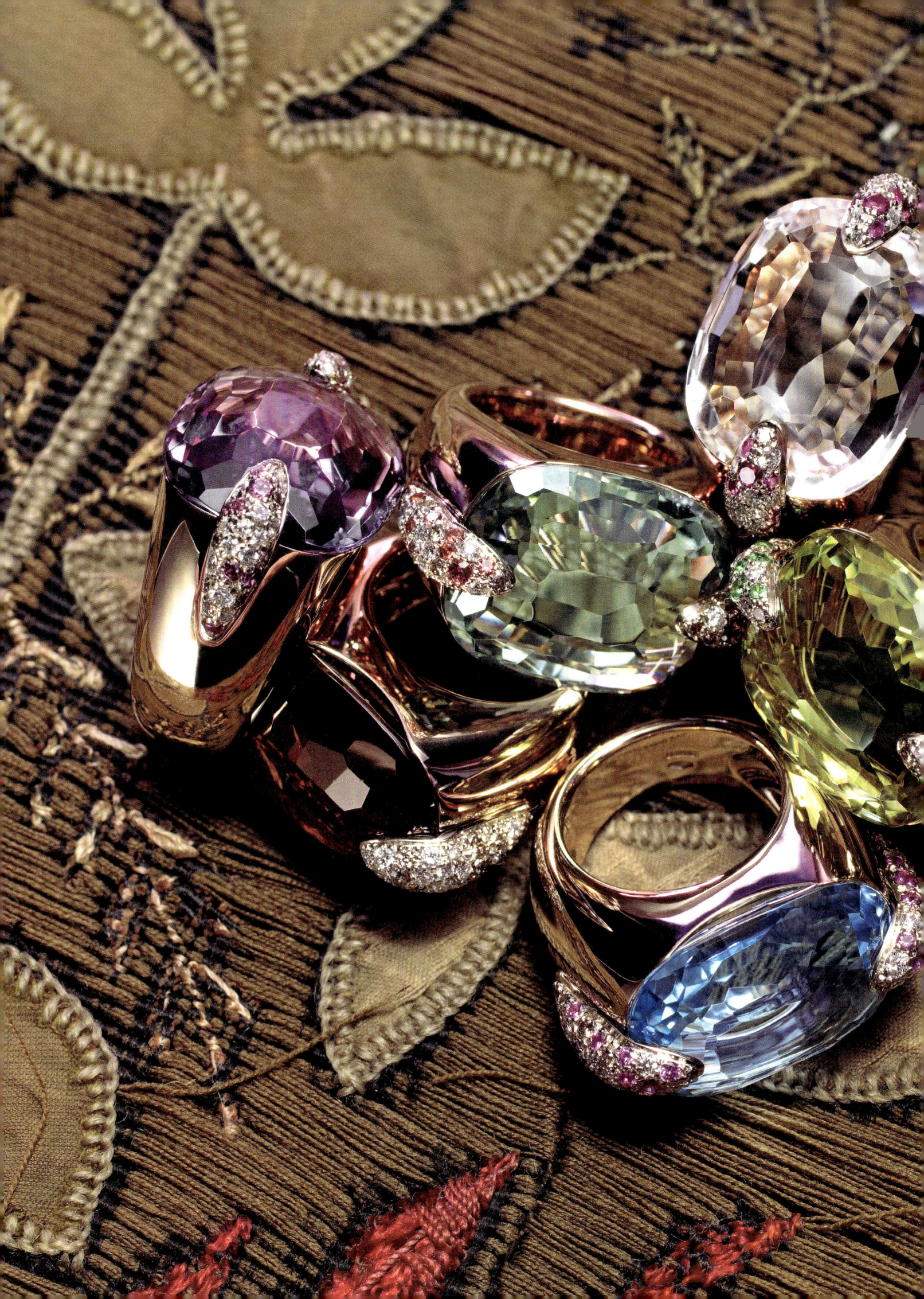

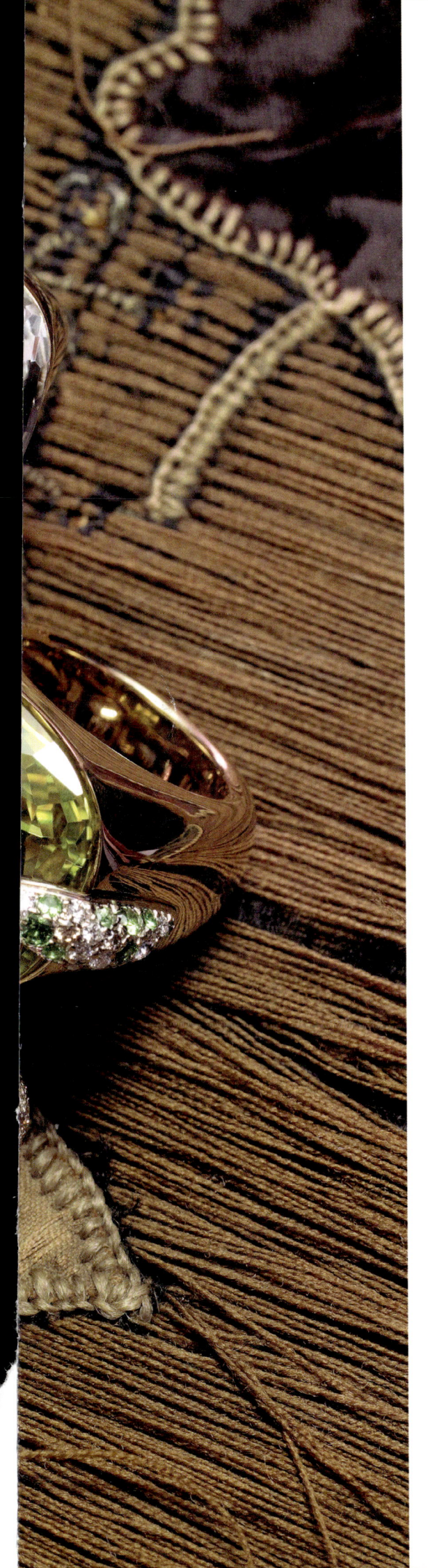

OPPOSITE: In the *Pin Up* collection, sinuous shapes emphasize bold transparent stones

FOLLOWING SPREAD: Someone in a crowd of hippies blows a giant bubble, which reflects the view of the crowd during a love-in at San Francisco's Golden Gate Park, Ted Streshinsky, 1967

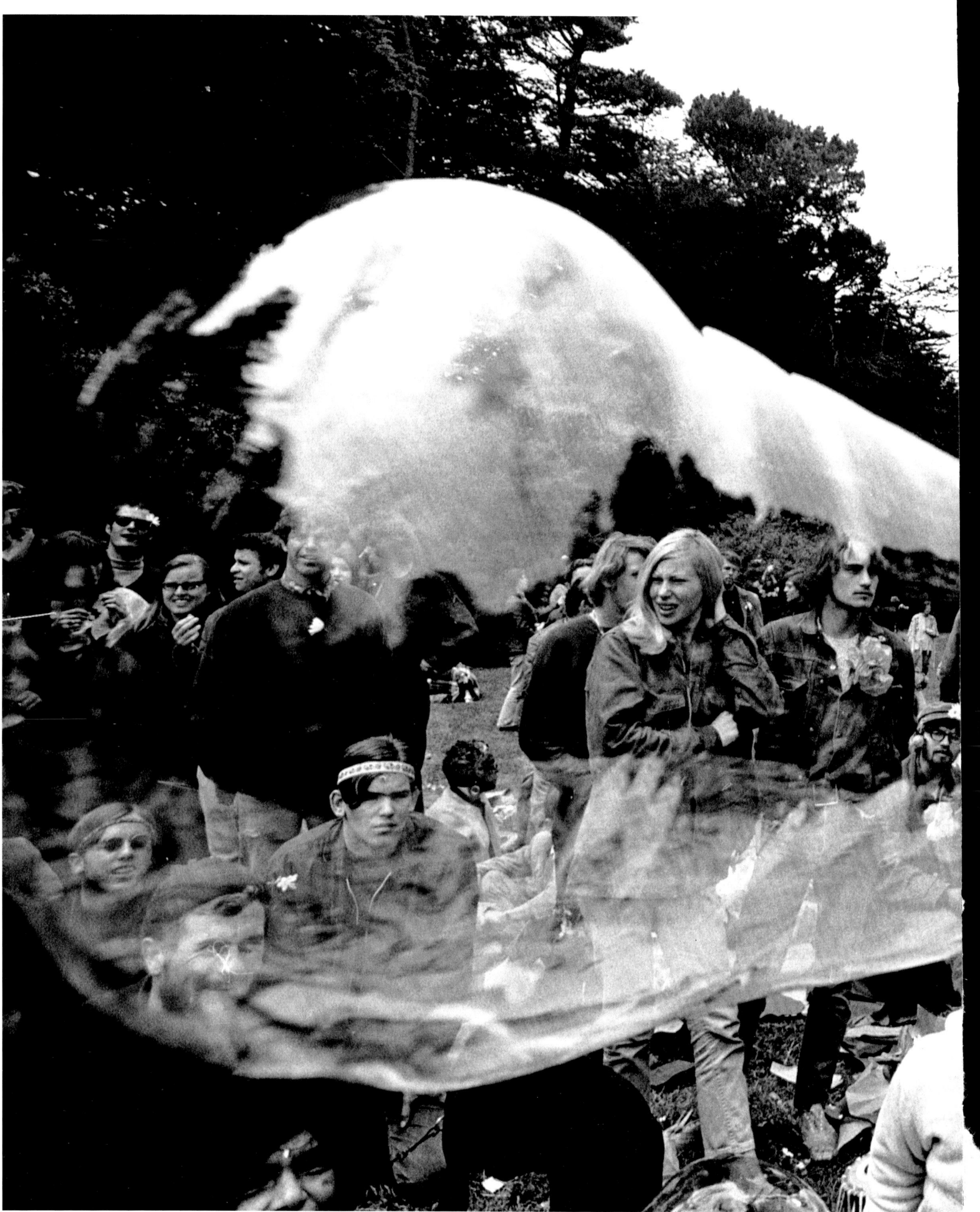

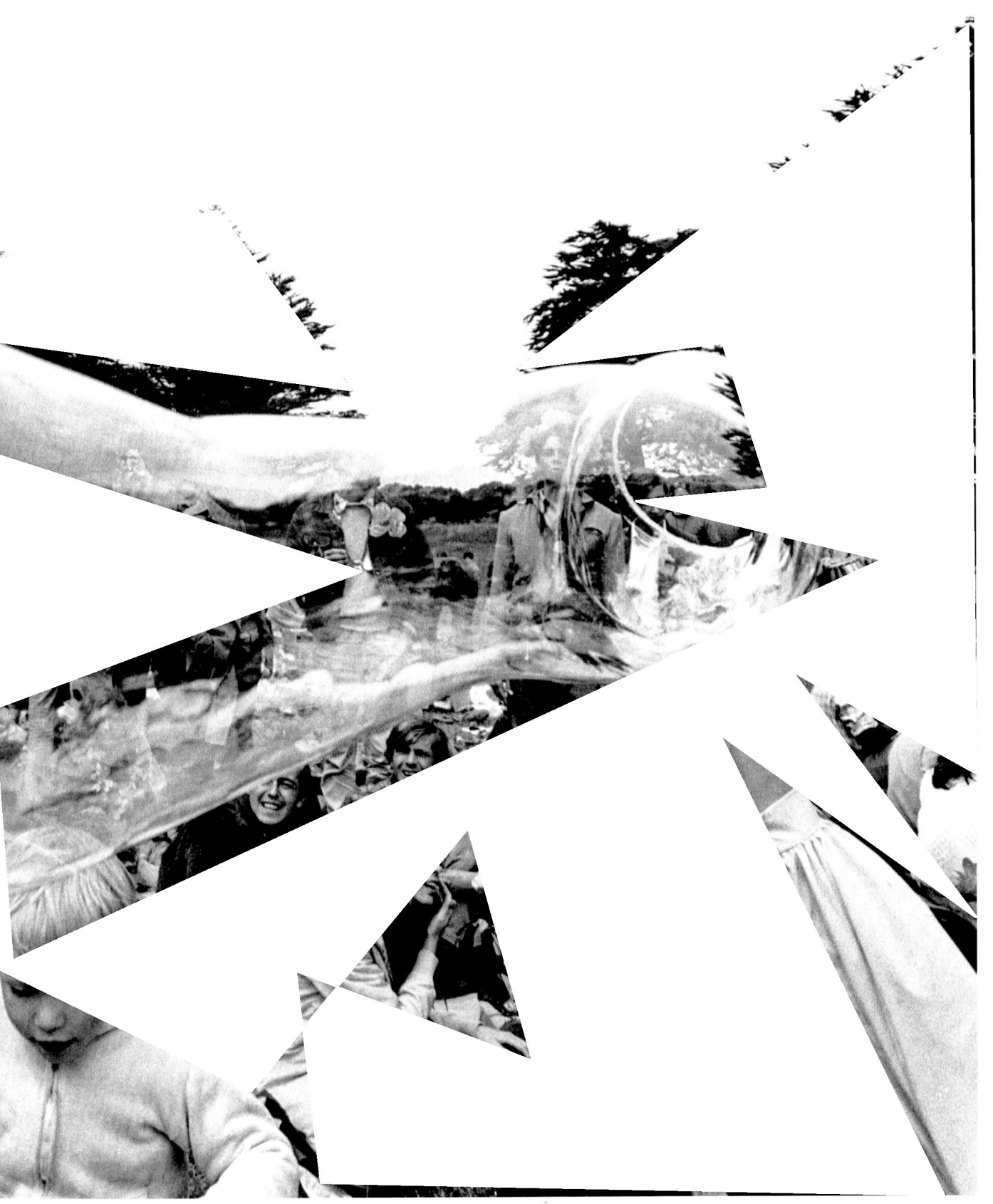

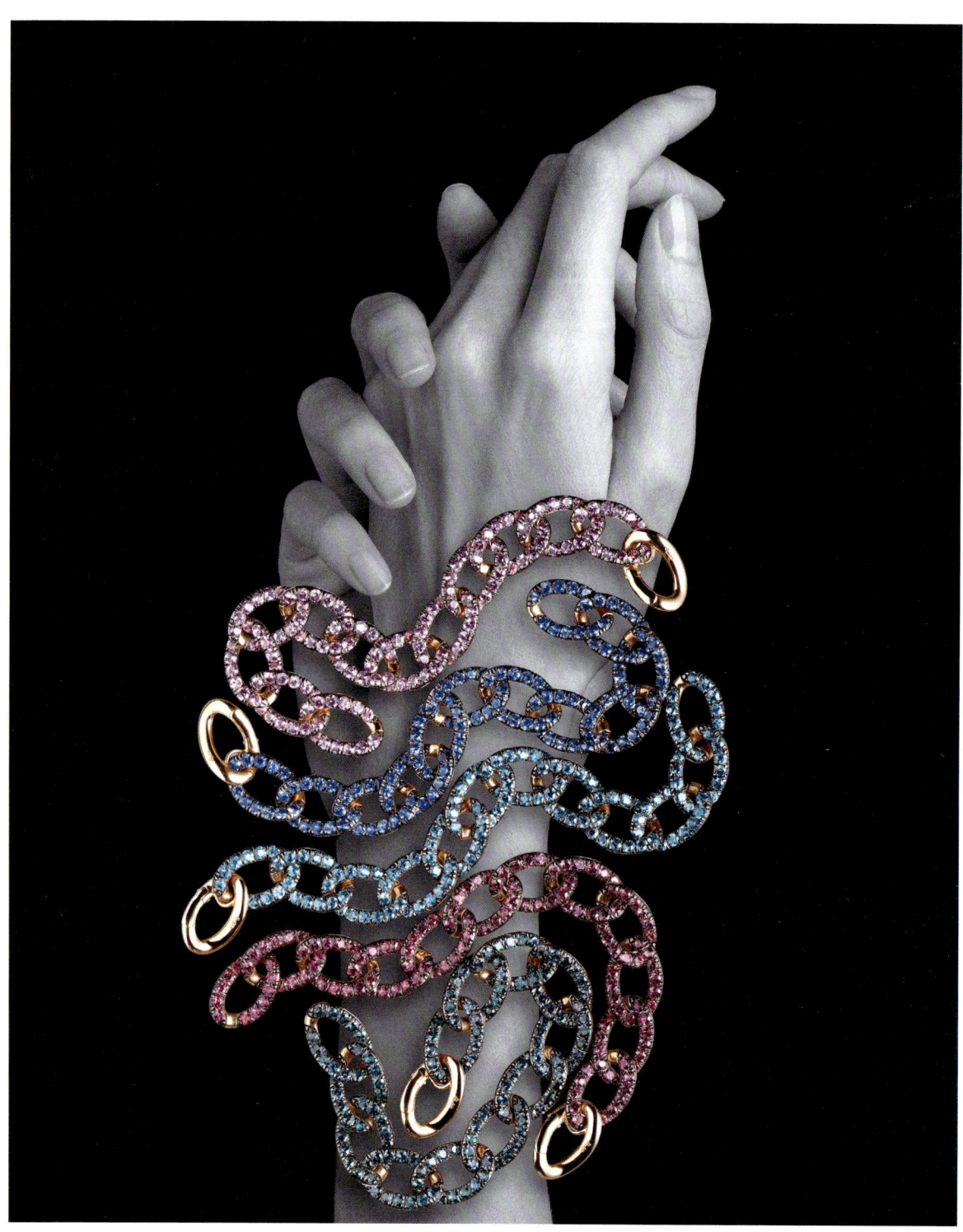

ABOVE: The vibrant colors of *Tango* bracelets

OPPOSITE: Belted gray jacket over a plaid dirndl, David McCabe, 1967

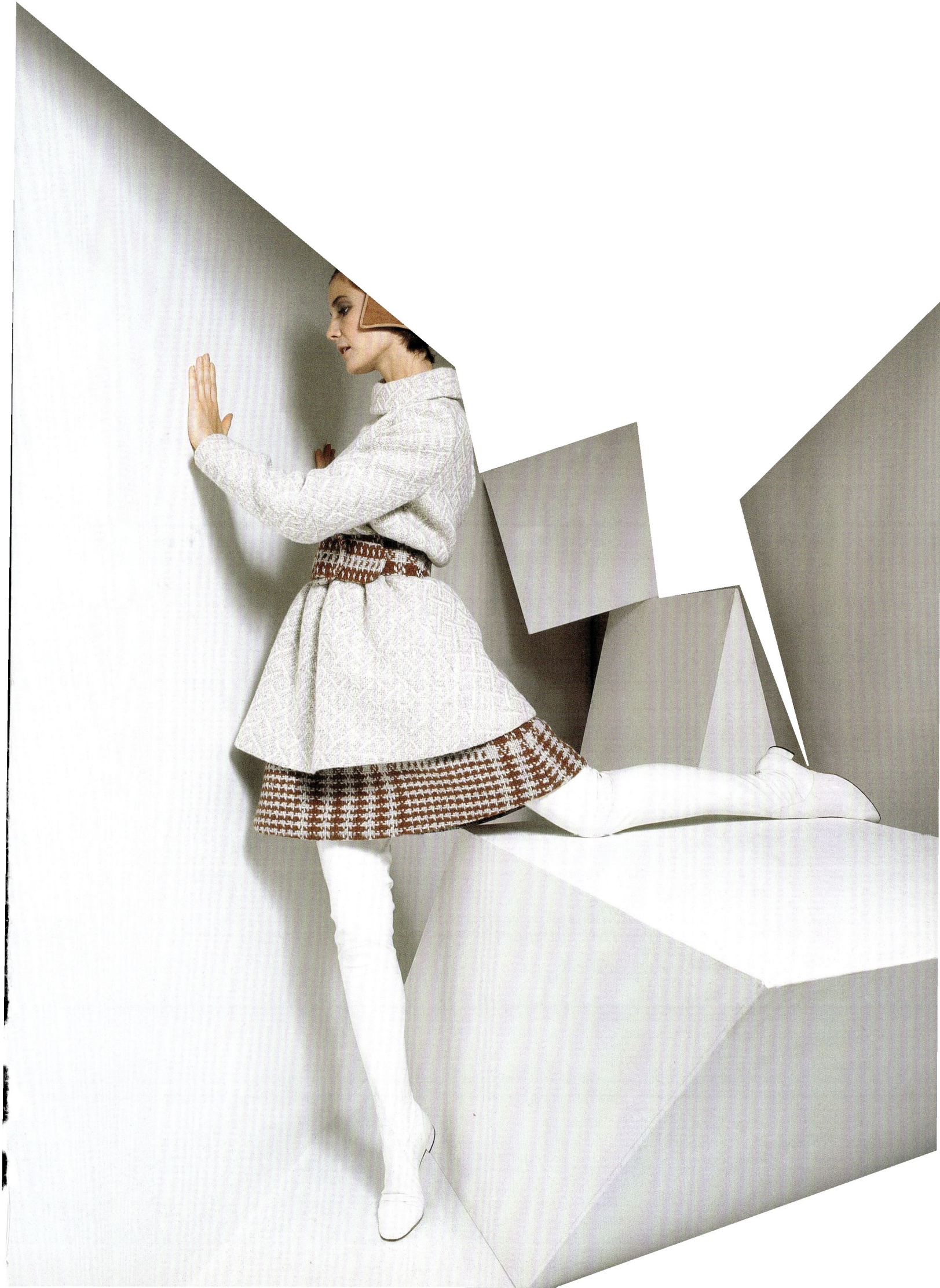

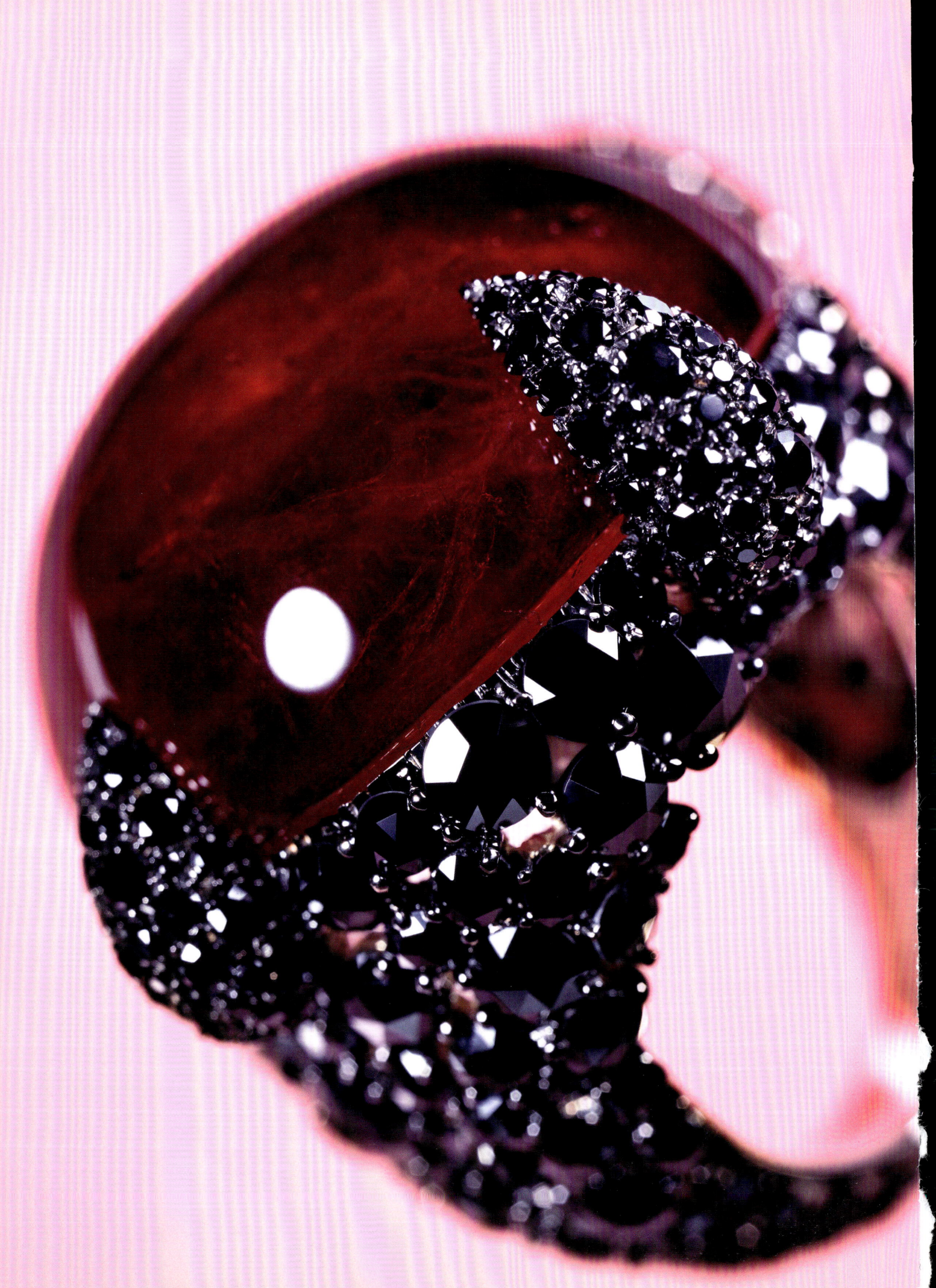

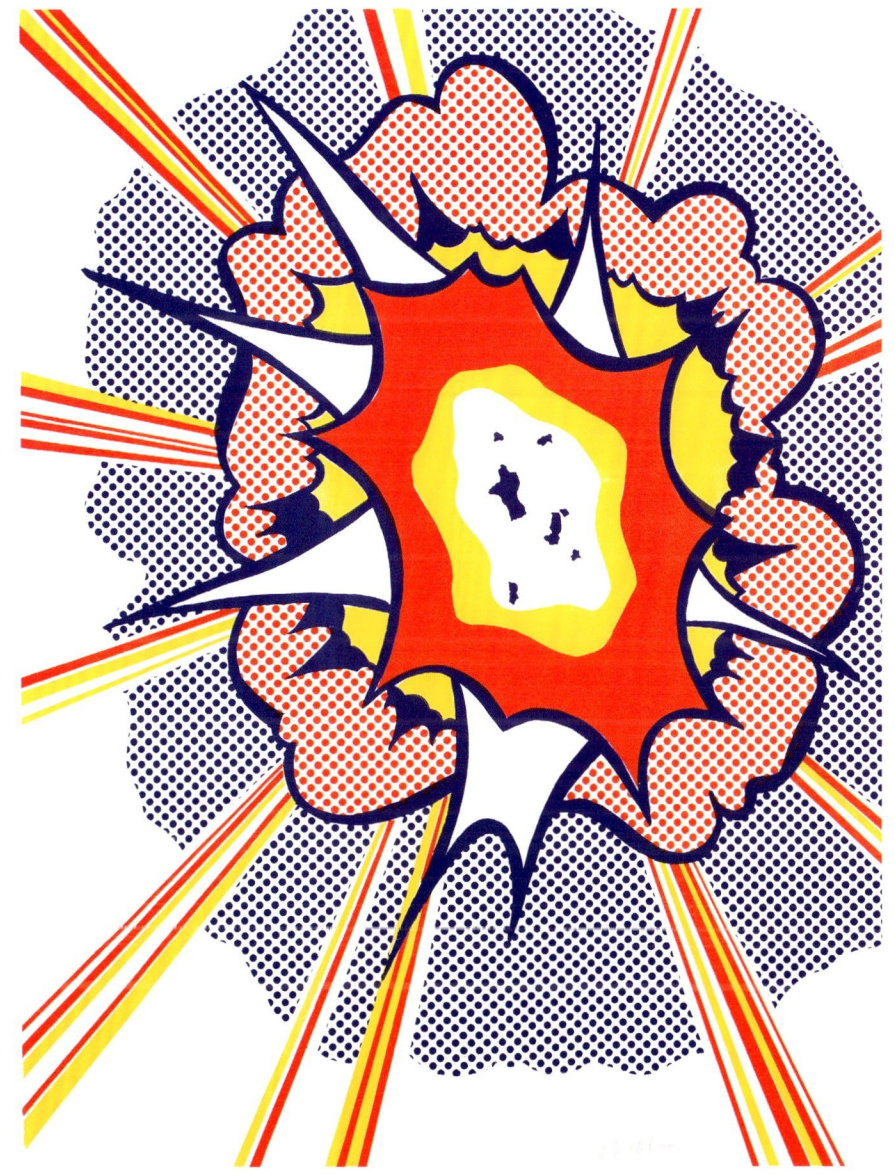

OPPOSITE: *Pom Pom* unique ring in red tourmaline and black diamonds

ABOVE: *Explosion* by Roy Lichtenstein, 1967

OPPOSITE: Gian Paolo Barbieri, *Le Mappe del Desiderio*, 1989

FOLLOWING SPREAD: *Arabesque* collection in matte rose gold
featuring precious transparent stones

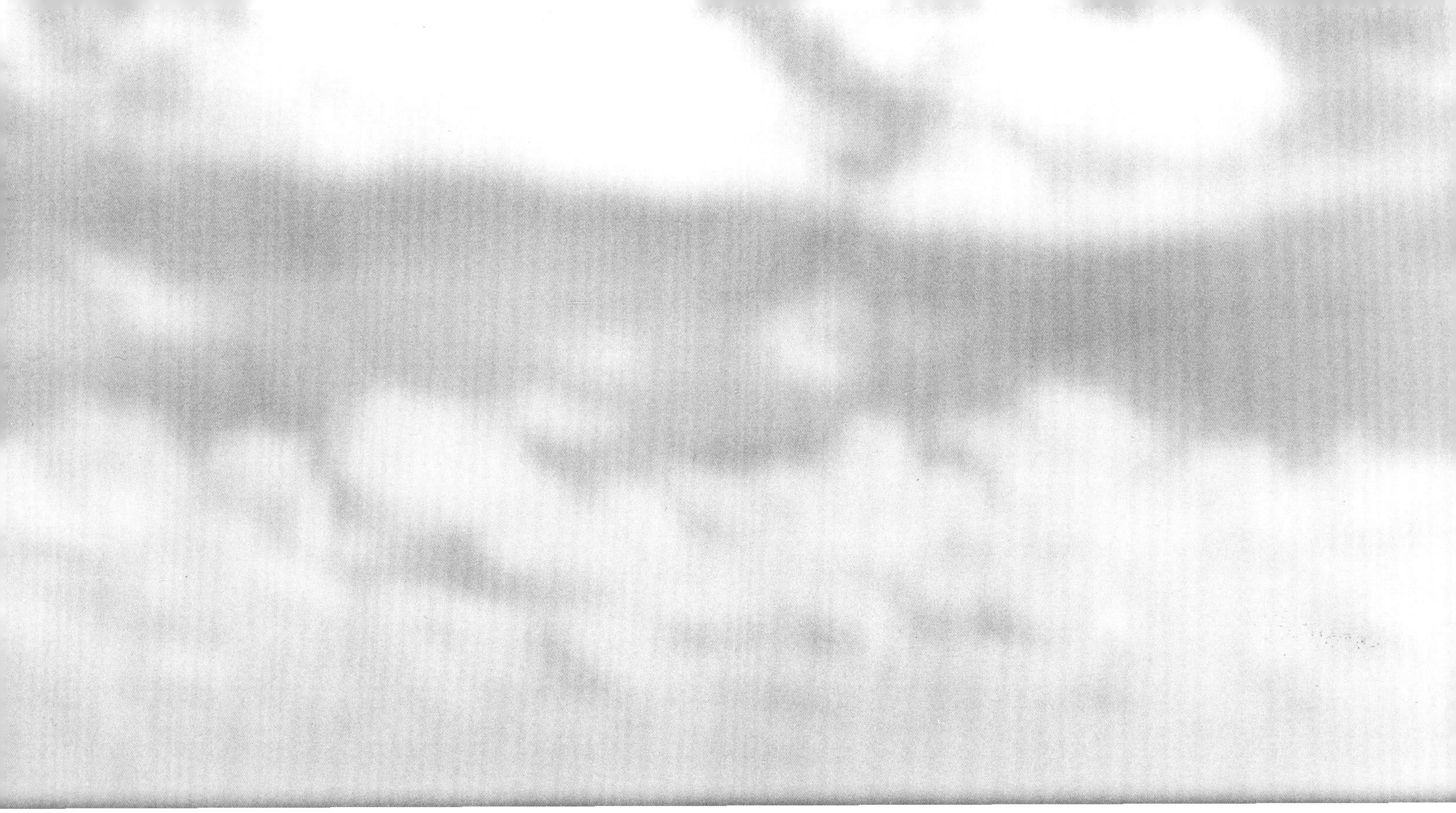

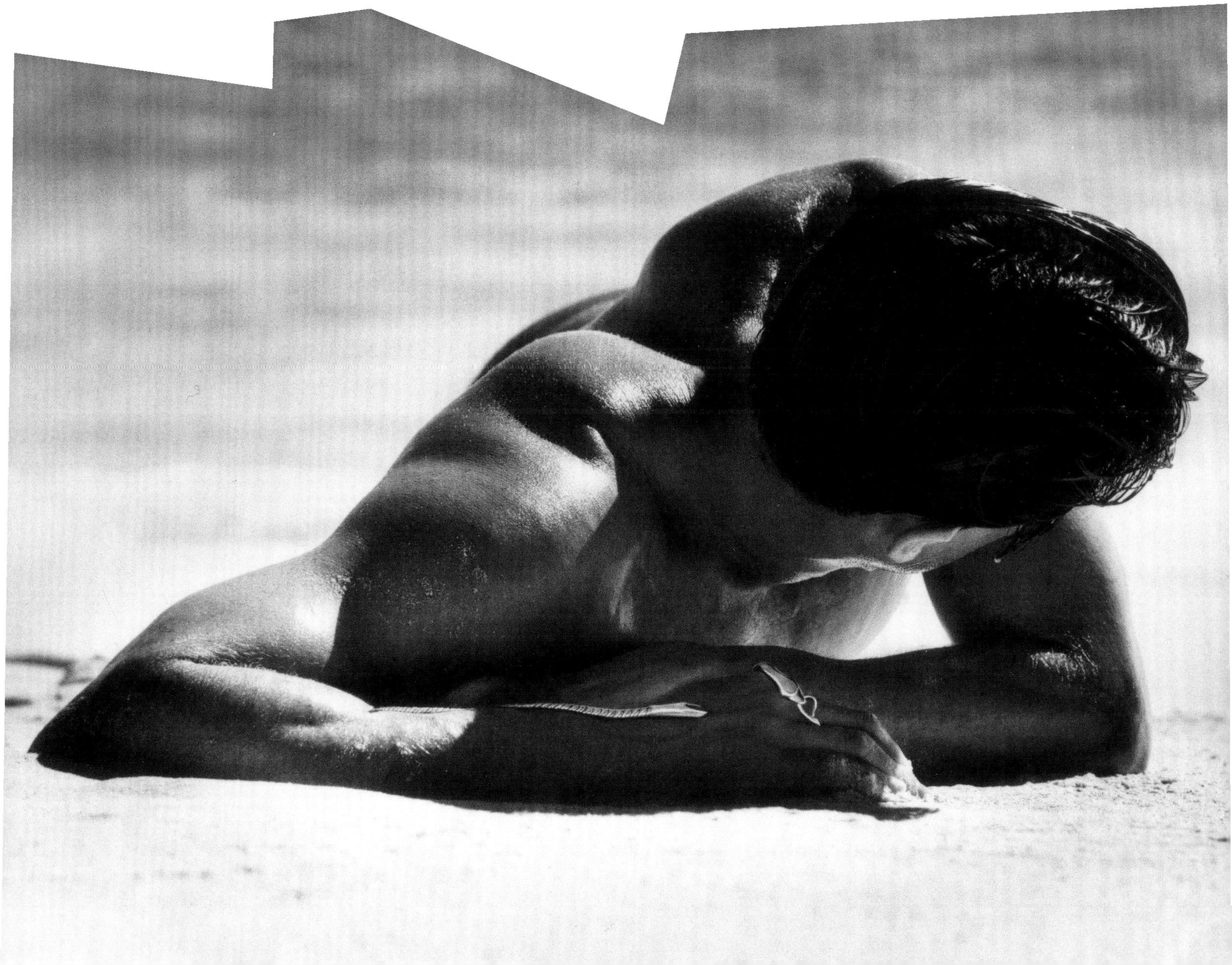

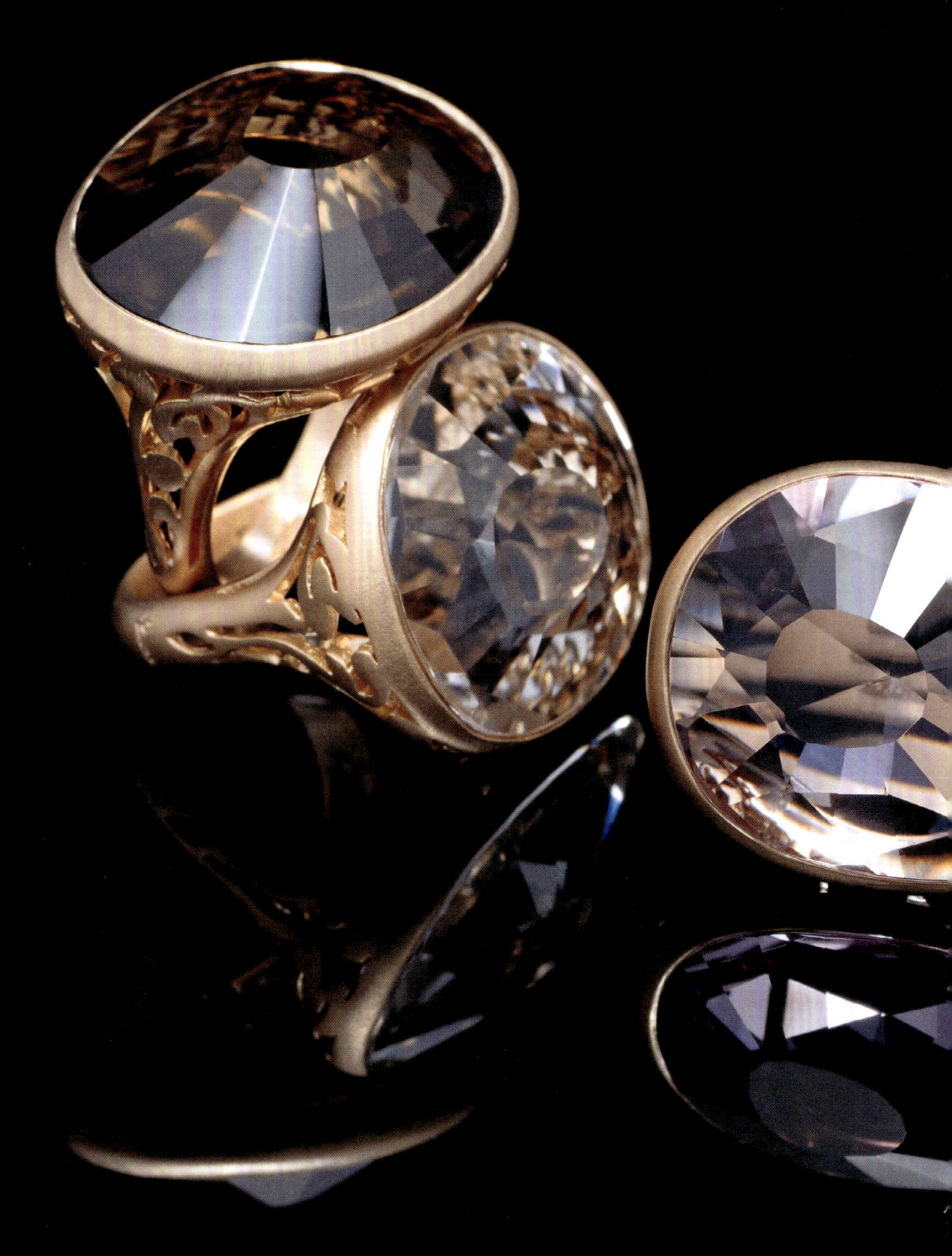

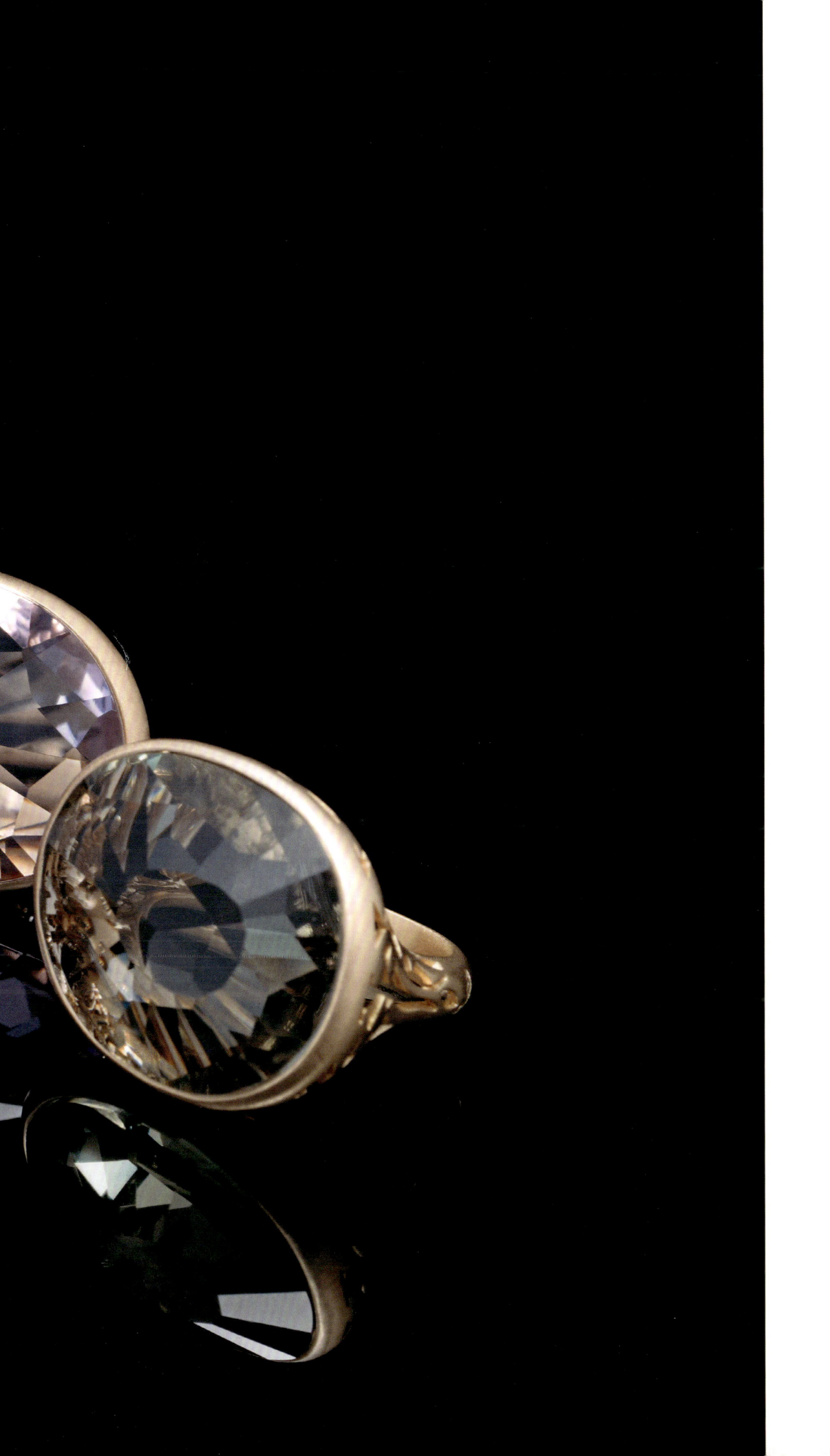

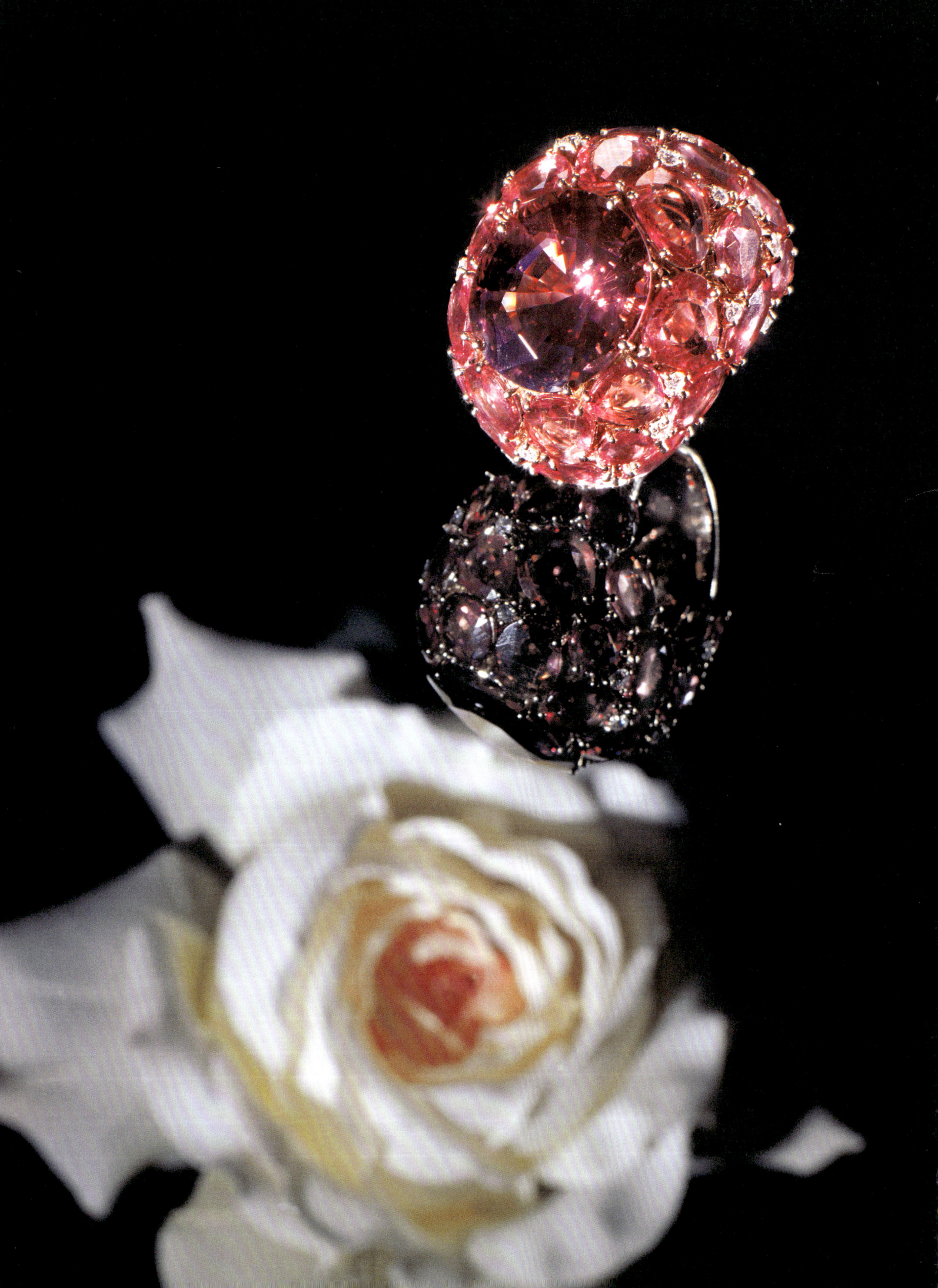

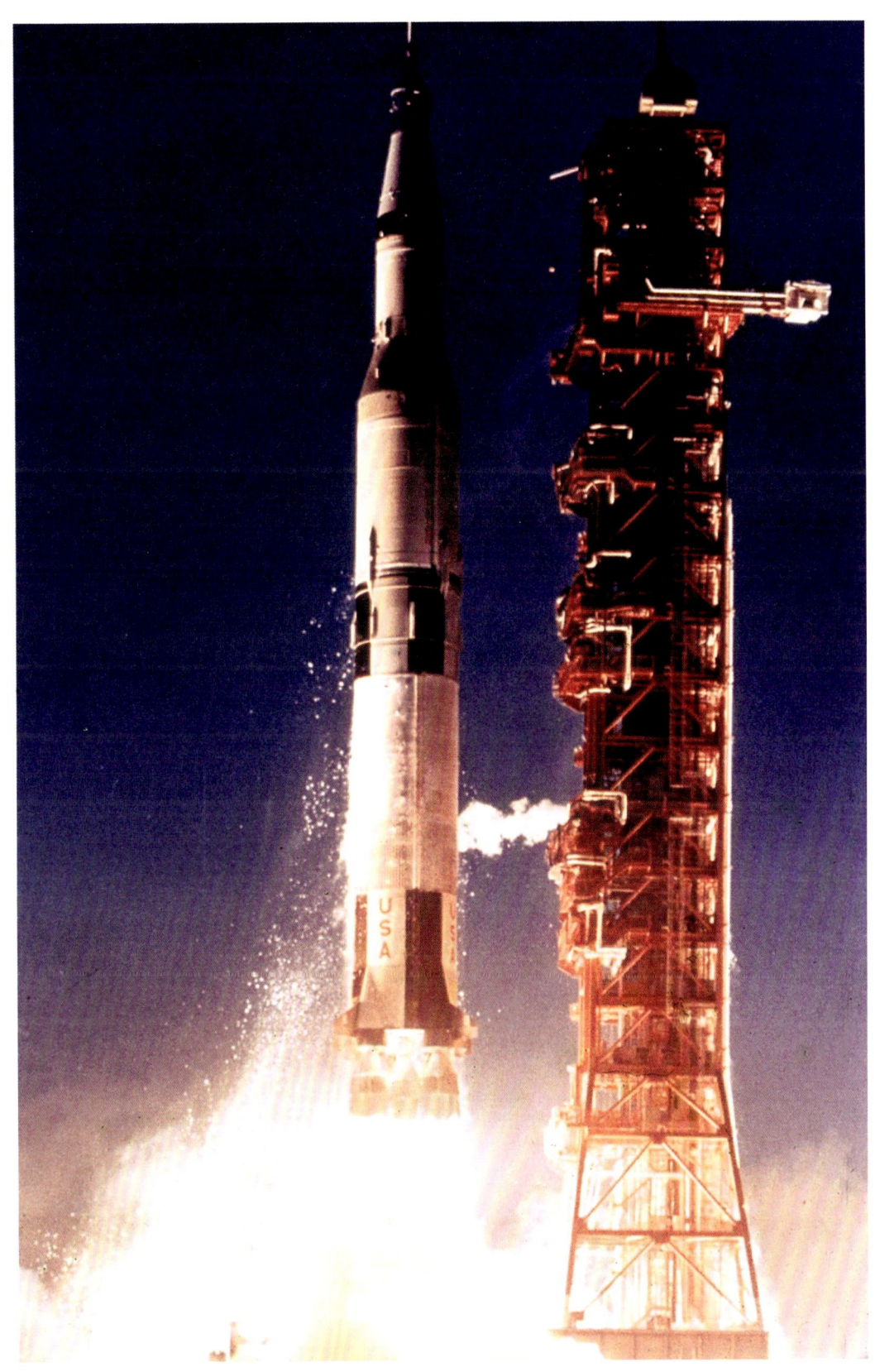

OPPOSITE: Pretty in pink: *Pom Pom* ring with spinel, rhodolites, and diamonds

ABOVE: Launch of the Apollo 4 unmanned spacecraft from Launch Complex 39 at the John F. Kennedy Space Center on Merritt Island, Florida, 1967

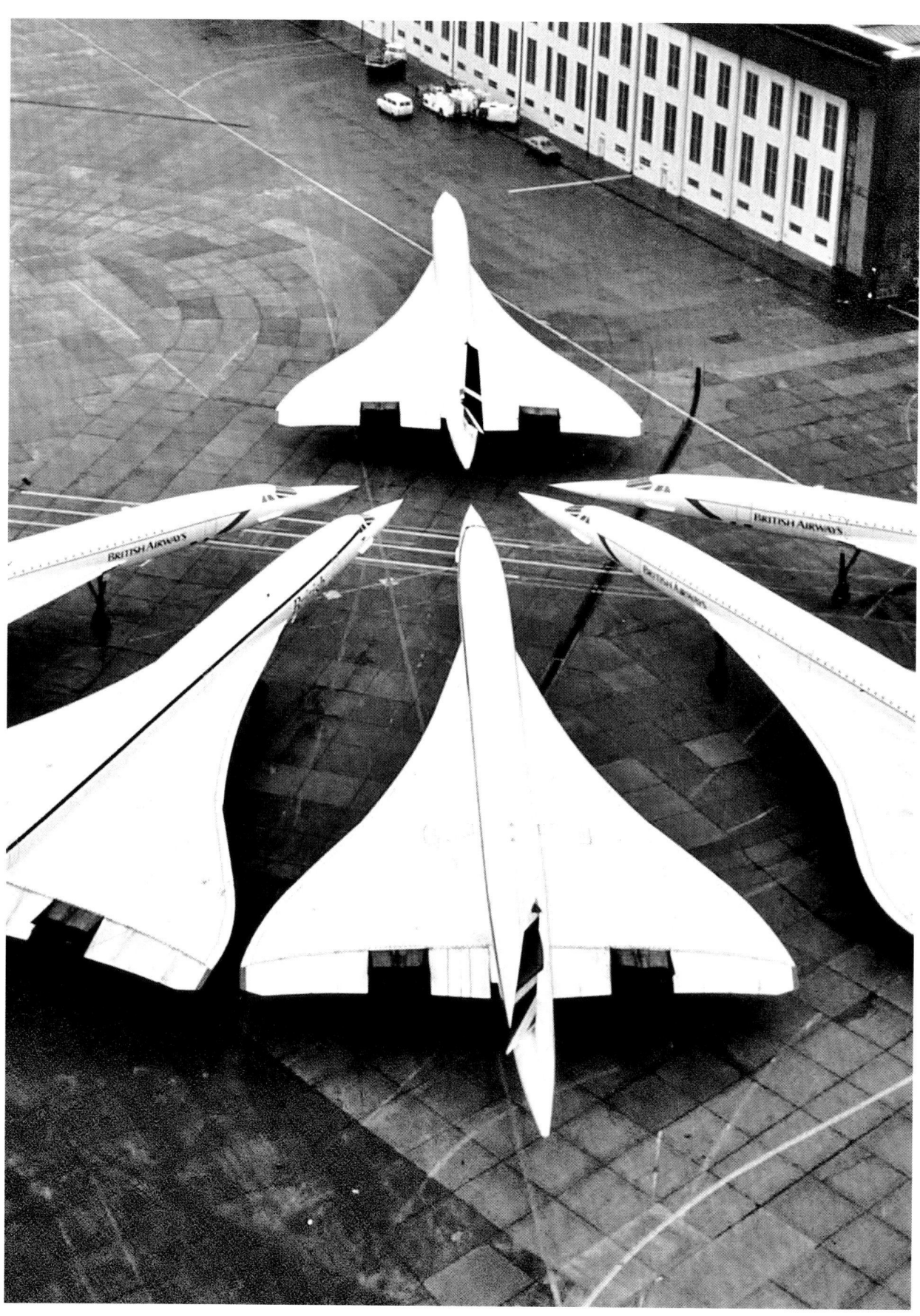

ABOVE: The first prototype of the Concorde was
rolled out in Toulouse, France, in 1967

OPPOSITE: Pomellato *Gourmette* chain and bracelets

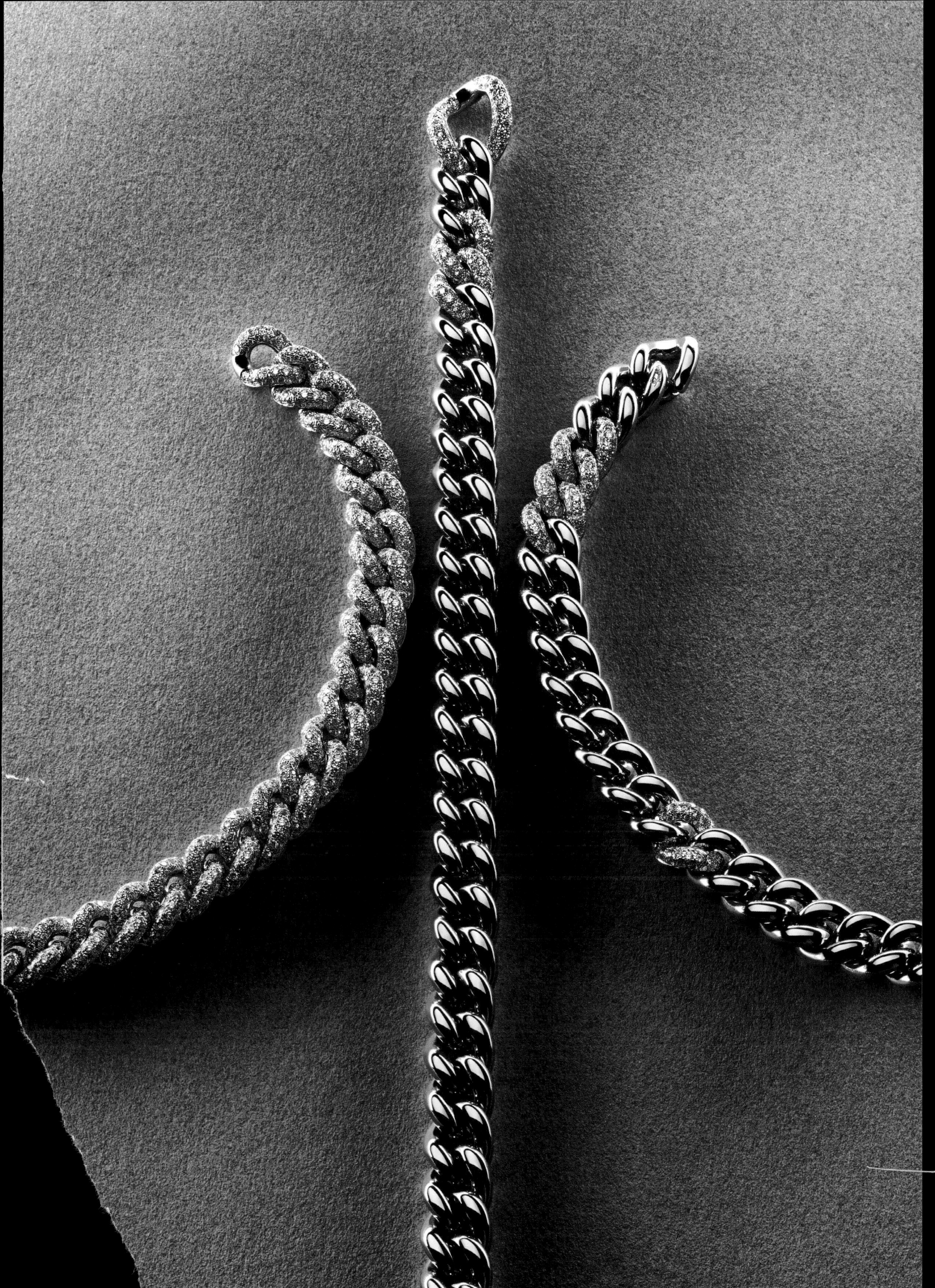

Sabbia collection bracelet mingling wi

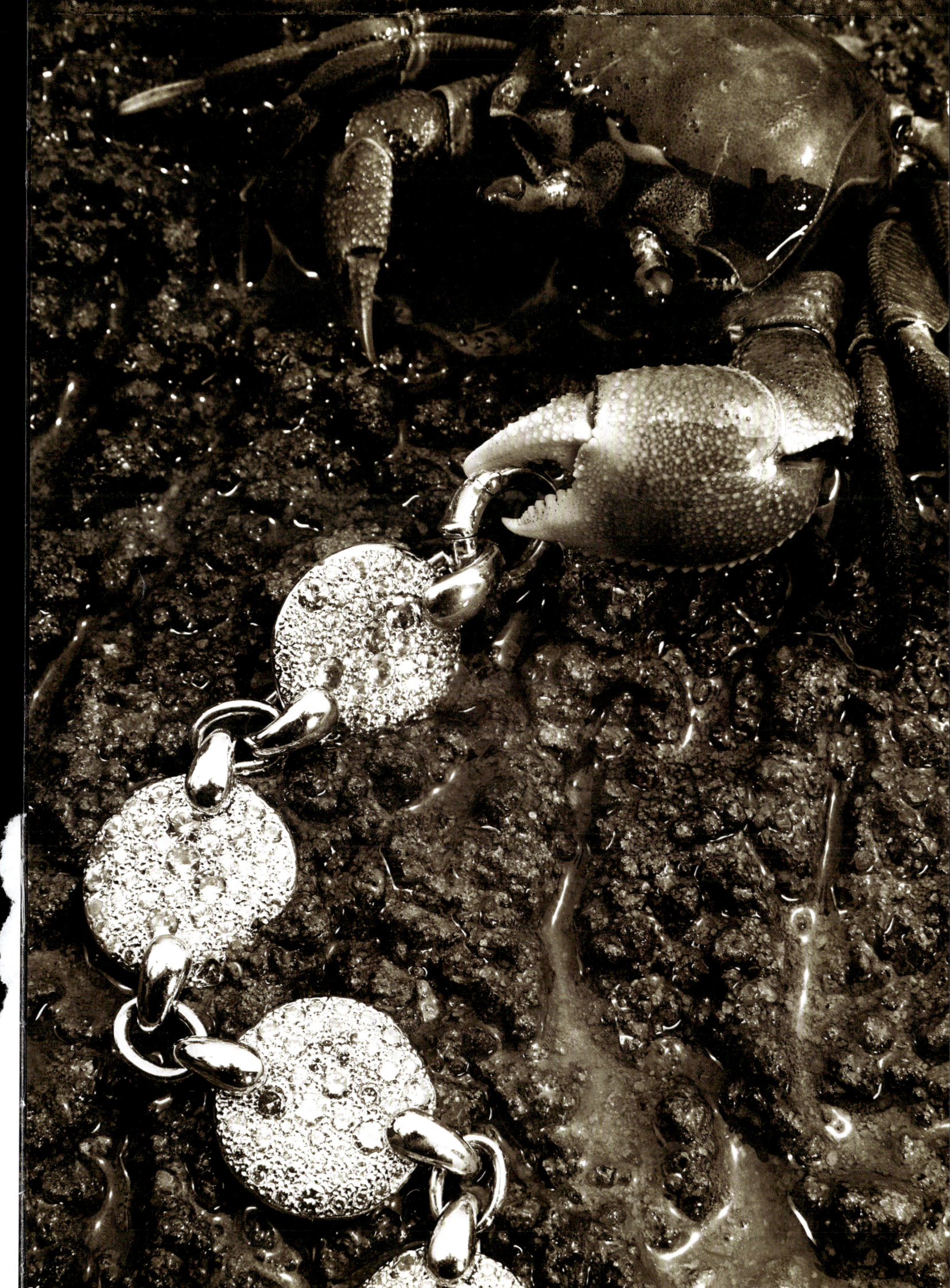

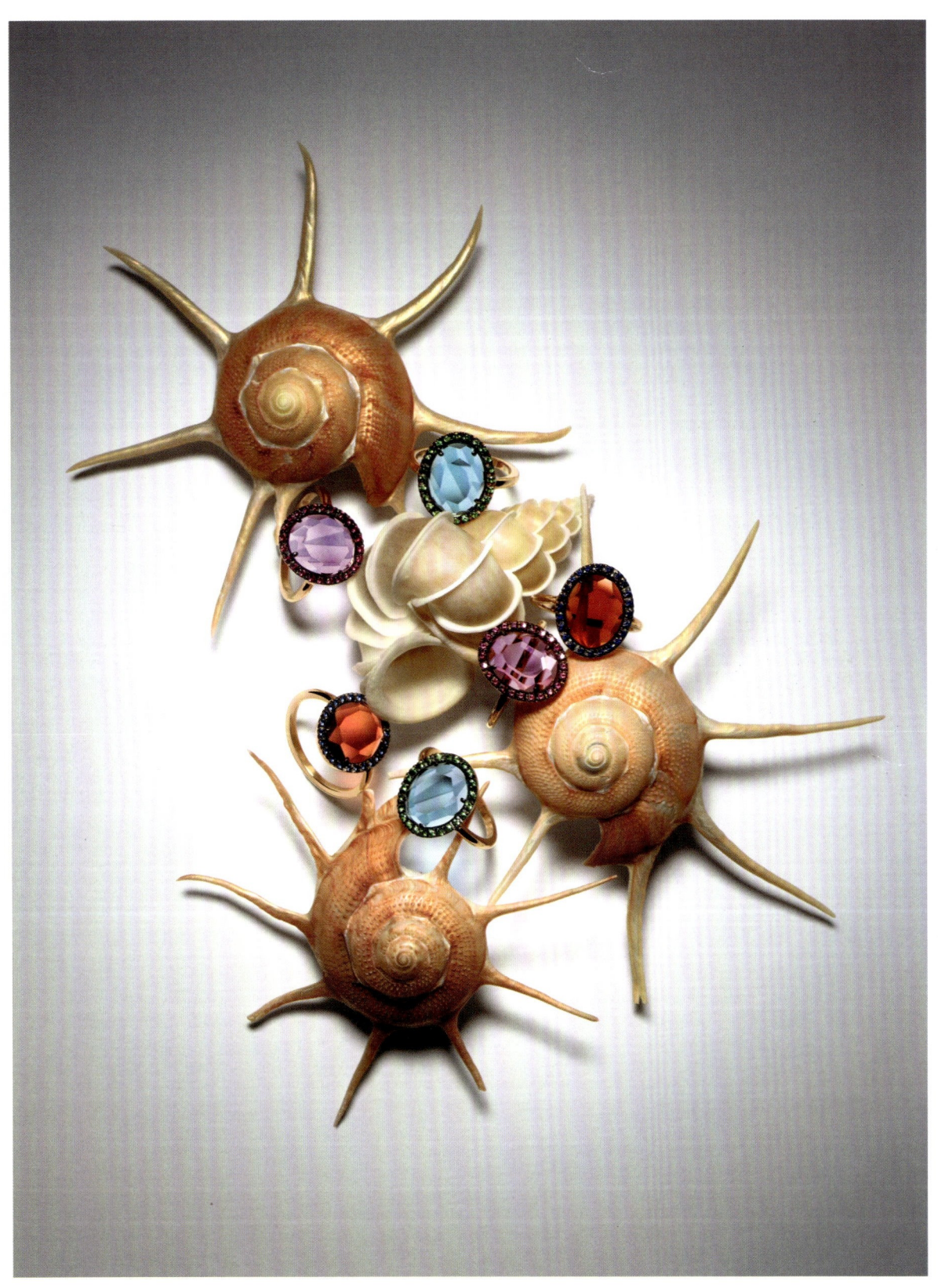

ABOVE: Pomellato *Colpo di Fulmine* collection

OPPOSITE: The colorful touch of the *Tango* collection

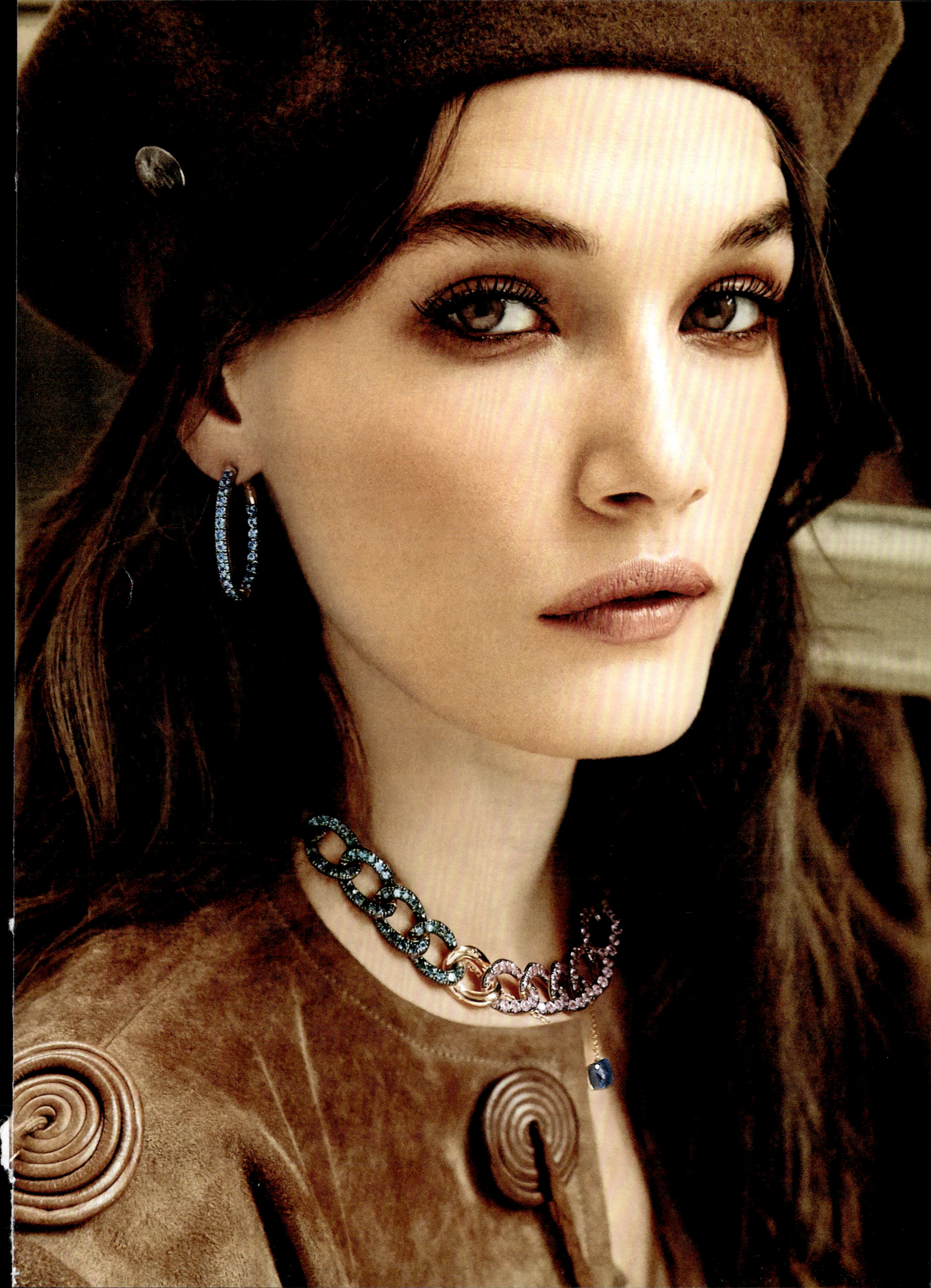

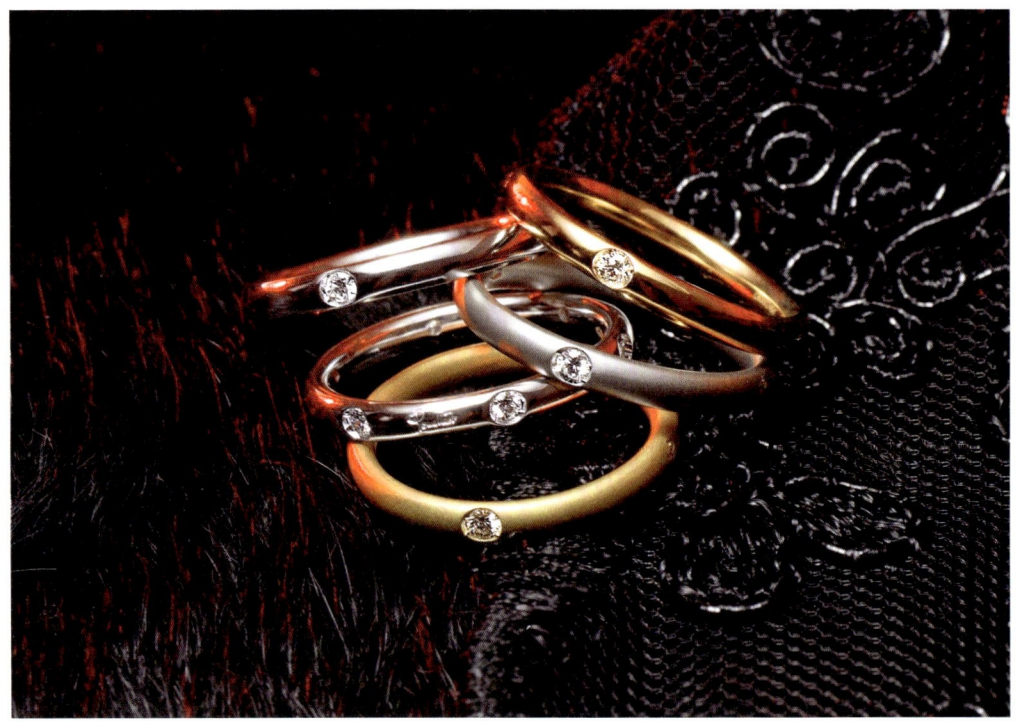

ABOVE: Bright as their namesake: the *Lucciole* rings

OPPOSITE: Portrait by Gian Paolo Barbieri for *Le Mappe del Desiderio*, 1989

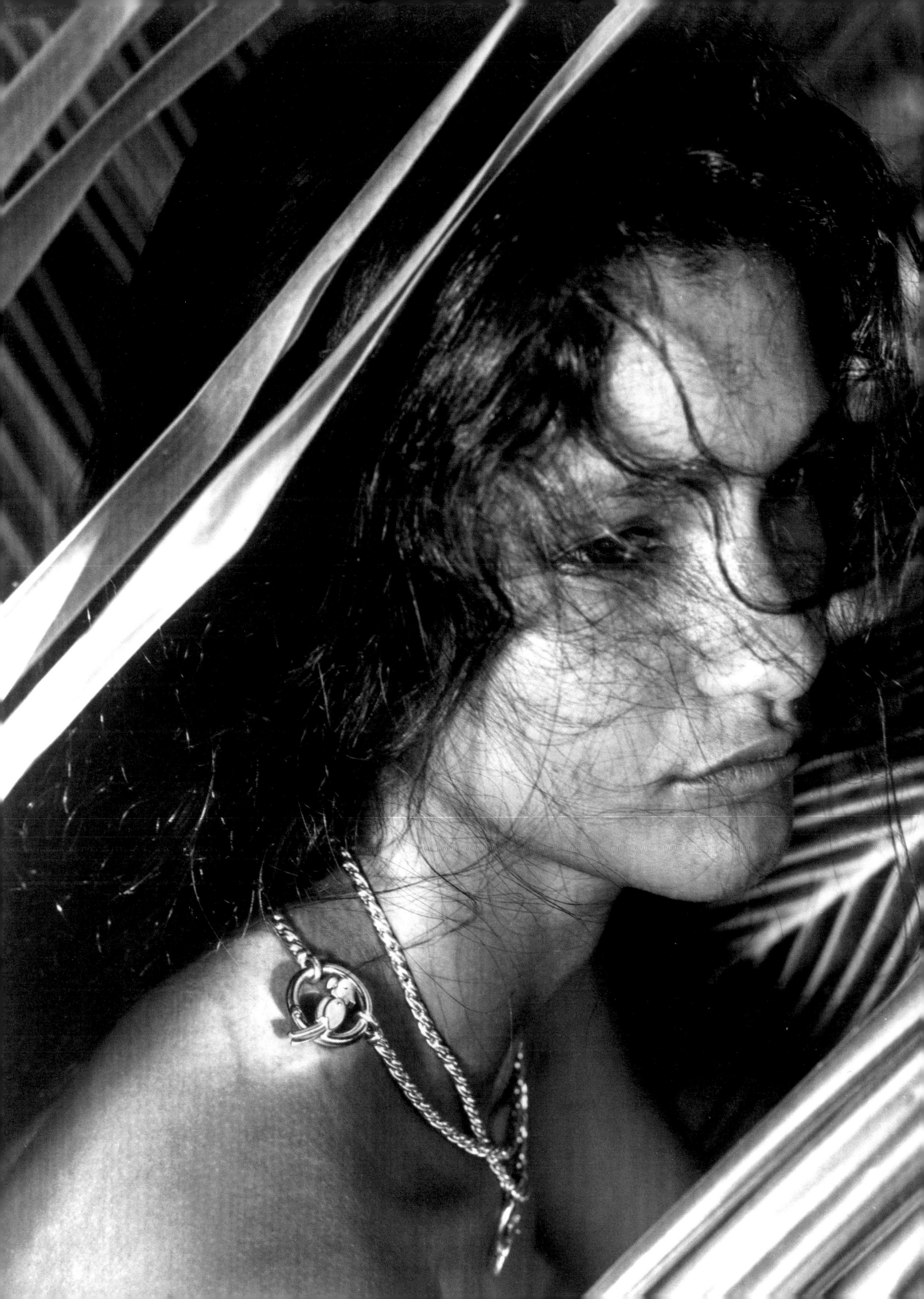

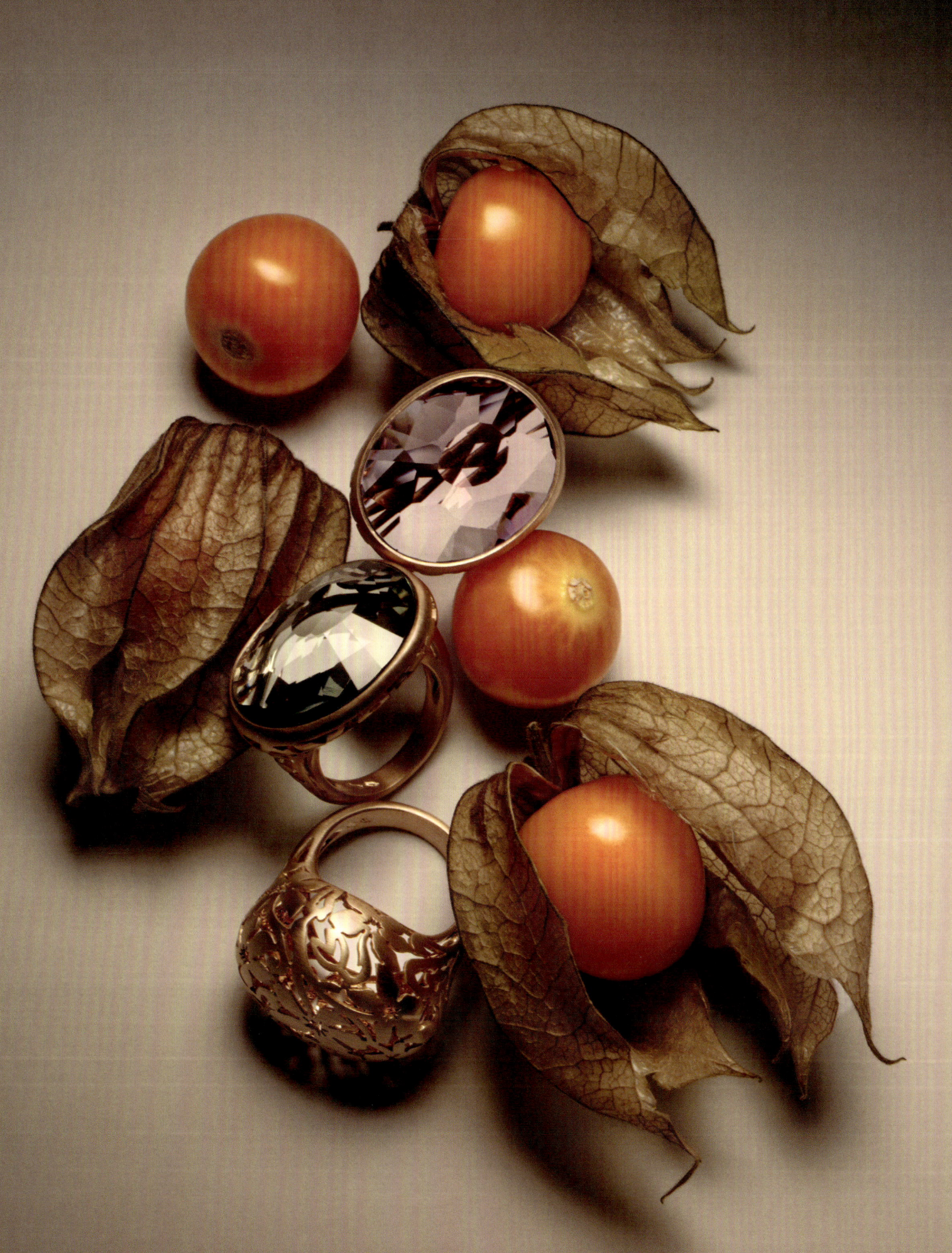

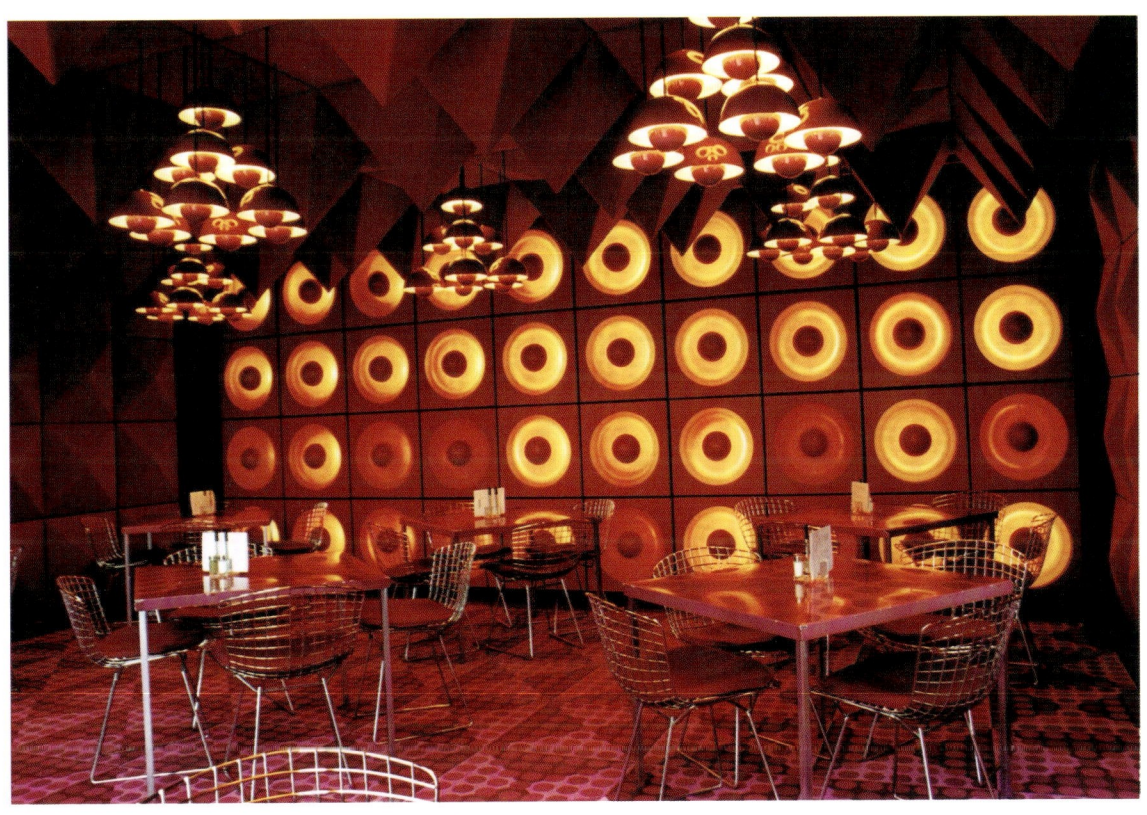

OPPOSITE: *Arabesque* rings by Guido Mocafico

ABOVE: The canteen of *Spiegel* magazine's headquarters in
Hamburg, Germany, designed by Verner Panton in 1969

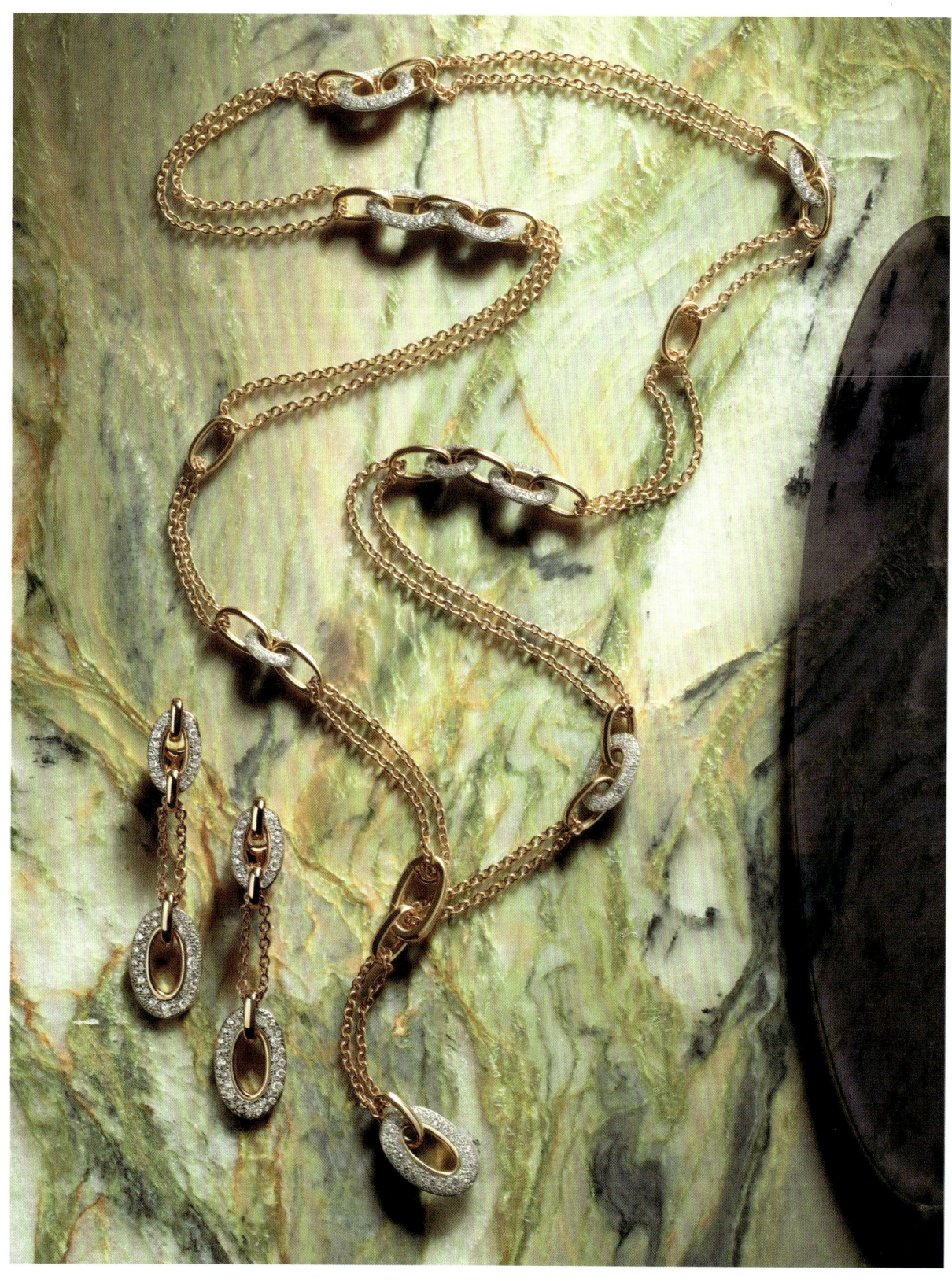

ABOVE AND OPPOSITE: The sophisticated beauty of the *Tango* collection

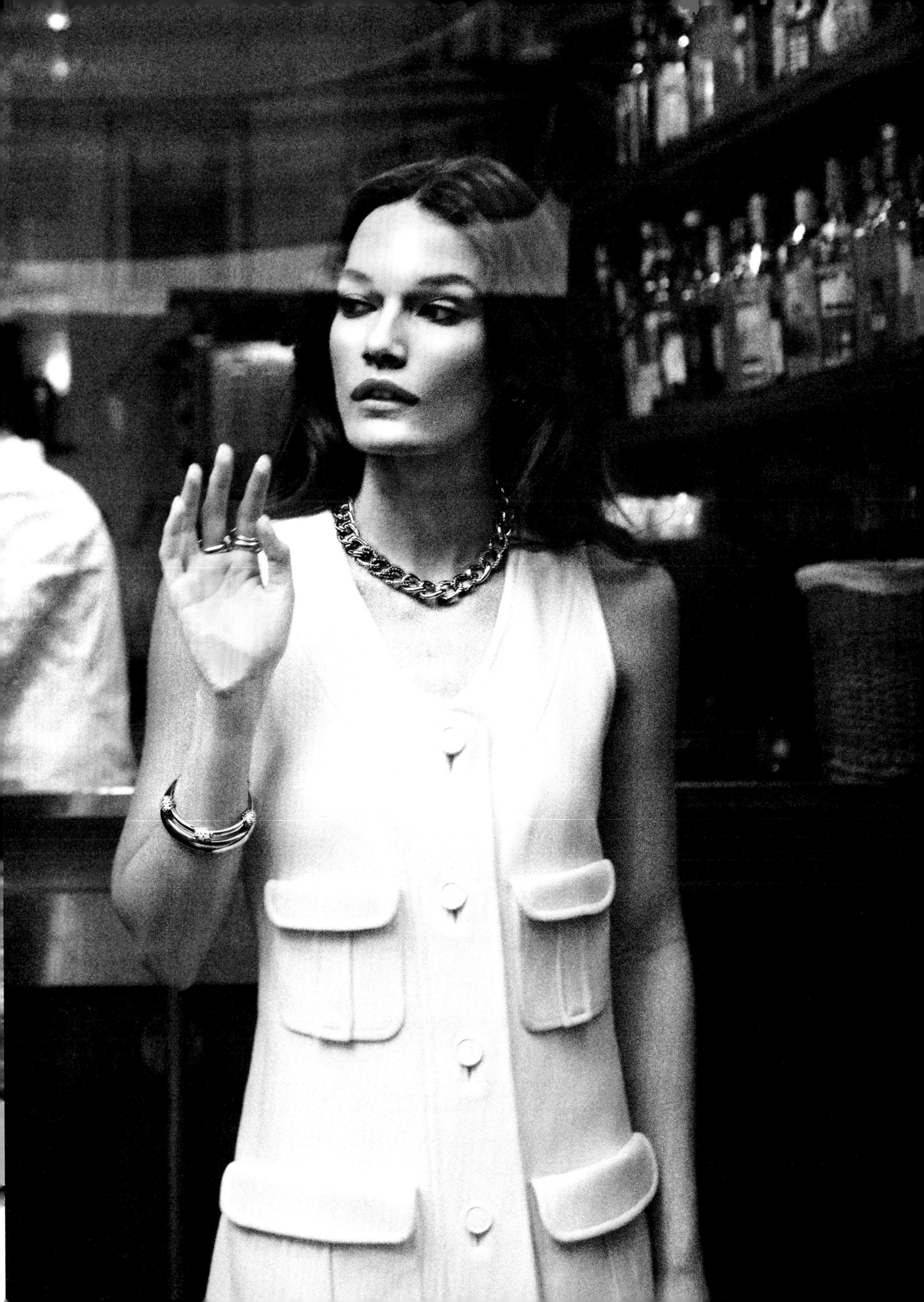

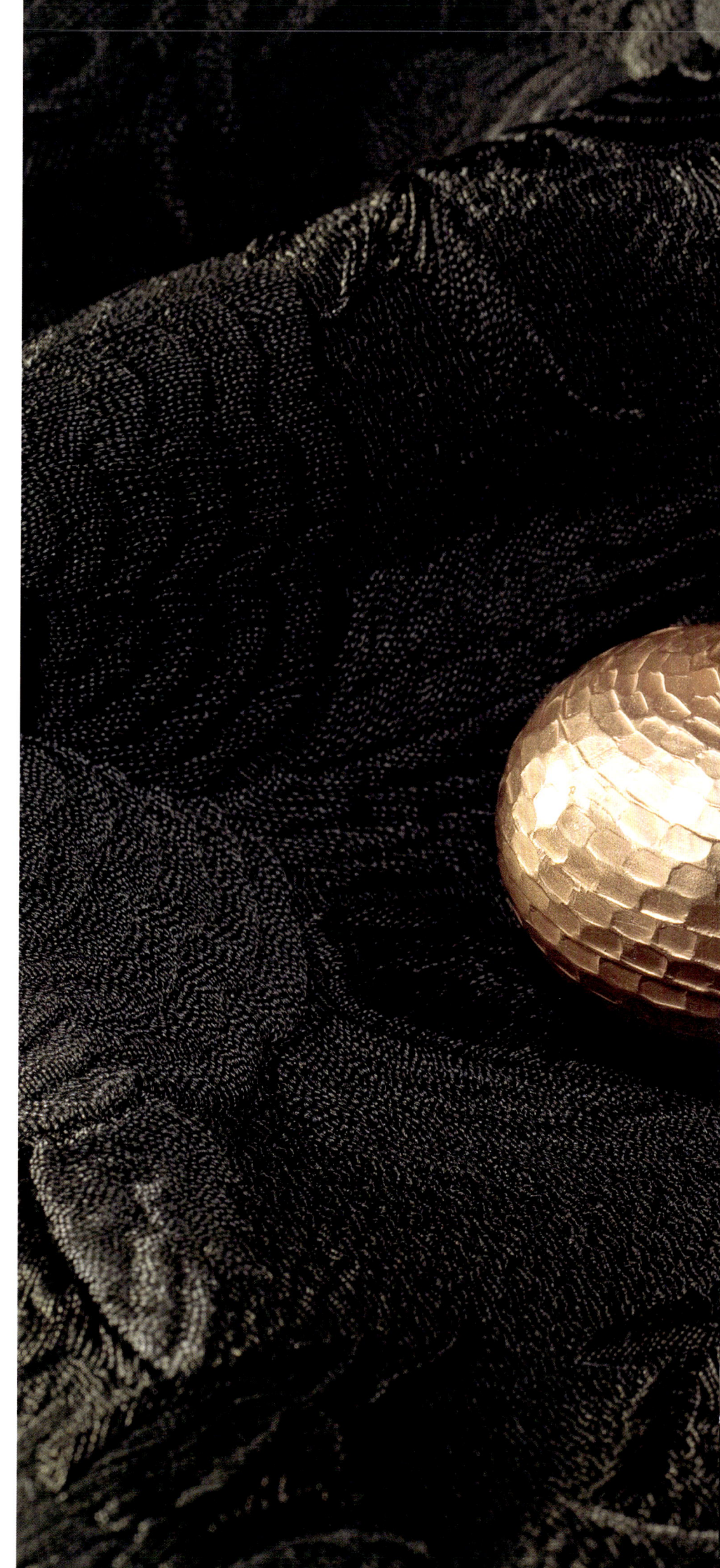

The sinuous volumes of *Duna* collection
rings in rose gold and brown diamonds

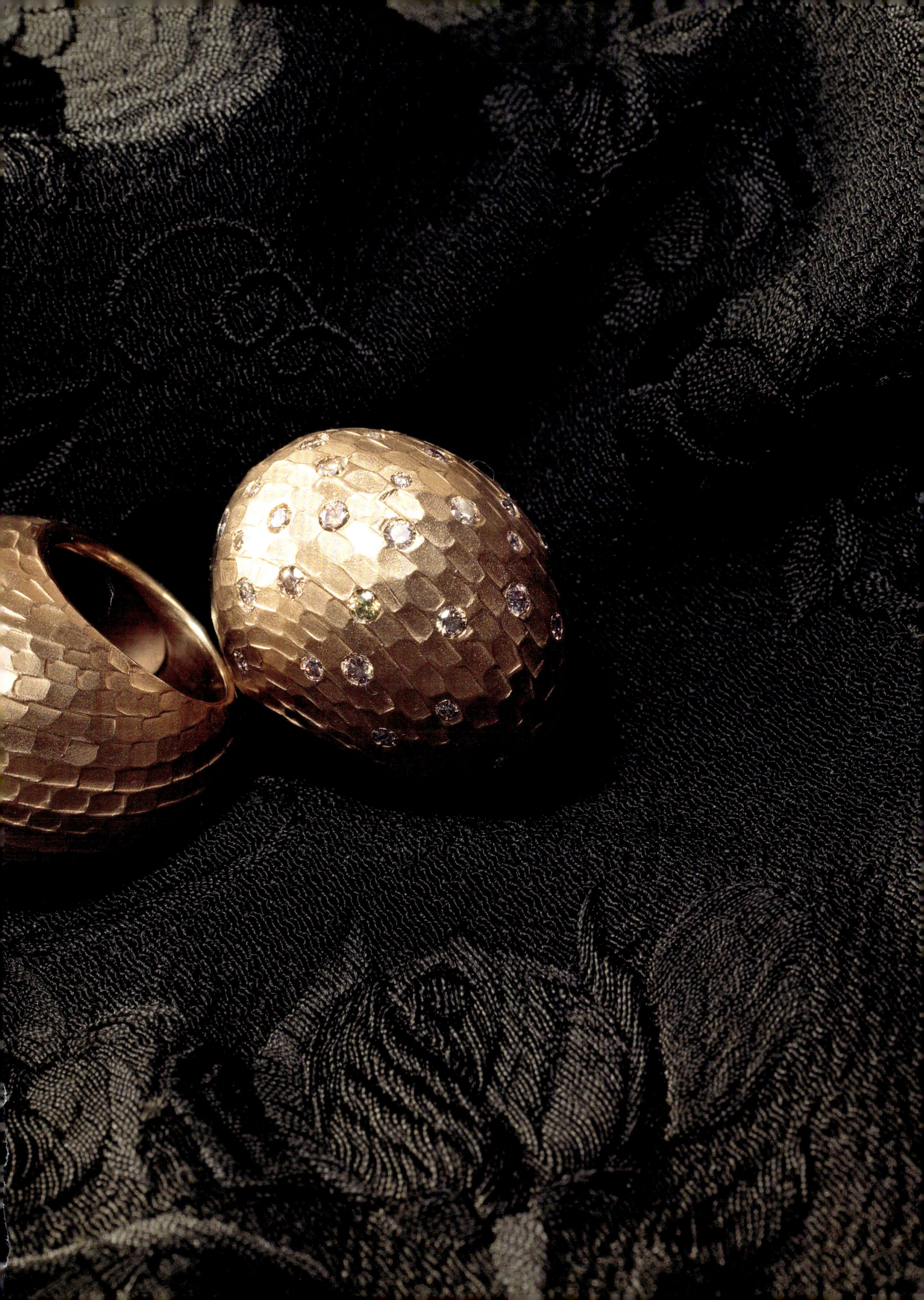

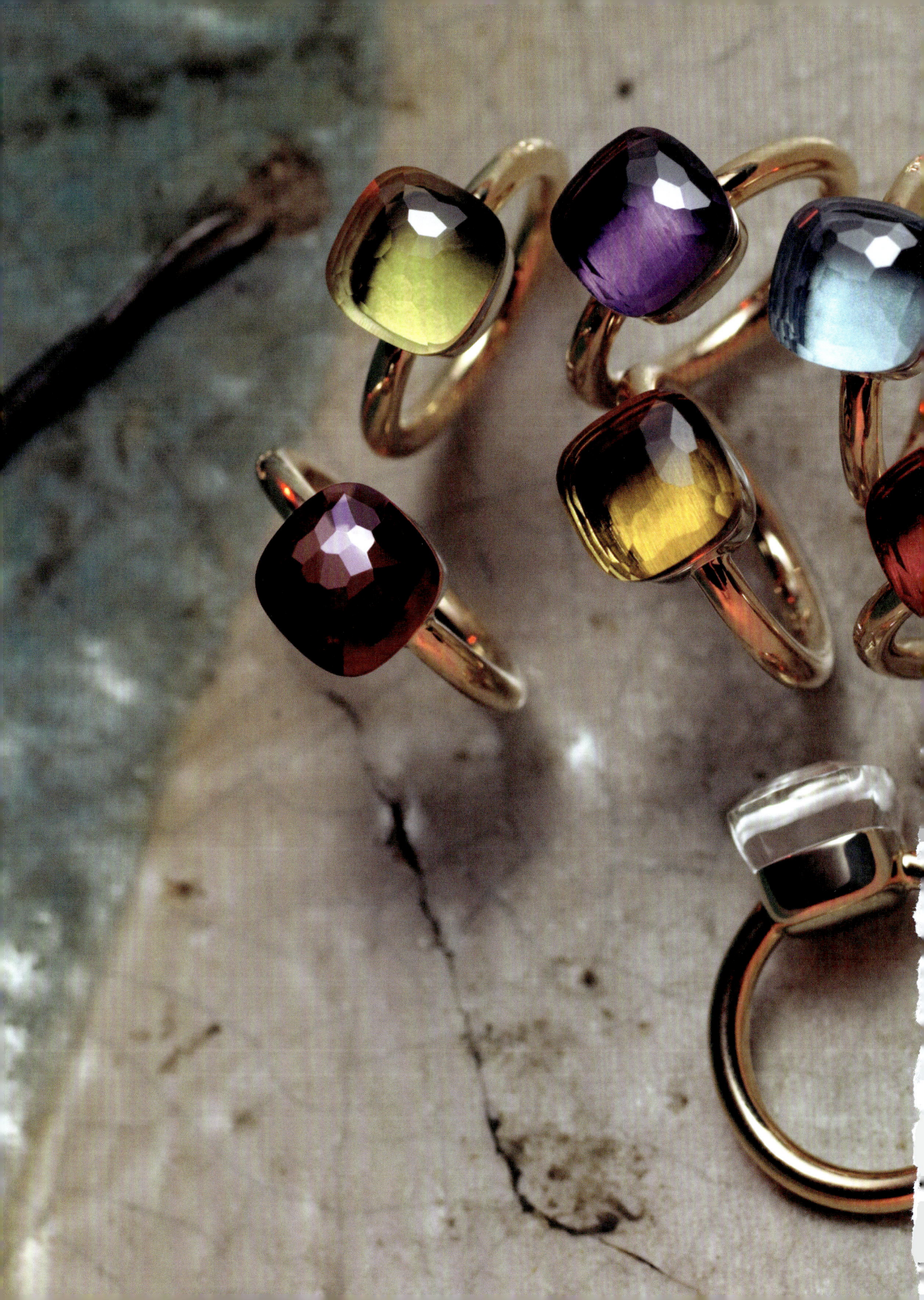

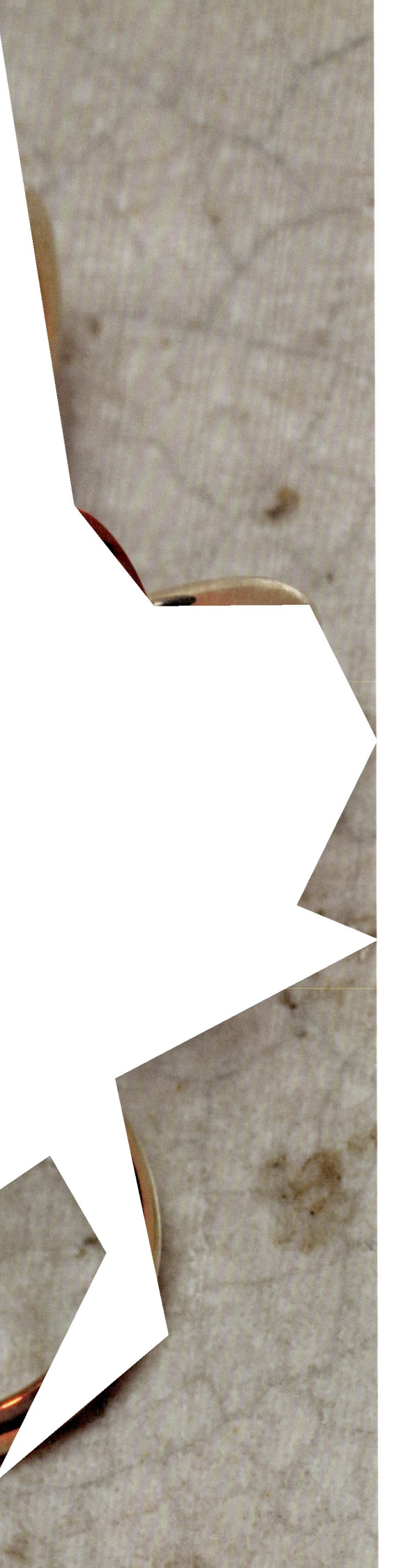

Need: a *Nudo* for each day of the week

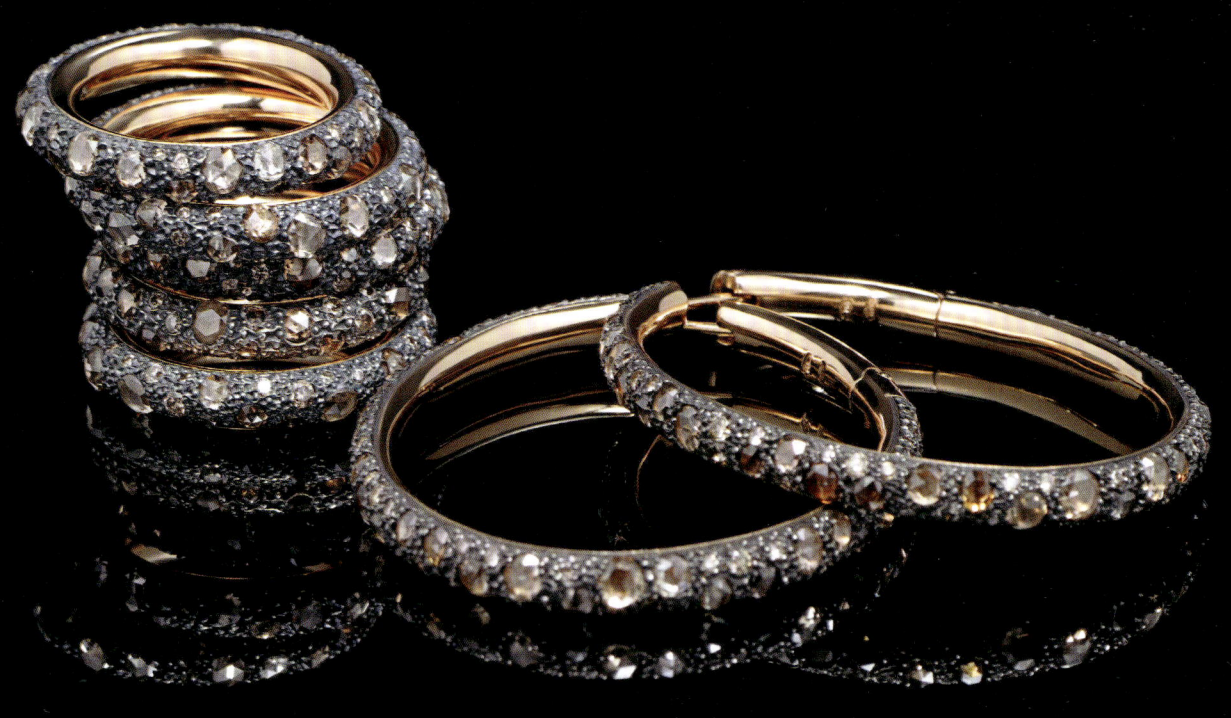

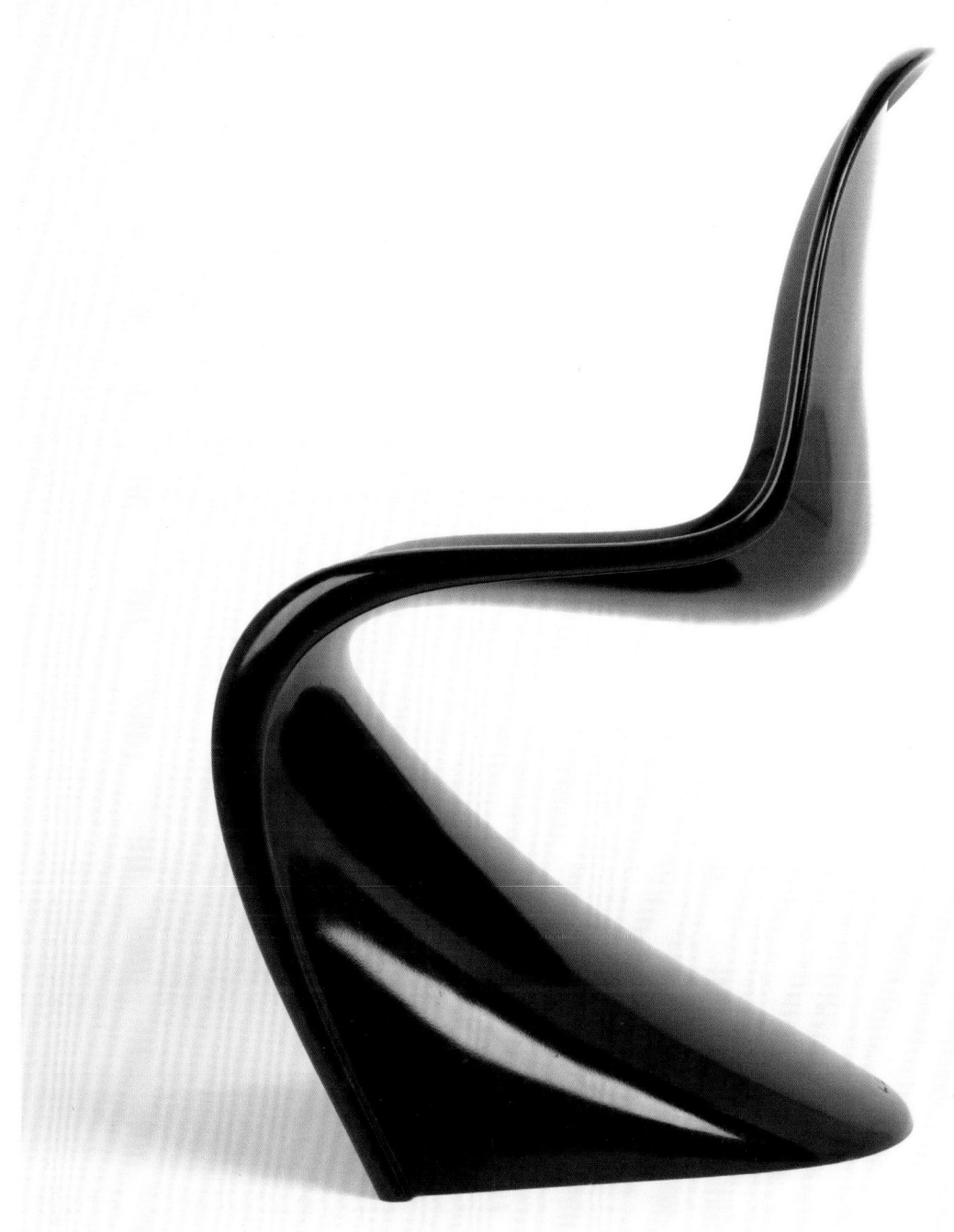

OPPOSITE: Champagne and cognac diamonds adorning the *Tango* collection, here rings and earrings

ABOVE: Design masterpiece *Panton Chair* by Verner Panton, 1967

FOLLOWING SPREAD, LEFT TO RIGHT: Makeup shades for summer 1967, by Horst P. Horst; a fresh color contrast for the *Bahia* and *Capri* collection rings

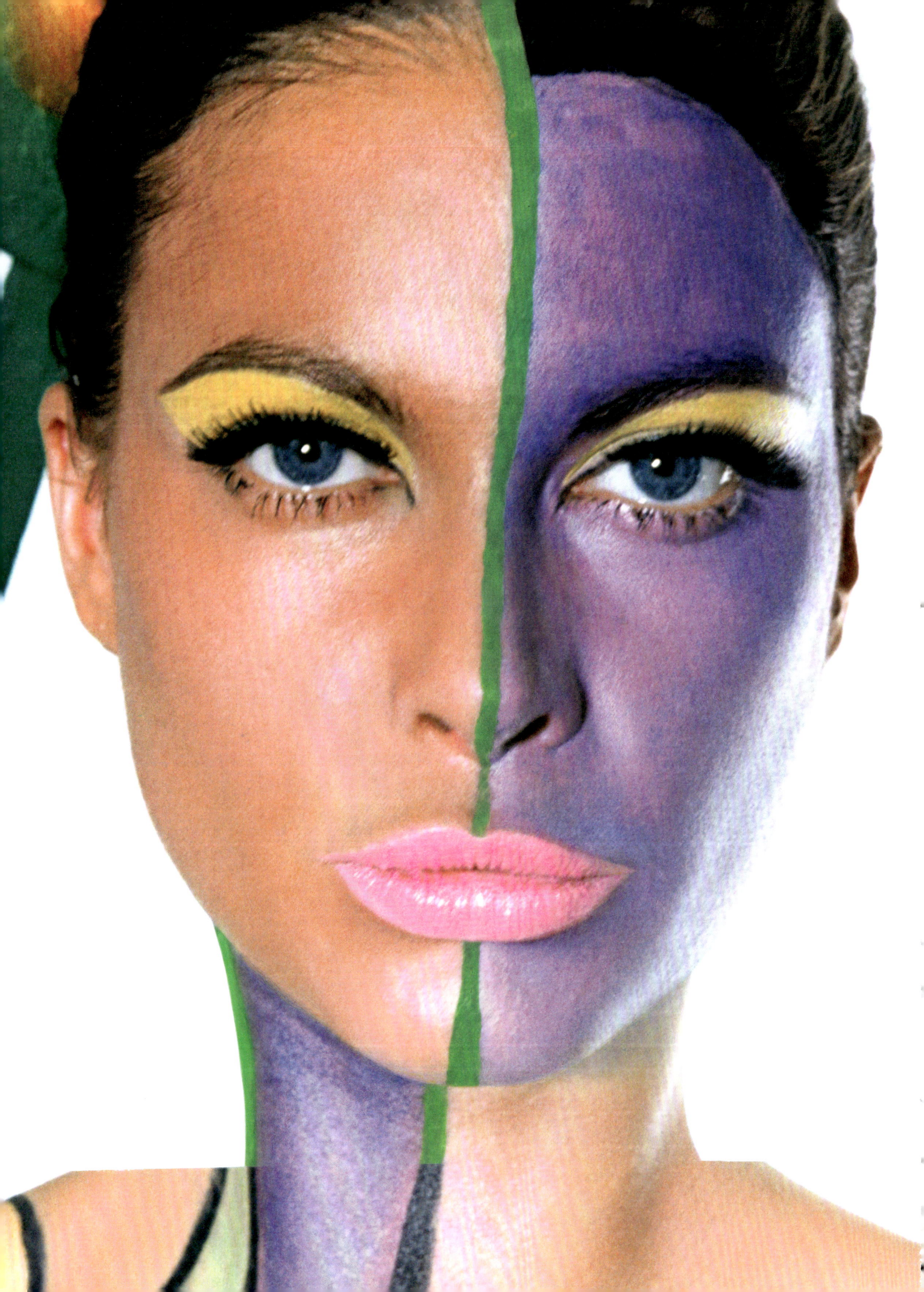

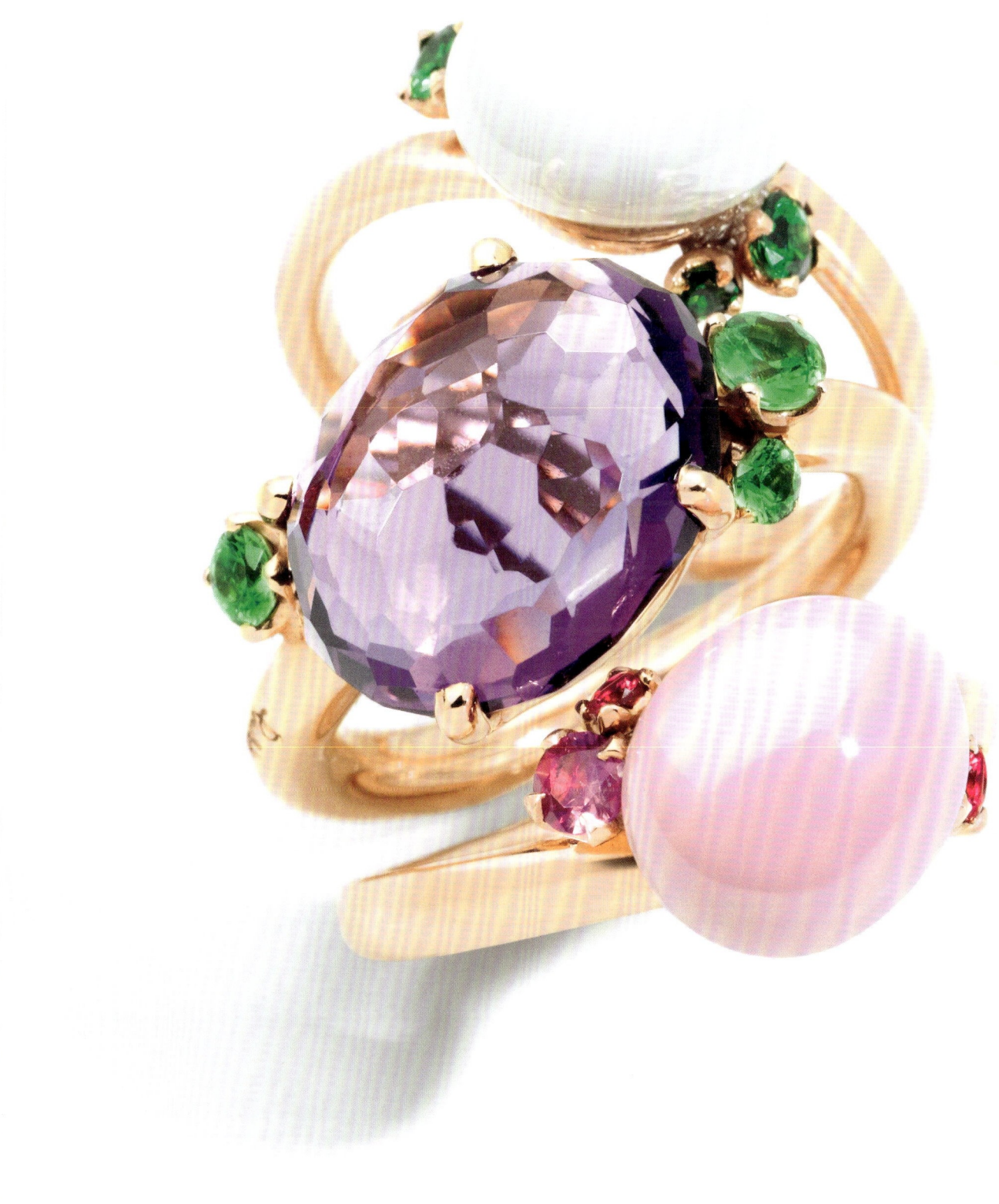

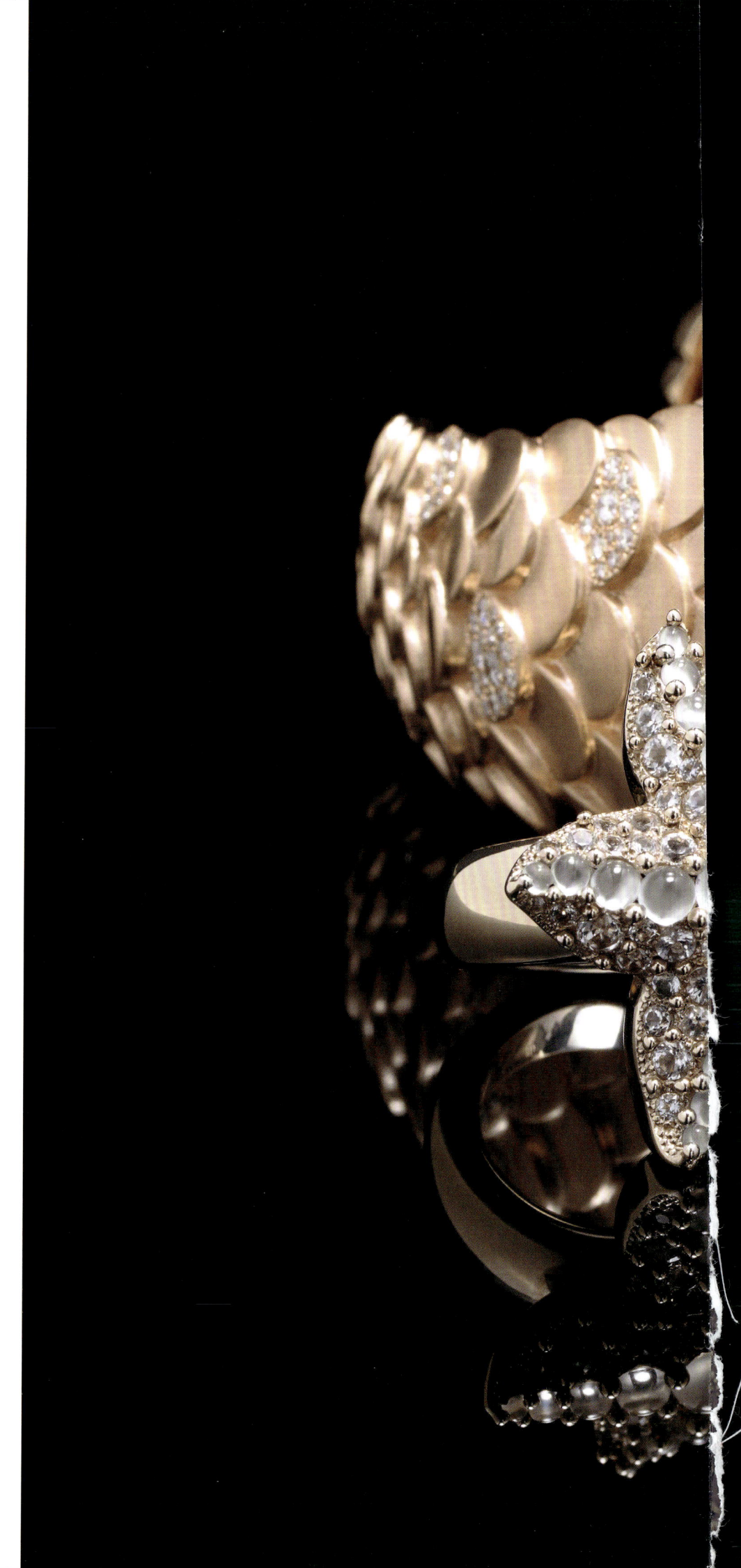

Echoing the seashore with the *Sirene*
collection rings and bracelet

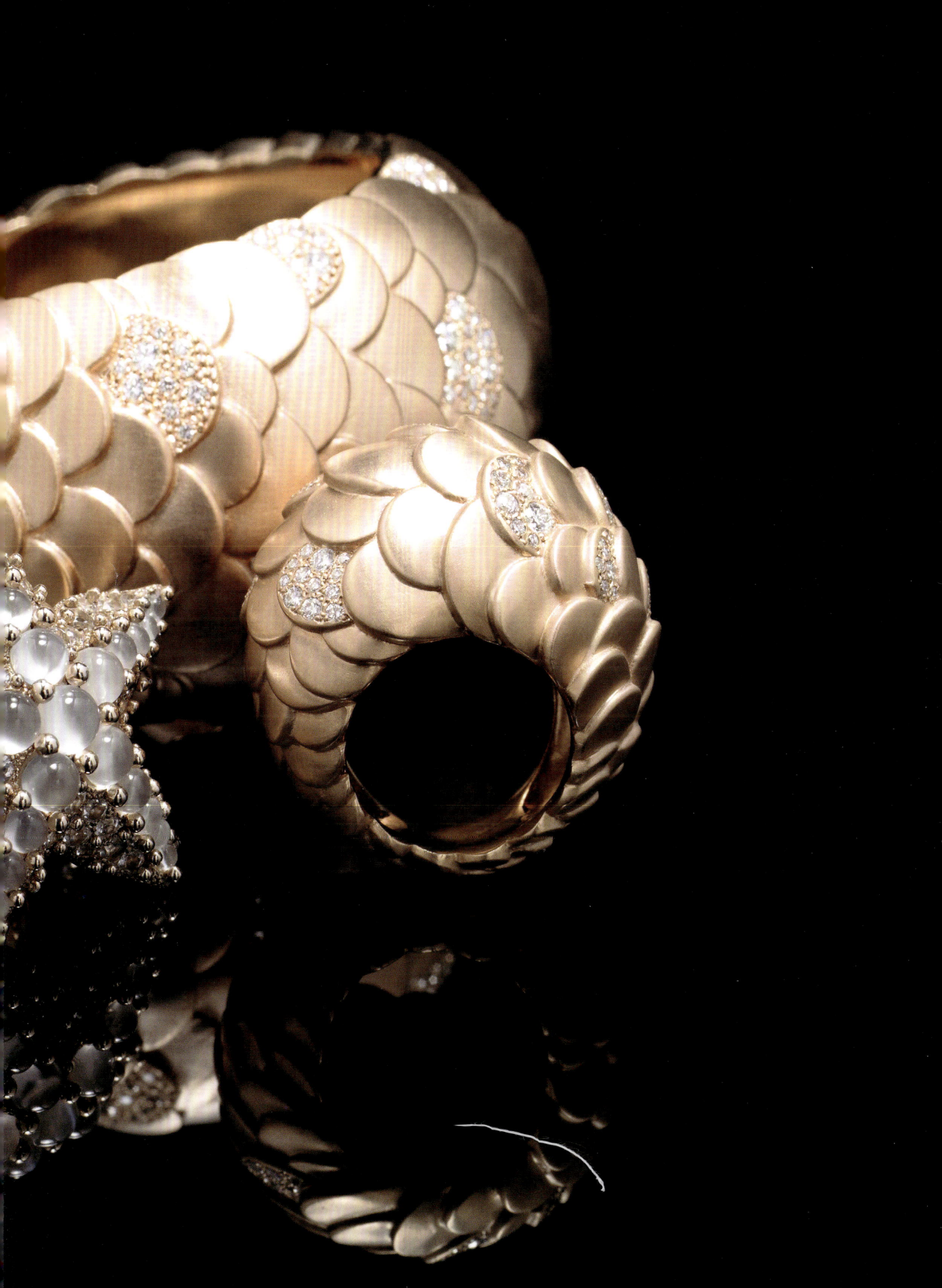

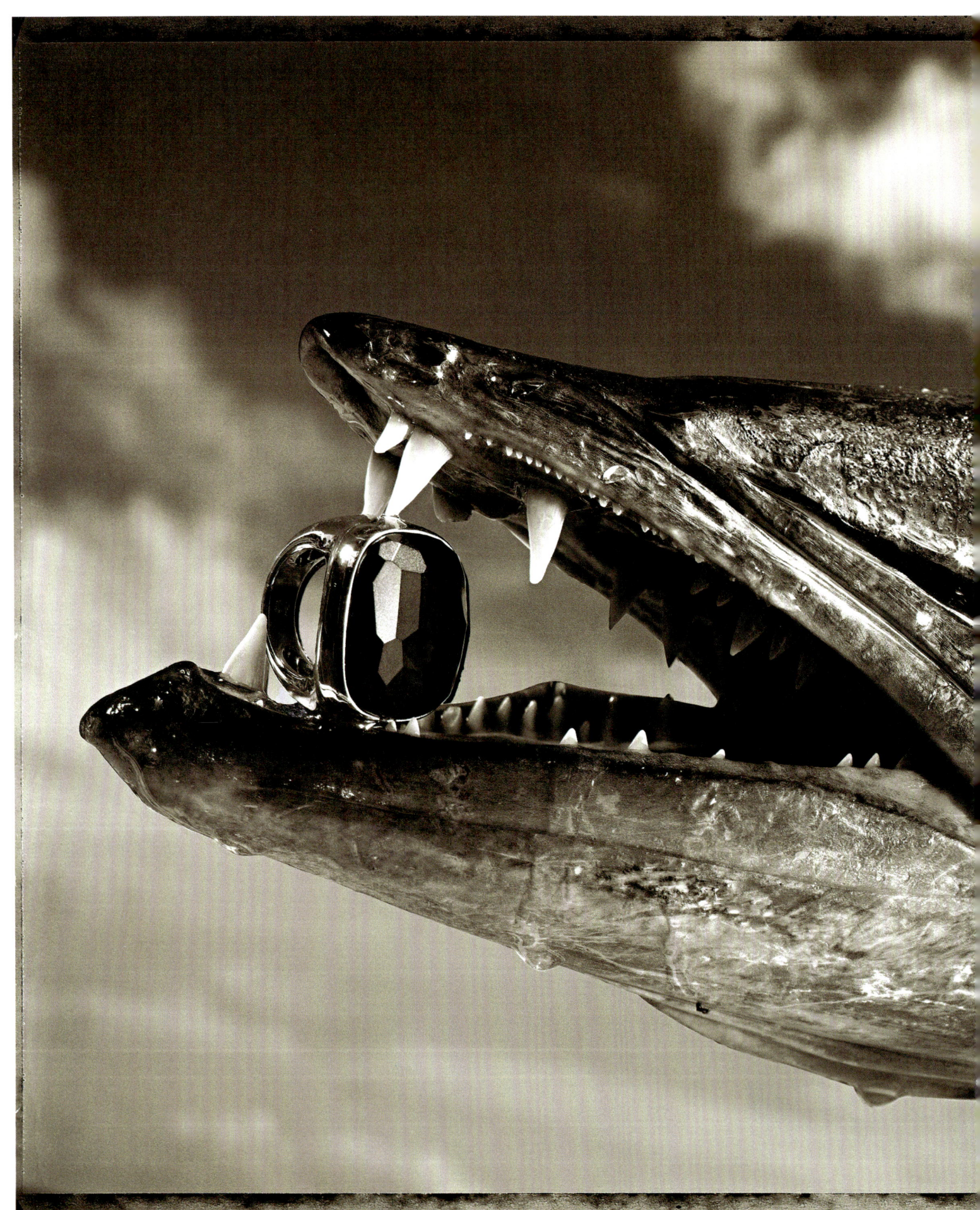

Victoria collection ring from *Innatural* by Gian Paolo Barbieri, 2004

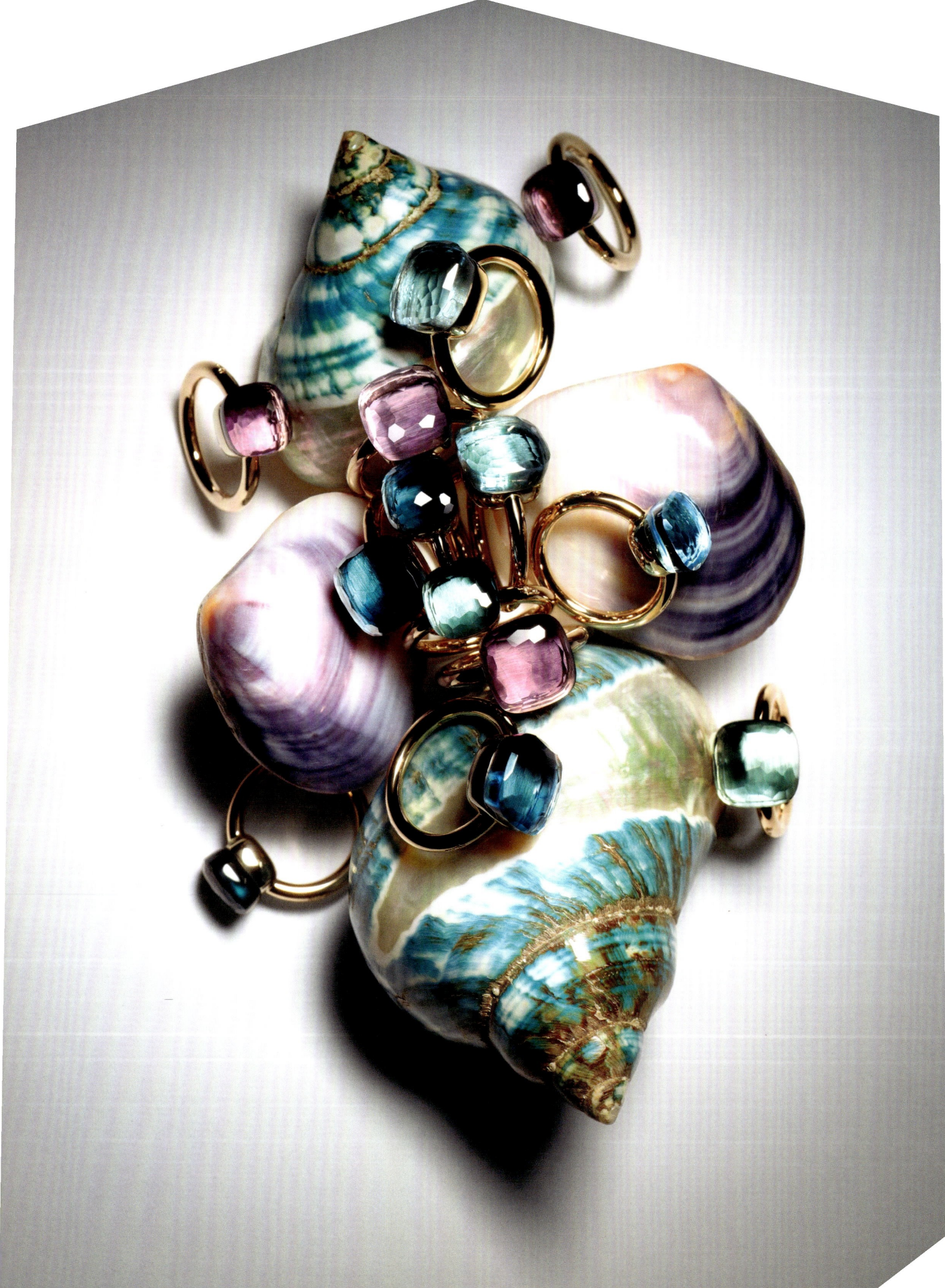

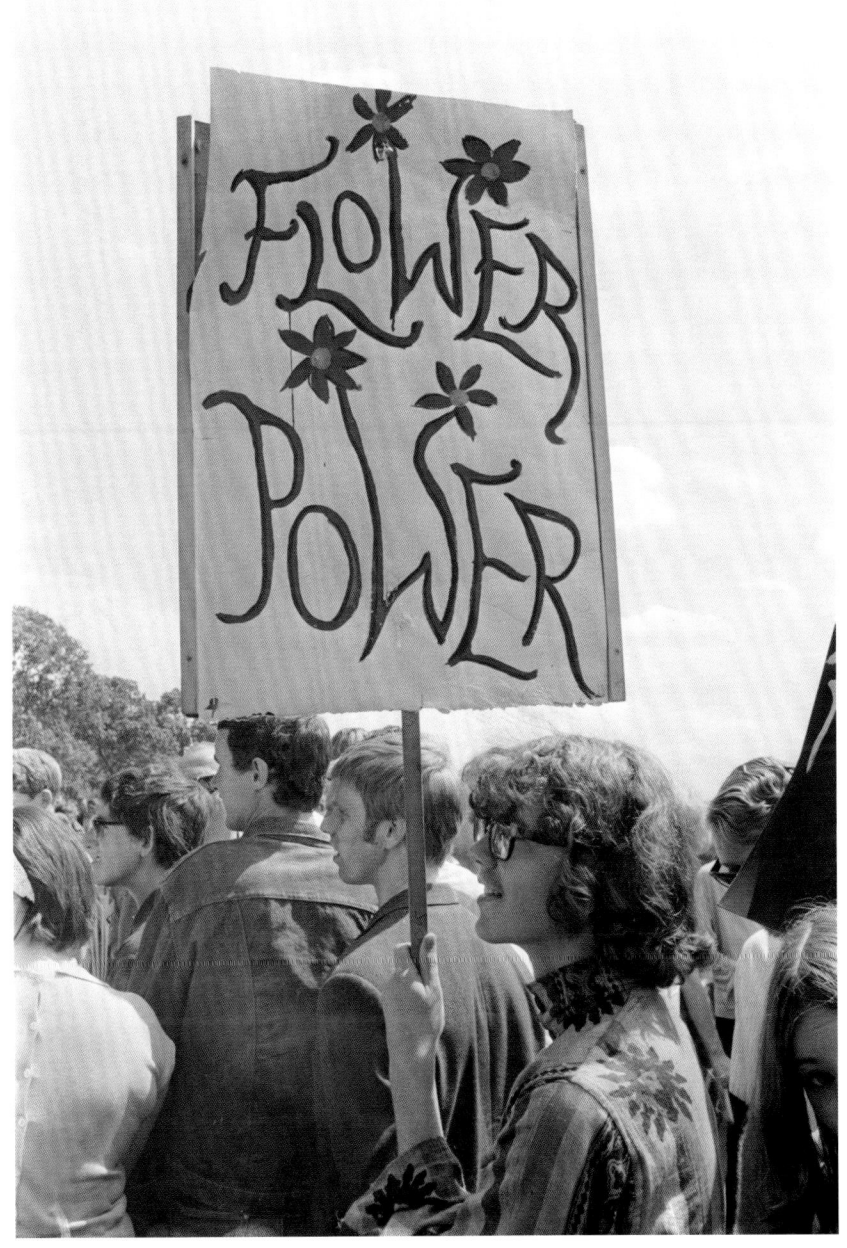

OPPOSITE: *Nudo* rings in amethyst and blue topaz

ABOVE: Fifty years of free-thinking: demonstrating flower power, Hyde Park, London, 1967

The *Tango* collection comes in all the shades of a rainbow

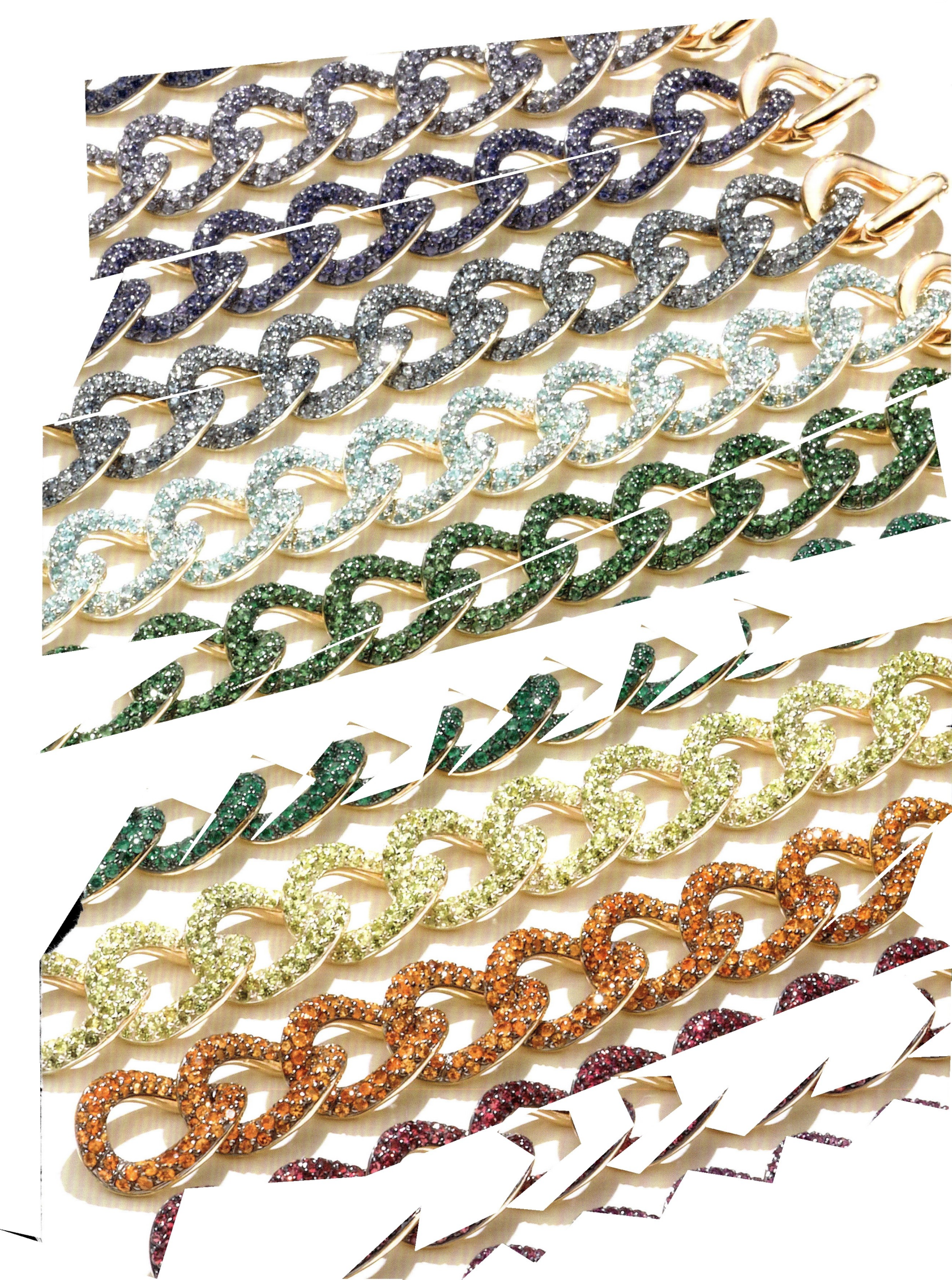

#POMELLATOFORWOMEN

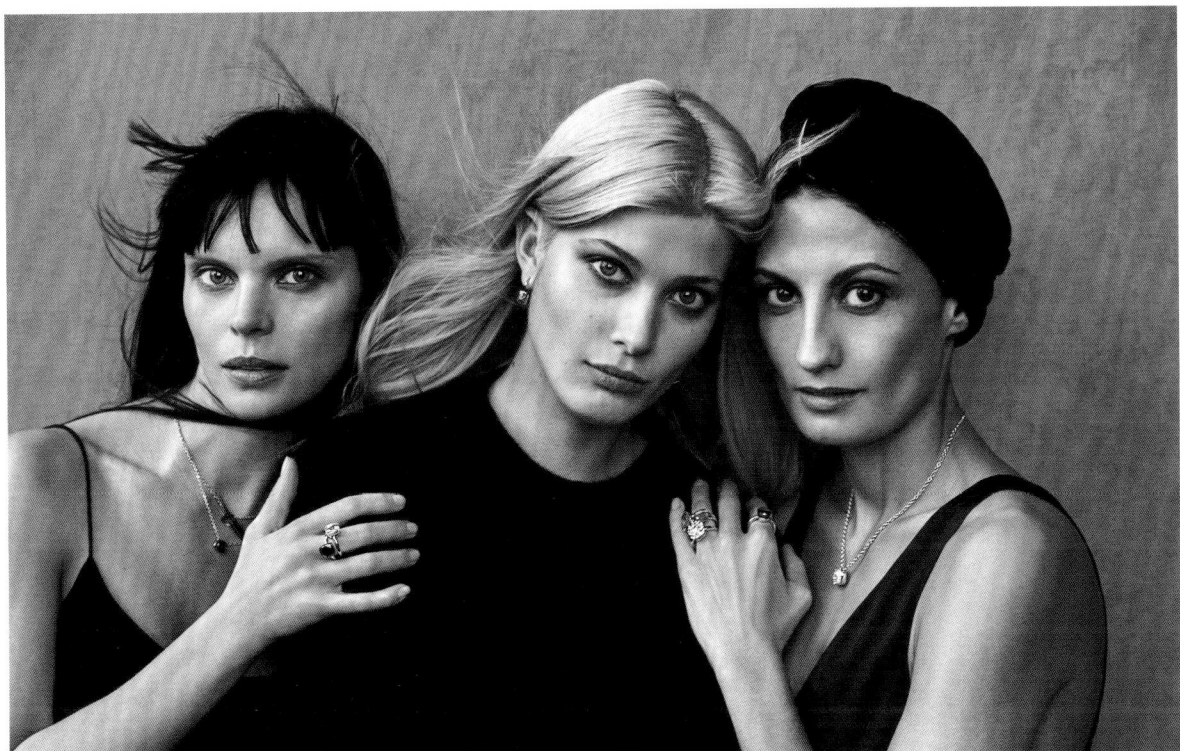

Pomellato is ultimately a women's affair. Its jewels are something women buy for themselves, in an act of self-gratification that is empowering, self-affirming, and joyous.

Time is to nurture and promote self-consciousness and personality, and to get as far away as possible from preconceived and ultimately oppressive ideas of beauty.

Embracing diversity means amplifying and glorifying the unique strength every woman has inside of herself.

Through the #PomellatoForWomen platform, Pomellato has created a community of like-minded women who are willing to share part of themselves with others, thus inspiring other women.

PHOTOGRAPHIC CREDITS

p. 110: Michael Ochs Archives/Getty Images
p. 111: Michael Ochs Archives/Getty Images
pp. 112–113: Patricia Schwoerer, 2007
p. 114: Patricia Schwoerer, 2009
p. 115: Albert Watson, 1984
p. 116: 1998 Kate Rothko Prizel & Christopher Rothko/
Artists Rights Society (ARS), New York
p. 117: Guido Mocafico, 2015
pp. 118–119: Lord Snowdon/Trunk Archive, 1992
pp. 120–121: Jean-Claude Deutsch/Paris Match via
Getty Images
p. 122: Victoria and Albert Museum, London
p. 123: Guido Mocafico, 2013
pp. 124–125: David Hockney Collection. Tate, London 2017
p. 126: Bodha D'Erasmo & Gilda, 2017
p. 127: Ernesto Gismondi/Artemide
p. 128: Ted Streshinsky/Corbis via Getty Images
p. 129: Patricia Schwoerer, 2009
pp. 130–131: The Helmut Newton Estate/Maconochie
Photography, 1982
p. 132: Popperfoto/Getty Images
p. 133: Bodha D'Erasmo & Gilda, 2017
pp. 134–135: Yoshie Nishikawa, 2011
p. 136: Enrico Suà Ummarino, 2017
p. 137: Alberto Zanetti, 2017
pp. 138–139: Javier Vallhonrat, 1993
p. 140: Guido Mocafico, 2015
p. 141: © 2017 Trustees of the Paolozzi Foundation,
Licensed by DACS/Artists Rights Society (ARS), New York
© Tate, London 2017
p. 142: © Tate, London/Art Resource, NY Miro, Joan
(1893–1983) © ARS, NY
p. 143: Bodha D'Erasmo & Gilda, 2017
p. 144: Frank Horvat/Conde Nast via Getty Images
p. 145: Enrico Suà Ummarino, 2013
p. 146: Yoshie Nishikawa, 2011
p. 147: Michael Ochs Archives/Getty Images
pp. 148–149: Philippe Le Tellier/Paris Match via Getty Images
p. 150: NASA/Central Press/Getty Images
p. 151: Bodha D'Erasmo & Gilda, 2017
p. 152: Guido Mocafico, 2009
p. 153: Giorgio Lotti/Mondadori Portfolio via Getty Images

p. 154: Bodha D'Erasmo & Gilda, 2017
p. 155: © David Hockney/Victoria and Albert Museum, London
p. 156: Yoshie Nishikawa, 2011
p. 157: Slim Aarons/Getty Images
p. 158: Gian Paolo Barbieri, 2007
p. 159: Duffy/Getty Images
p. 161: Guido Mocafico, 2010
pp. 162–163: Patricia Schwoerer, 2007
pp. 164–165: Ted Streshinsky/Corbis via Getty Images
p. 166: Oriani & Origone, 2016
p. 167: David McCabe/Conde Nast via Getty Images
p. 168: Guido Mocafico, 2009
p. 169: © Estate of Roy Lichtenstein
p. 171: Gian Paolo Barbieri, 1989
pp. 172–173: Patricia Schwoerer, 2009
p. 174: Gian Paolo Barbieri, 2007
p. 175: NASA/Interim Archives/Getty Images
p. 176: © Adrian Meredith Photography
p. 177: Bodha D'Erasmo & Gilda, 2017
p. 179: Gian Paolo Barbieri, 2004
p. 180: Guido Mocafico, 2013
p. 181: Lorenzo Bringheli, 2016
p. 182: Patricia Schwoerer, 2007
p. 183: Gian Paolo Barbieri, 1989
p. 184: Guido Mocafico, 2011
p. 185: Heilke Heller/ullstein bild via Getty Images
p. 186: Bodha D'Erasmo & Gilda, 2017
p. 187: Lorenzo Bringheli, 2016
pp. 188–189: Patricia Schwoerer, 2007
pp. 190–191: Patricia Schwoerer, 2007
p. 192: Patricia Schwoerer, 2009
p. 193: © Courtesy of Design Museum
p. 194: Horst P. Horst/Conde Nast via Getty Images
p. 195: Enrico Suà Ummarino, 2016
pp. 196–197: Patricia Schwoerer, 2009
pp. 198–199: Gian Paolo Barbieri, 2004
p. 200: Guido Mocafico, 2013
p. 201: Stanley Sherman/Express/Hulton Archive/Getty Images
p. 203: Enrico Suà Ummarino, 2012
p. 205: Peter Lindbergh, 2017

ACKNOWLEDGMENTS

Our first thanks go to Pino Rabolini who helped us reconnect with the origins of Pomellato.

Our gratitude goes to Gian Paolo Barbieri, Catherine Bonifassi, Duncan Campbell and Charlotte Rey, Bodha D'Erasmo & Gilda, Giusi Ferré, Peter Lindbergh, Maconochie photography for the Helmut Newton images, Katja Martinez, Charles Miers, Guido Mocafico, Yoshie Nishikawa, Patricia Schwoerer, Enrico Suà Ummarino, Trunk Archive for the Herb Ritts images and Lord Snowdon images, Javier Vallhonrat, Lucia Vietri, and Sheila Weller.

Rizzoli New York would like to thank all the Pomellato employees and associates who generously contributed to the creation of this book, women and men who share their passion, creativity, and joy, with special thanks to Stéphane Gerschel and Francesca Artaria.